Freefall Romance

Hyouta Fujiyama

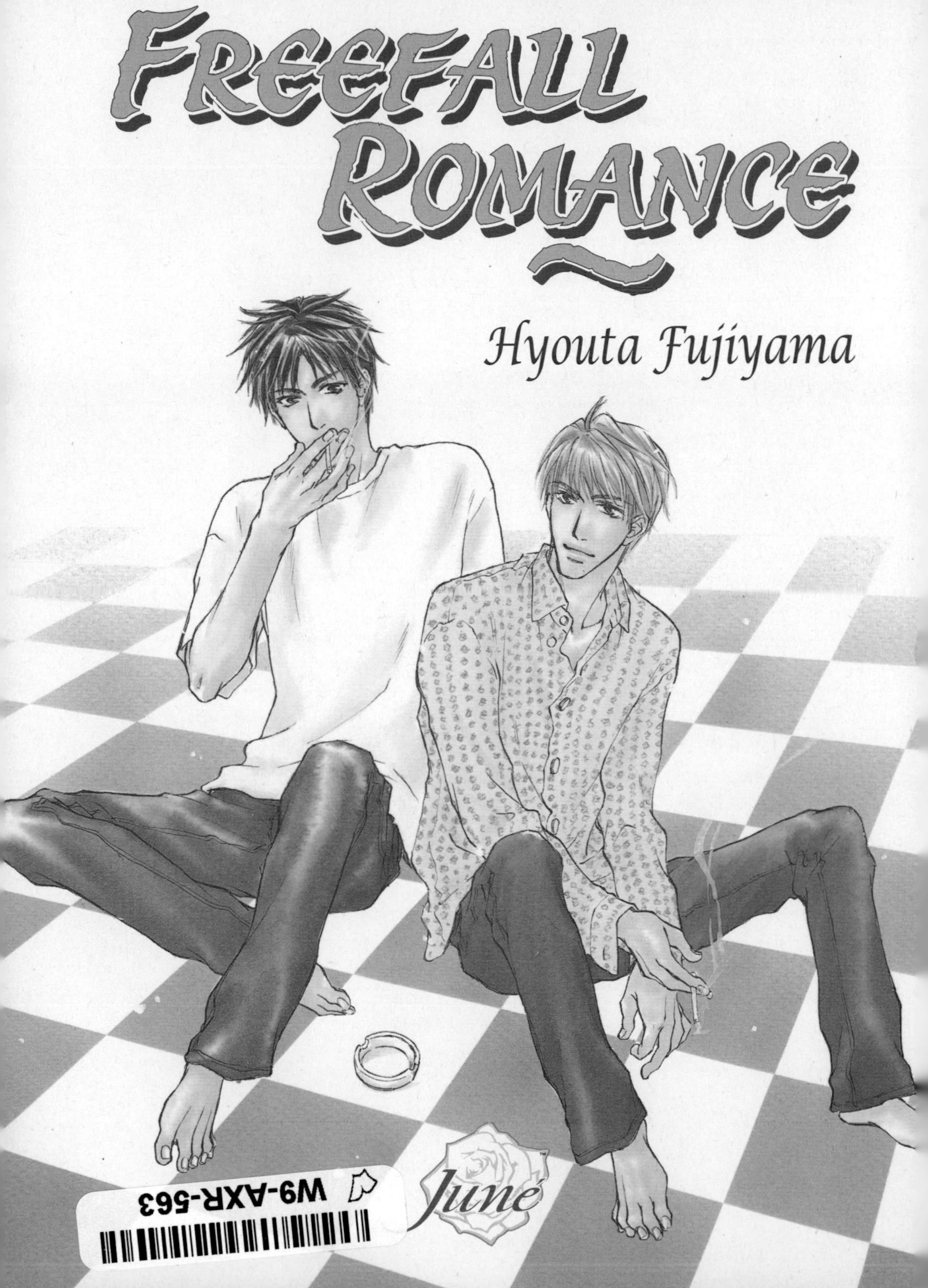

Juné

Translation	Emily Ohno
Lettering	Shelby Peak
Graphic Design	Wendy Lee/Fred Lui
Editing	Wendy Lee
Editor in Chief	Fred Lui
Publisher	Hikaru Sasahara

English Edition Published by
DIGITAL MANGA PUBLISHING
A division of DIGITAL MANGA, Inc.
1487 W 178th Street, Suite 300
Gardena, CA 90248

www.dmpbooks.com

First Edition: September 2007
ISBN-10: 1-56970-803-7
ISBN-13: 978-1-56970-803-3

1 3 5 7 9 10 8 6 4 2

Printed in China

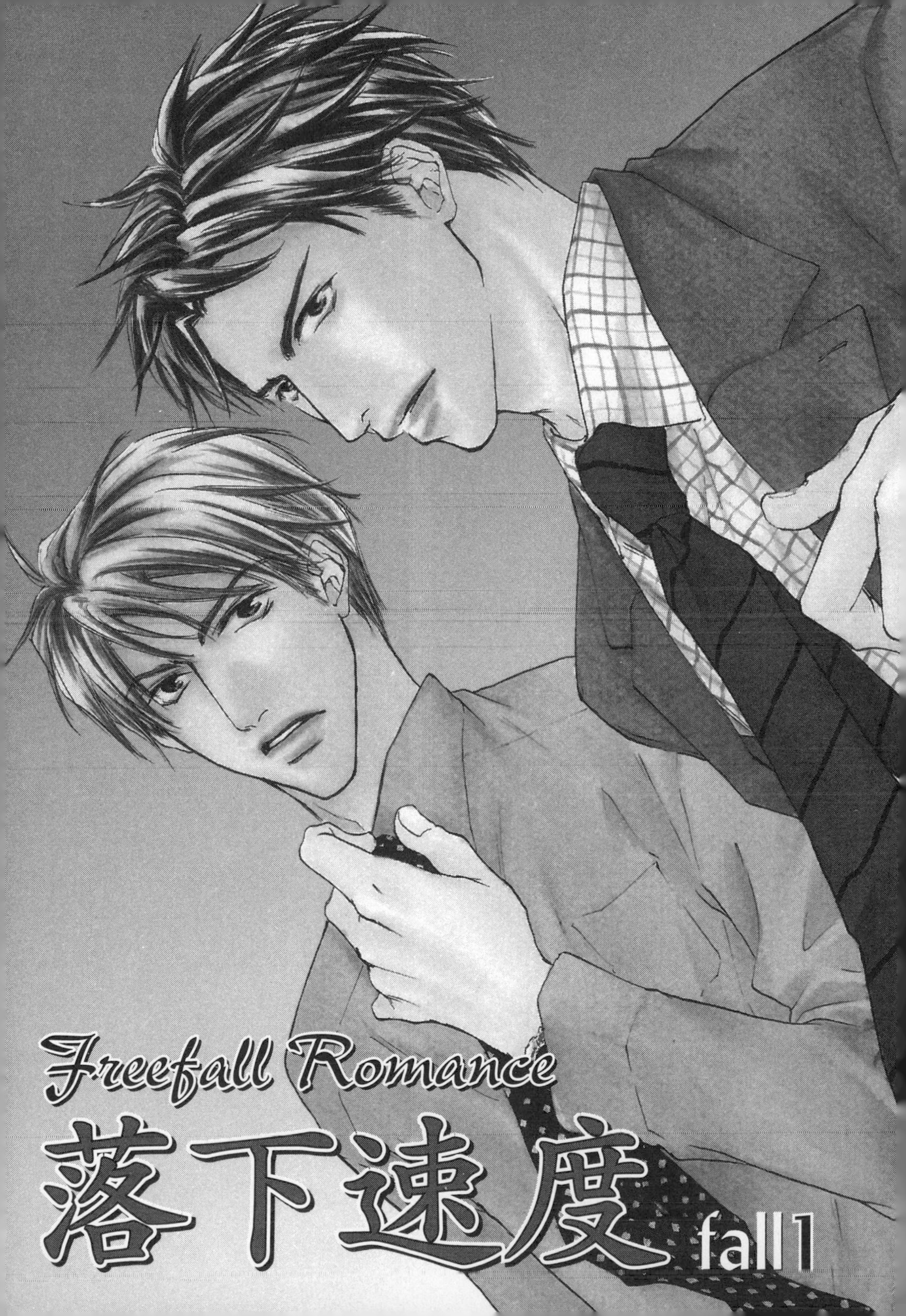
Freefall Romance
落下速度
fall 1

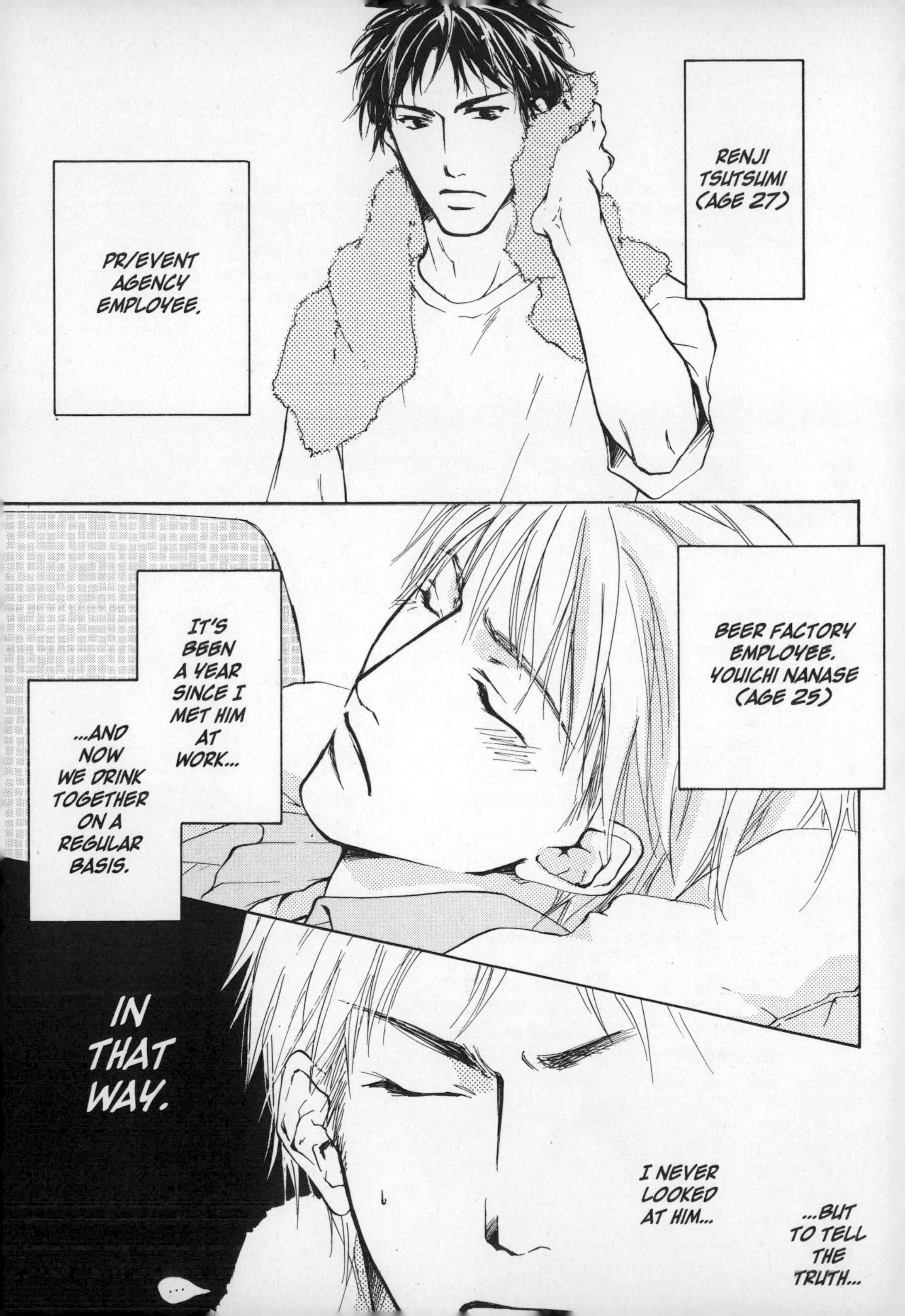
RENJI TSUTSUMI (AGE 27)
PR/EVENT AGENCY EMPLOYEE.
BEER FACTORY EMPLOYEE. YOUICHI NANASE (AGE 25)
IT'S BEEN A YEAR SINCE I MET HIM AT WORK...
...AND NOW WE DRINK TOGETHER ON A REGULAR BASIS.
...BUT TO TELL THE TRUTH...
I NEVER LOOKED AT HIM...
IN THAT WAY.
...

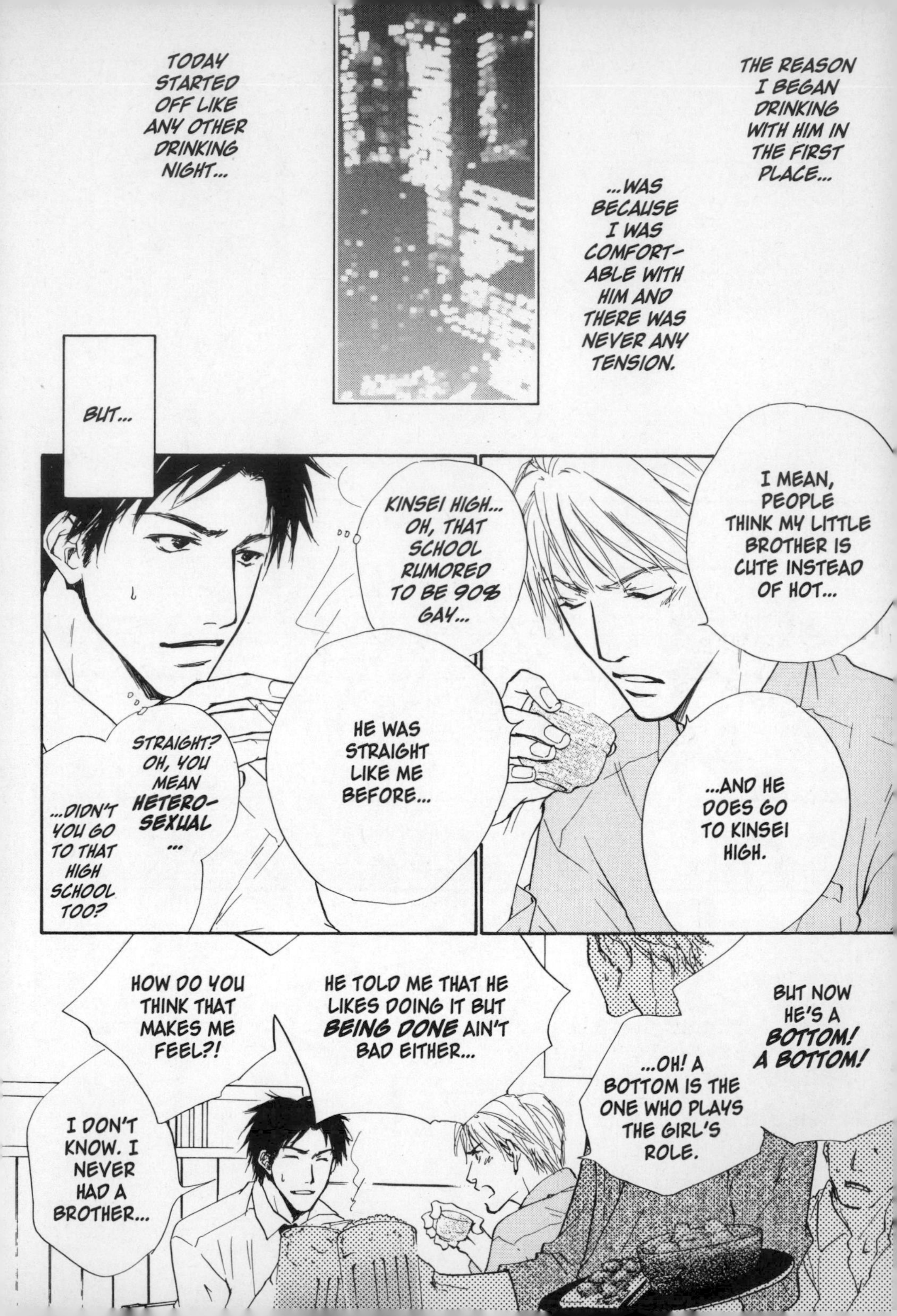

THE REASON I BEGAN DRINKING WITH HIM IN THE FIRST PLACE...
...WAS BECAUSE I WAS COMFORTABLE WITH HIM AND THERE WAS NEVER ANY TENSION.
TODAY STARTED OFF LIKE ANY OTHER DRINKING NIGHT...
BUT...
I MEAN, PEOPLE THINK MY LITTLE BROTHER IS CUTE INSTEAD OF HOT...
...AND HE DOES GO TO KINSEI HIGH.
KINSEI HIGH... OH, THAT SCHOOL RUMORED TO BE 90% GAY...
HE WAS STRAIGHT LIKE ME BEFORE...
STRAIGHT? OH, YOU MEAN HETERO-SEXUAL...
...DIDN'T YOU GO TO THAT HIGH SCHOOL TOO?
BUT NOW HE'S A BOTTOM! A BOTTOM!
...OH! A BOTTOM IS THE ONE WHO PLAYS THE GIRL'S ROLE.
HE TOLD ME THAT HE LIKES DOING IT BUT BEING DONE AIN'T BAD EITHER...
HOW DO YOU THINK THAT MAKES ME FEEL?!
I DON'T KNOW. I NEVER HAD A BROTHER...

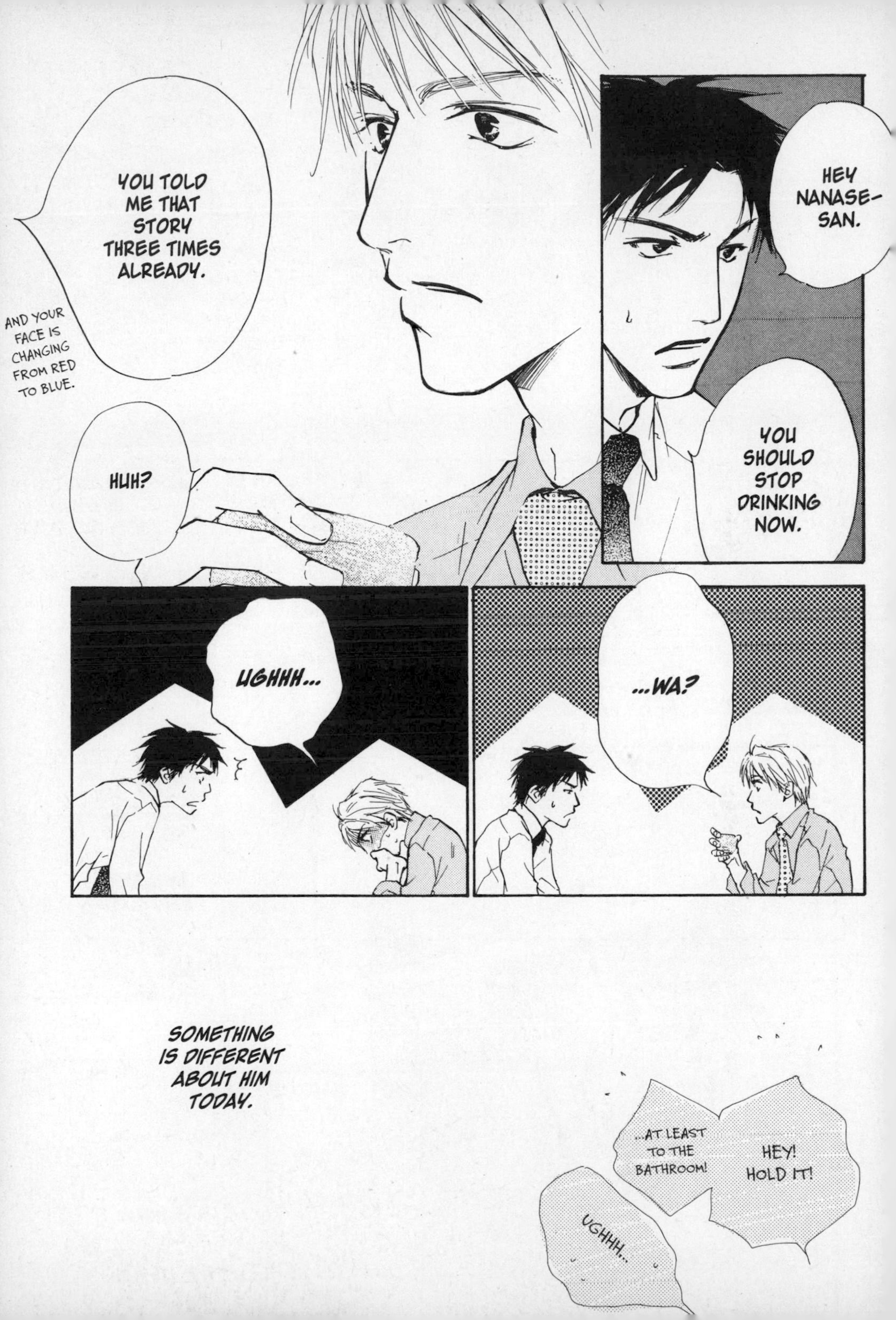
HEY NANASE-SAN.
YOU SHOULD STOP DRINKING NOW.
YOU TOLD ME THAT STORY THREE TIMES ALREADY.
AND YOUR FACE IS CHANGING FROM RED TO BLUE.
HUH?
...WA?
UGHHH...
SOMETHING IS DIFFERENT ABOUT HIM TODAY.
HEY! HOLD IT!
...AT LEAST TO THE BATHROOM!
UGHHH...

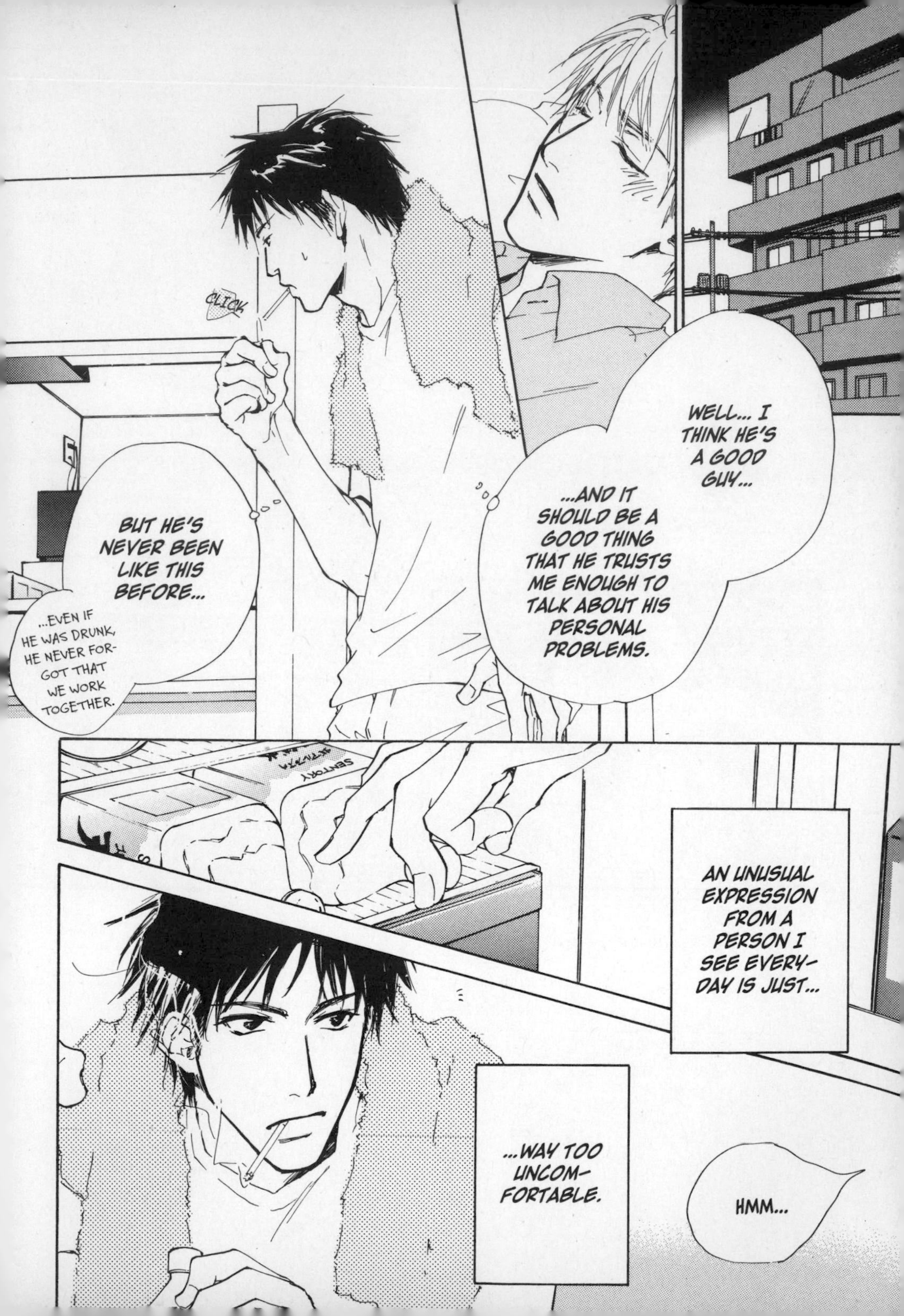
WELL... I THINK HE'S A GOOD GUY...
...AND IT SHOULD BE A GOOD THING THAT HE TRUSTS ME ENOUGH TO TALK ABOUT HIS PERSONAL PROBLEMS.
CLICK
BUT HE'S NEVER BEEN LIKE THIS BEFORE...
...EVEN IF HE WAS DRUNK, HE NEVER FOR-GOT THAT WE WORK TOGETHER.
SENTORY
AN UNUSUAL EXPRESSION FROM A PERSON I SEE EVERY-DAY IS JUST...
...WAY TOO UNCOM-FORTABLE.
HMM...

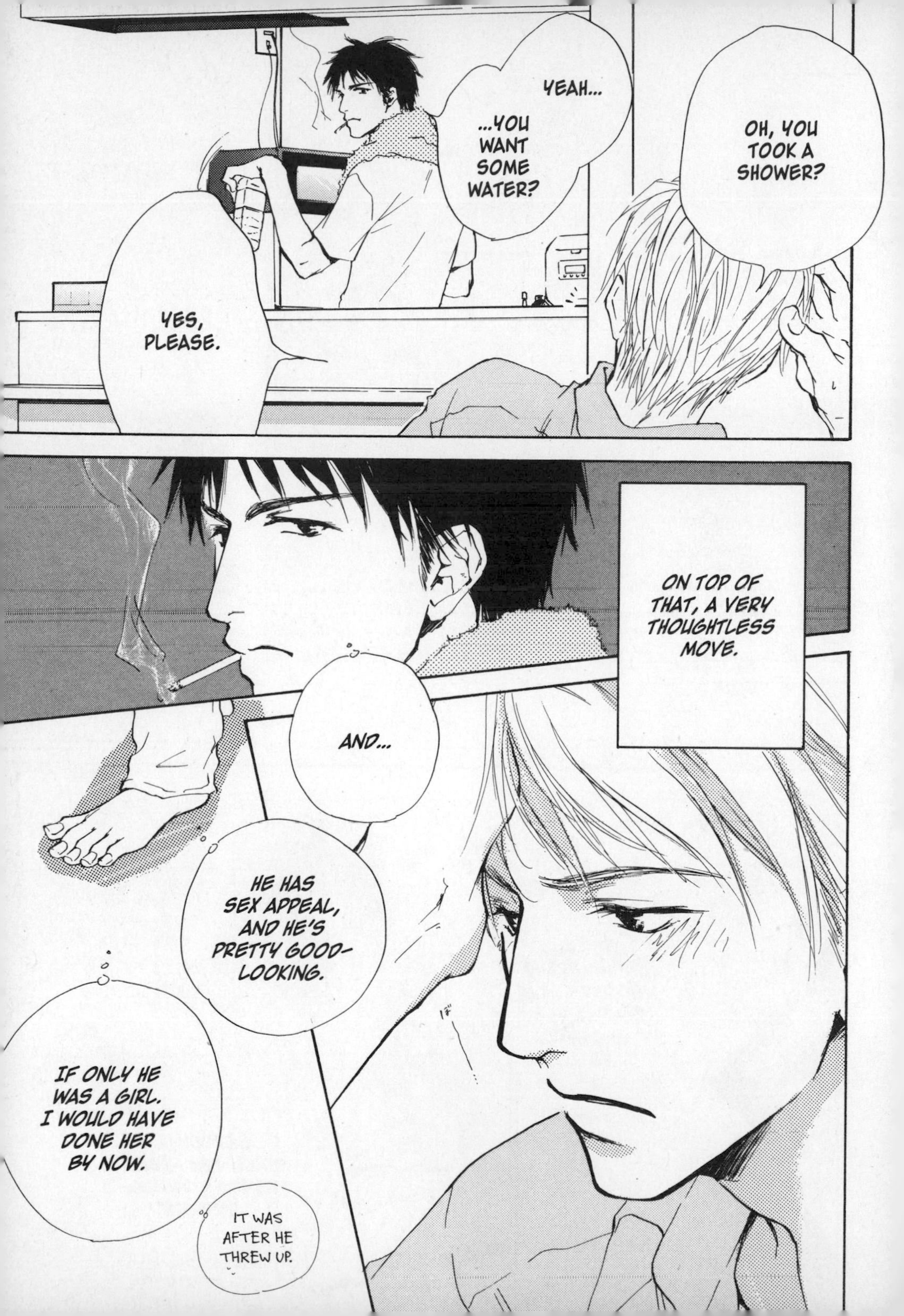
OH, YOU TOOK A SHOWER?
YEAH... ...YOU WANT SOME WATER?
YES, PLEASE.
ON TOP OF THAT, A VERY THOUGHTLESS MOVE.
AND...
HE HAS SEX APPEAL, AND HE'S PRETTY GOOD-LOOKING.
IF ONLY HE WAS A GIRL. I WOULD HAVE DONE HER BY NOW.
IT WAS AFTER HE THREW UP.

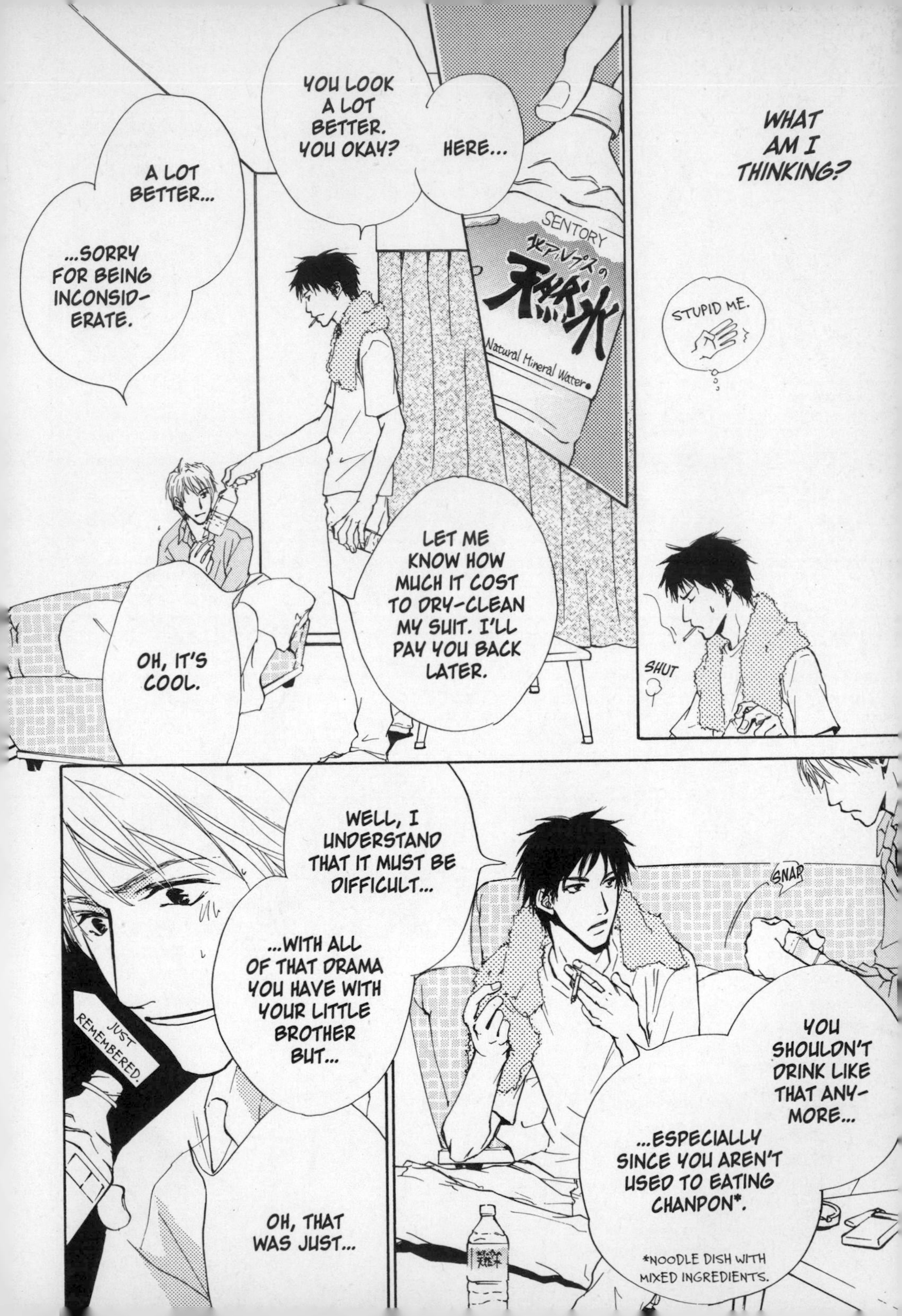
WHAT AM I THINKING?
STUPID ME.
SHUT
HERE...
YOU LOOK A LOT BETTER. YOU OKAY?
SENTORY
北アルプスの天然水
Natural Mineral Water
A LOT BETTER...
...SORRY FOR BEING INCONSIDERATE.
LET ME KNOW HOW MUCH IT COST TO DRY-CLEAN MY SUIT. I'LL PAY YOU BACK LATER.
OH, IT'S COOL.
SNAP
YOU SHOULDN'T DRINK LIKE THAT ANYMORE...
...ESPECIALLY SINCE YOU AREN'T USED TO EATING CHANPON*.
*NOODLE DISH WITH MIXED INGREDIENTS.
WELL, I UNDERSTAND THAT IT MUST BE DIFFICULT...
...WITH ALL OF THAT DRAMA YOU HAVE WITH YOUR LITTLE BROTHER BUT...
JUST REMEMBERED.
OH, THAT WAS JUST...

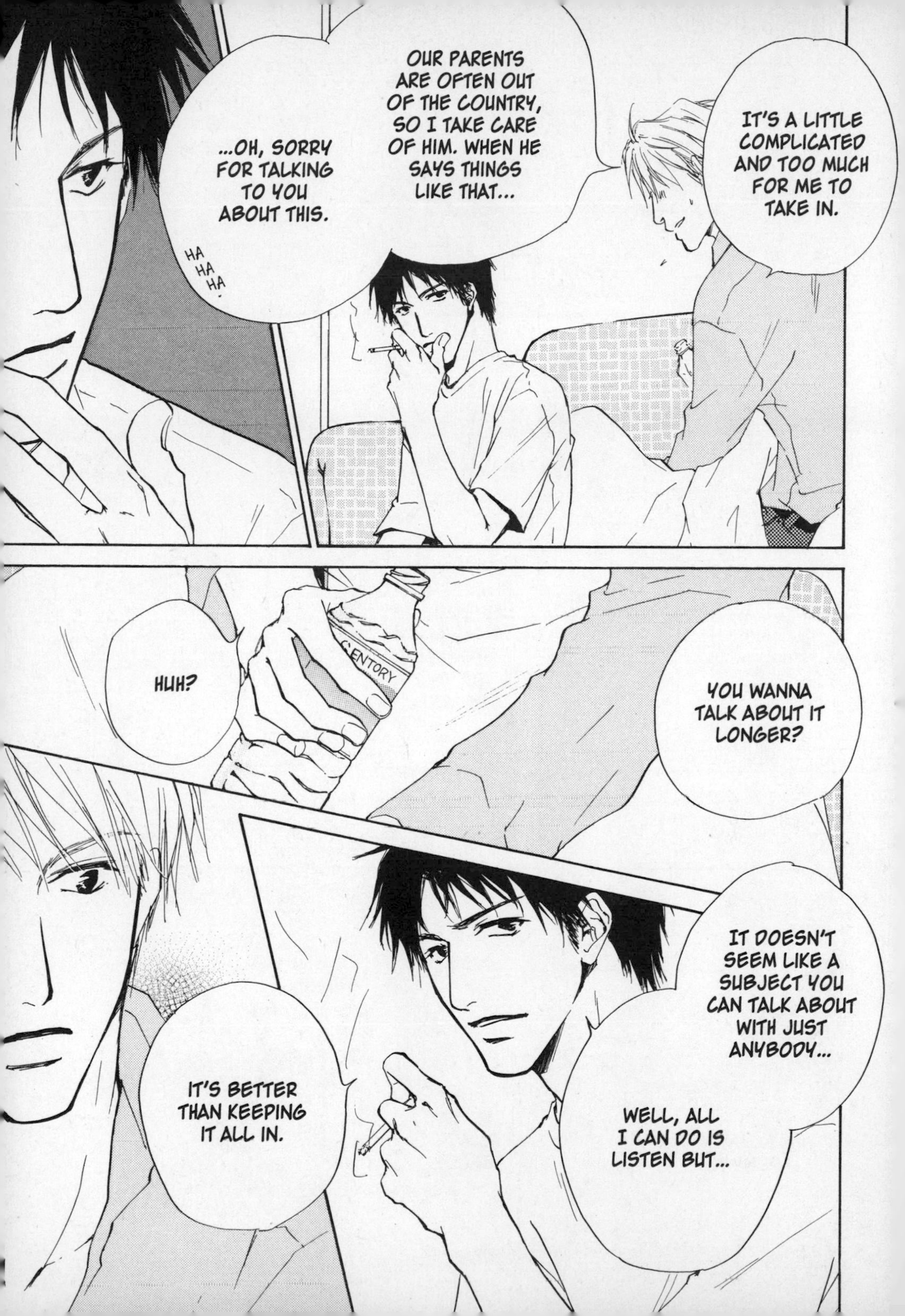
IT'S A LITTLE COMPLICATED AND TOO MUCH FOR ME TO TAKE IN.
OUR PARENTS ARE OFTEN OUT OF THE COUNTRY, SO I TAKE CARE OF HIM. WHEN HE SAYS THINGS LIKE THAT...
...OH, SORRY FOR TALKING TO YOU ABOUT THIS.
HA HA HA
YOU WANNA TALK ABOUT IT LONGER?
HUH?
IT DOESN'T SEEM LIKE A SUBJECT YOU CAN TALK ABOUT WITH JUST ANYBODY...
WELL, ALL I CAN DO IS LISTEN BUT...
IT'S BETTER THAN KEEPING IT ALL IN.

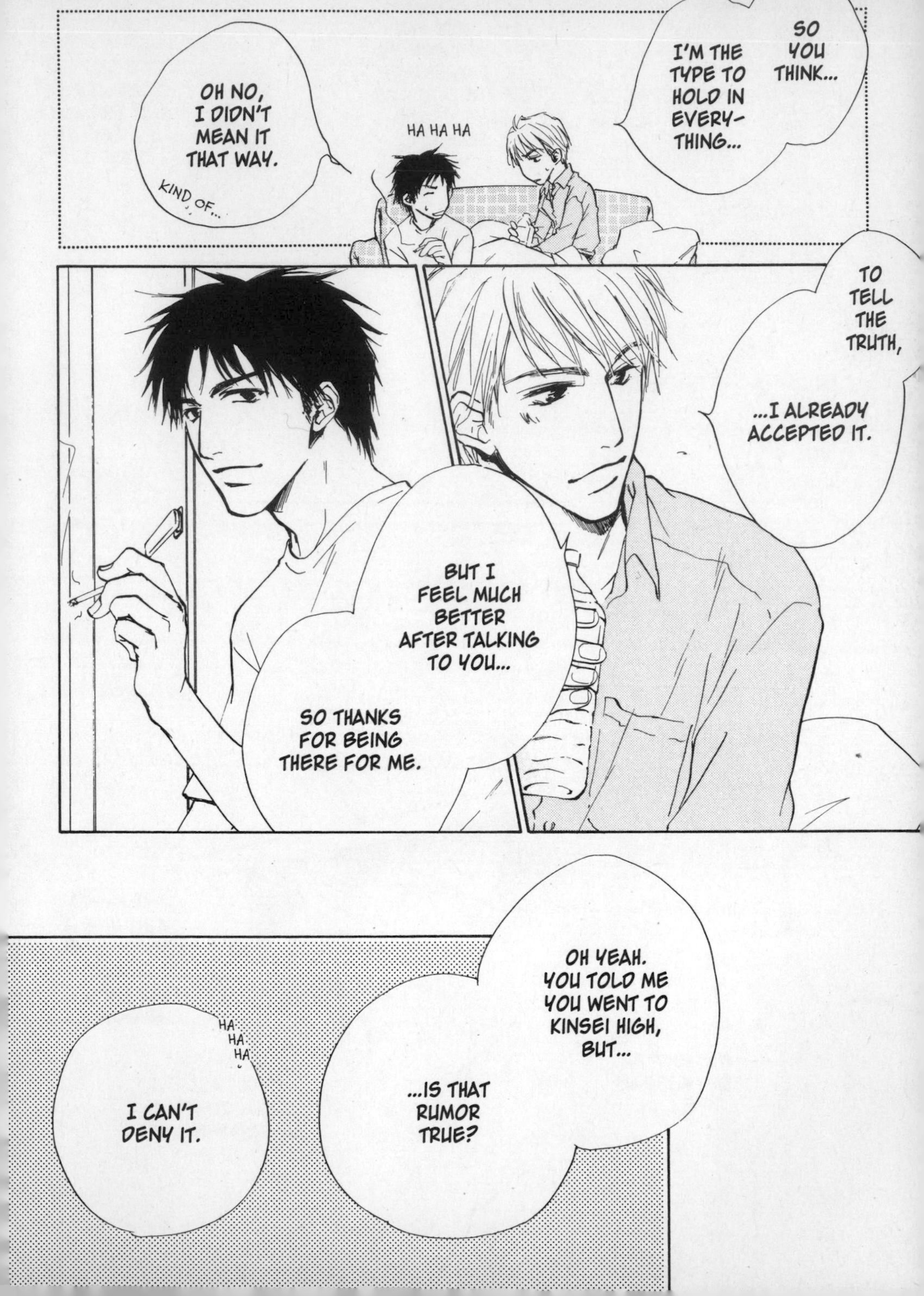
SO YOU THINK...
I'M THE TYPE TO HOLD IN EVERY-THING...
HA HA HA
OH NO, I DIDN'T MEAN IT THAT WAY.
KIND OF...
TO TELL THE TRUTH,
...I ALREADY ACCEPTED IT.
BUT I FEEL MUCH BETTER AFTER TALKING TO YOU...
SO THANKS FOR BEING THERE FOR ME.
OH YEAH. YOU TOLD ME YOU WENT TO KINSEI HIGH, BUT...
...IS THAT RUMOR TRUE?
HA HA HA
I CAN'T DENY IT.

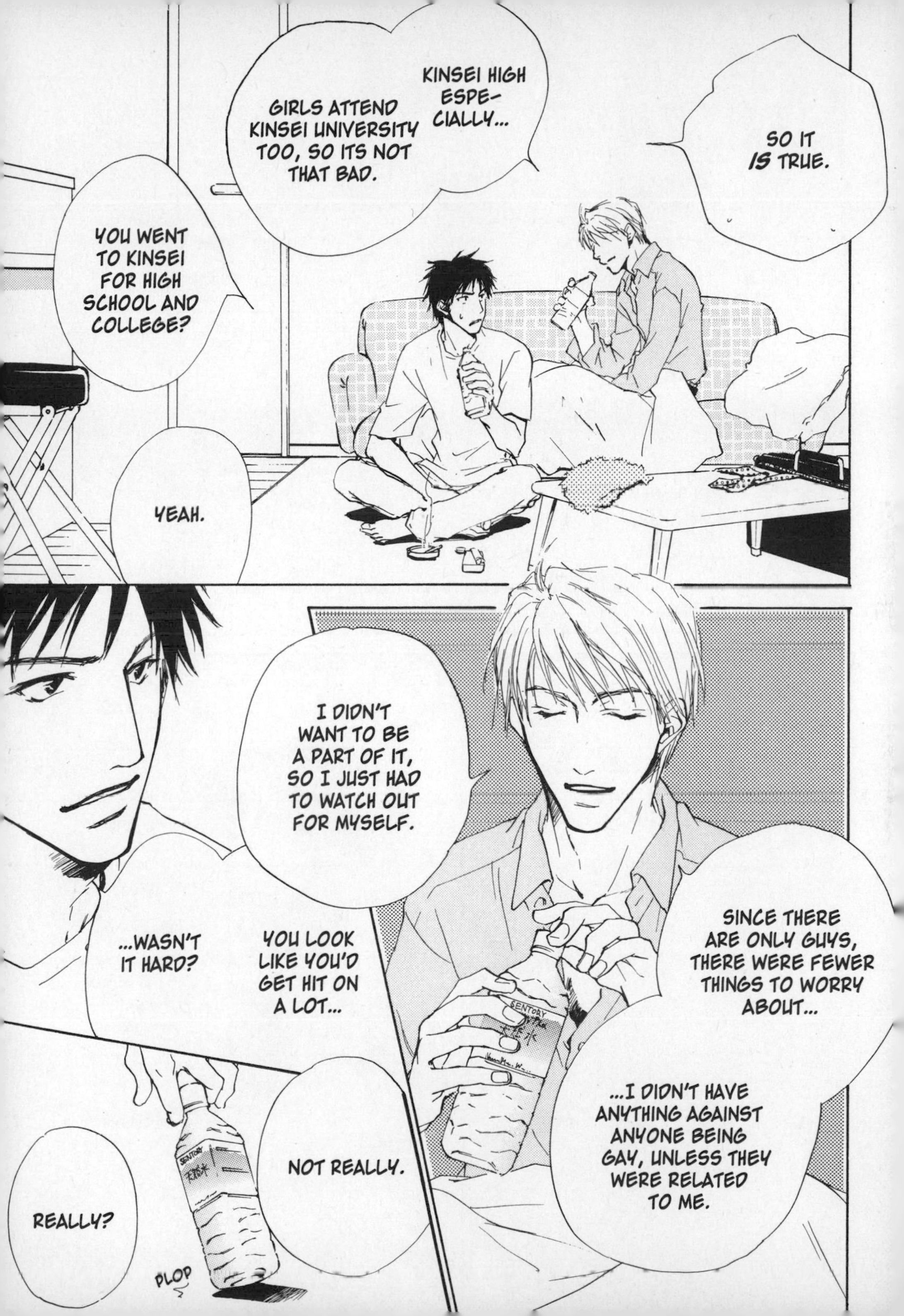
SO IT *IS* TRUE.
KINSEI HIGH ESPE- CIALLY...
GIRLS ATTEND KINSEI UNIVERSITY TOO, SO ITS NOT THAT BAD.
YOU WENT TO KINSEI FOR HIGH SCHOOL AND COLLEGE?
YEAH.
I DIDN'T WANT TO BE A PART OF IT, SO I JUST HAD TO WATCH OUT FOR MYSELF.
SINCE THERE ARE ONLY GUYS, THERE WERE FEWER THINGS TO WORRY ABOUT...
...I DIDN'T HAVE ANYTHING AGAINST ANYONE BEING GAY, UNLESS THEY WERE RELATED TO ME.
YOU LOOK LIKE YOU'D GET HIT ON A LOT...
...WASN'T IT HARD?
NOT REALLY.
REALLY?
PLOP

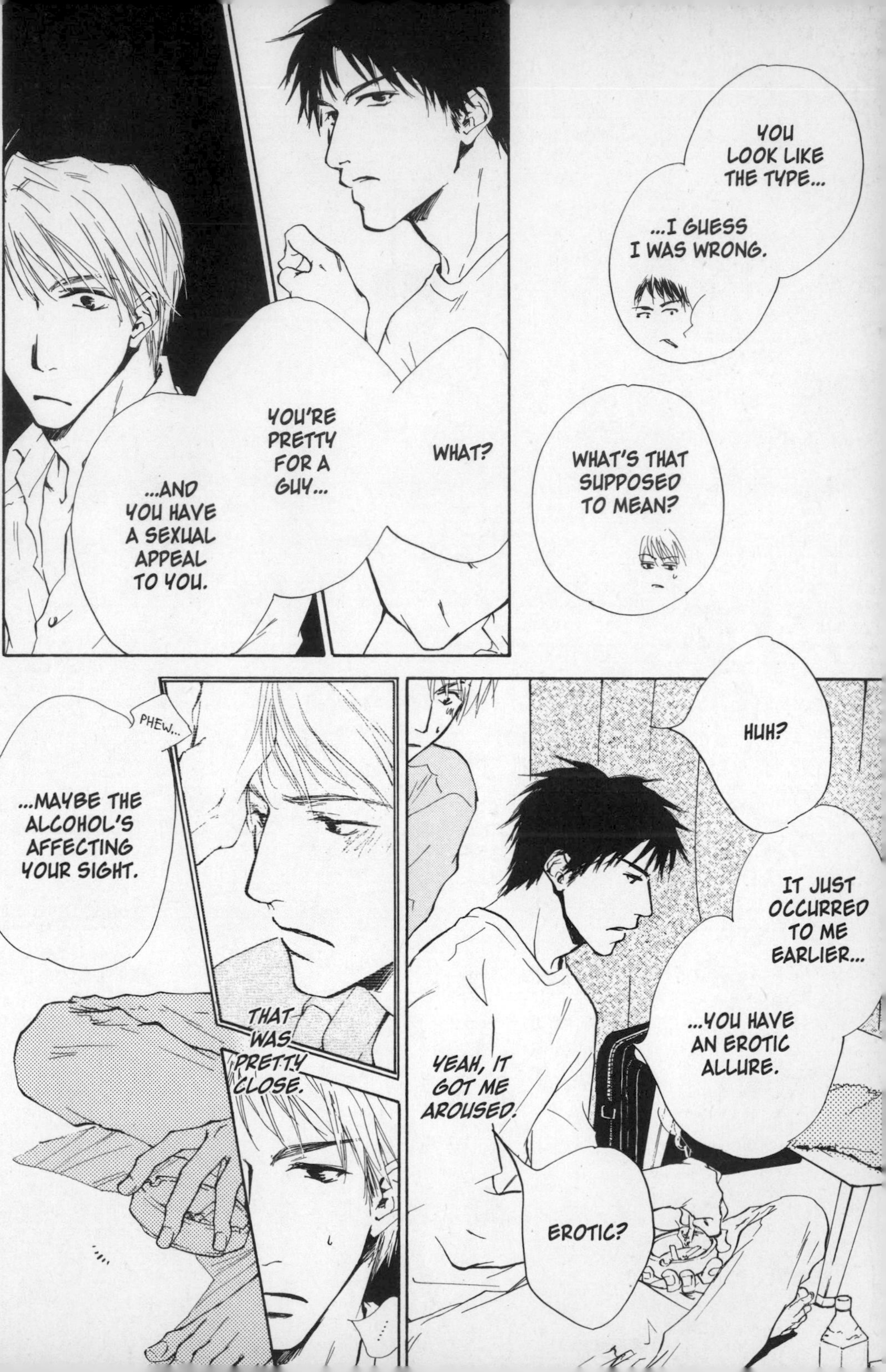
YOU LOOK LIKE THE TYPE...
...I GUESS I WAS WRONG.
WHAT'S THAT SUPPOSED TO MEAN?
WHAT?
YOU'RE PRETTY FOR A GUY...
...AND YOU HAVE A SEXUAL APPEAL TO YOU.
HUH?
IT JUST OCCURRED TO ME EARLIER...
...YOU HAVE AN EROTIC ALLURE.
EROTIC?
YEAH, IT GOT ME AROUSED.
THAT WAS PRETTY CLOSE.
PHEW...
...MAYBE THE ALCOHOL'S AFFECTING YOUR SIGHT.

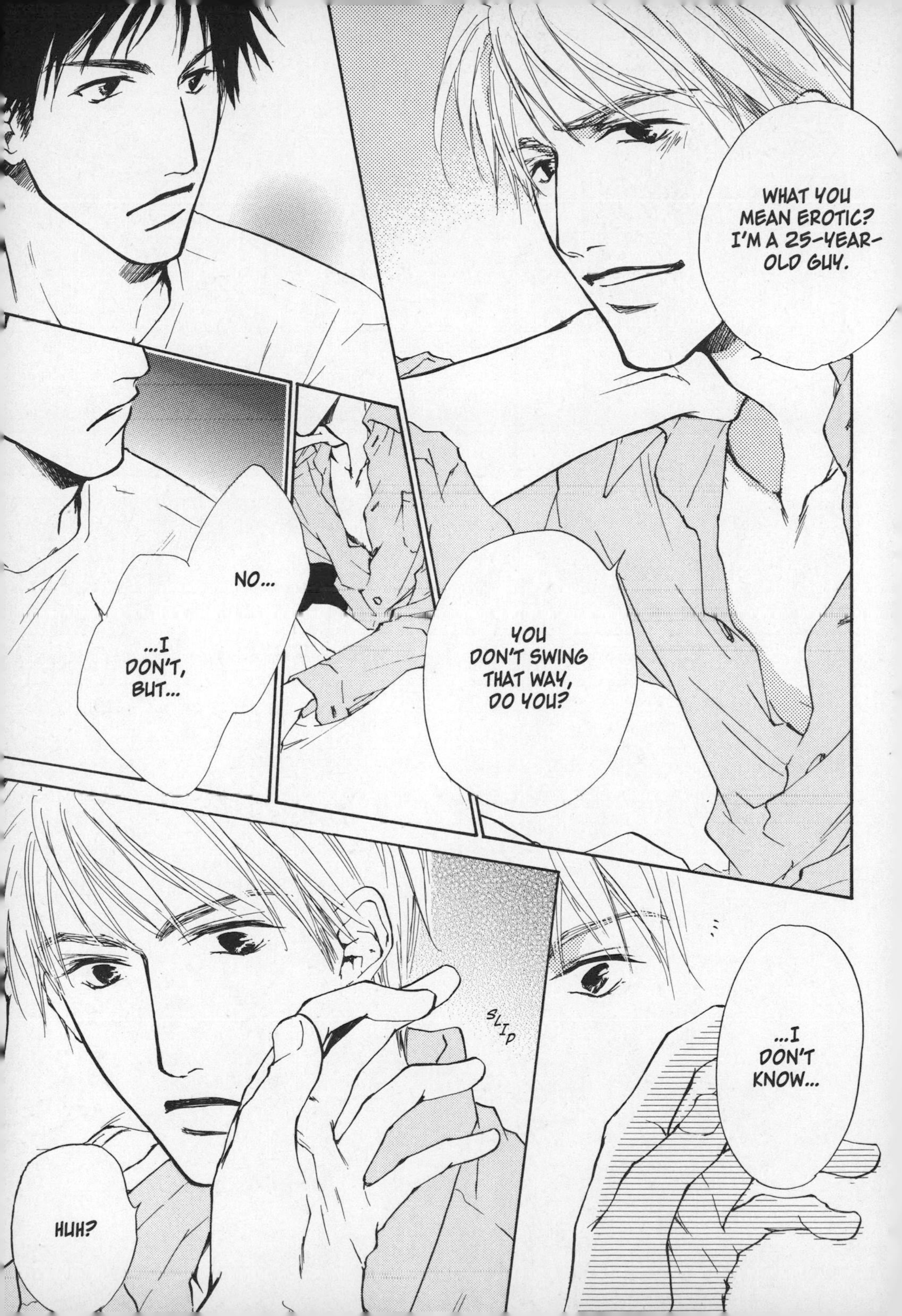
WHAT YOU MEAN EROTIC? I'M A 25-YEAR-OLD GUY.
YOU DON'T SWING THAT WAY, DO YOU?
NO...
...I DON'T, BUT...
...I DON'T KNOW...
SLIP
HUH?

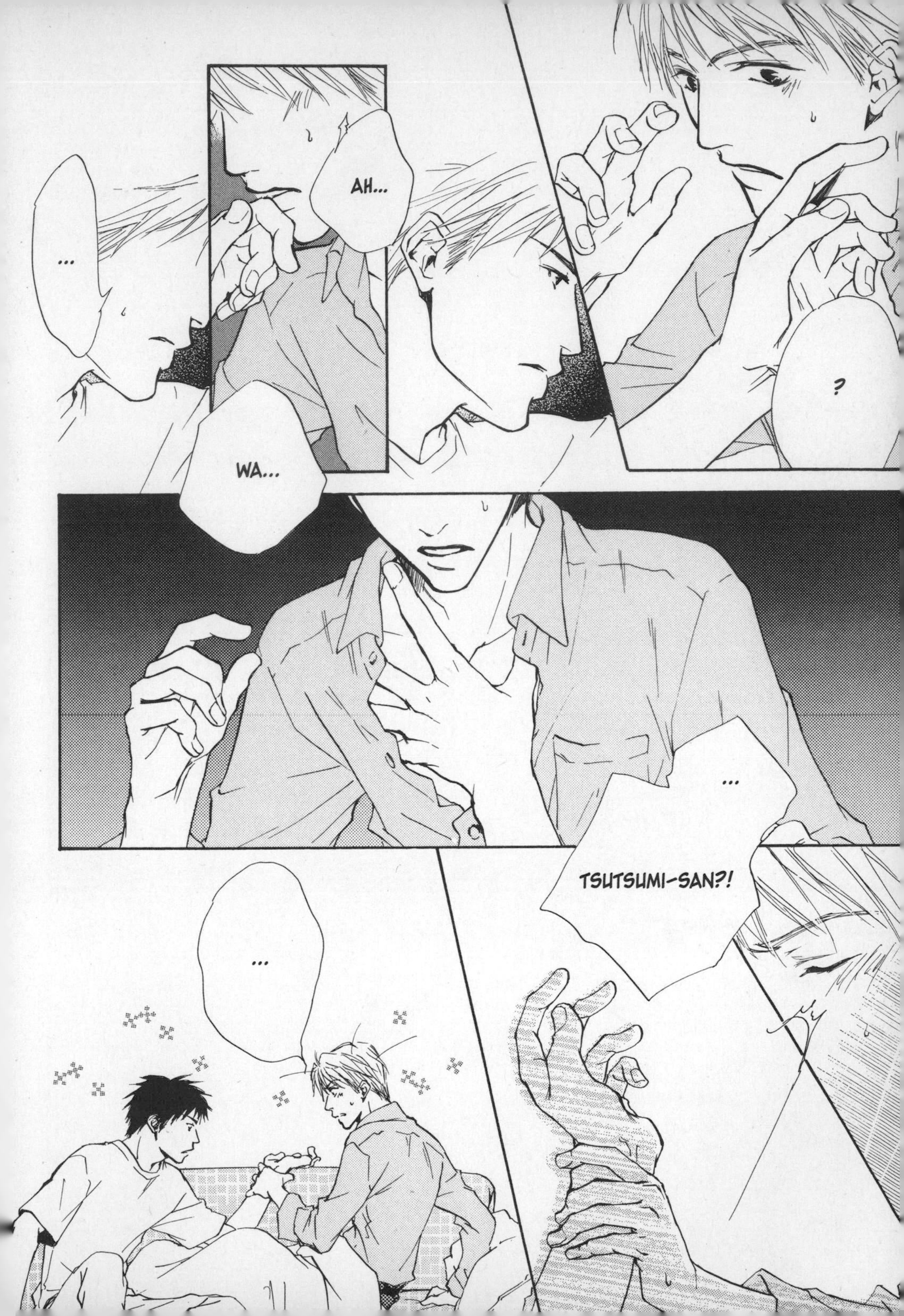
?
AH...
WA...
...
...
TSUTSUMI-SAN?!
...

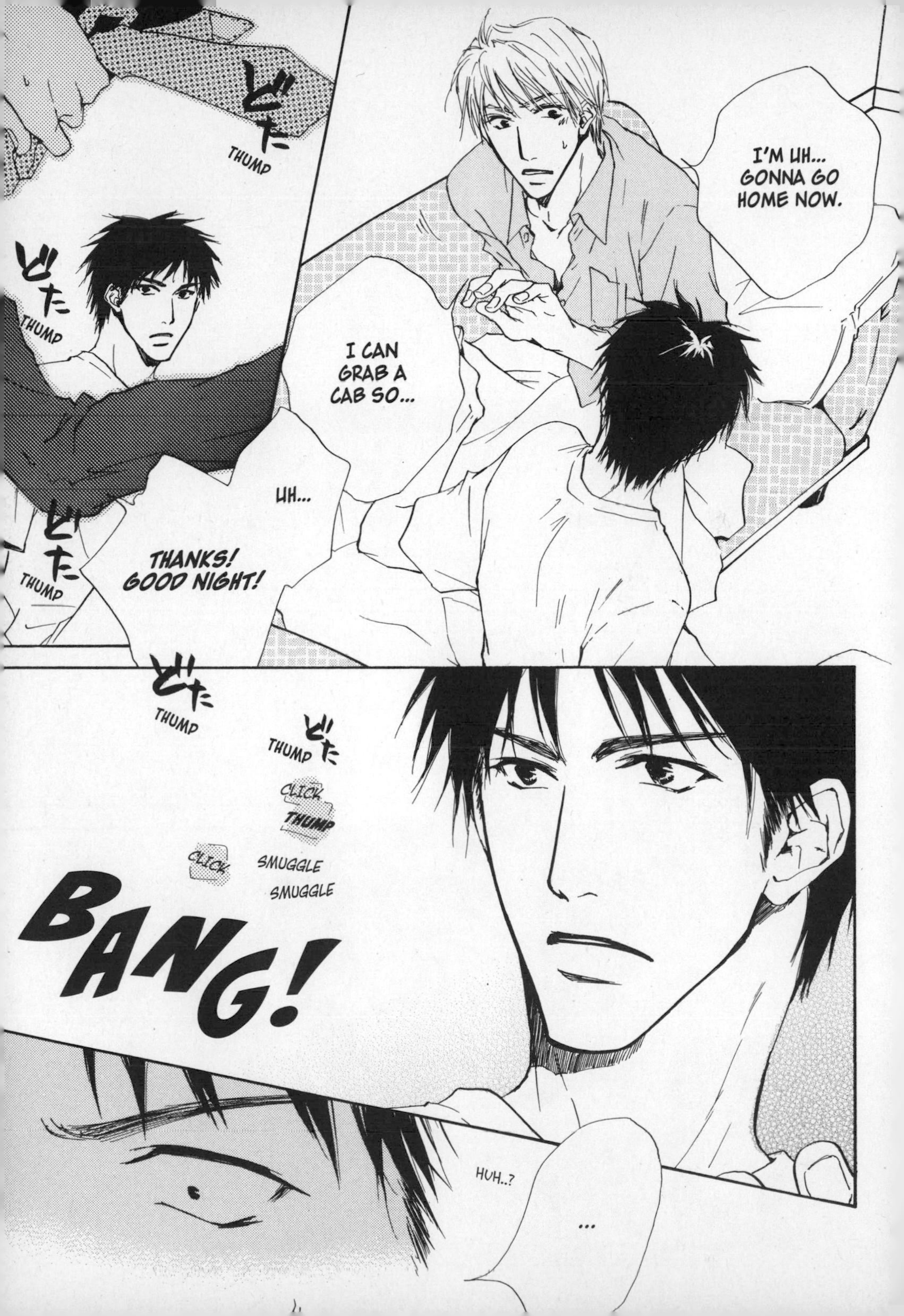
I'M UH... GONNA GO HOME NOW.
I CAN GRAB A CAB SO...
UH...
THANKS! GOOD NIGHT!
どた
THUMP
どた
THUMP
どた
THUMP
どた
THUMP
どた
THUMP
CLICK
THUMP
CLICK
SMUGGLE
SMUGGLE
BANG!
HUH..?
...

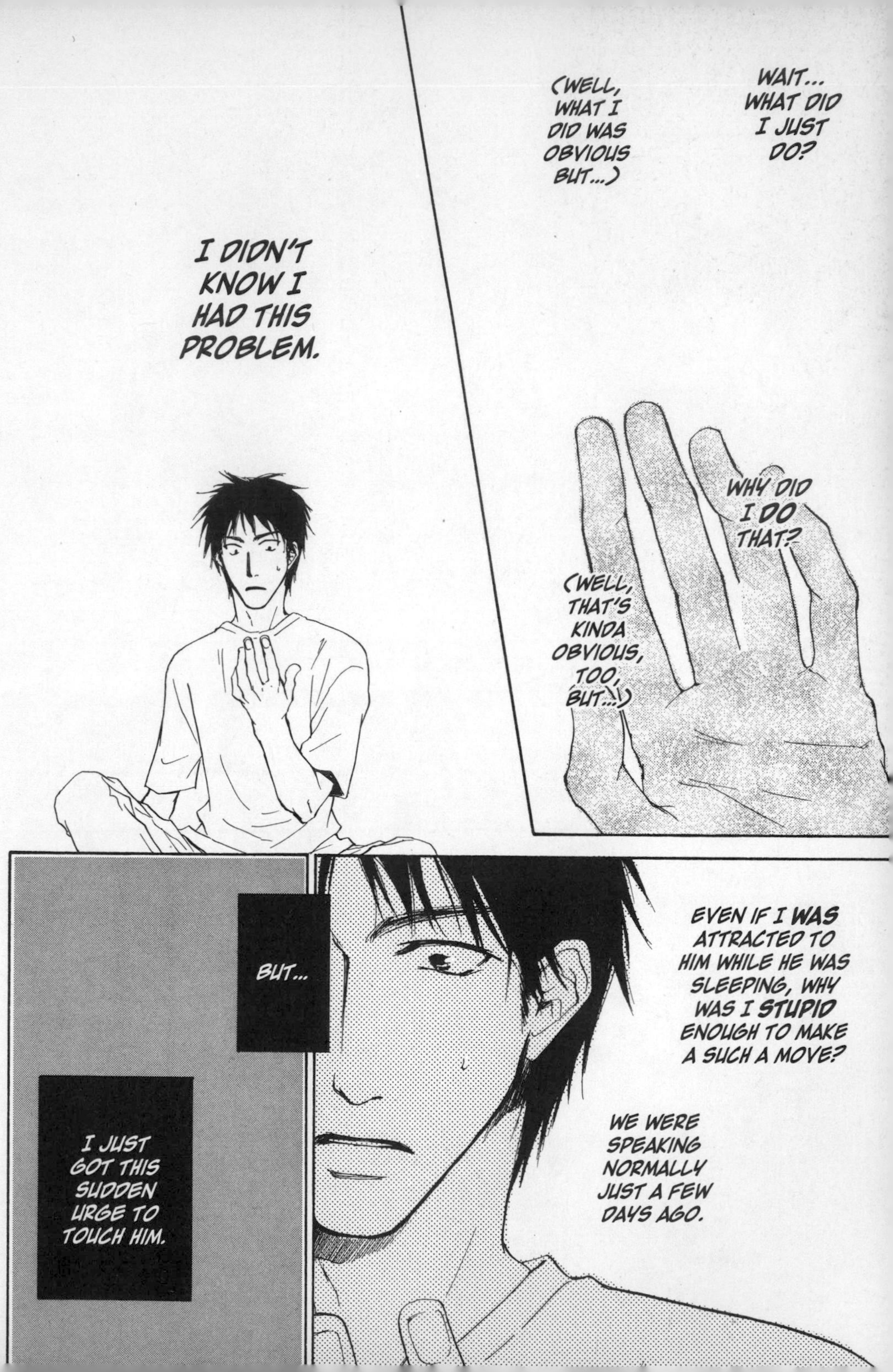
WAIT... WHAT DID I JUST DO?
(WELL, WHAT I DID WAS OBVIOUS BUT...)
WHY DID I DO THAT?
(WELL, THAT'S KINDA OBVIOUS, TOO, BUT...)
I DIDN'T KNOW I HAD THIS PROBLEM.
EVEN IF I WAS ATTRACTED TO HIM WHILE HE WAS SLEEPING, WHY WAS I STUPID ENOUGH TO MAKE A SUCH A MOVE?
WE WERE SPEAKING NORMALLY JUST A FEW DAYS AGO.
BUT...
I JUST GOT THIS SUDDEN URGE TO TOUCH HIM.

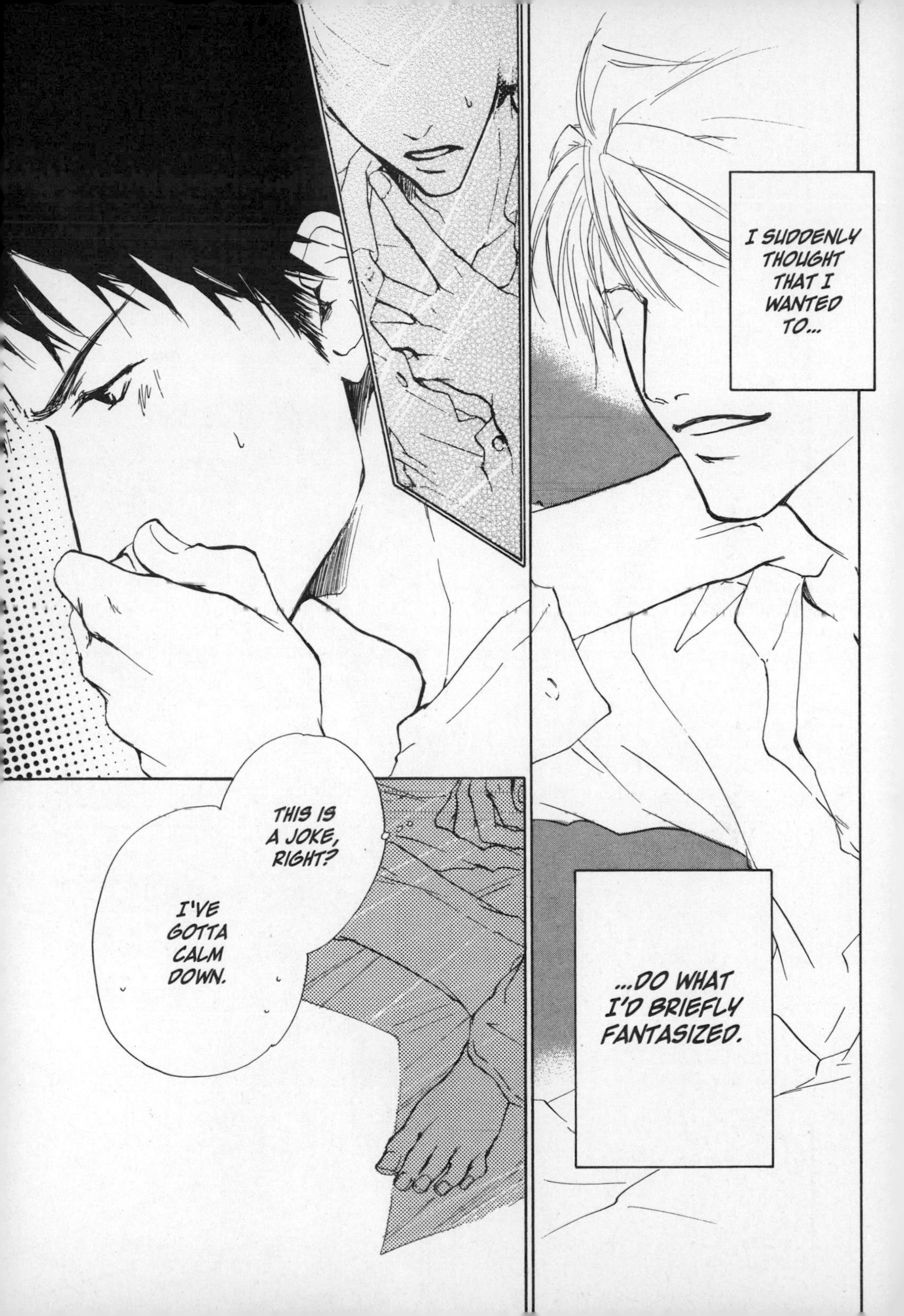
I SUDDENLY THOUGHT THAT I WANTED TO...
...DO WHAT I'D BRIEFLY FANTASIZED.
THIS IS A JOKE, RIGHT?
I'VE GOTTA CALM DOWN.

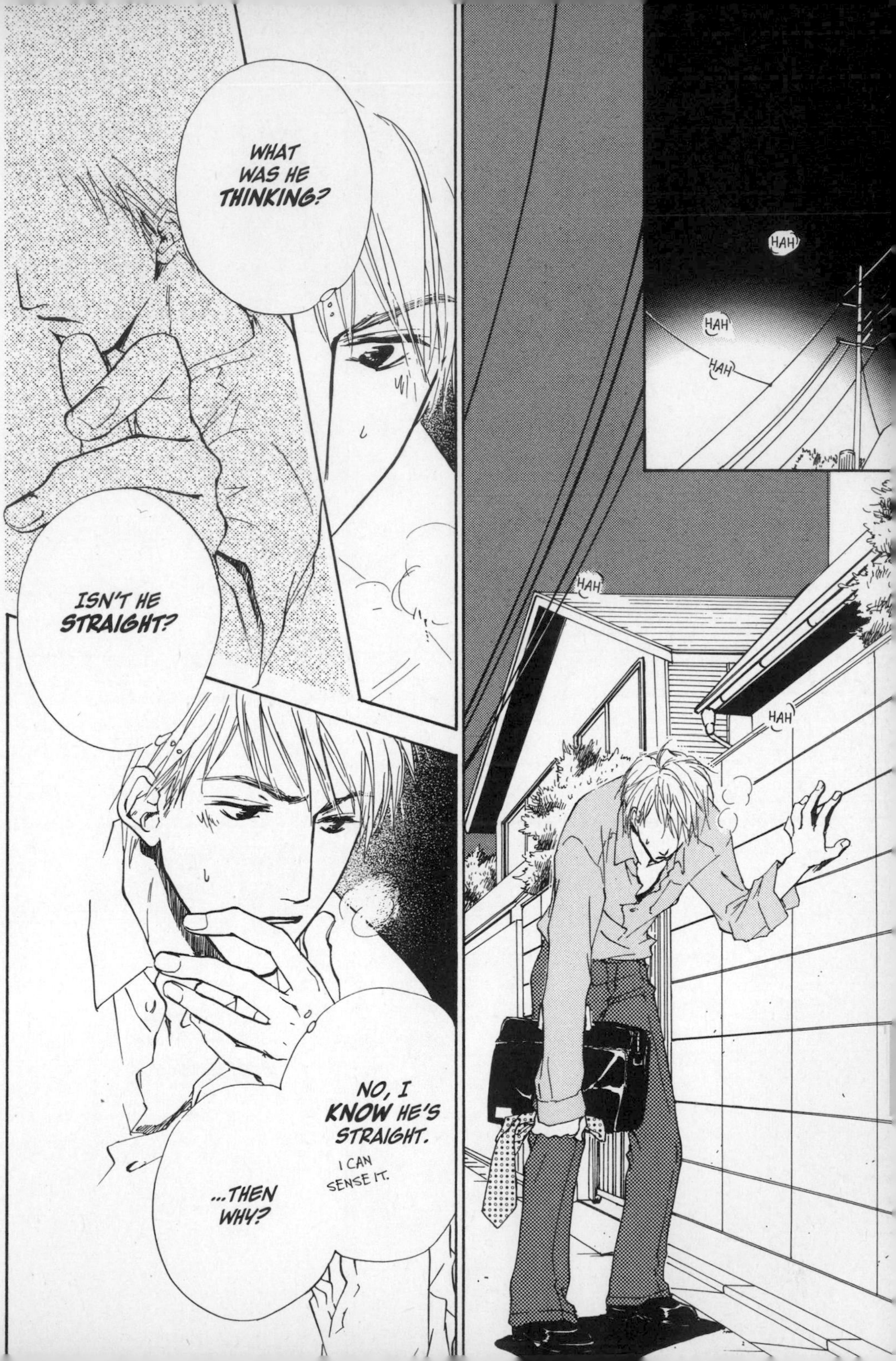
HAH
HAH
HAH
HAH
HAH
WHAT WAS HE THINKING?
ISN'T HE STRAIGHT?
NO, I KNOW HE'S STRAIGHT.
I CAN SENSE IT.
...THEN WHY?

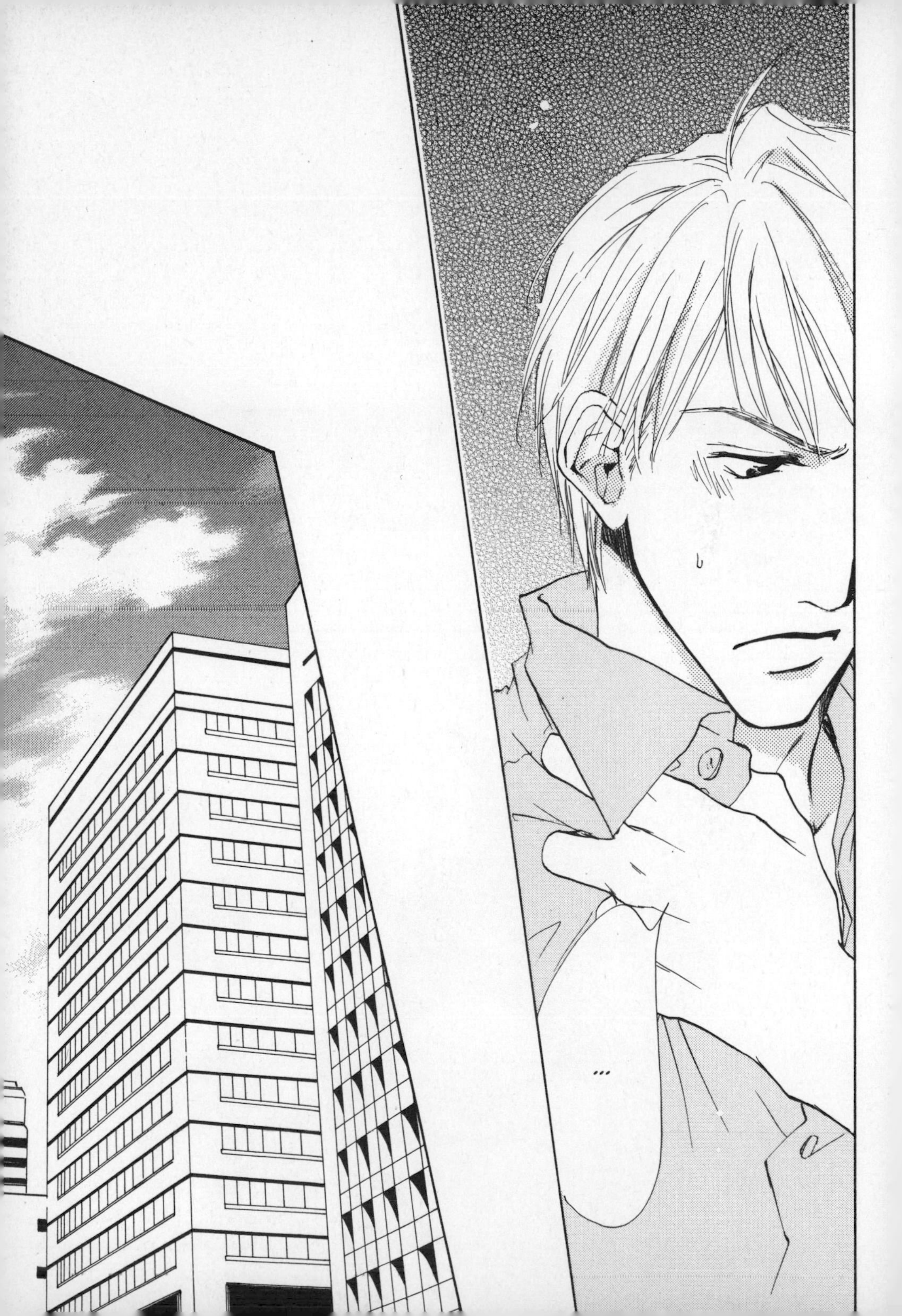
...

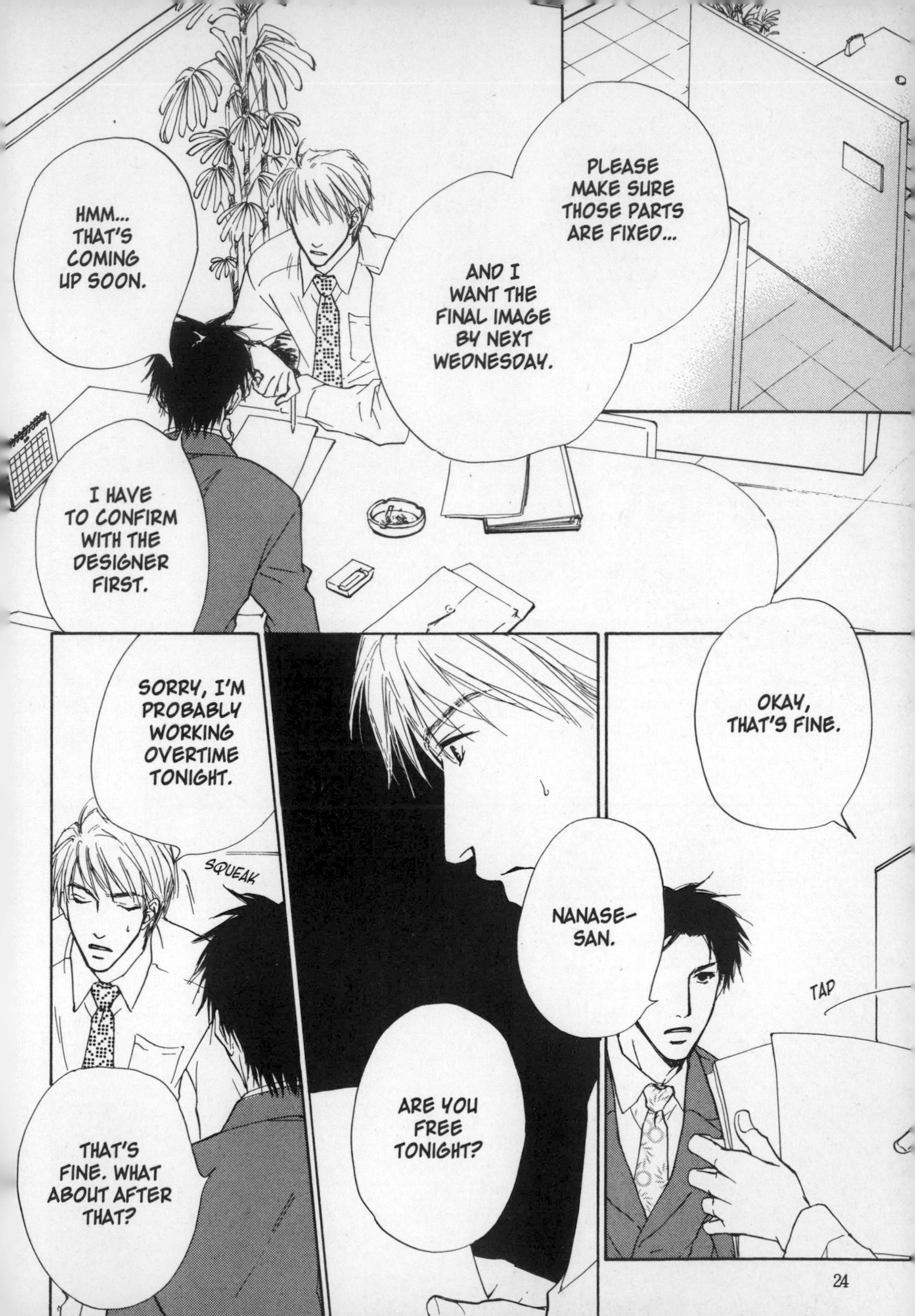
PLEASE MAKE SURE THOSE PARTS ARE FIXED...
AND I WANT THE FINAL IMAGE BY NEXT WEDNESDAY.
HMM... THAT'S COMING UP SOON.
I HAVE TO CONFIRM WITH THE DESIGNER FIRST.
OKAY, THAT'S FINE.
NANASE-SAN.
TAP
ARE YOU FREE TONIGHT?
SORRY, I'M PROBABLY WORKING OVERTIME TONIGHT.
SQUEAK
THAT'S FINE. WHAT ABOUT AFTER THAT?

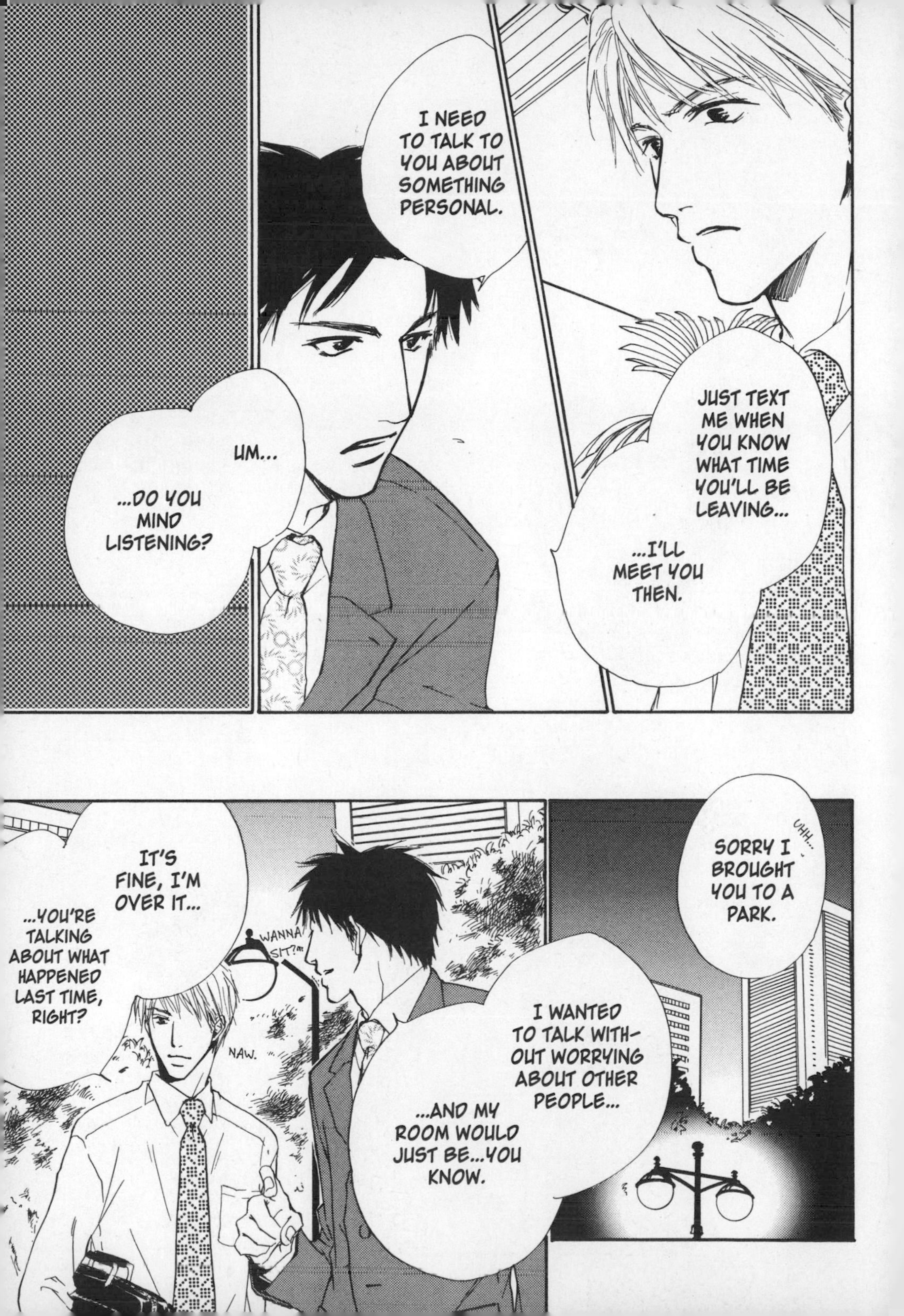
I NEED TO TALK TO YOU ABOUT SOMETHING PERSONAL.
JUST TEXT ME WHEN YOU KNOW WHAT TIME YOU'LL BE LEAVING...
...I'LL MEET YOU THEN.
UM...
...DO YOU MIND LISTENING?
UHH...
SORRY I BROUGHT YOU TO A PARK.
I WANTED TO TALK WITH-OUT WORRYING ABOUT OTHER PEOPLE...
...AND MY ROOM WOULD JUST BE...YOU KNOW.
IT'S FINE, I'M OVER IT...
...YOU'RE TALKING ABOUT WHAT HAPPENED LAST TIME, RIGHT?
WANNA SIT?
NAW.

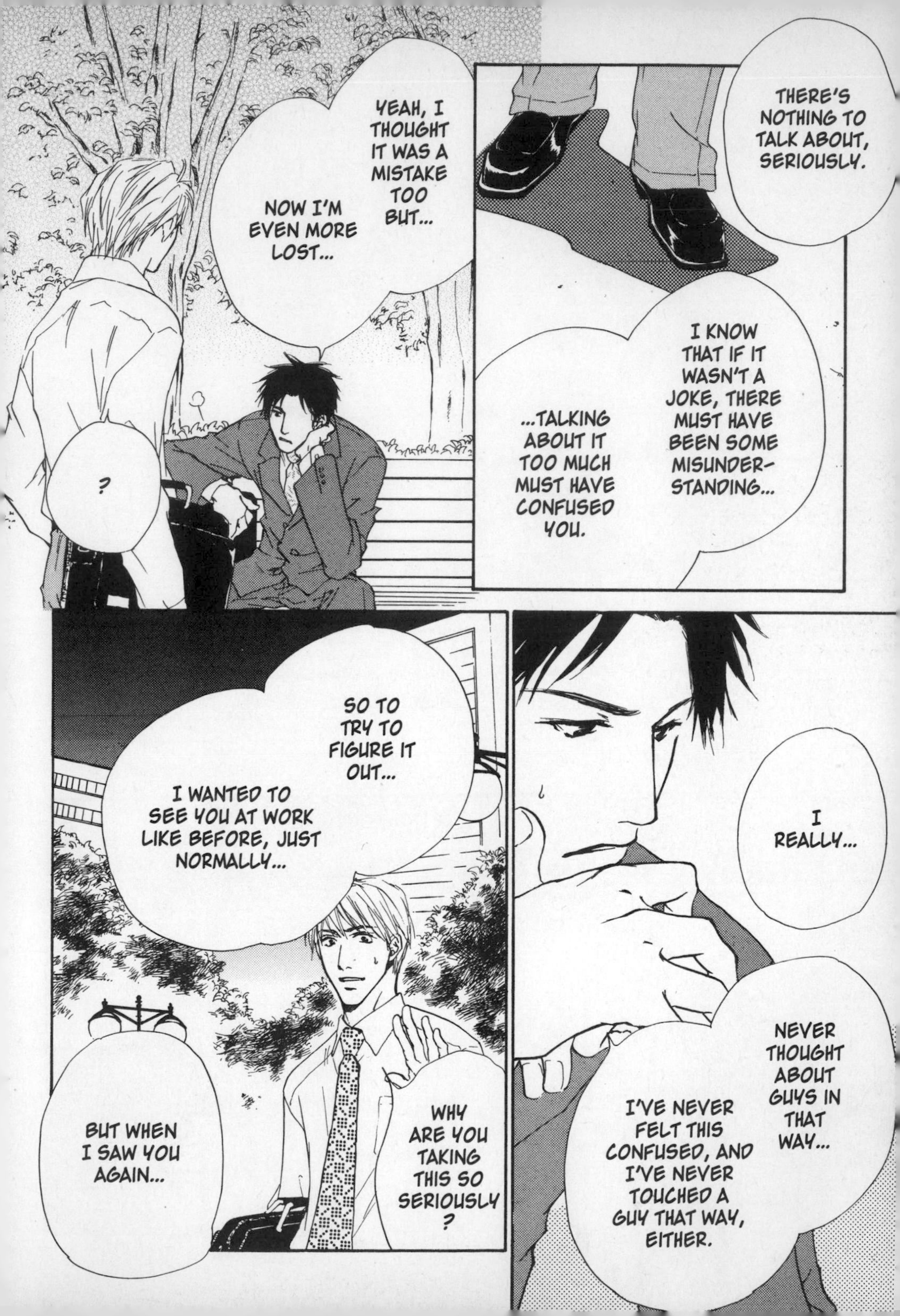
THERE'S NOTHING TO TALK ABOUT, SERIOUSLY.
I KNOW THAT IF IT WASN'T A JOKE, THERE MUST HAVE BEEN SOME MISUNDER-STANDING...
...TALKING ABOUT IT TOO MUCH MUST HAVE CONFUSED YOU.
YEAH, I THOUGHT IT WAS A MISTAKE TOO BUT...
NOW I'M EVEN MORE LOST...
?
I REALLY...
NEVER THOUGHT ABOUT GUYS IN THAT WAY...
I'VE NEVER FELT THIS CONFUSED, AND I'VE NEVER TOUCHED A GUY THAT WAY, EITHER.
SO TO TRY TO FIGURE IT OUT...
I WANTED TO SEE YOU AT WORK LIKE BEFORE, JUST NORMALLY...
WHY ARE YOU TAKING THIS SO SERIOUSLY?
BUT WHEN I SAW YOU AGAIN...

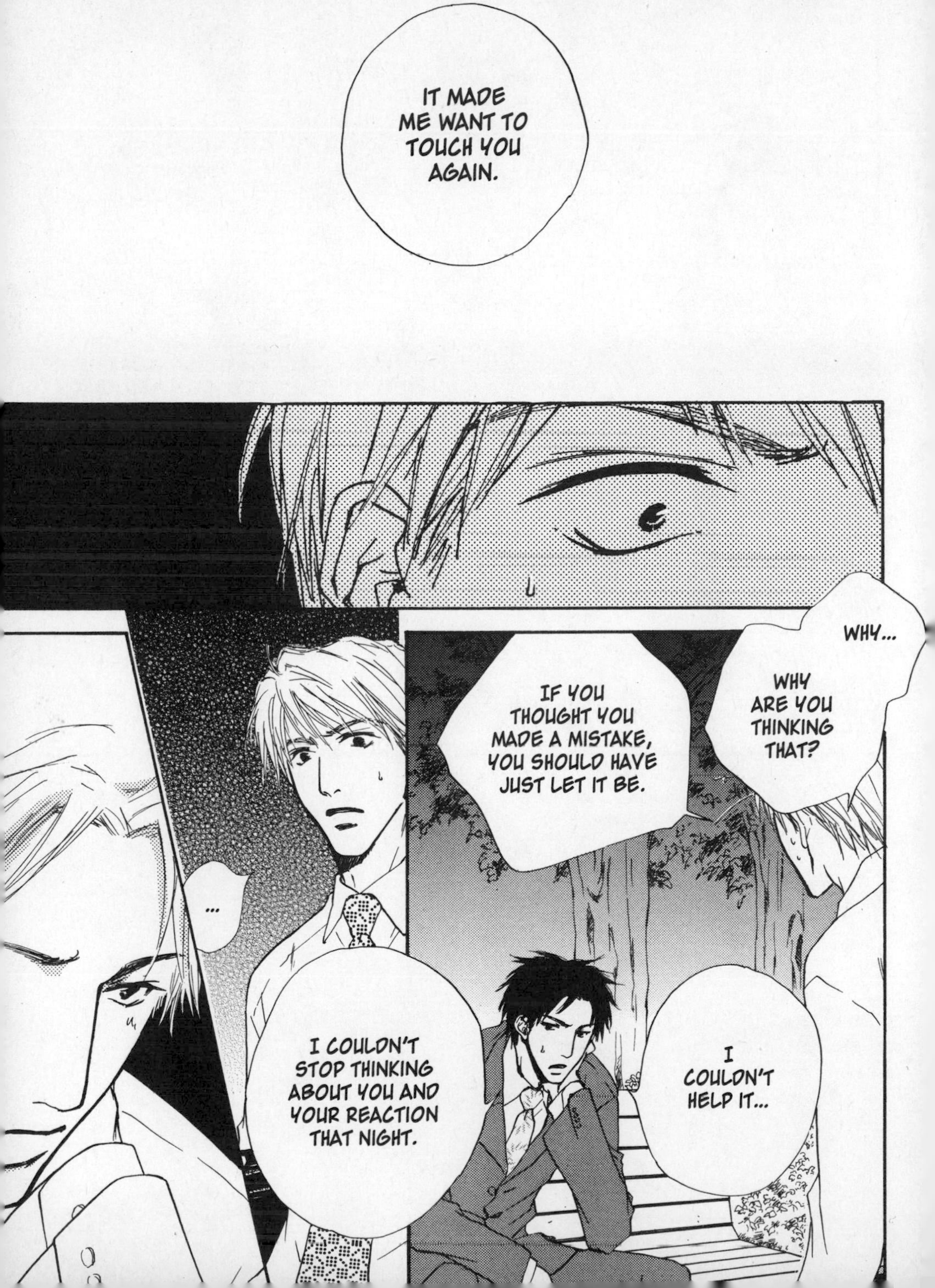
IT MADE ME WANT TO TOUCH YOU AGAIN.
WHY...
WHY ARE YOU THINKING THAT?
IF YOU THOUGHT YOU MADE A MISTAKE, YOU SHOULD HAVE JUST LET IT BE.
I COULDN'T HELP IT...
...
I COULDN'T STOP THINKING ABOUT YOU AND YOUR REACTION THAT NIGHT.

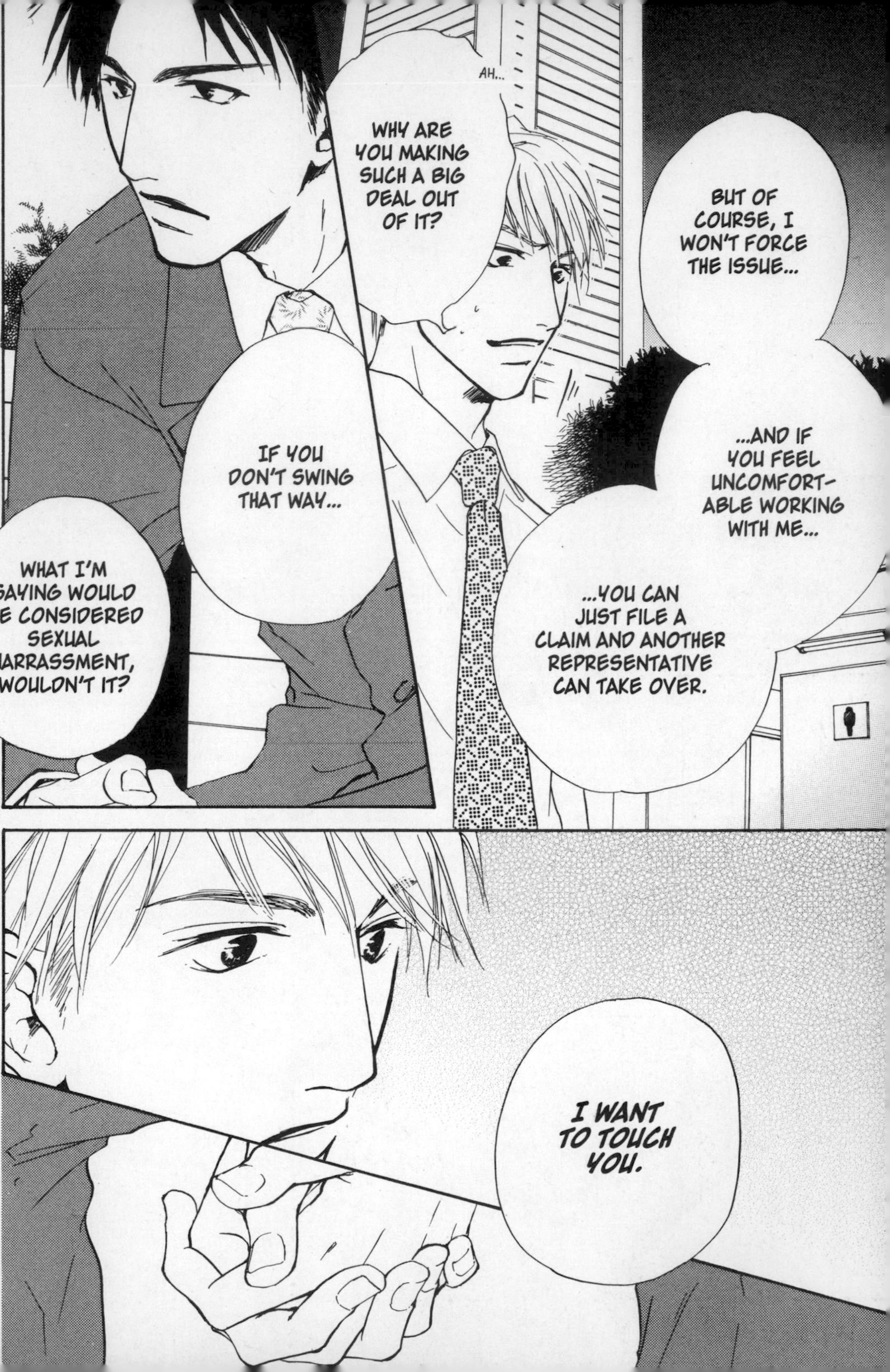
AH...
WHY ARE YOU MAKING SUCH A BIG DEAL OUT OF IT?
BUT OF COURSE, I WON'T FORCE THE ISSUE...
...AND IF YOU FEEL UNCOMFORT-ABLE WORKING WITH ME...
...YOU CAN JUST FILE A CLAIM AND ANOTHER REPRESENTATIVE CAN TAKE OVER.
IF YOU DON'T SWING THAT WAY...
WHAT I'M SAYING WOULD BE CONSIDERED SEXUAL HARRASSMENT, WOULDN'T IT?
I WANT TO TOUCH YOU.

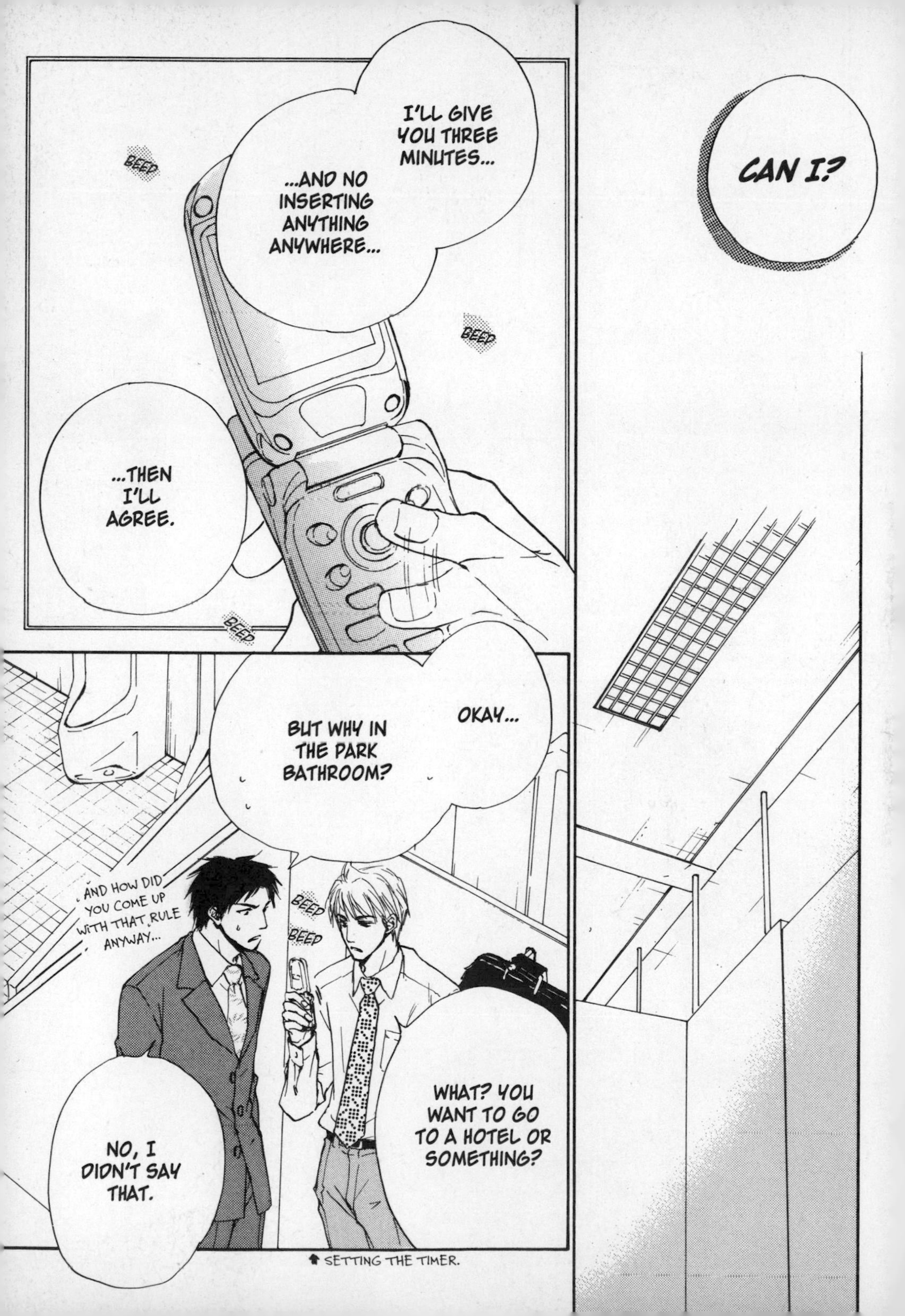
CAN I?
I'LL GIVE YOU THREE MINUTES...
...AND NO INSERTING ANYTHING ANYWHERE...
BEEP
BEEP
...THEN I'LL AGREE.
BEEP
OKAY...
BUT WHY IN THE PARK BATHROOM?
BEEP
BEEP
AND HOW DID YOU COME UP WITH THAT RULE ANYWAY...
WHAT? YOU WANT TO GO TO A HOTEL OR SOMETHING?
NO, I DIDN'T SAY THAT.
SETTING THE TIMER.

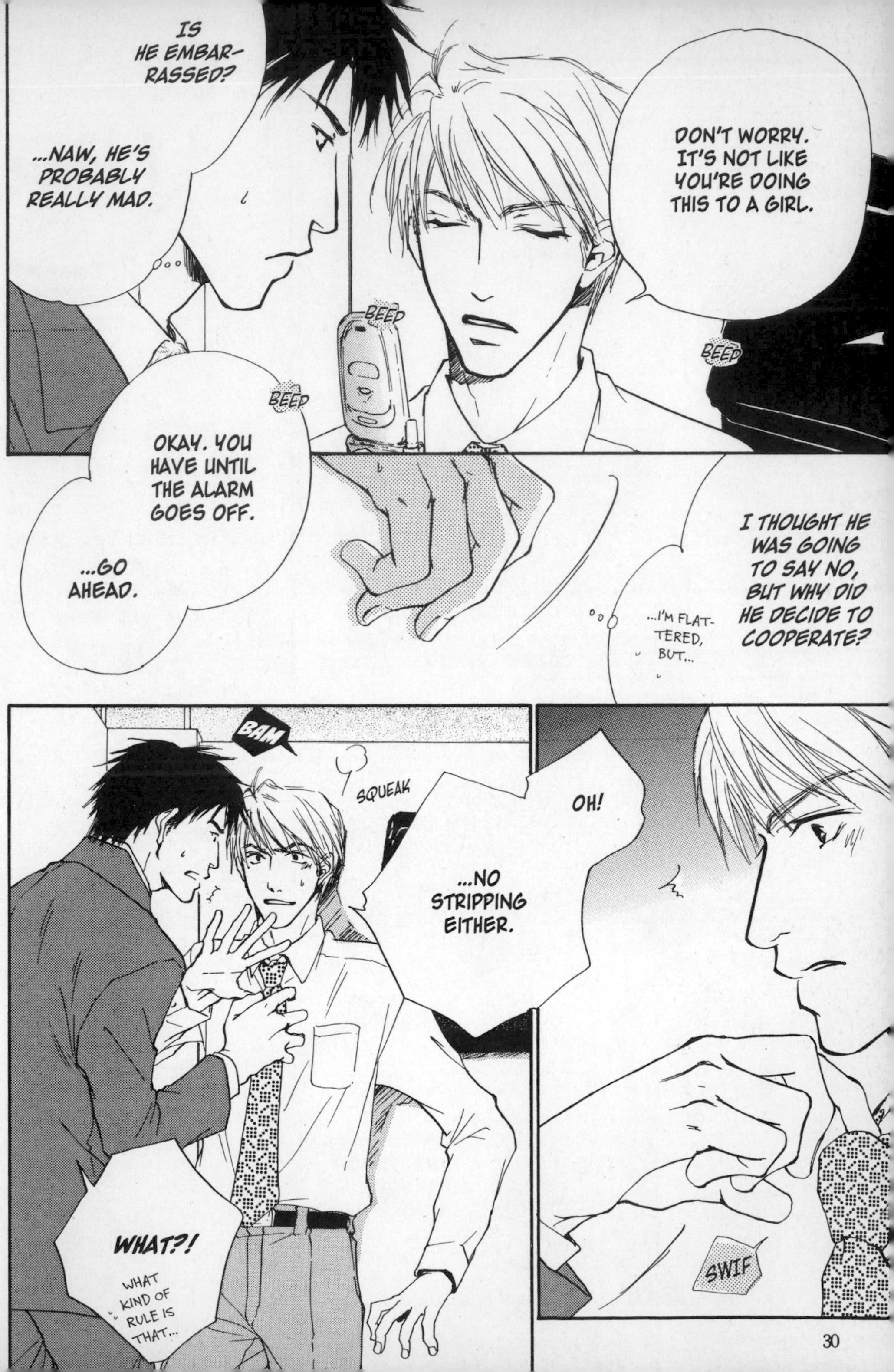
DON'T WORRY. IT'S NOT LIKE YOU'RE DOING THIS TO A GIRL.
BEEP
BEEP
BEEP
OKAY. YOU HAVE UNTIL THE ALARM GOES OFF.
...GO AHEAD.
IS HE EMBAR-RASSED?
...NAW, HE'S PROBABLY REALLY MAD.
I THOUGHT HE WAS GOING TO SAY NO, BUT WHY DID HE DECIDE TO COOPERATE?
...I'M FLAT-TERED, BUT...
OH!
...NO STRIPPING EITHER.
SWIF
BAM
SQUEAK
WHAT?!
WHAT KIND OF RULE IS THAT...

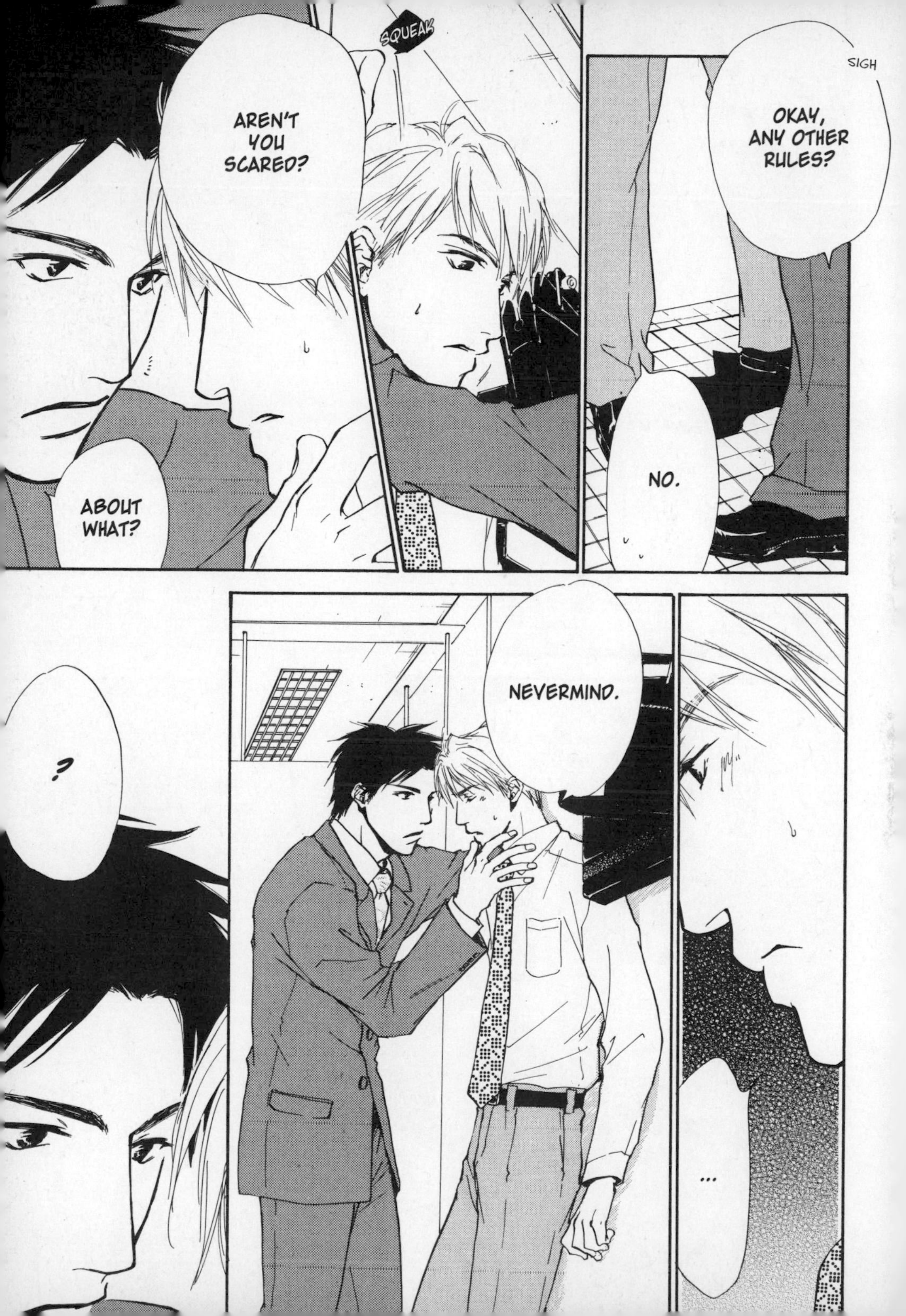
SIGH
OKAY, ANY OTHER RULES?
NO.
SQUEAK
AREN'T YOU SCARED?
ABOUT WHAT?
...
NEVERMIND.
?

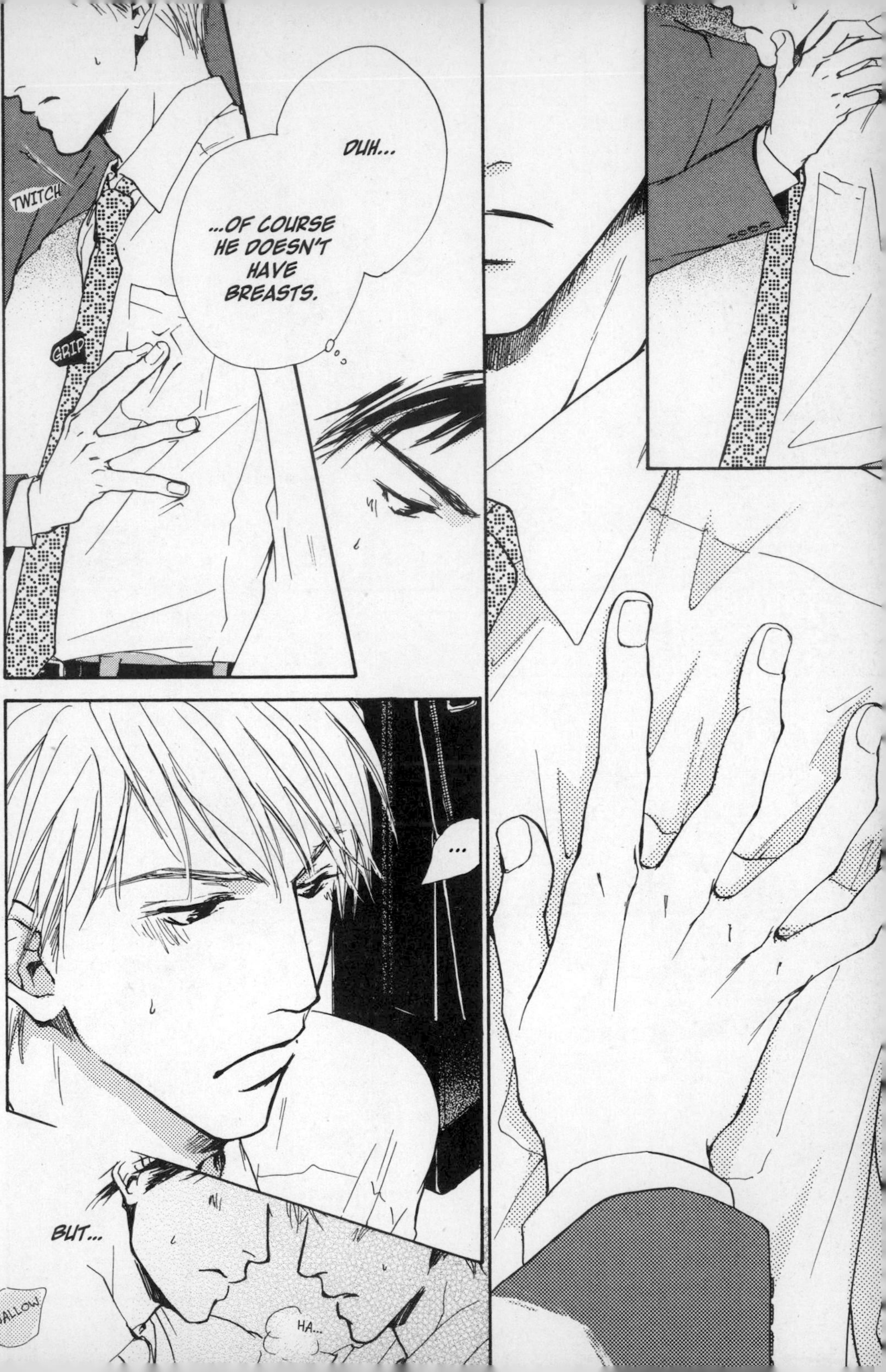
DUH...
...OF COURSE HE DOESN'T HAVE BREASTS.
TWITCH
GRIP
...
BUT...
SWALLOW
HA...

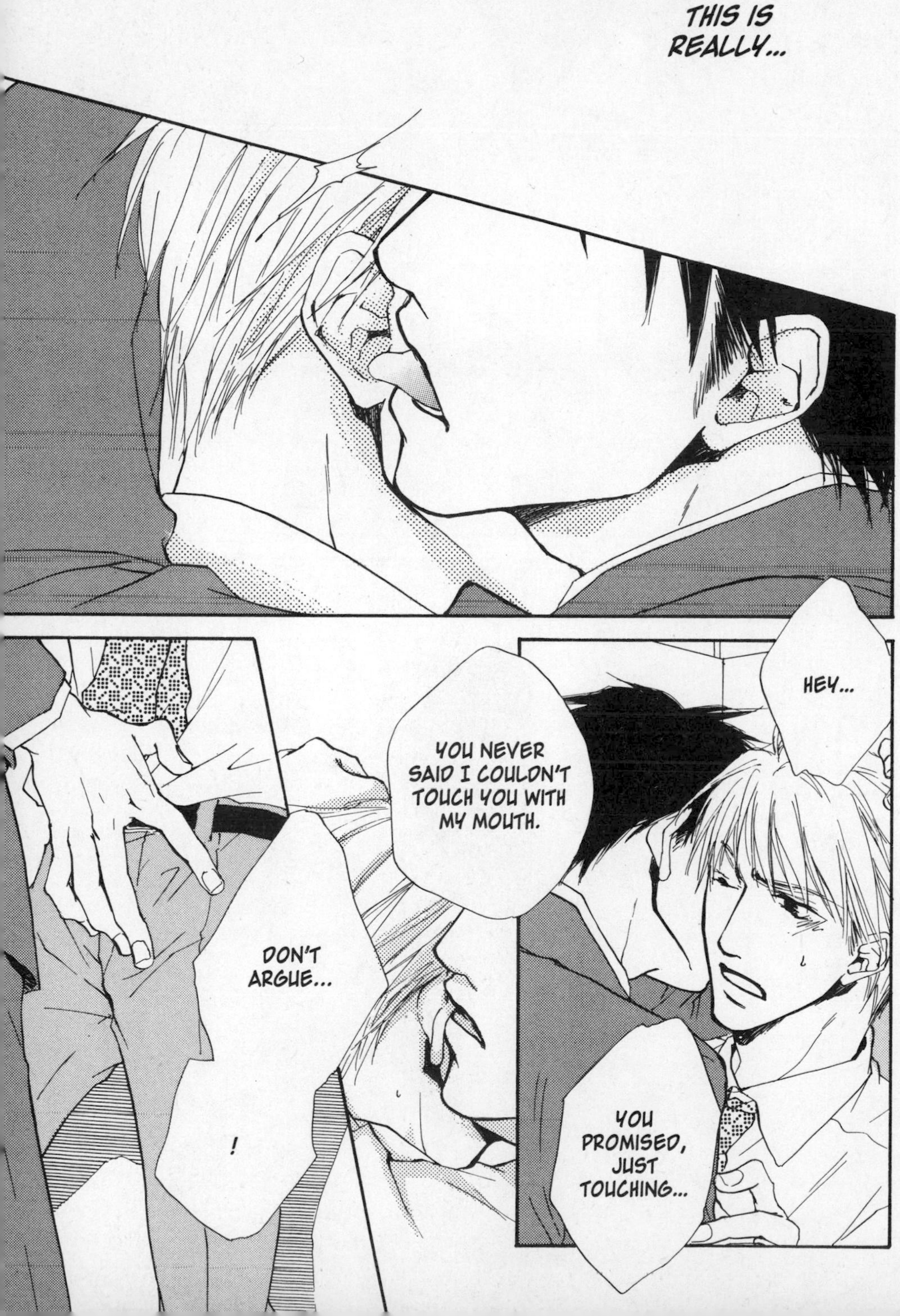
THIS IS REALLY...
HEY...
YOU PROMISED, JUST TOUCHING...
YOU NEVER SAID I COULDN'T TOUCH YOU WITH MY MOUTH.
DON'T ARGUE...
!

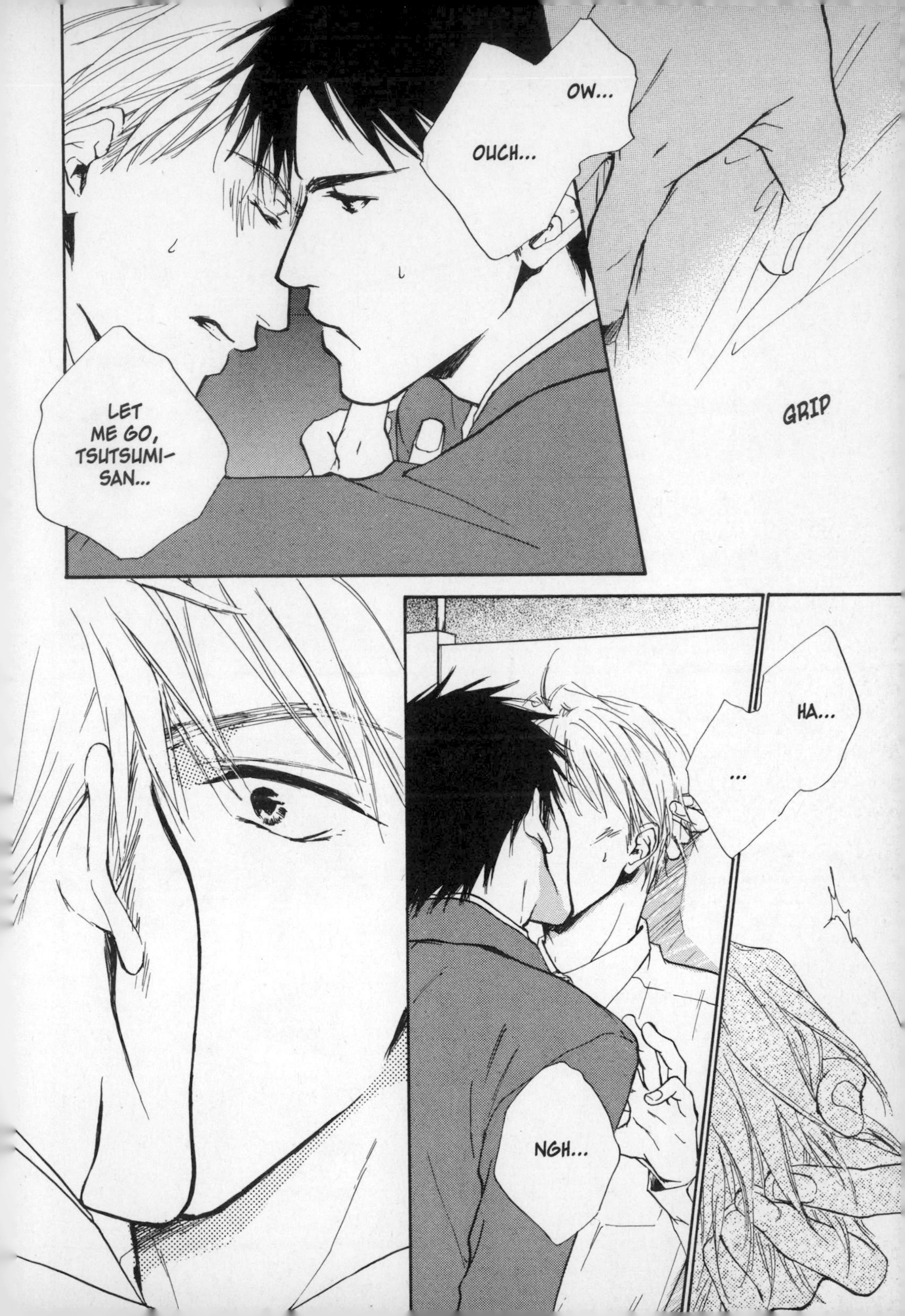
OW...
OUCH...
GRIP
LET ME GO, TSUTSUMI-SAN...
HA...
...
NGH...

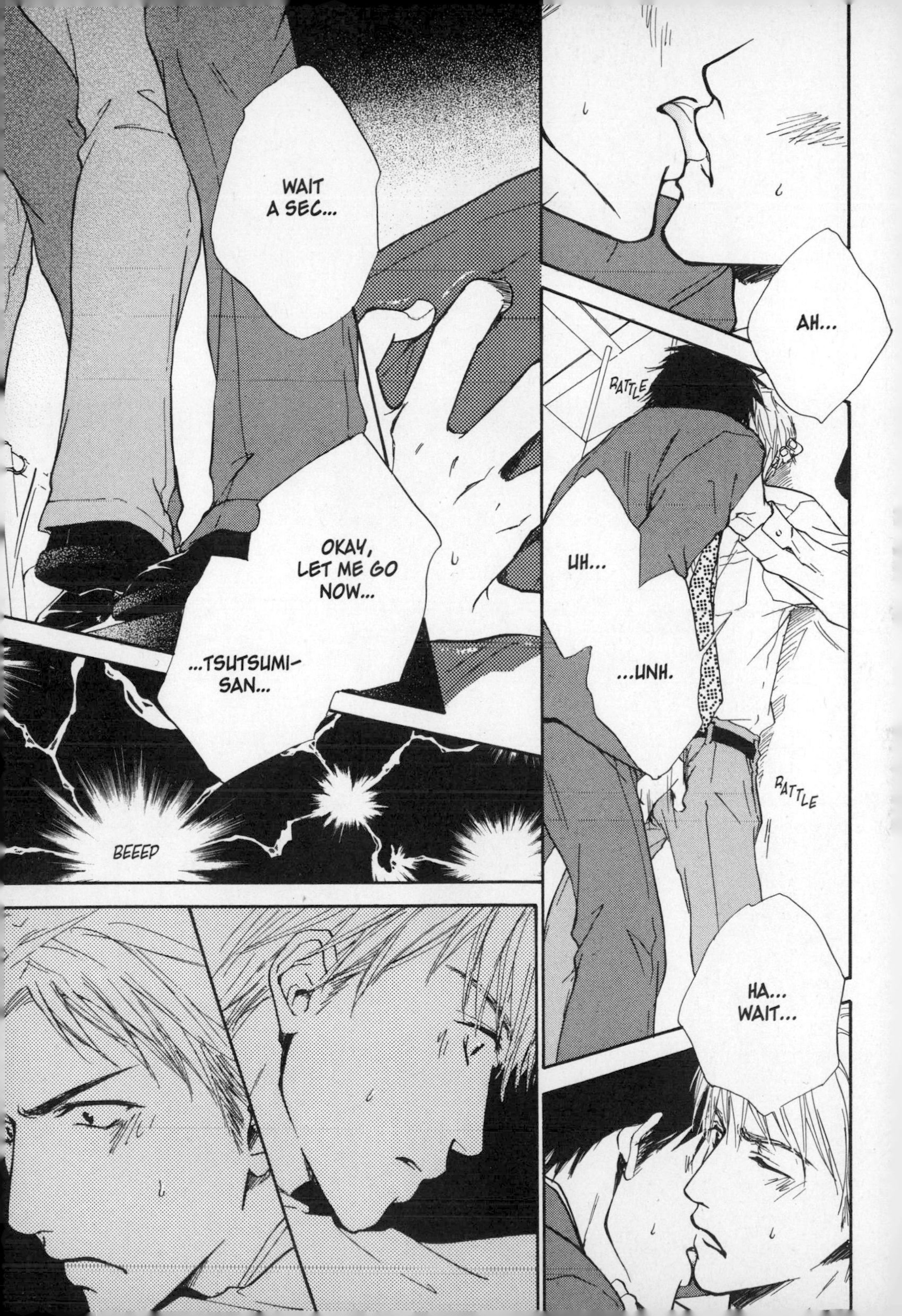
AH...
RATTLE
UH...
...UNH.
RATTLE
HA... WAIT...
WAIT A SEC...
OKAY, LET ME GO NOW...
...TSUTSUMI-SAN...
BEEEP

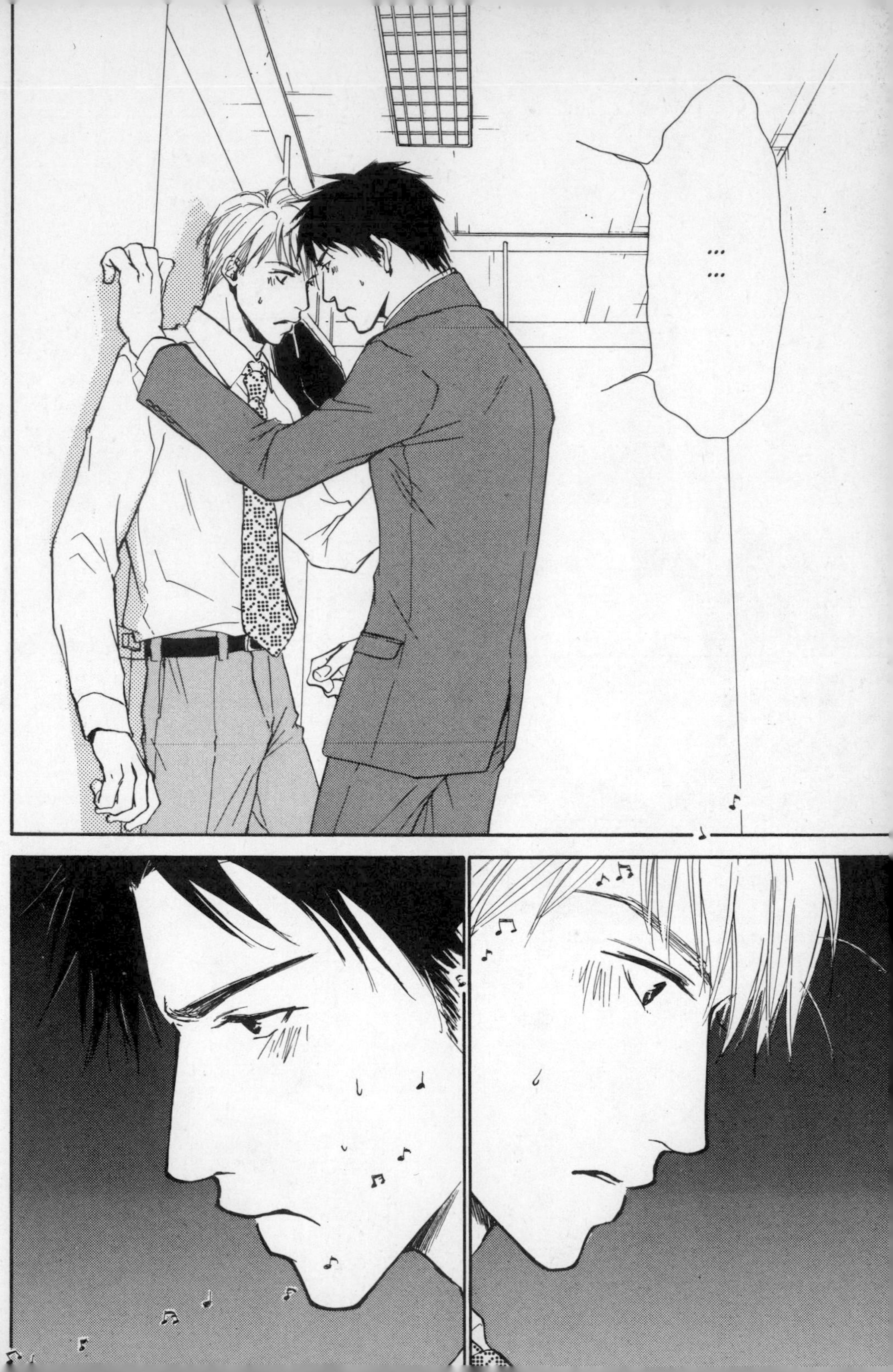
…
…

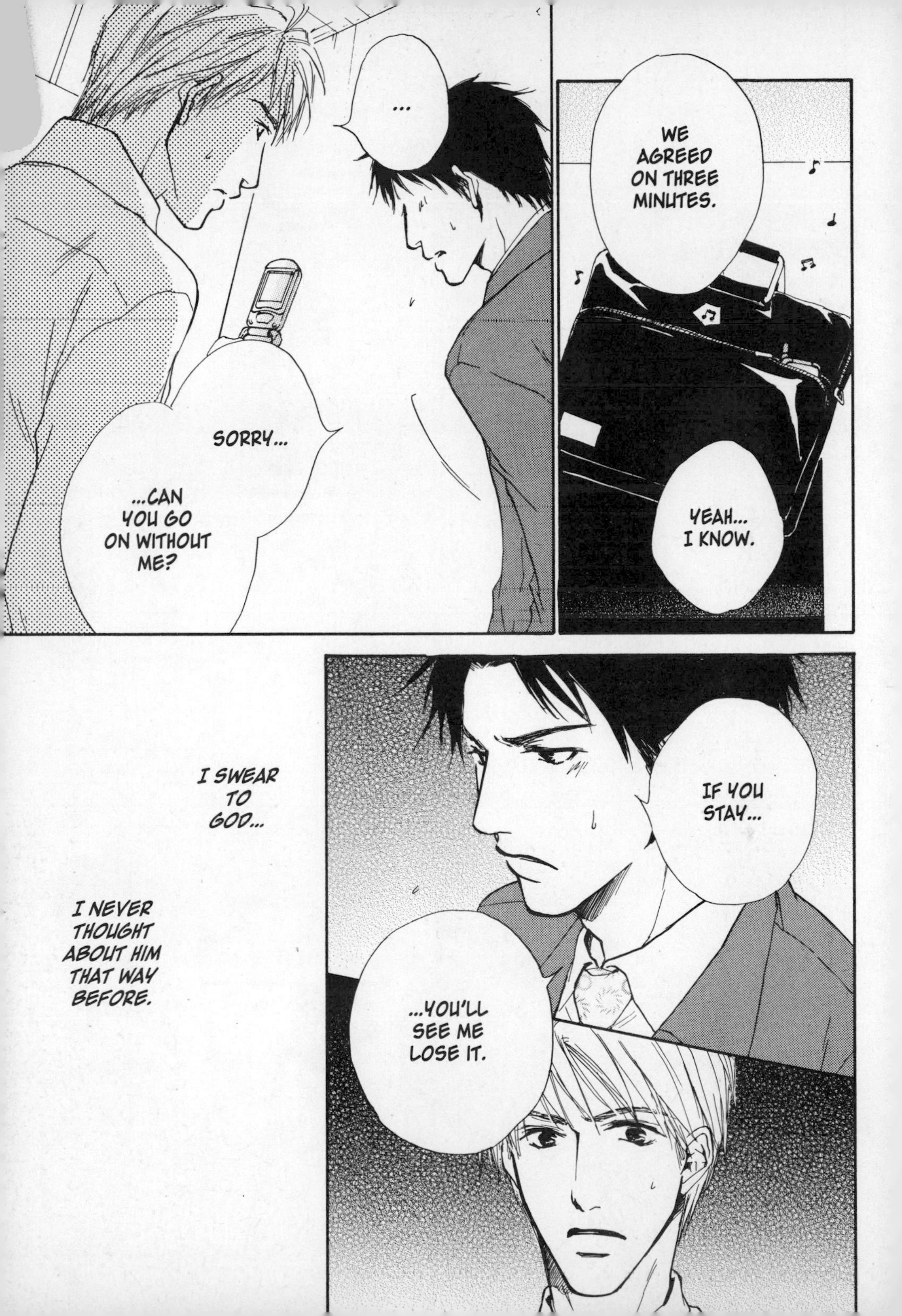
WE AGREED ON THREE MINUTES.
YEAH... I KNOW.
...
SORRY...
...CAN YOU GO ON WITHOUT ME?
IF YOU STAY...
...YOU'LL SEE ME LOSE IT.
I SWEAR TO GOD...
I NEVER THOUGHT ABOUT HIM THAT WAY BEFORE.

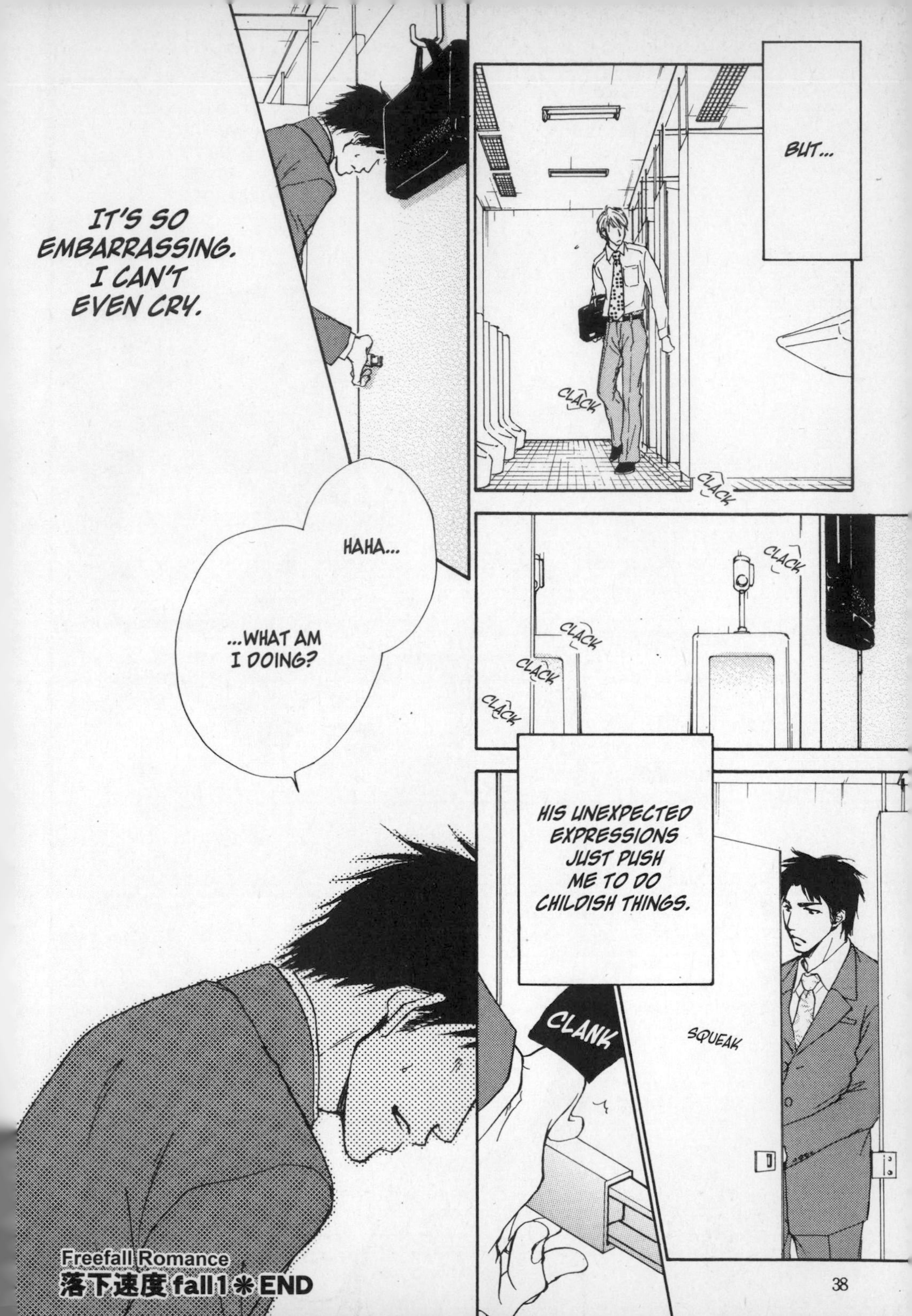
BUT...
CLACK
CLACK
CLACK
CLACK
CLACK
CLACK
HIS UNEXPECTED EXPRESSIONS JUST PUSH ME TO DO CHILDISH THINGS.
SQUEAK
CLANK
IT'S SO EMBARRASSING. I CAN'T EVEN CRY.
HAHA...
...WHAT AM I DOING?

Freefall Romance
落下速度 fall 1 ✻ END

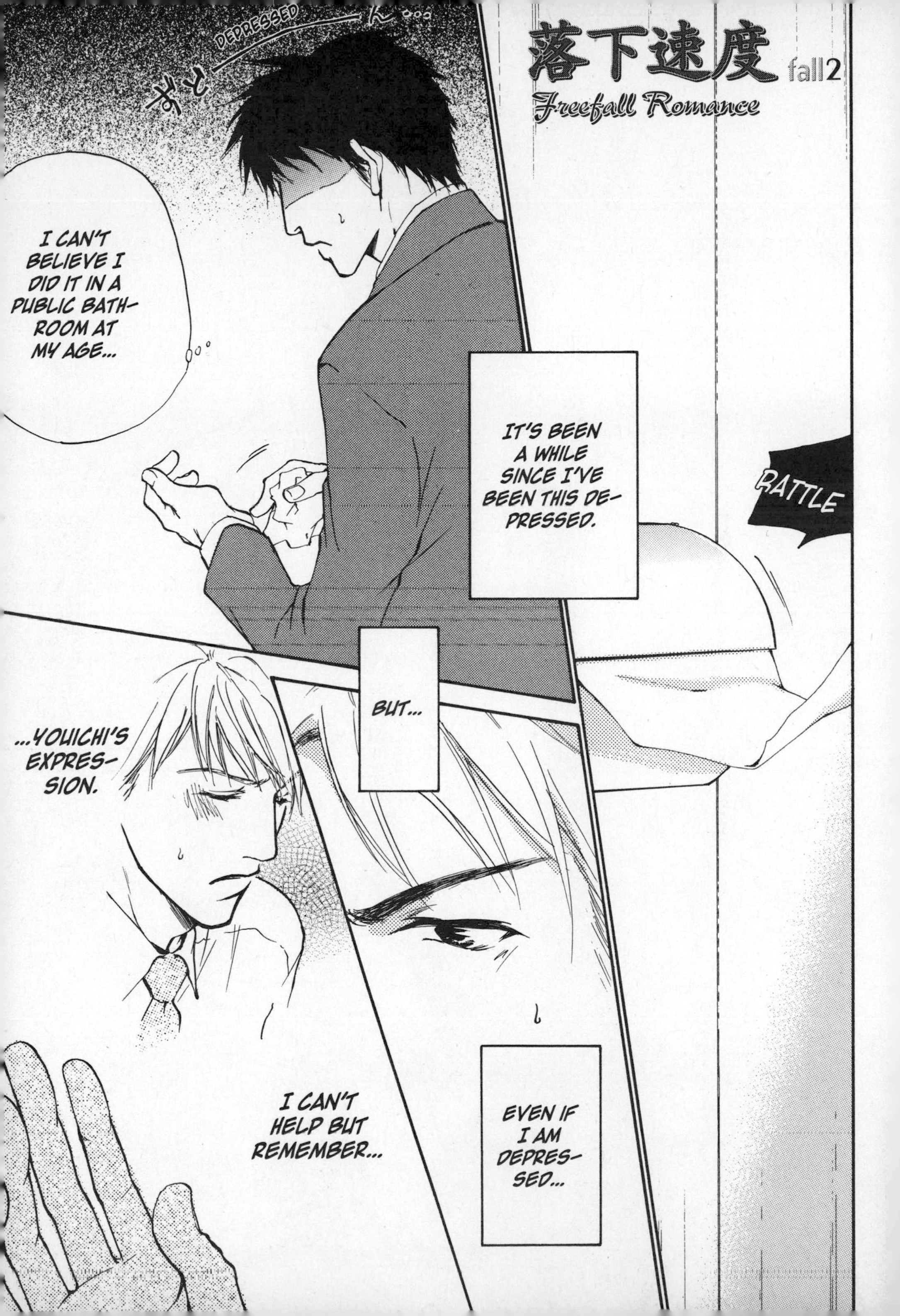
落下速度 fall2
Freefall Romance
IT'S BEEN A WHILE SINCE I'VE BEEN THIS DE-PRESSED.
RATTLE
DEPRESSED
I CAN'T BELIEVE I DID IT IN A PUBLIC BATH-ROOM AT MY AGE...
BUT...
...YOUICHI'S EXPRES-SION.
EVEN IF I AM DEPRES-SED...
I CAN'T HELP BUT REMEMBER...

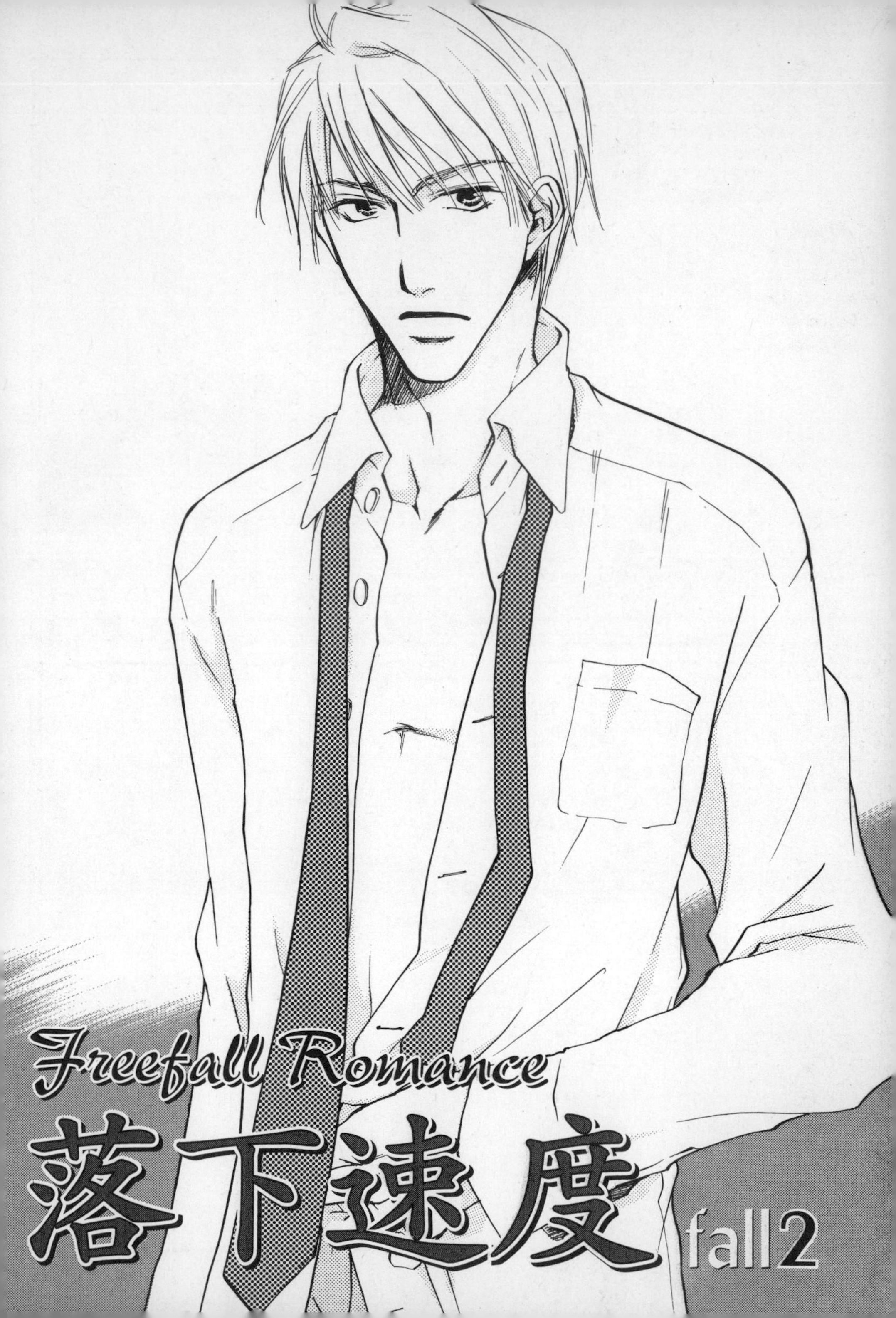
Freefall Romance
落下速度
fall2

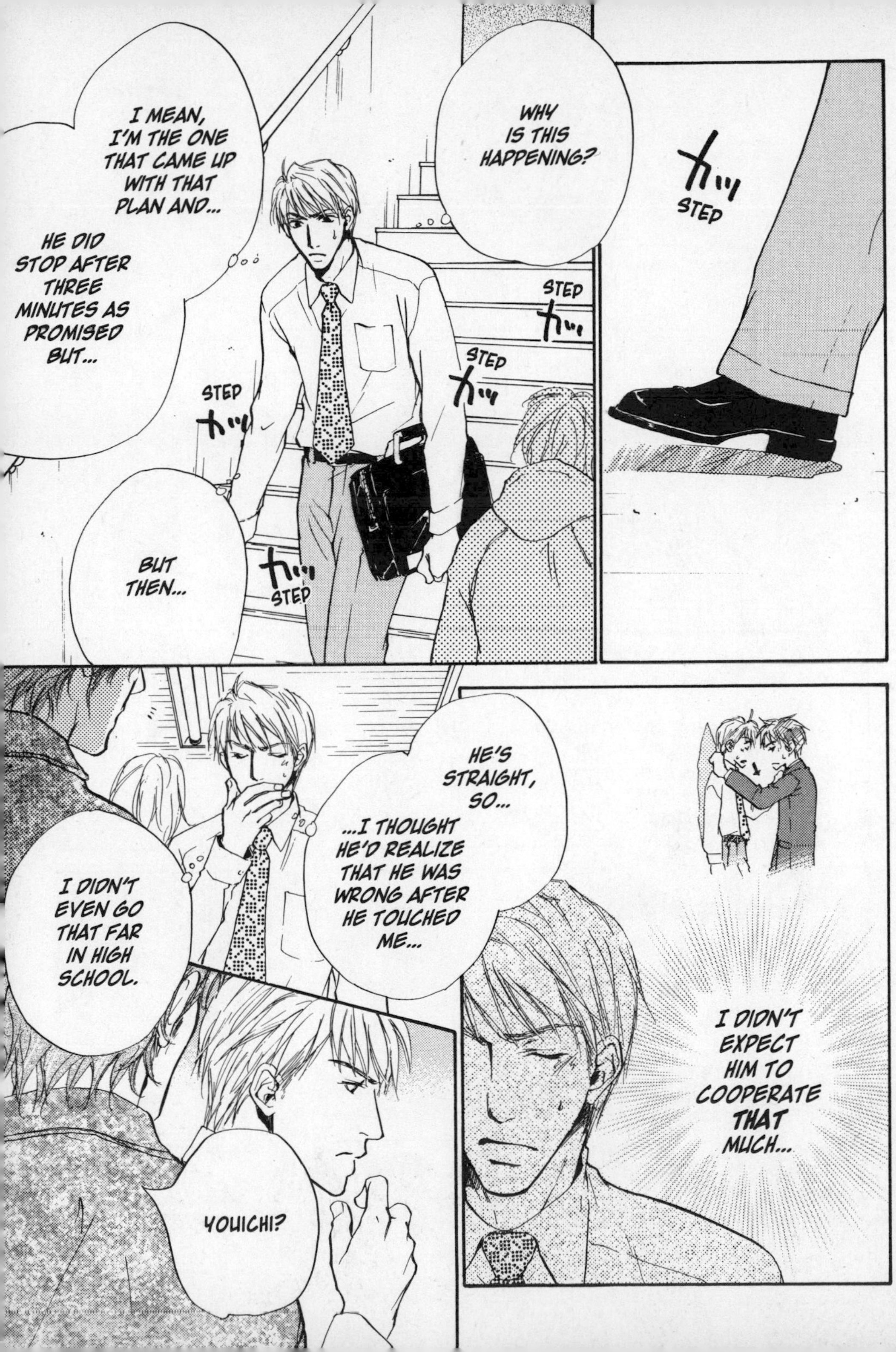
カッ
STEP
WHY IS THIS HAPPENING?
I MEAN, I'M THE ONE THAT CAME UP WITH THAT PLAN AND...
HE DID STOP AFTER THREE MINUTES AS PROMISED BUT...
STEP
カッ
STEP
カッ
STEP
カッ
BUT THEN...
カッ
STEP
I DIDN'T EXPECT HIM TO COOPERATE THAT MUCH...
HE'S STRAIGHT, SO...
...I THOUGHT HE'D REALIZE THAT HE WAS WRONG AFTER HE TOUCHED ME...
I DIDN'T EVEN GO THAT FAR IN HIGH SCHOOL.
YOUICHI?

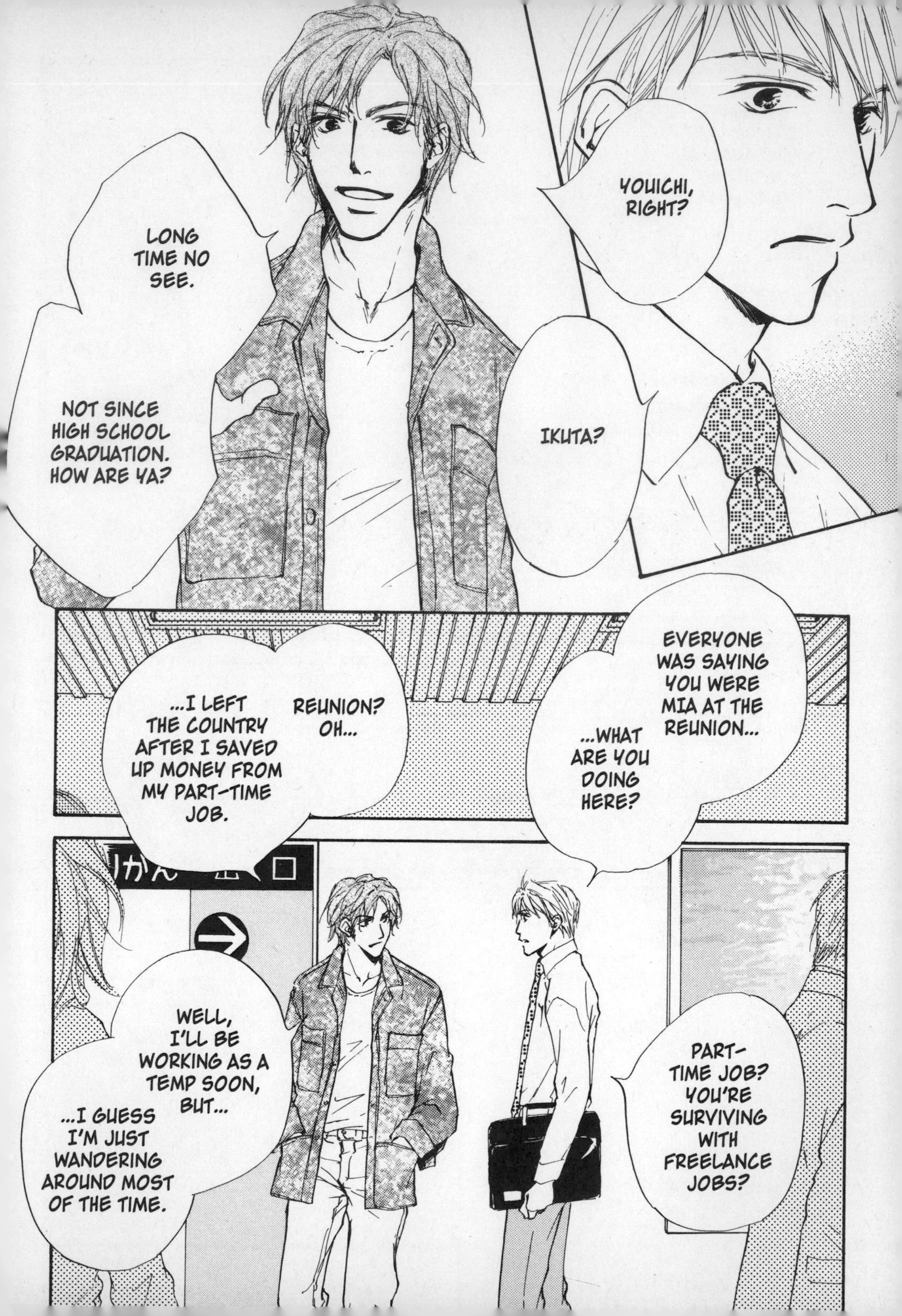
YOUICHI, RIGHT?
IKUTA?
LONG TIME NO SEE.
NOT SINCE HIGH SCHOOL GRADUATION. HOW ARE YA?
EVERYONE WAS SAYING YOU WERE MIA AT THE REUNION...
...WHAT ARE YOU DOING HERE?
REUNION? OH...
...I LEFT THE COUNTRY AFTER I SAVED UP MONEY FROM MY PART-TIME JOB.
PART-TIME JOB? YOU'RE SURVIVING WITH FREELANCE JOBS?
WELL, I'LL BE WORKING AS A TEMP SOON, BUT...
...I GUESS I'M JUST WANDERING AROUND MOST OF THE TIME.

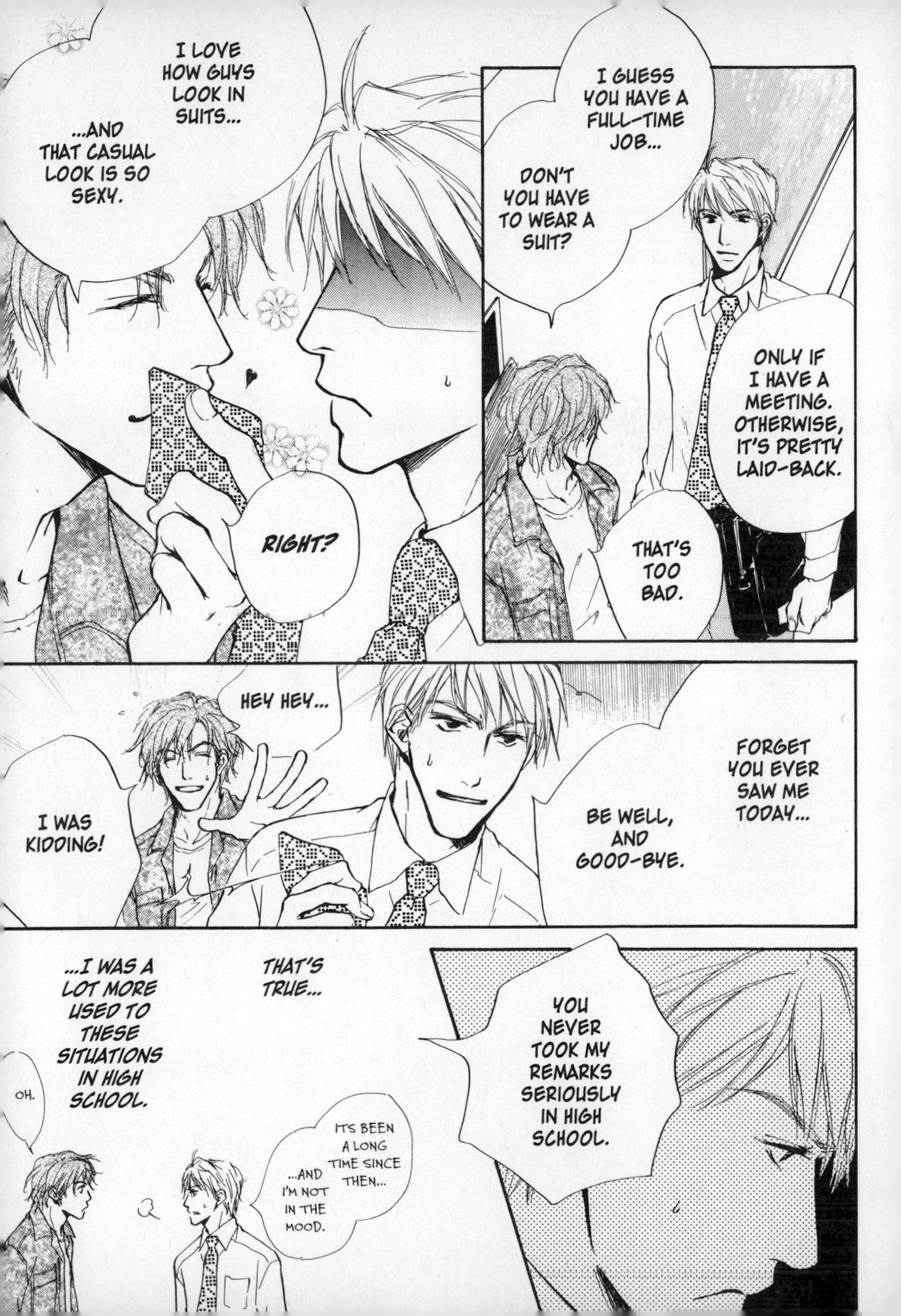
I GUESS YOU HAVE A FULL-TIME JOB...
DON'T YOU HAVE TO WEAR A SUIT?
ONLY IF I HAVE A MEETING. OTHERWISE, IT'S PRETTY LAID-BACK.
THAT'S TOO BAD.
I LOVE HOW GUYS LOOK IN SUITS...
...AND THAT CASUAL LOOK IS SO SEXY.
RIGHT?
FORGET YOU EVER SAW ME TODAY...
BE WELL, AND GOOD-BYE.
HEY HEY...
I WAS KIDDING!
YOU NEVER TOOK MY REMARKS SERIOUSLY IN HIGH SCHOOL.
THAT'S TRUE...
...I WAS A LOT MORE USED TO THESE SITUATIONS IN HIGH SCHOOL.
ITS BEEN A LONG TIME SINCE THEN...
...AND I'M NOT IN THE MOOD.
OH.

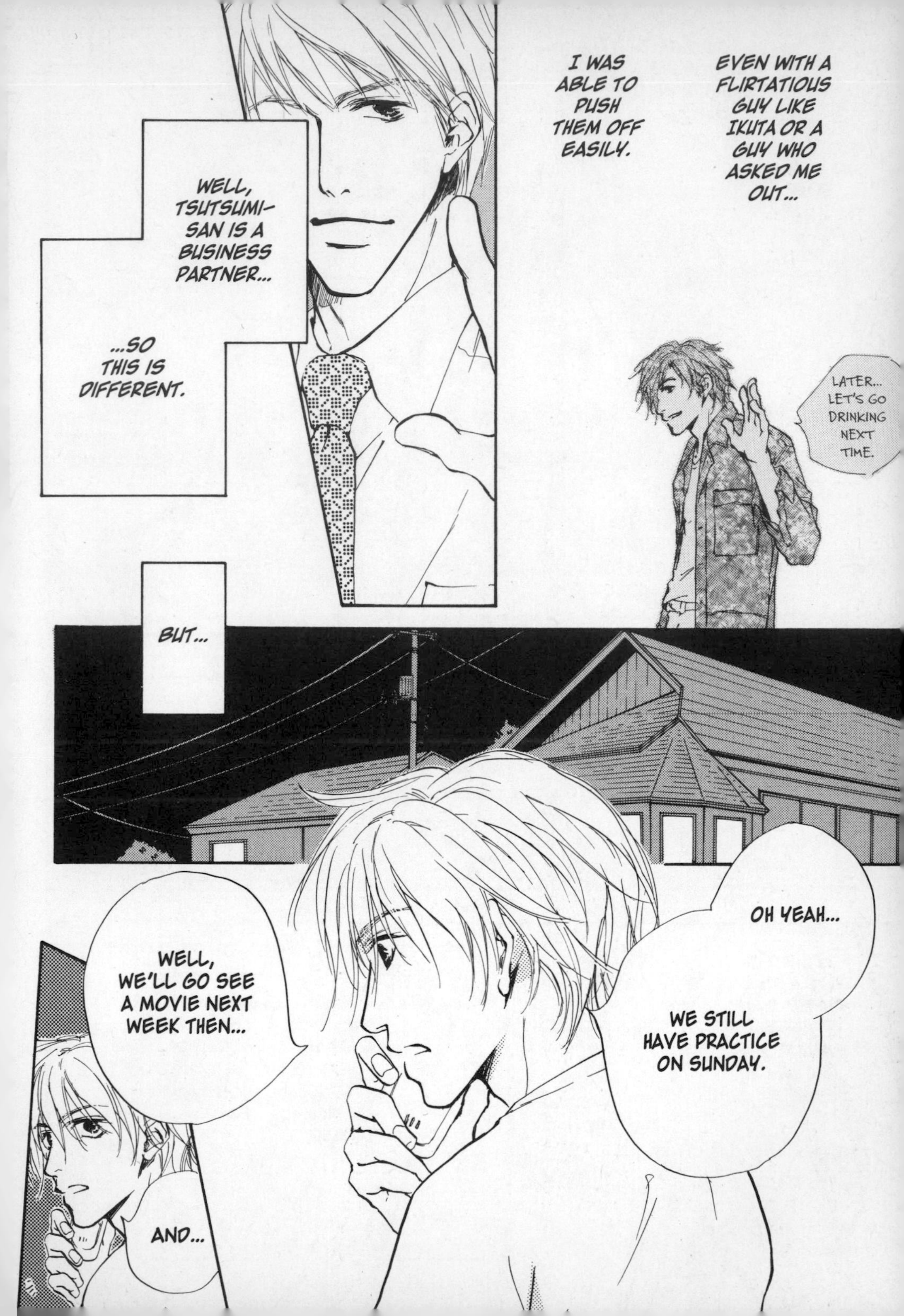
EVEN WITH A FLIRTATIOUS GUY LIKE IKUTA OR A GUY WHO ASKED ME OUT...
I WAS ABLE TO PUSH THEM OFF EASILY.
LATER... LET'S GO DRINKING NEXT TIME.
WELL, TSUTSUMI-SAN IS A BUSINESS PARTNER...
...SO THIS IS DIFFERENT.
BUT...
OH YEAH...
WE STILL HAVE PRACTICE ON SUNDAY.
WELL, WE'LL GO SEE A MOVIE NEXT WEEK THEN...
AND...

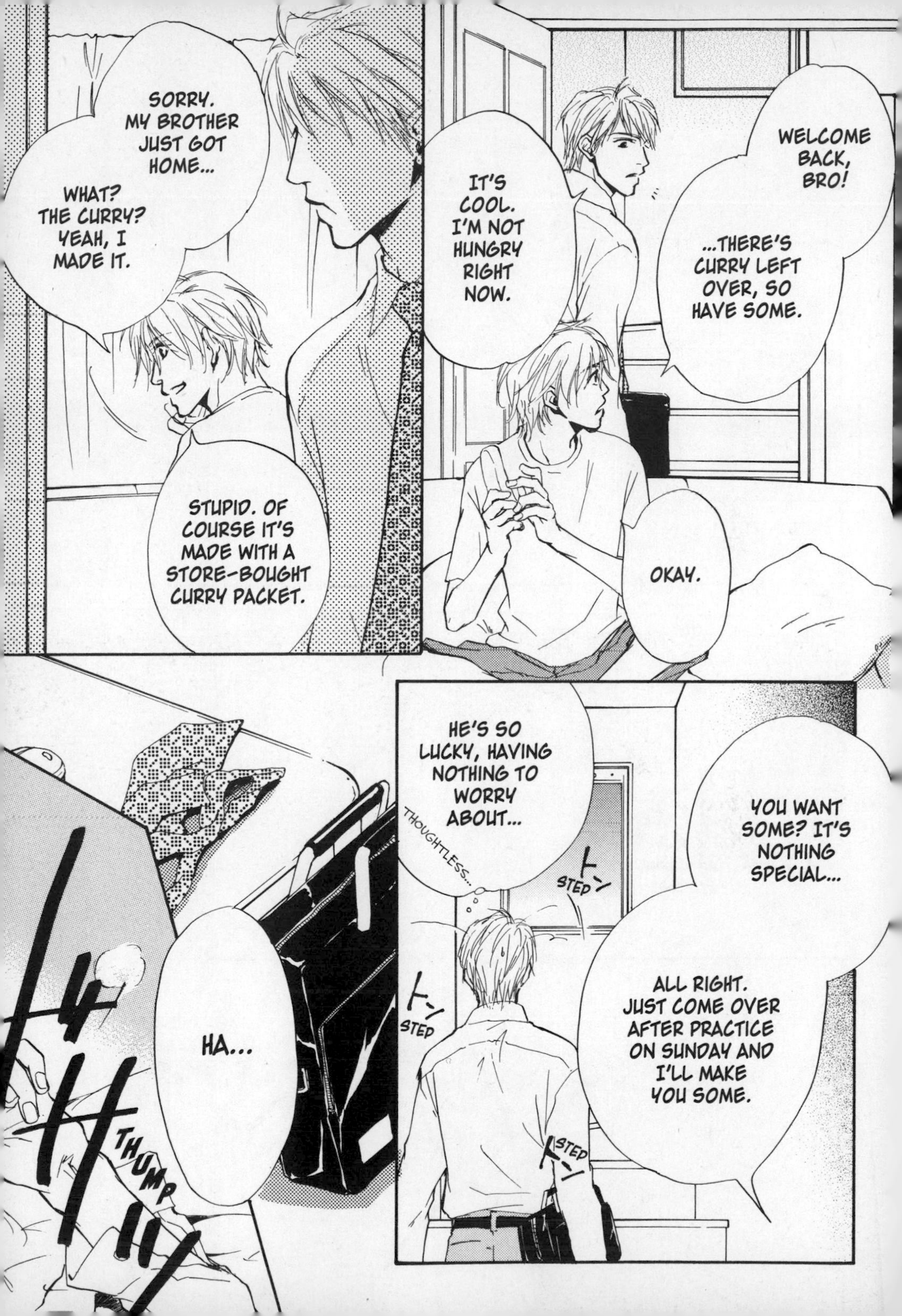
WELCOME BACK, BRO!
...THERE'S CURRY LEFT OVER, SO HAVE SOME.
IT'S COOL. I'M NOT HUNGRY RIGHT NOW.
OKAY.
SORRY. MY BROTHER JUST GOT HOME...
WHAT? THE CURRY? YEAH, I MADE IT.
STUPID. OF COURSE IT'S MADE WITH A STORE-BOUGHT CURRY PACKET.
YOU WANT SOME? IT'S NOTHING SPECIAL...
ALL RIGHT. JUST COME OVER AFTER PRACTICE ON SUNDAY AND I'LL MAKE YOU SOME.
STEP
STEP
STEP
HE'S SO LUCKY, HAVING NOTHING TO WORRY ABOUT...
THOUGHTLESS...
HA...
THUMP

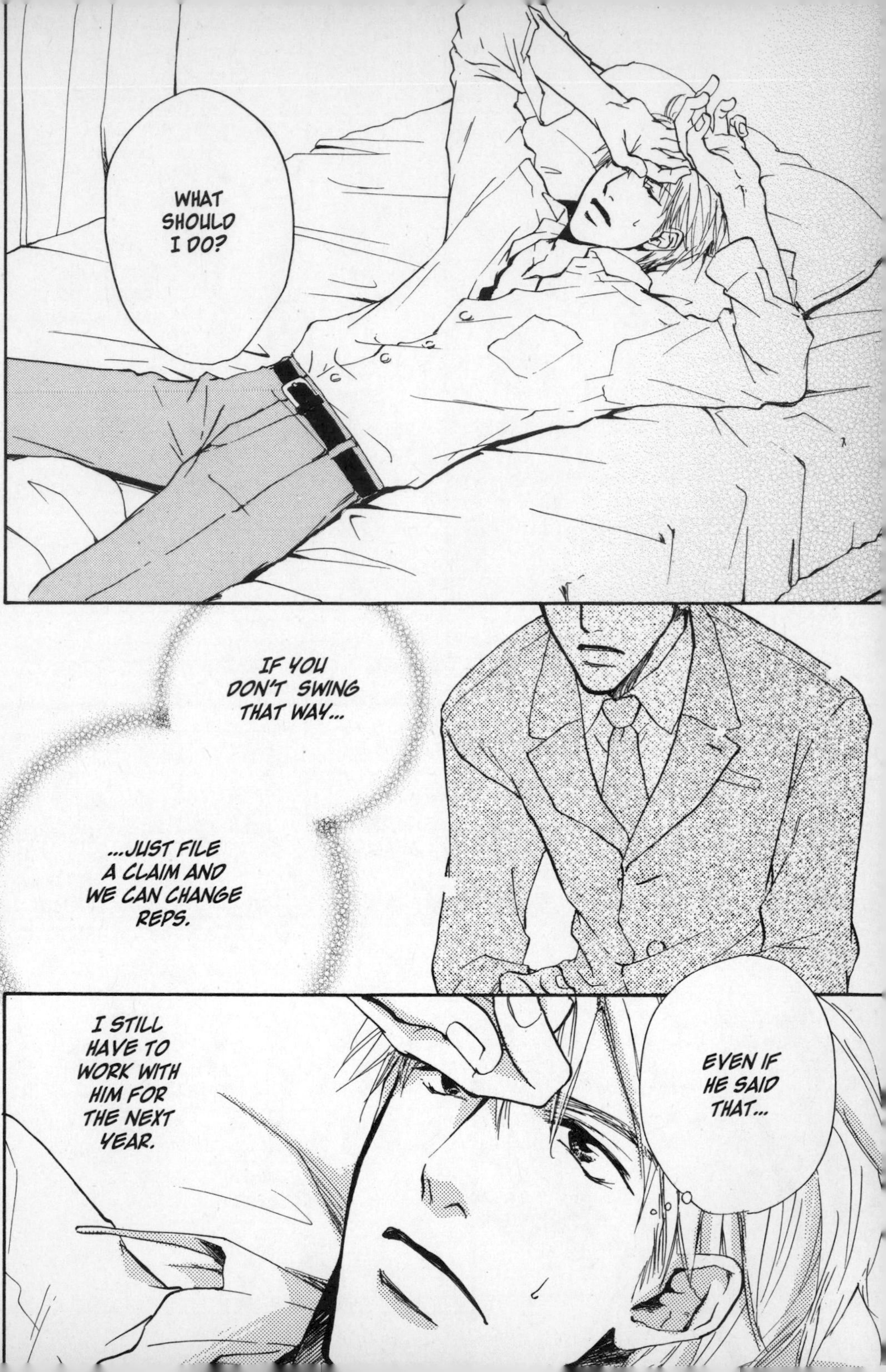
WHAT SHOULD I DO?
IF YOU DON'T SWING THAT WAY...
...JUST FILE A CLAIM AND WE CAN CHANGE REPS.
EVEN IF HE SAID THAT...
I STILL HAVE TO WORK WITH HIM FOR THE NEXT YEAR.

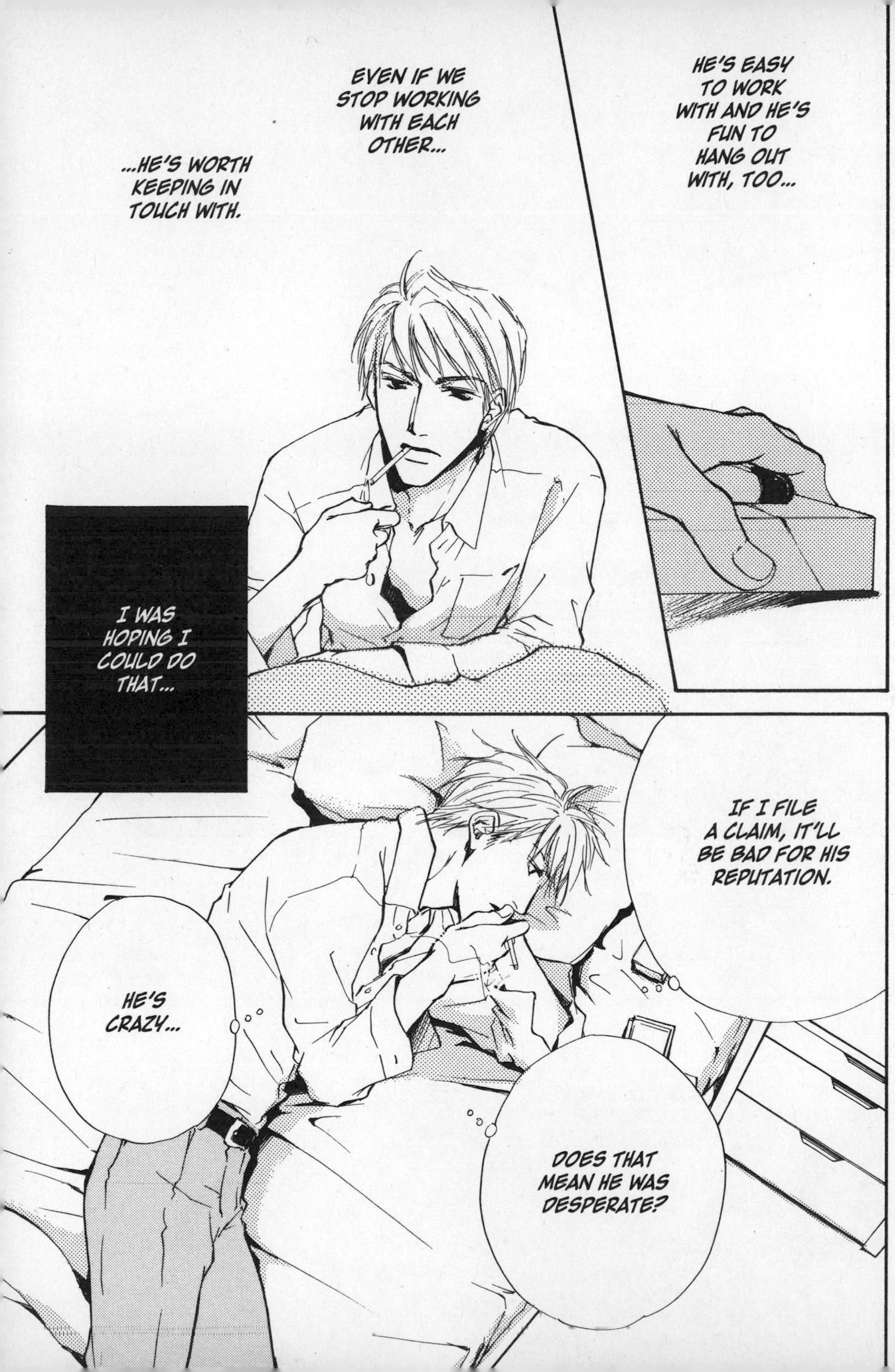
HE'S EASY TO WORK WITH AND HE'S FUN TO HANG OUT WITH, TOO...
EVEN IF WE STOP WORKING WITH EACH OTHER...
...HE'S WORTH KEEPING IN TOUCH WITH.
I WAS HOPING I COULD DO THAT...
IF I FILE A CLAIM, IT'LL BE BAD FOR HIS REPUTATION.
DOES THAT MEAN HE WAS DESPERATE?
HE'S CRAZY...

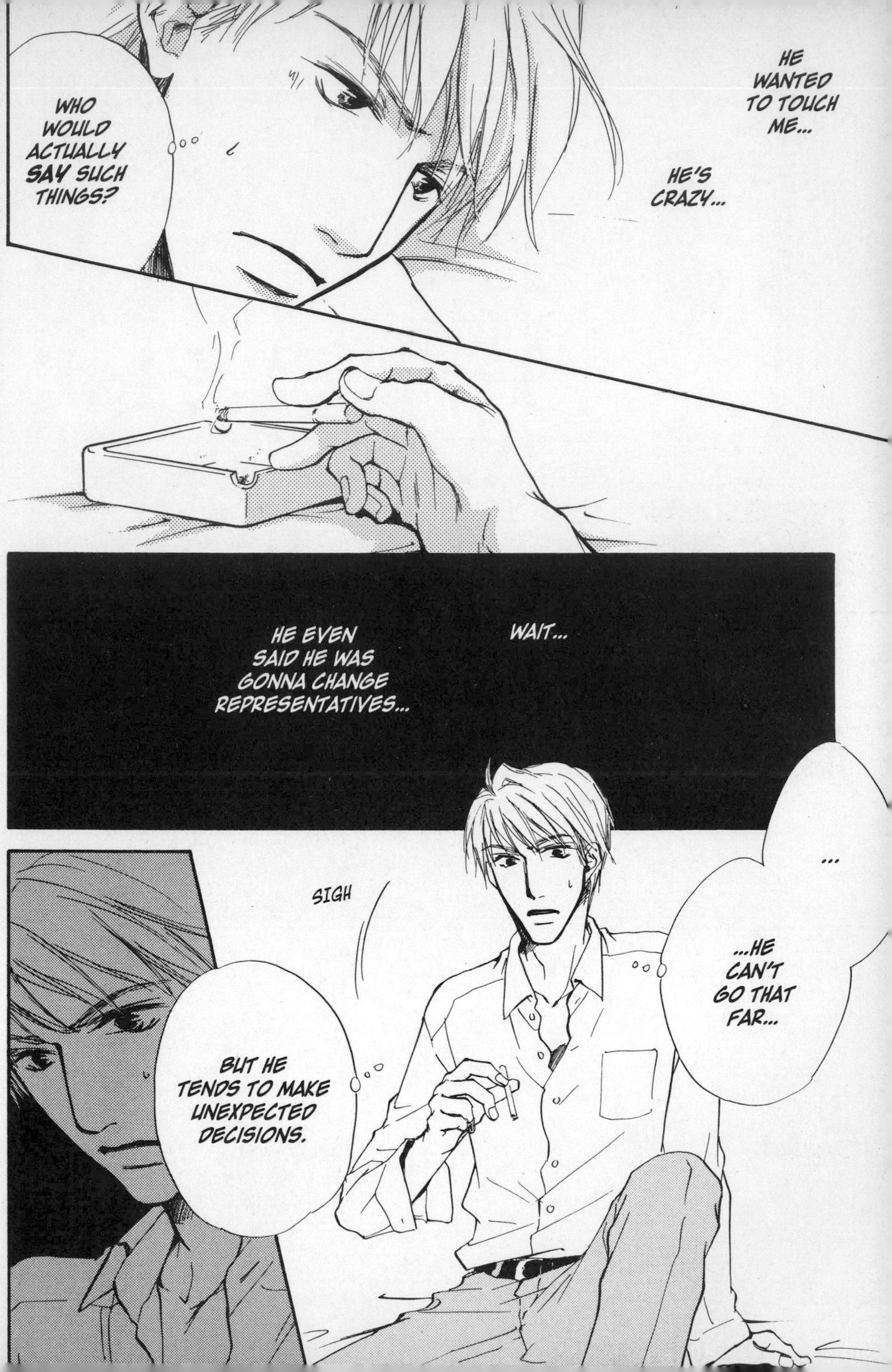
HE WANTED TO TOUCH ME...
HE'S CRAZY...
WHO WOULD ACTUALLY SAY SUCH THINGS?
WAIT...
HE EVEN SAID HE WAS GONNA CHANGE REPRESENTATIVES...
...
...HE CAN'T GO THAT FAR...
SIGH
BUT HE TENDS TO MAKE UNEXPECTED DECISIONS.

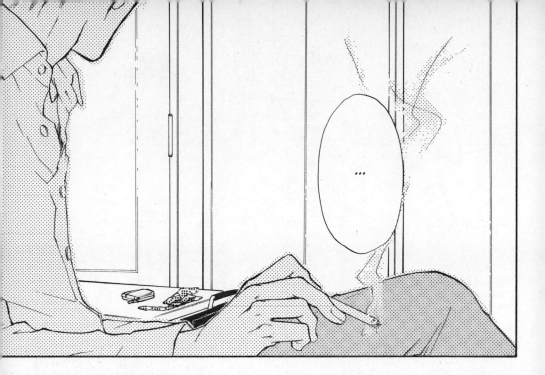

...

TSUTSUMI.

YOU'VE REEKED OF ALCOHOL *ALL MORNING.*

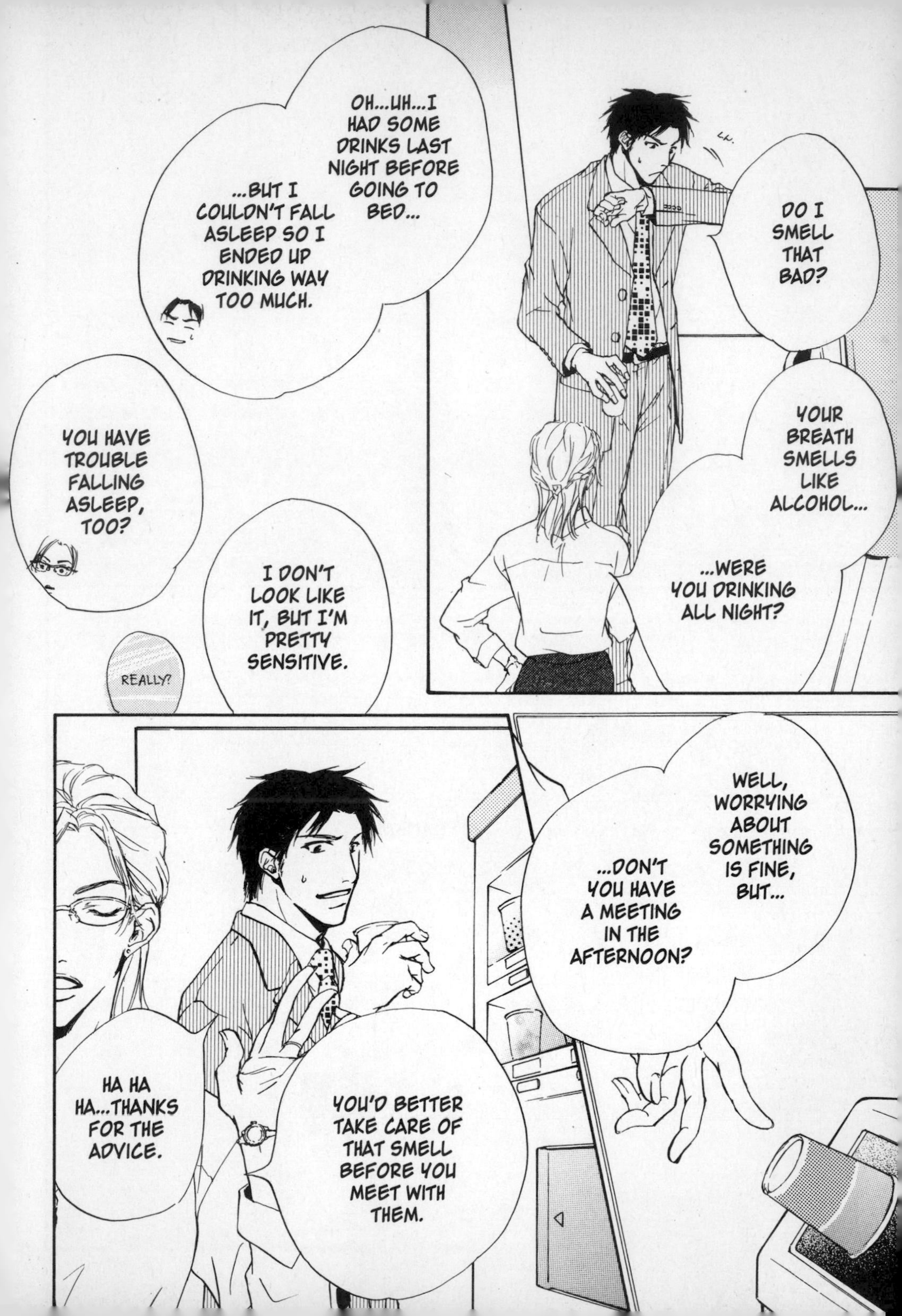
DO I SMELL THAT BAD?
YOUR BREATH SMELLS LIKE ALCOHOL...
...WERE YOU DRINKING ALL NIGHT?
OH...UH...I HAD SOME DRINKS LAST NIGHT BEFORE GOING TO BED...
...BUT I COULDN'T FALL ASLEEP SO I ENDED UP DRINKING WAY TOO MUCH.
YOU HAVE TROUBLE FALLING ASLEEP, TOO?
I DON'T LOOK LIKE IT, BUT I'M PRETTY SENSITIVE.
REALLY?
WELL, WORRYING ABOUT SOMETHING IS FINE, BUT...
...DON'T YOU HAVE A MEETING IN THE AFTERNOON?
YOU'D BETTER TAKE CARE OF THAT SMELL BEFORE YOU MEET WITH THEM.
HA HA HA...THANKS FOR THE ADVICE.

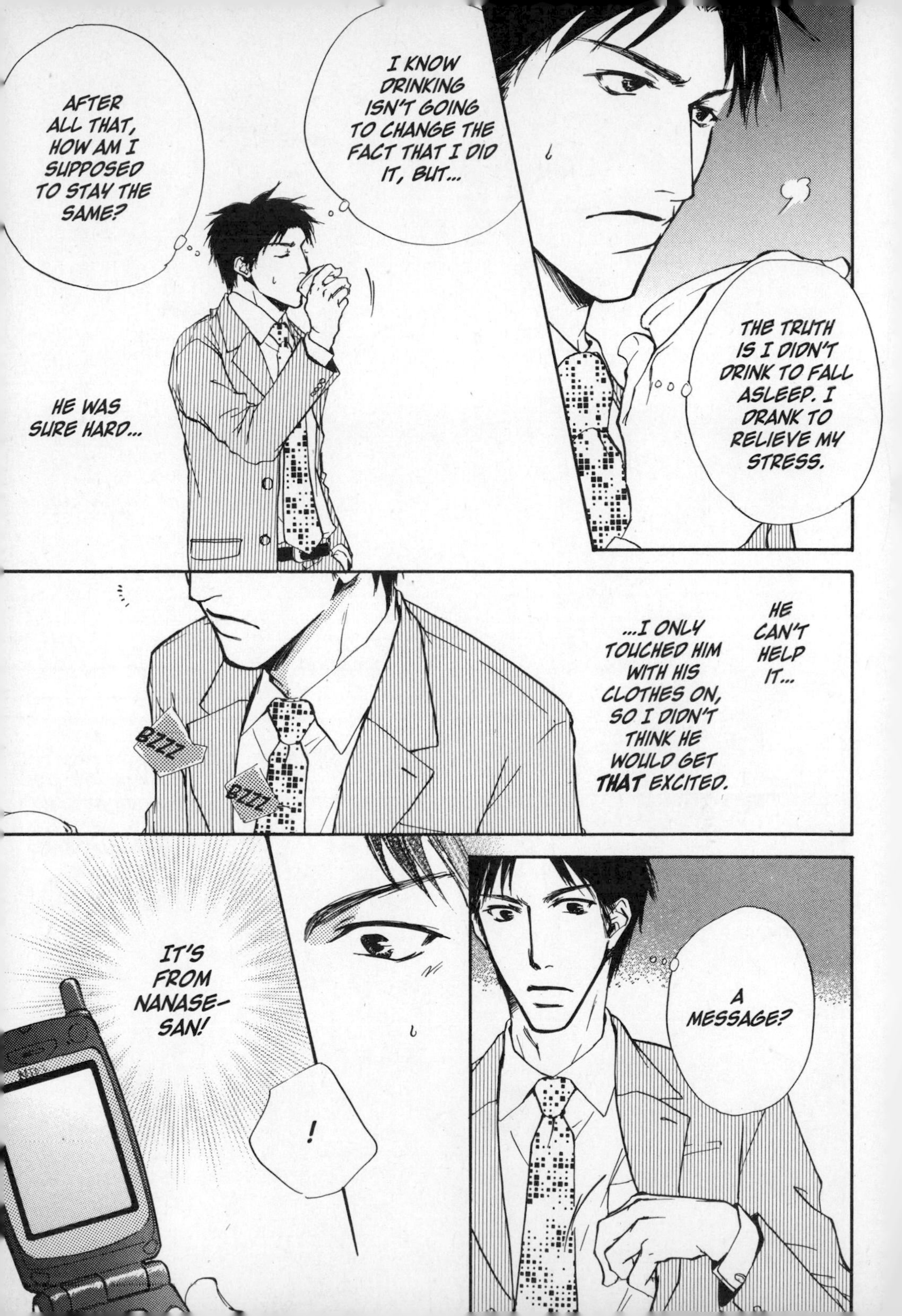
THE TRUTH IS I DIDN'T DRINK TO FALL ASLEEP. I DRANK TO RELIEVE MY STRESS.
I KNOW DRINKING ISN'T GOING TO CHANGE THE FACT THAT I DID IT, BUT...
AFTER ALL THAT, HOW AM I SUPPOSED TO STAY THE SAME?
HE WAS SURE HARD...
HE CAN'T HELP IT...
...I ONLY TOUCHED HIM WITH HIS CLOTHES ON, SO I DIDN'T THINK HE WOULD GET **THAT** EXCITED.
BZZZ
BZZZ
A MESSAGE?
!
IT'S FROM NANASE-SAN!

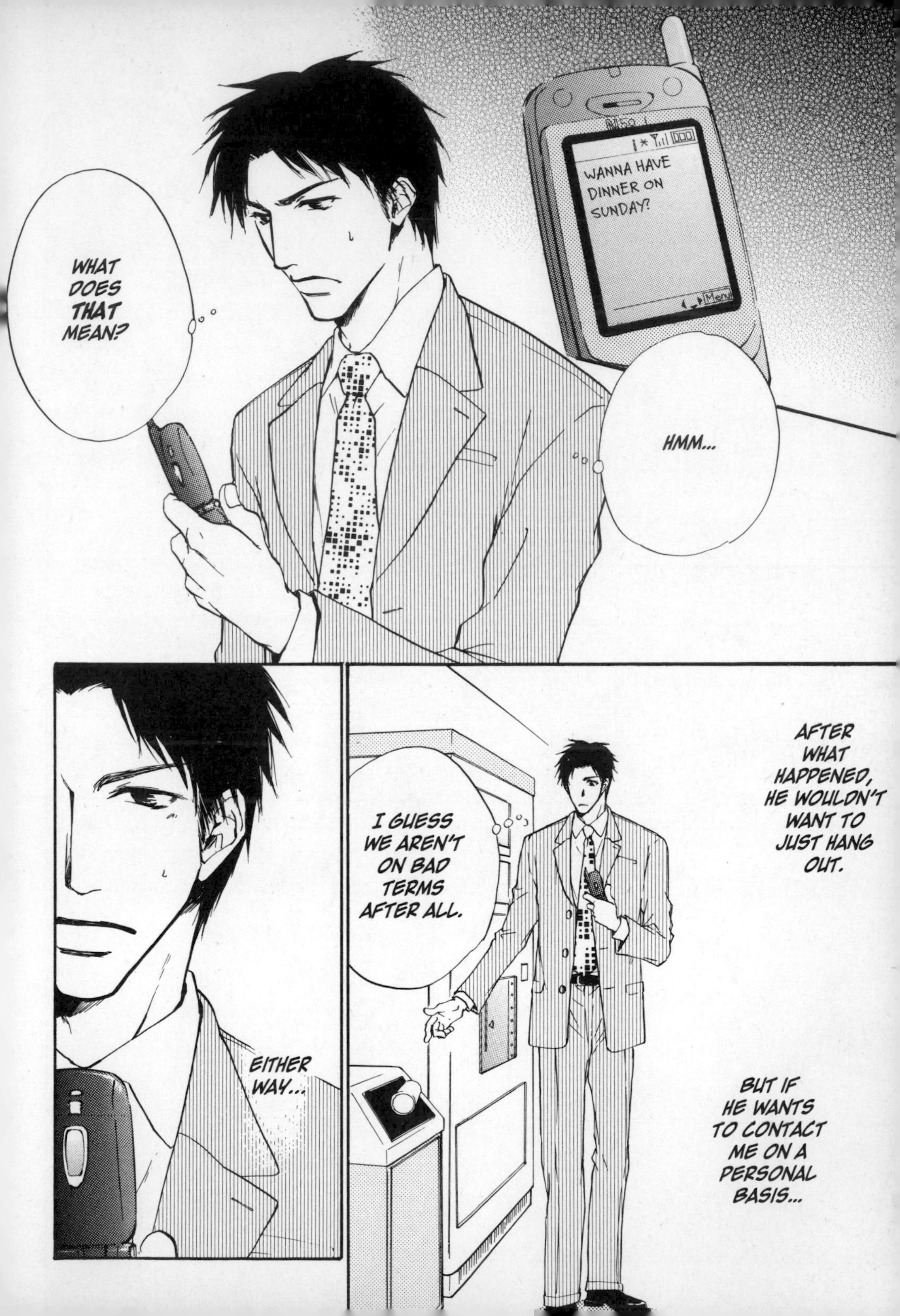
WANNA HAVE DINNER ON SUNDAY?
HMM...
WHAT DOES THAT MEAN?
AFTER WHAT HAPPENED, HE WOULDN'T WANT TO JUST HANG OUT.
I GUESS WE AREN'T ON BAD TERMS AFTER ALL.
BUT IF HE WANTS TO CONTACT ME ON A PERSONAL BASIS...
EITHER WAY...

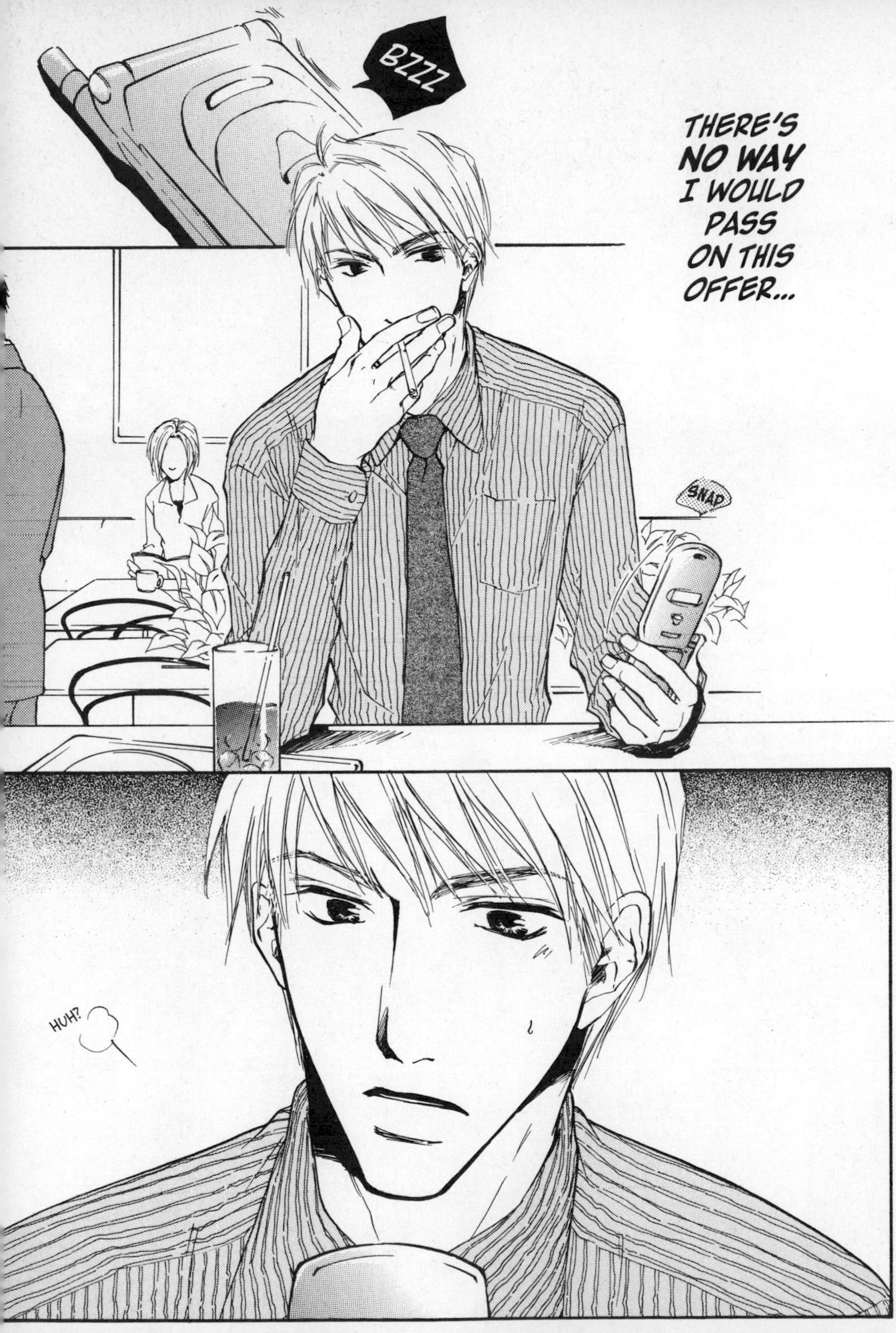
THERE'S NO WAY I WOULD PASS ON THIS OFFER...
BZZZ
SNAP
HUH?

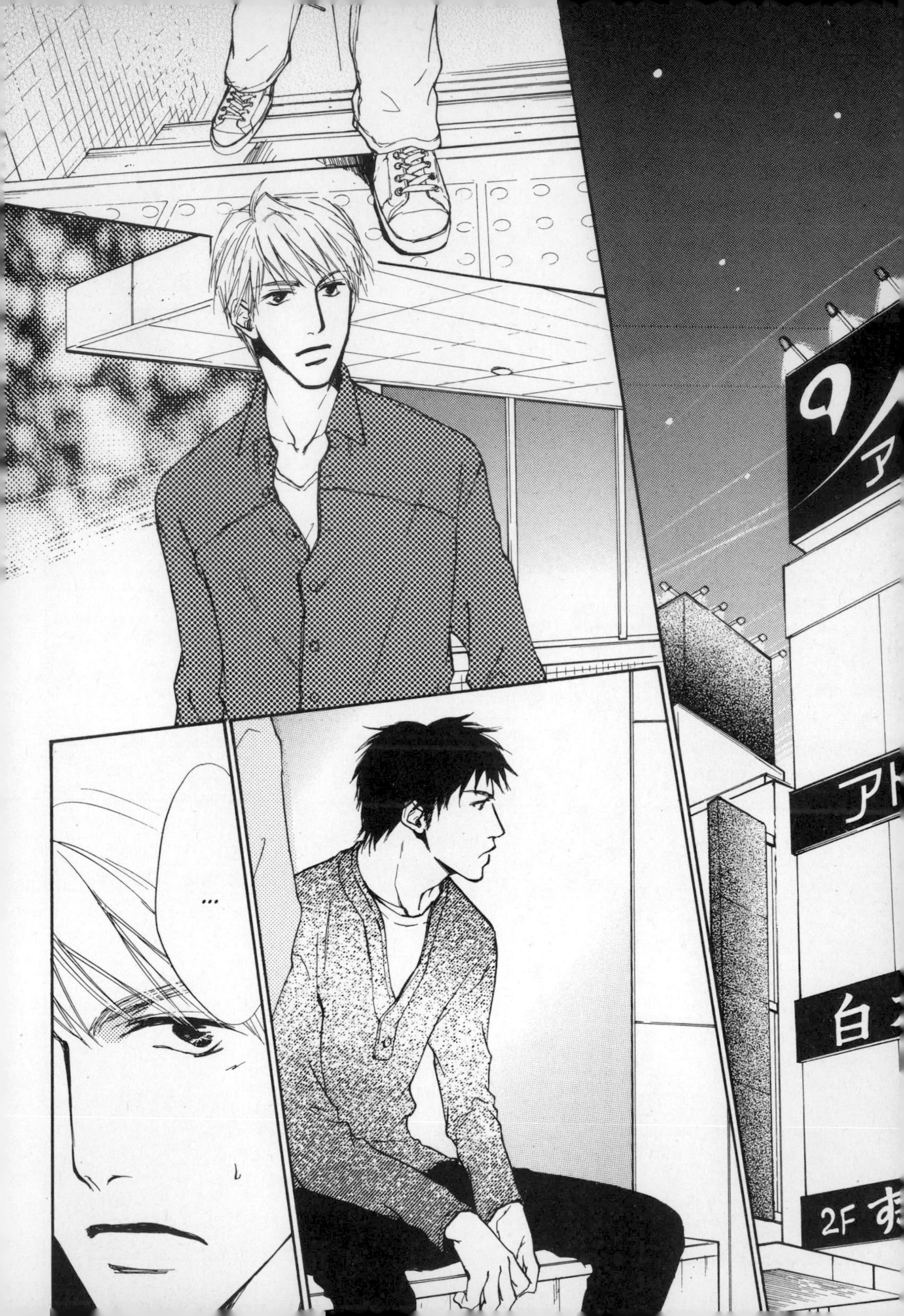
ア
アト
白
2F す
…

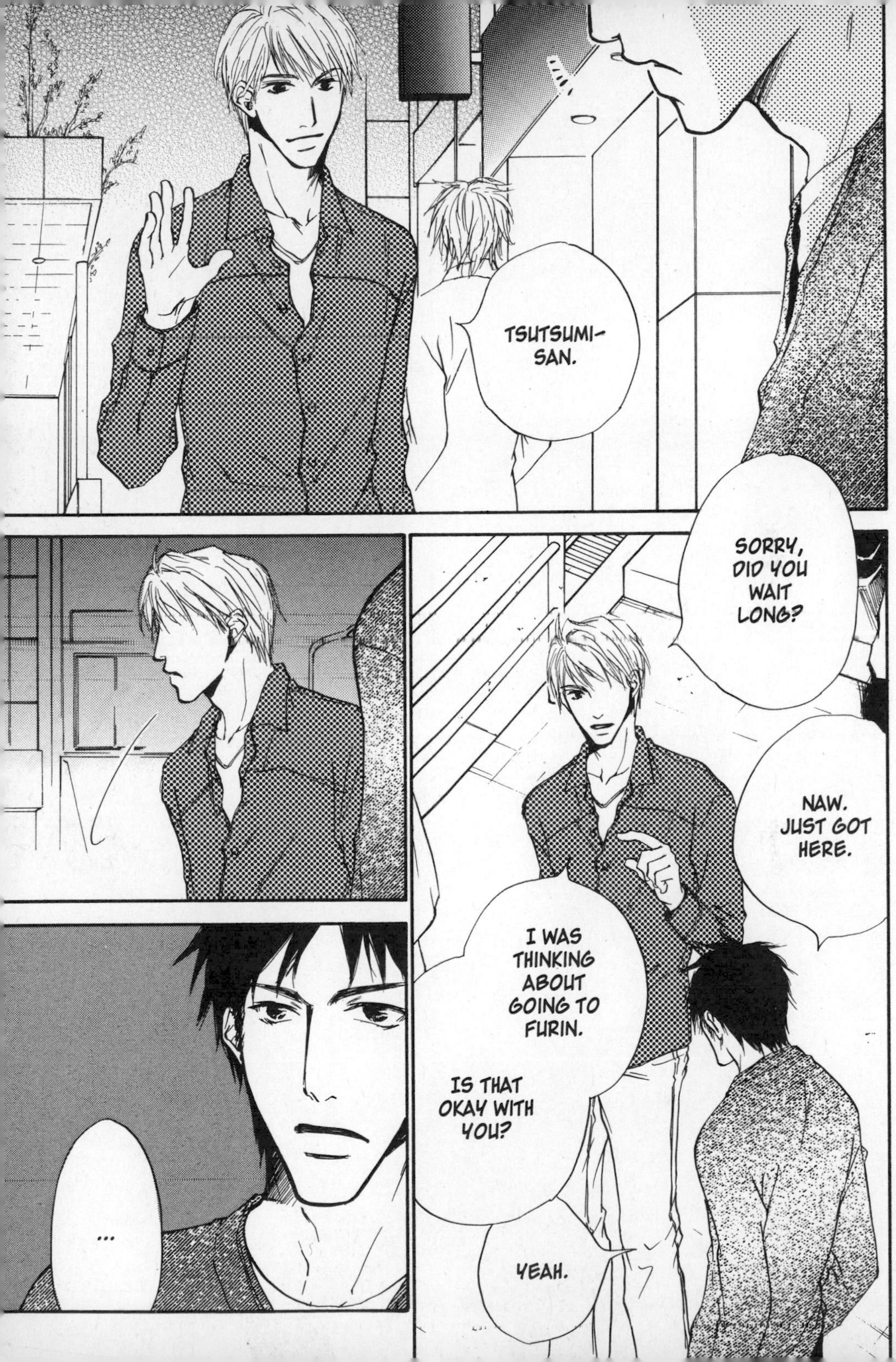
TSUTSUMI-SAN.
SORRY, DID YOU WAIT LONG?
NAW. JUST GOT HERE.
I WAS THINKING ABOUT GOING TO FURIN.
IS THAT OKAY WITH YOU?
YEAH.
...

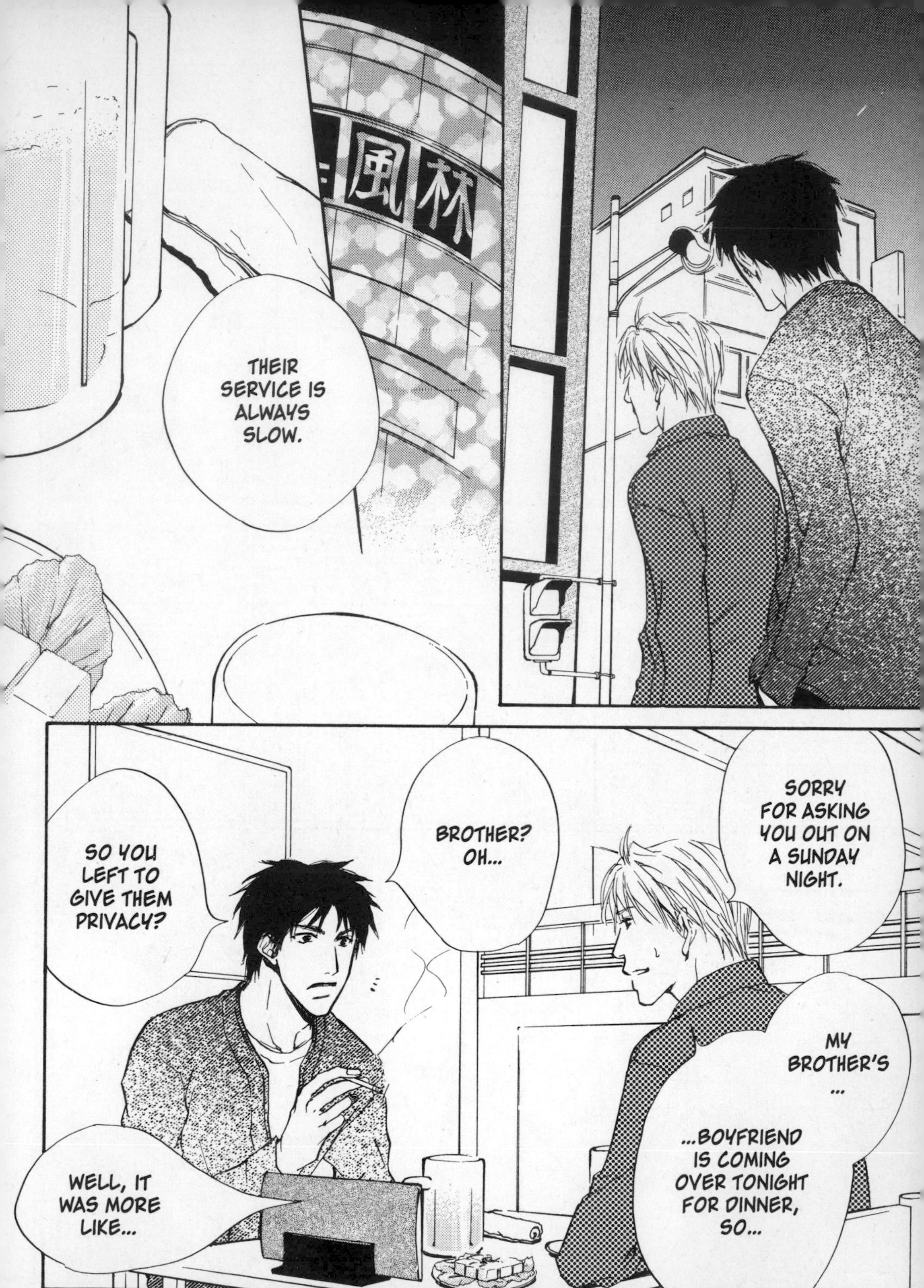
THEIR SERVICE IS ALWAYS SLOW.
SORRY FOR ASKING YOU OUT ON A SUNDAY NIGHT.
MY BROTHER'S ...
...BOYFRIEND IS COMING OVER TONIGHT FOR DINNER, SO...
BROTHER? OH...
SO YOU LEFT TO GIVE THEM PRIVACY?
WELL, IT WAS MORE LIKE...

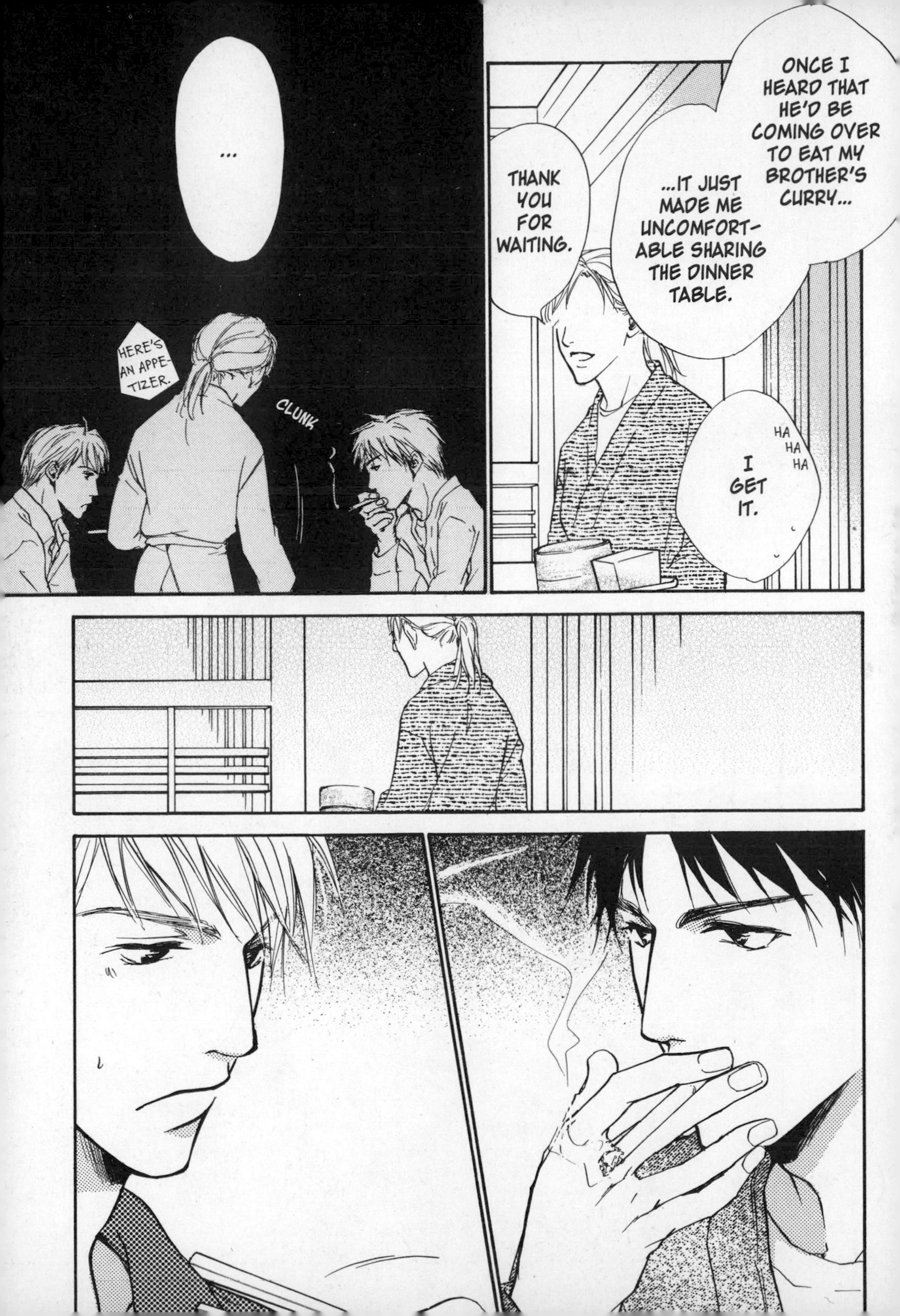
ONCE I HEARD THAT HE'D BE COMING OVER TO EAT MY BROTHER'S CURRY...
...IT JUST MADE ME UNCOMFORTABLE SHARING THE DINNER TABLE.
THANK YOU FOR WAITING.
HA HA HA
I GET IT.
...
HERE'S AN APPETIZER.
CLUNK

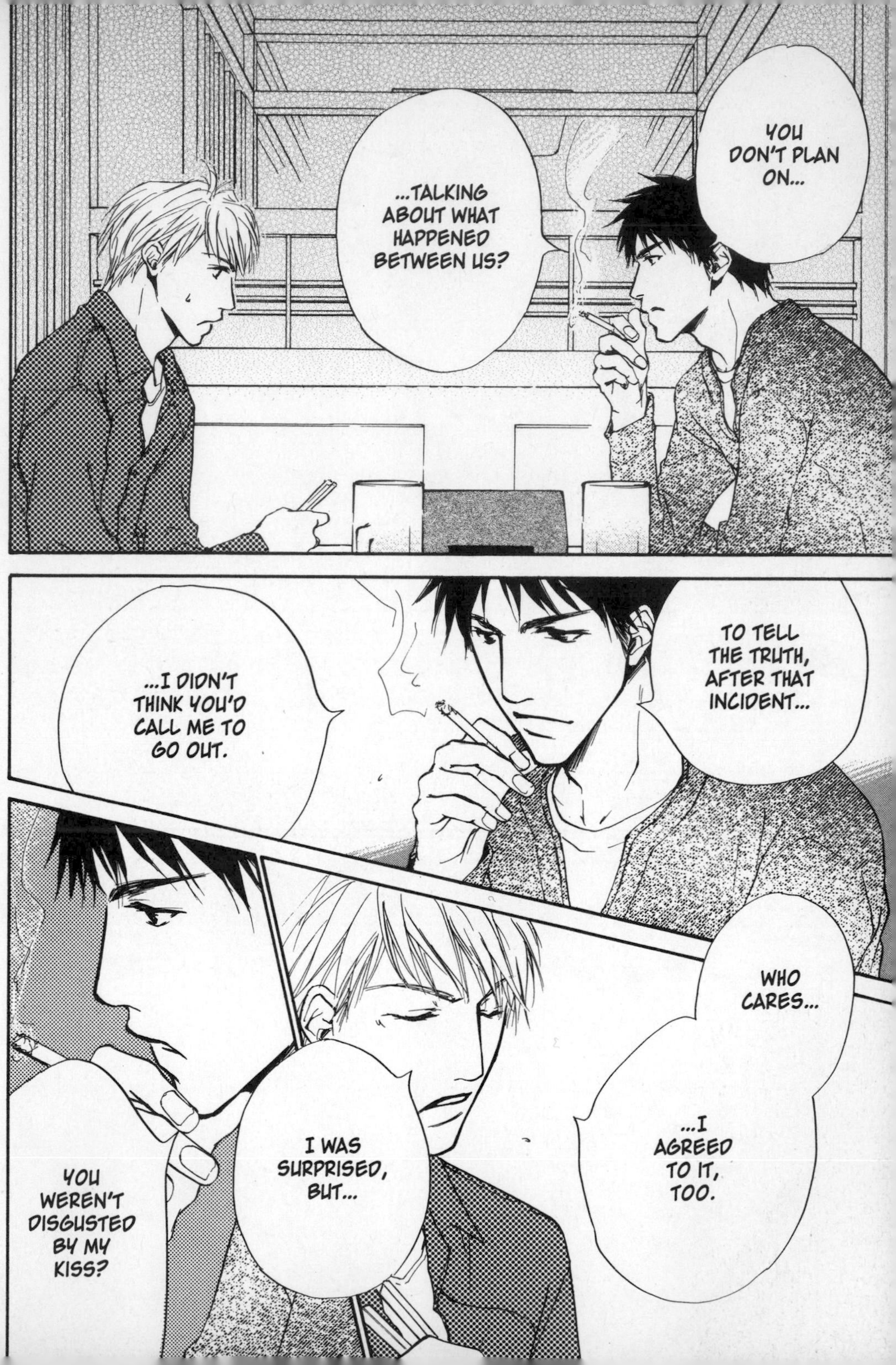
YOU DON'T PLAN ON...
...TALKING ABOUT WHAT HAPPENED BETWEEN US?
TO TELL THE TRUTH, AFTER THAT INCIDENT...
...I DIDN'T THINK YOU'D CALL ME TO GO OUT.
WHO CARES...
...I AGREED TO IT, TOO.
I WAS SURPRISED, BUT...
YOU WEREN'T DISGUSTED BY MY KISS?

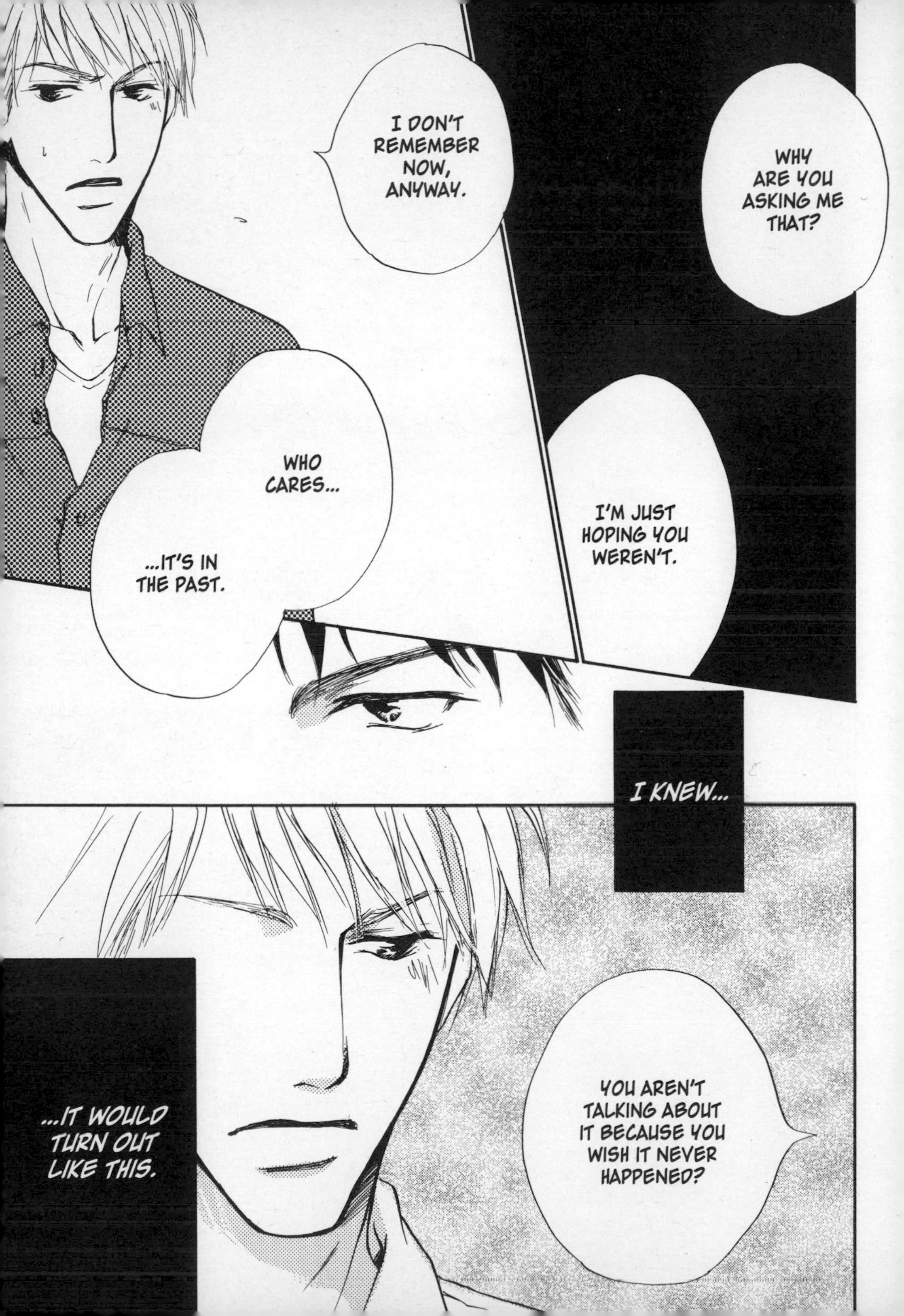
WHY ARE YOU ASKING ME THAT?
I'M JUST HOPING YOU WEREN'T.
I DON'T REMEMBER NOW, ANYWAY.
WHO CARES...
...IT'S IN THE PAST.
I KNEW...
YOU AREN'T TALKING ABOUT IT BECAUSE YOU WISH IT NEVER HAPPENED?
...IT WOULD TURN OUT LIKE THIS.

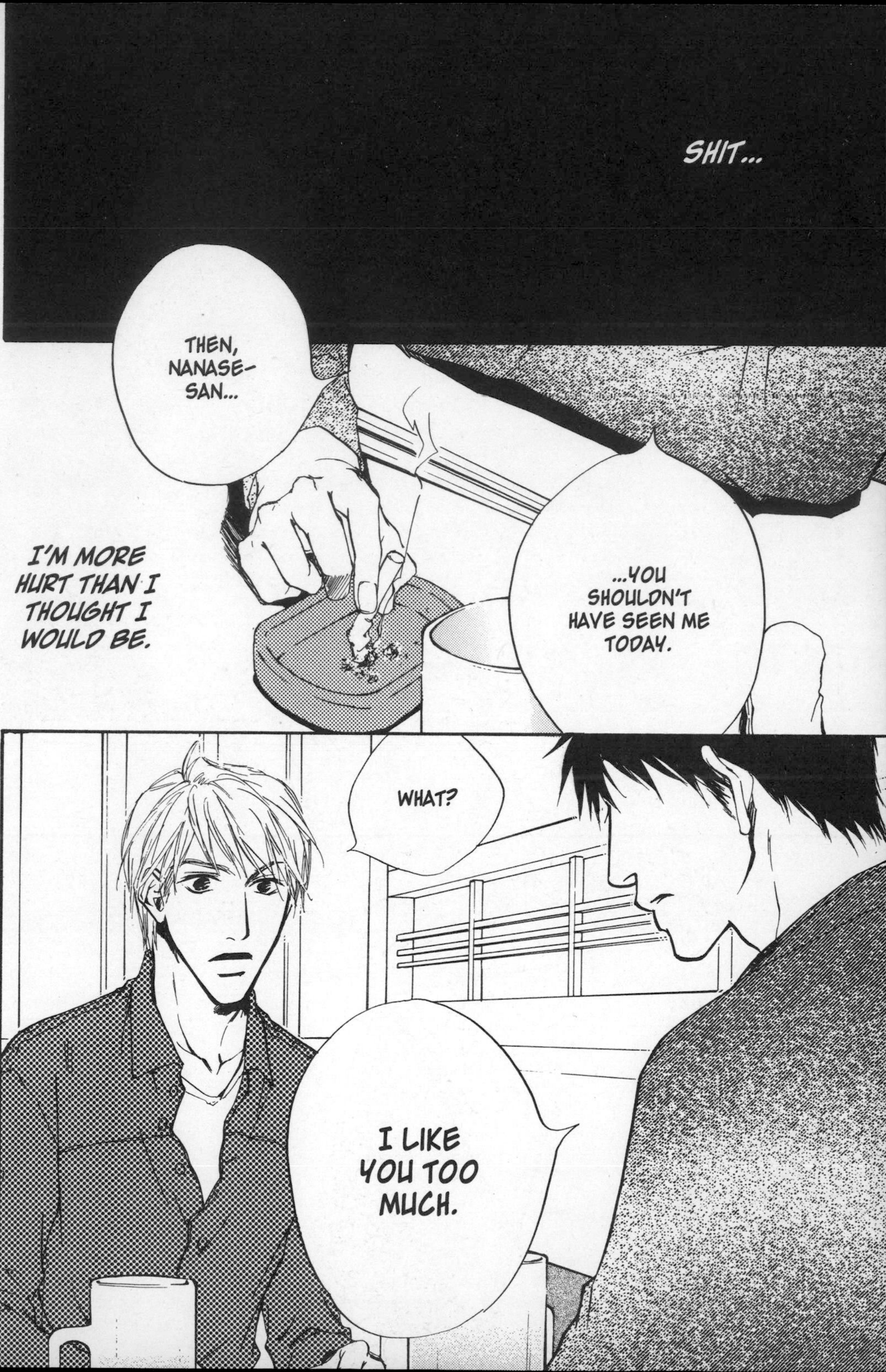
SHIT...
THEN, NANASE-SAN...
...YOU SHOULDN'T HAVE SEEN ME TODAY.
I'M MORE HURT THAN I THOUGHT I WOULD BE.
WHAT?
I LIKE YOU TOO MUCH.

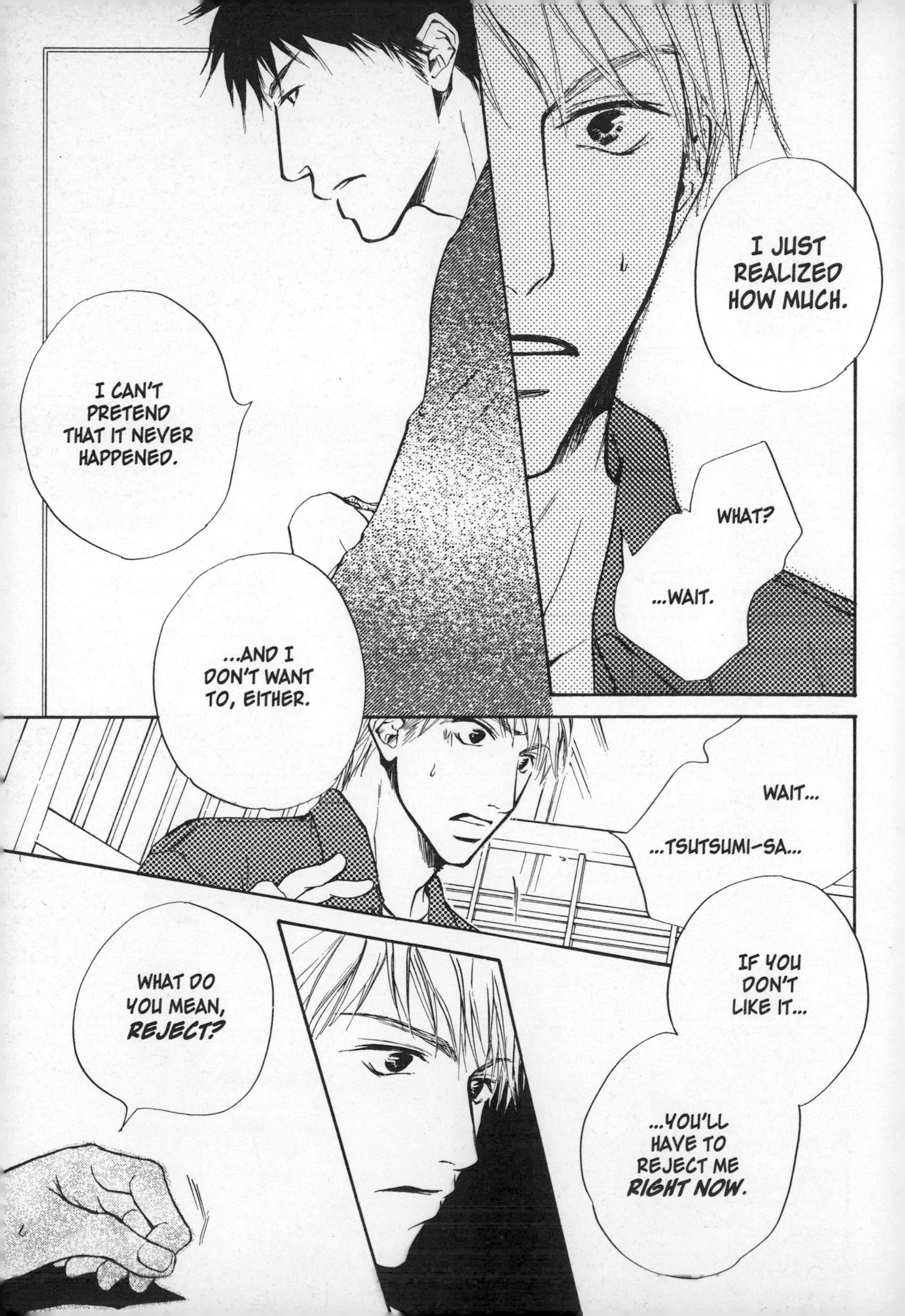
I JUST REALIZED HOW MUCH.
I CAN'T PRETEND THAT IT NEVER HAPPENED.
WHAT?
...WAIT.
...AND I DON'T WANT TO, EITHER.
WAIT...
...TSUTSUMI-SA...
IF YOU DON'T LIKE IT...
...YOU'LL HAVE TO REJECT ME **RIGHT NOW**.
WHAT DO YOU MEAN, ***REJECT?***

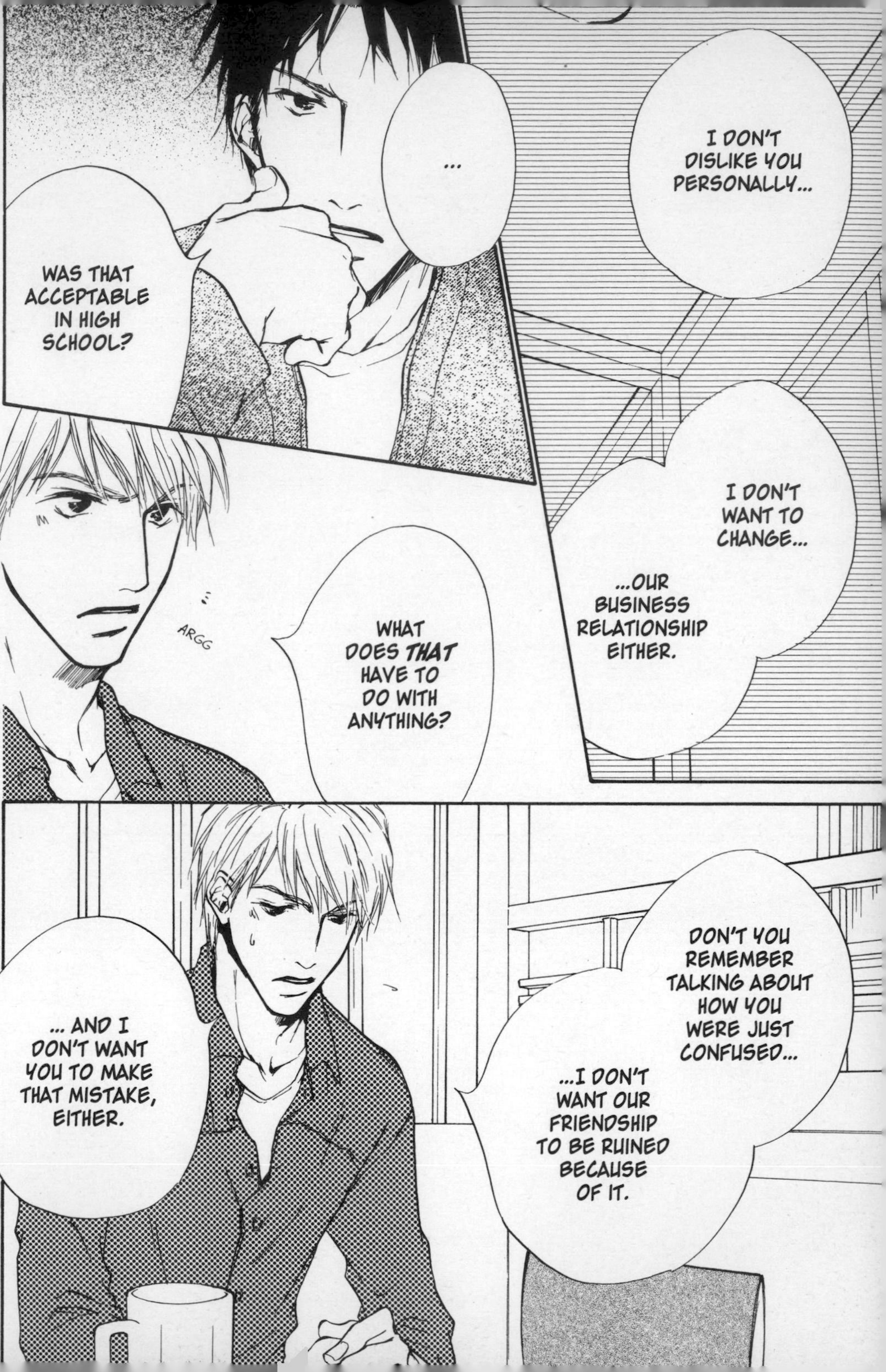
I DON'T DISLIKE YOU PERSONALLY...
I DON'T WANT TO CHANGE...
...OUR BUSINESS RELATIONSHIP EITHER.
...
WAS THAT ACCEPTABLE IN HIGH SCHOOL?
WHAT DOES *THAT* HAVE TO DO WITH ANYTHING?
ARGG
DON'T YOU REMEMBER TALKING ABOUT HOW YOU WERE JUST CONFUSED...
...I DON'T WANT OUR FRIENDSHIP TO BE RUINED BECAUSE OF IT.
... AND I DON'T WANT YOU TO MAKE THAT MISTAKE, EITHER.

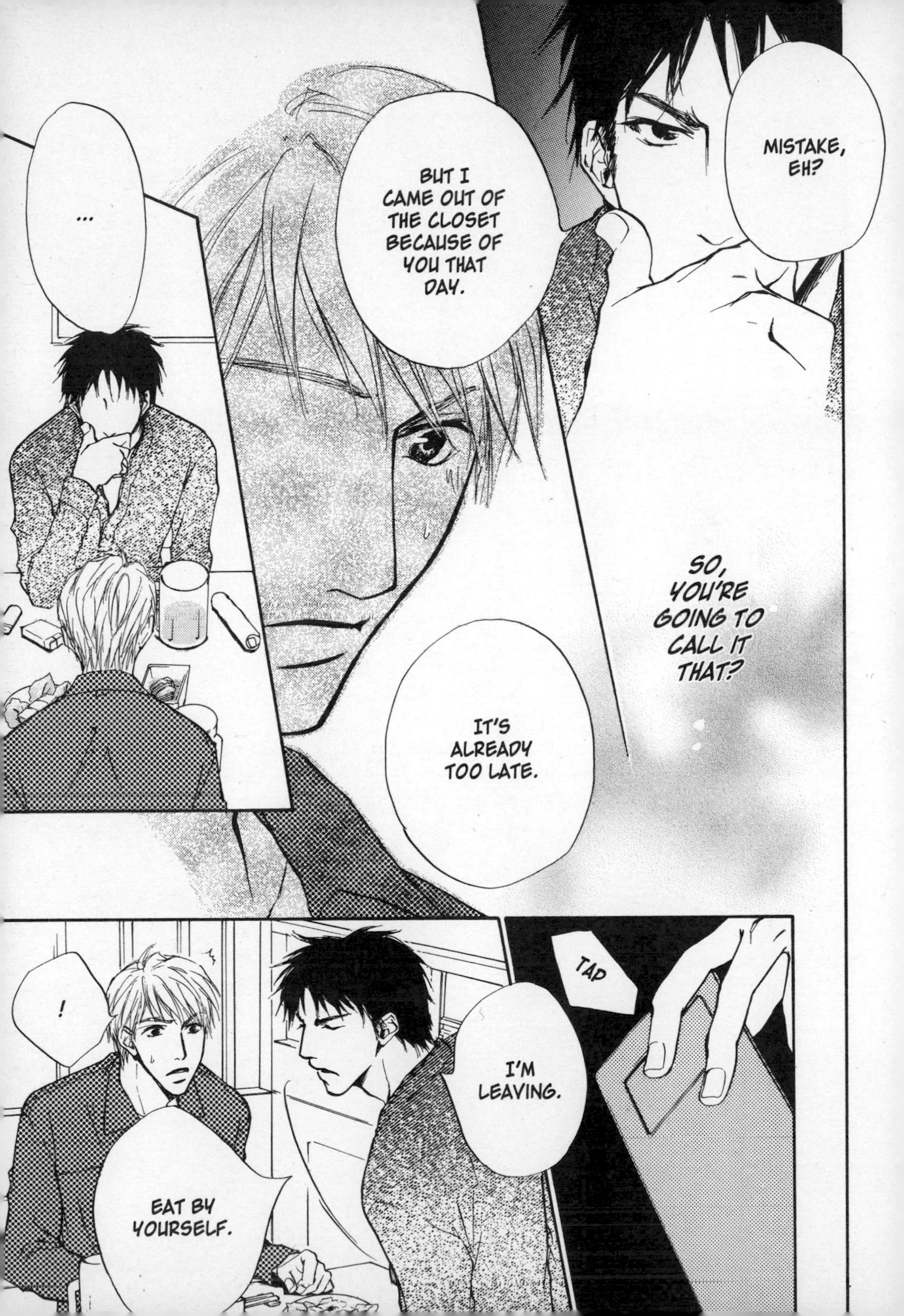
MISTAKE, EH?
BUT I CAME OUT OF THE CLOSET BECAUSE OF YOU THAT DAY.
...
SO, YOU'RE GOING TO CALL IT THAT?
IT'S ALREADY TOO LATE.
TAP
I'M LEAVING.
!
EAT BY YOURSELF.

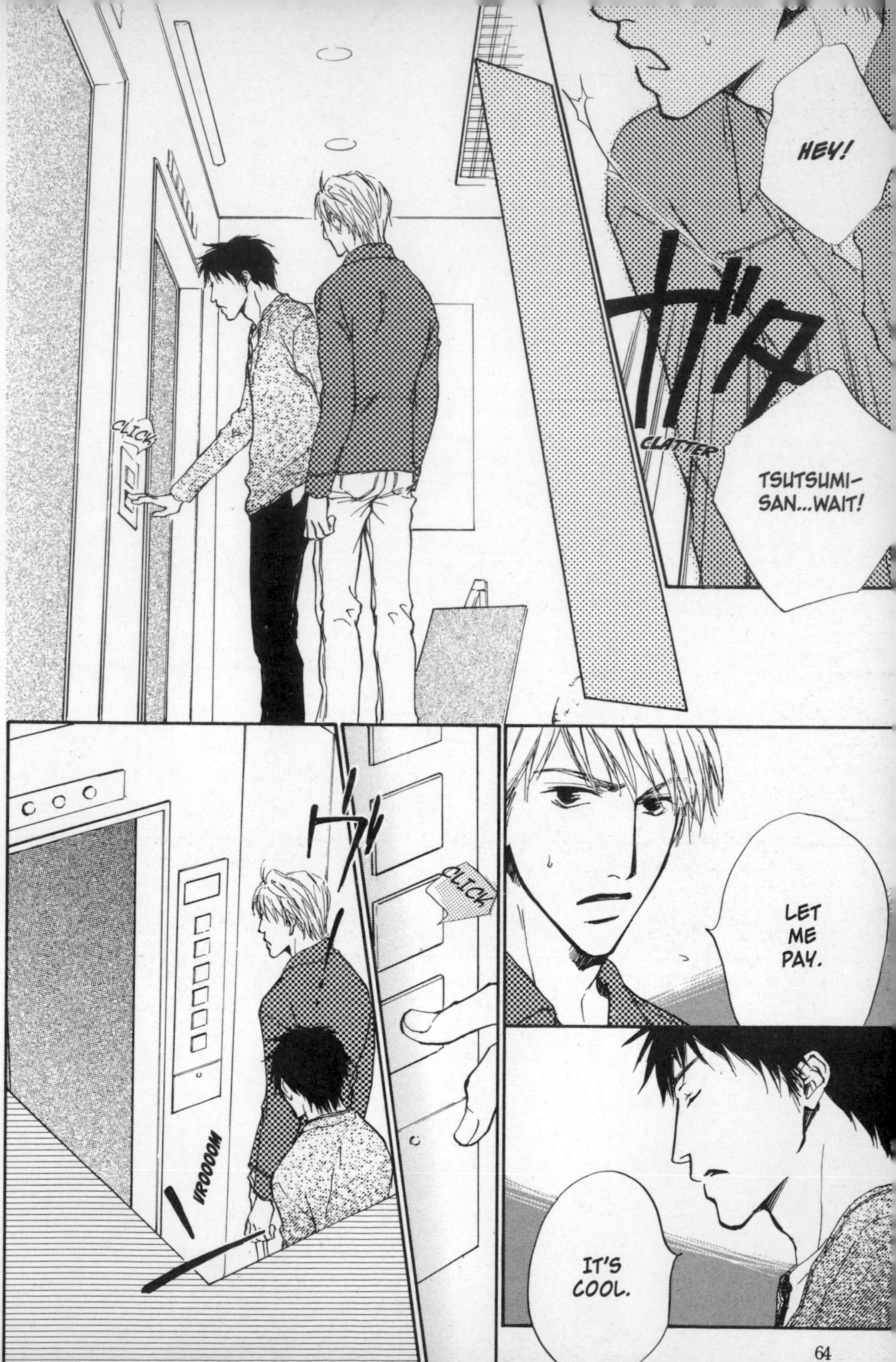
HEY!
ガタ
CLATTER
TSUTSUMI-SAN...WAIT!
CLICK
LET ME PAY.
IT'S COOL.
CLICK
VROOOOM

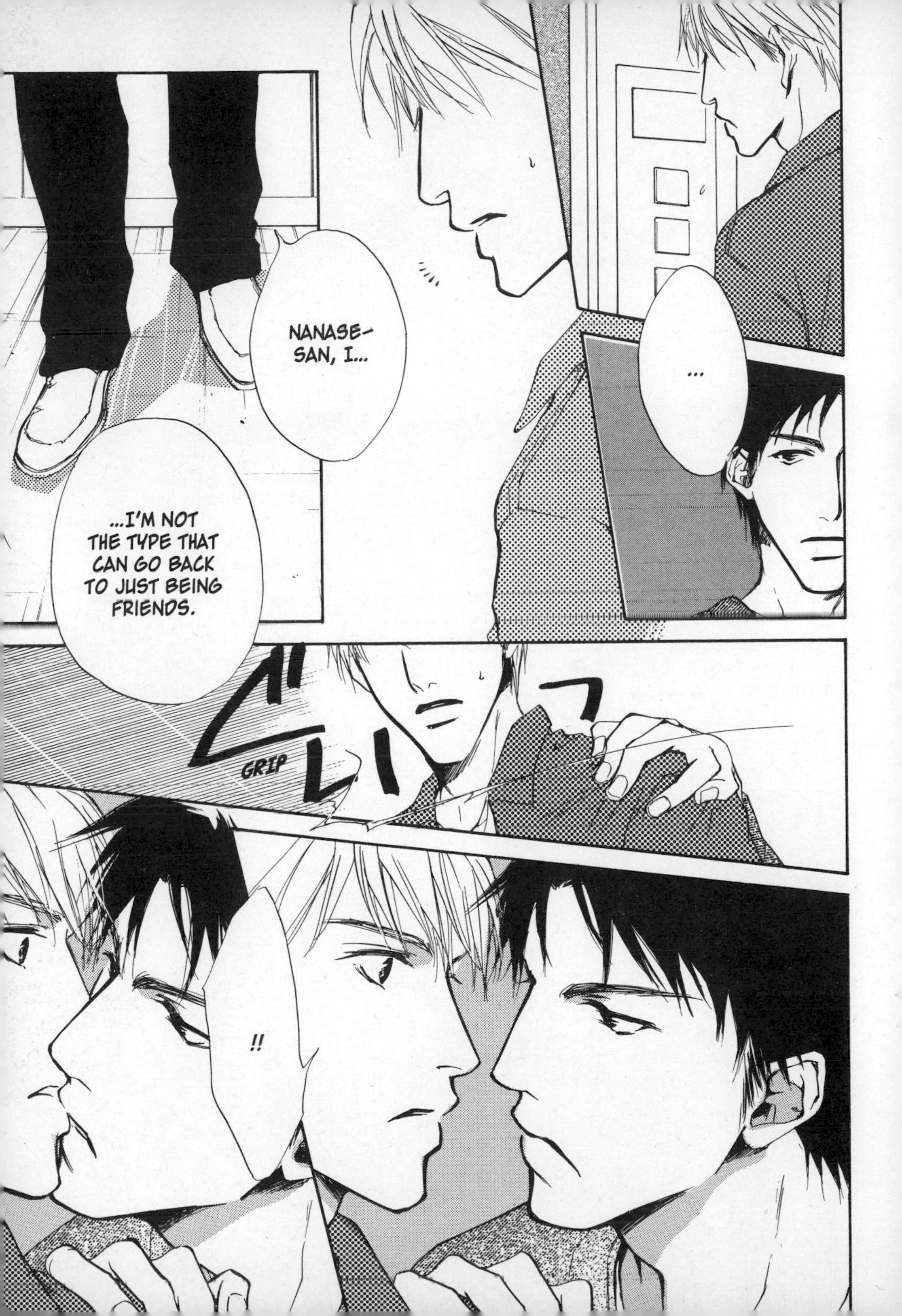
...
NANASE-SAN, I...
...I'M NOT THE TYPE THAT CAN GO BACK TO JUST BEING FRIENDS.
GRIP
!!

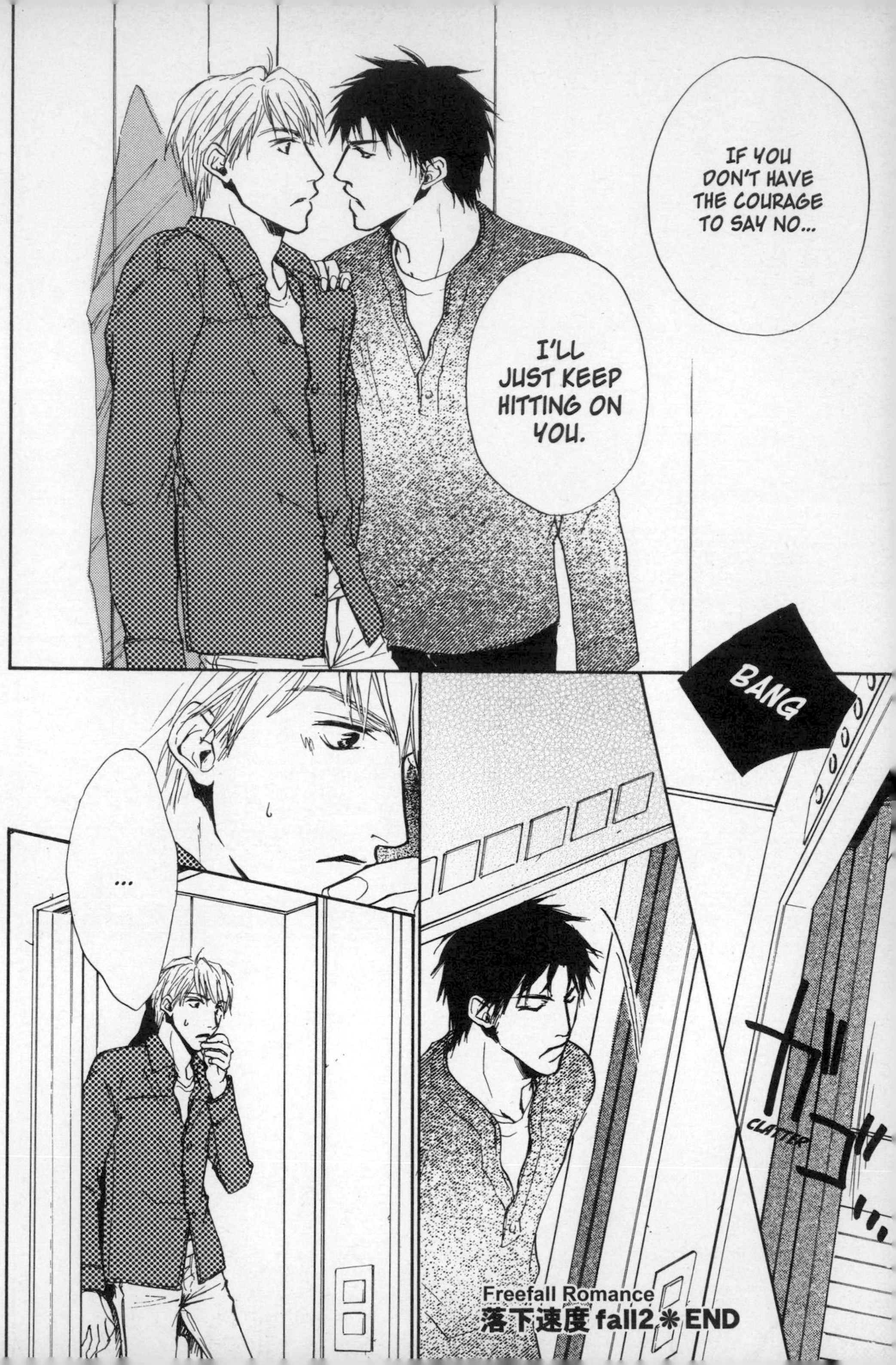
IF YOU DON'T HAVE THE COURAGE TO SAY NO...
I'LL JUST KEEP HITTING ON YOU.
BANG
CLATTER
...
Freefall Romance
落下速度 fall2 ＊ END

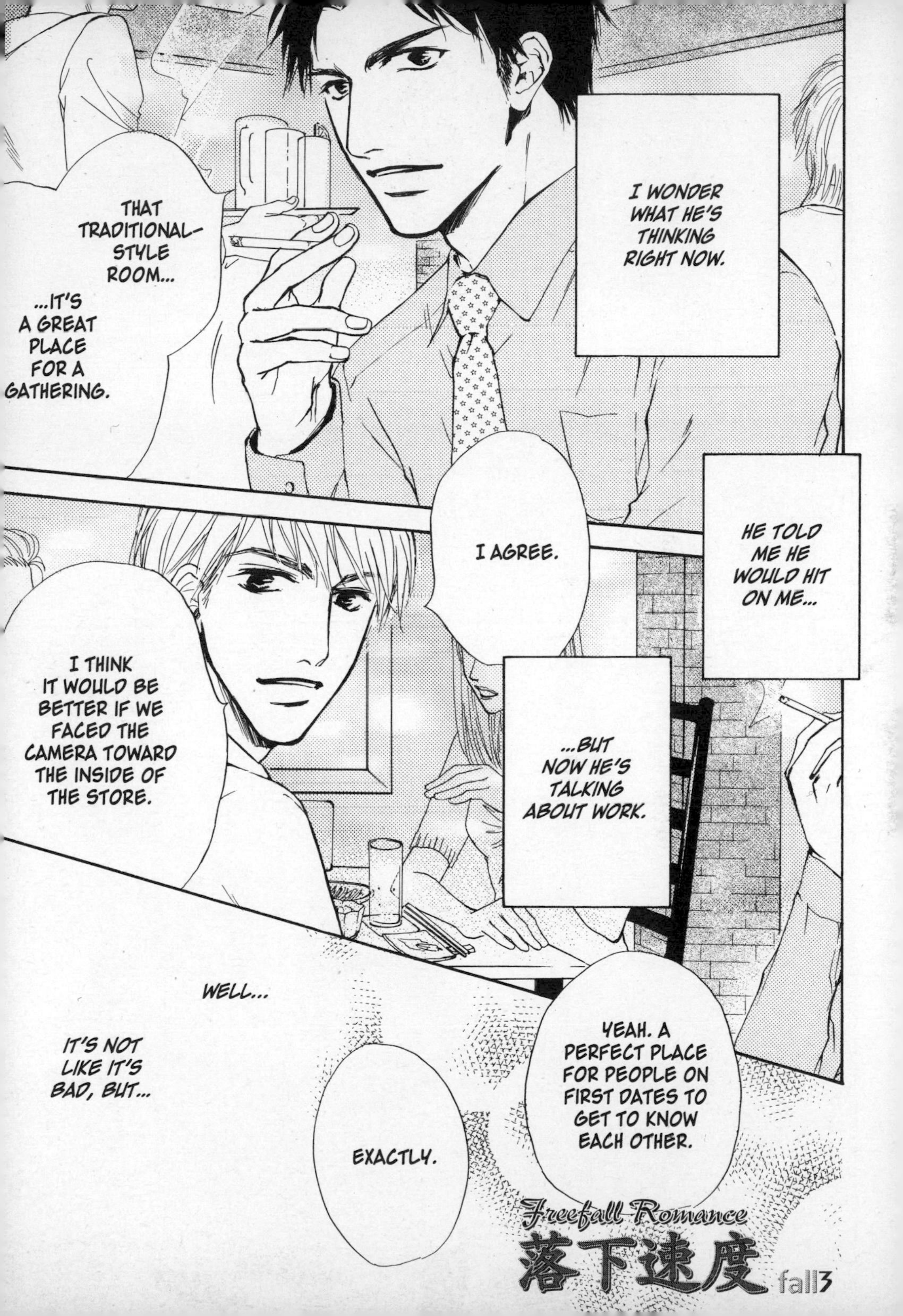
I WONDER WHAT HE'S THINKING RIGHT NOW.
THAT TRADITIONAL-STYLE ROOM...
...IT'S A GREAT PLACE FOR A GATHERING.
HE TOLD ME HE WOULD HIT ON ME...
I AGREE.
...BUT NOW HE'S TALKING ABOUT WORK.
I THINK IT WOULD BE BETTER IF WE FACED THE CAMERA TOWARD THE INSIDE OF THE STORE.
YEAH. A PERFECT PLACE FOR PEOPLE ON FIRST DATES TO GET TO KNOW EACH OTHER.
WELL...
EXACTLY.
IT'S NOT LIKE IT'S BAD, BUT...
Freefall Romance
落下速度
fall3

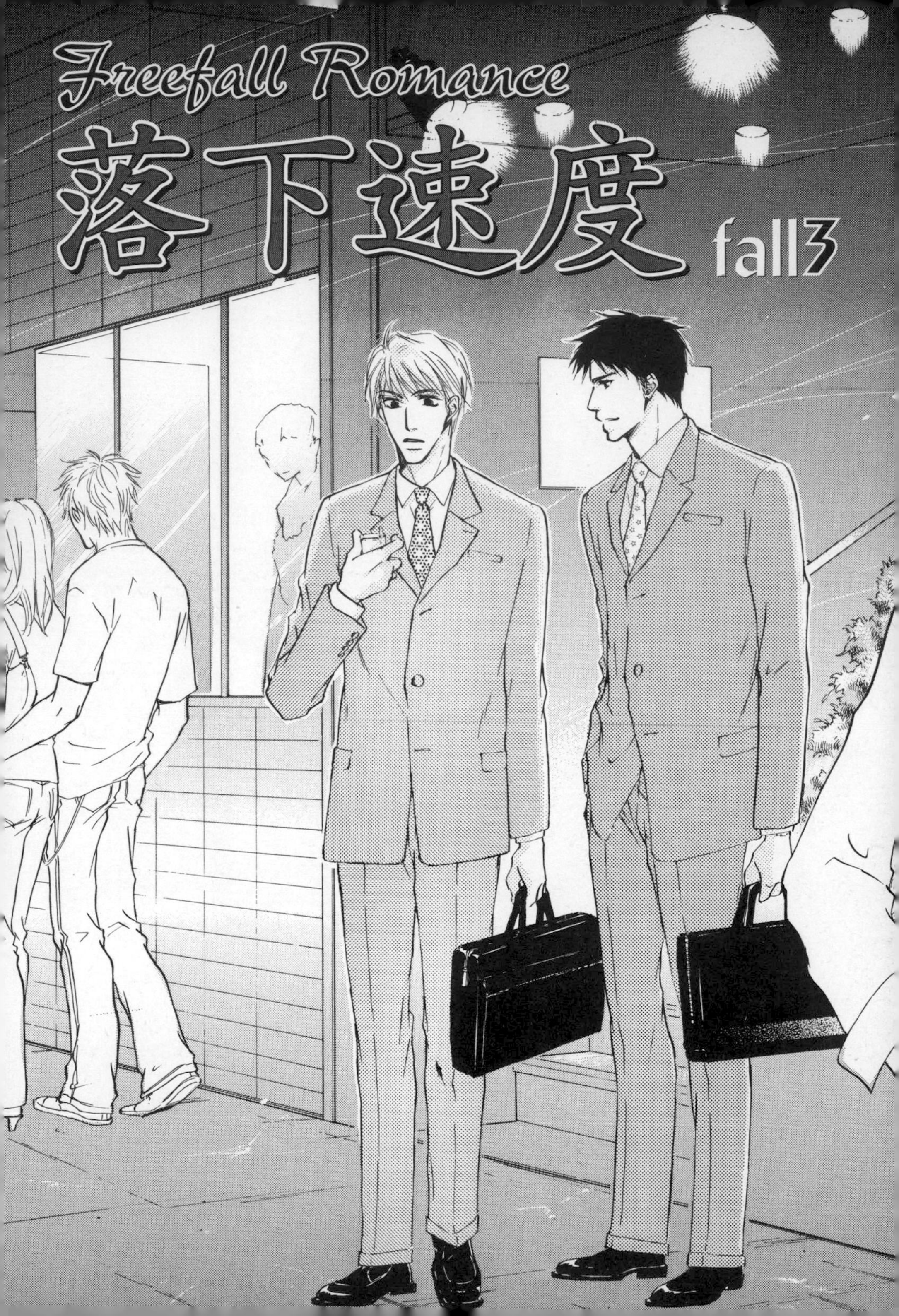
Freefall Romance
落下速度
fall3

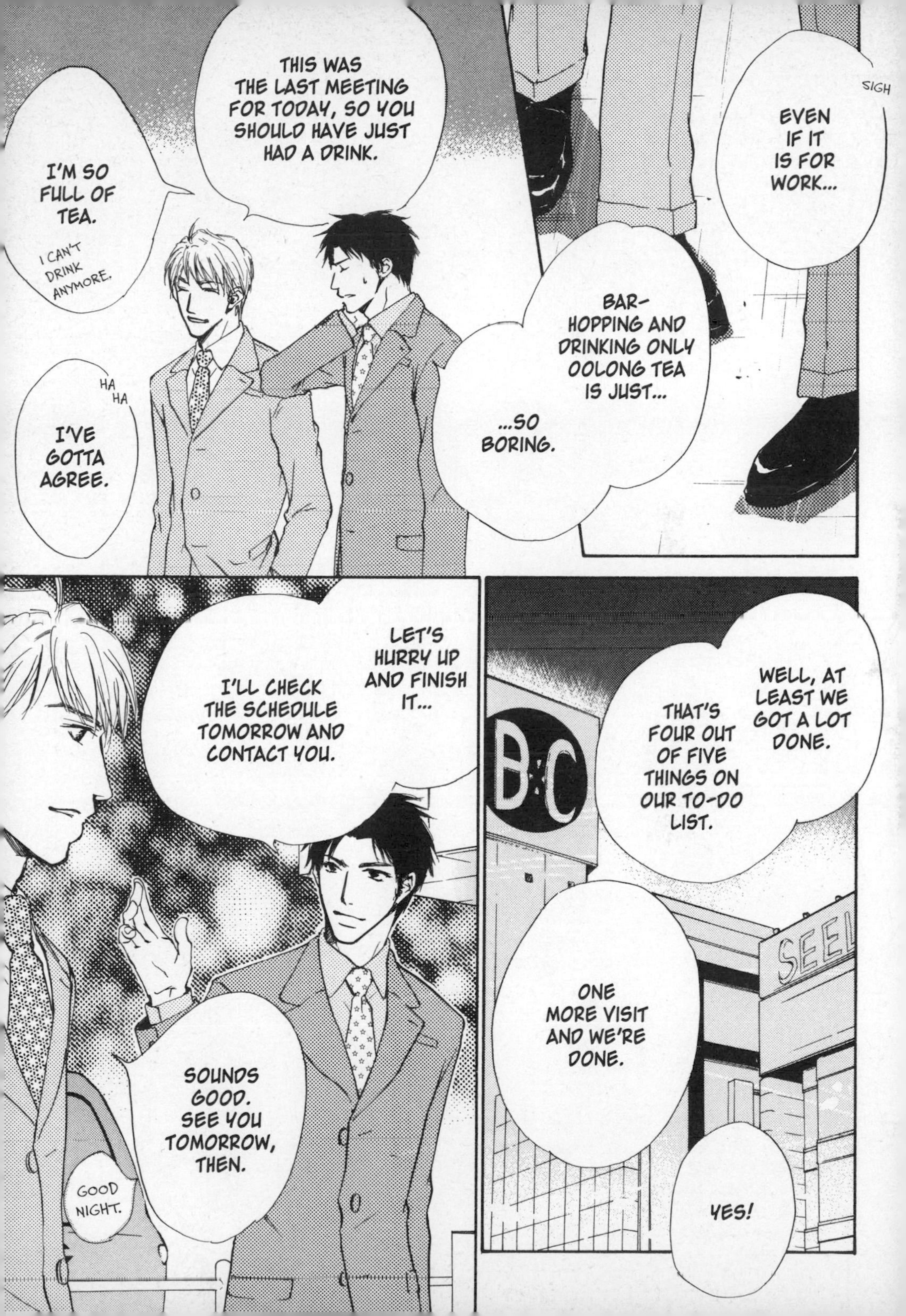
SIGH
EVEN IF IT IS FOR WORK...
BAR-HOPPING AND DRINKING ONLY OOLONG TEA IS JUST...
...SO BORING.
THIS WAS THE LAST MEETING FOR TODAY, SO YOU SHOULD HAVE JUST HAD A DRINK.
I'M SO FULL OF TEA.
I CAN'T DRINK ANYMORE.
HA HA
I'VE GOTTA AGREE.
WELL, AT LEAST WE GOT A LOT DONE.
THAT'S FOUR OUT OF FIVE THINGS ON OUR TO-DO LIST.
ONE MORE VISIT AND WE'RE DONE.
YES!
LET'S HURRY UP AND FINISH IT...
I'LL CHECK THE SCHEDULE TOMORROW AND CONTACT YOU.
SOUNDS GOOD. SEE YOU TOMORROW, THEN.
GOOD NIGHT.

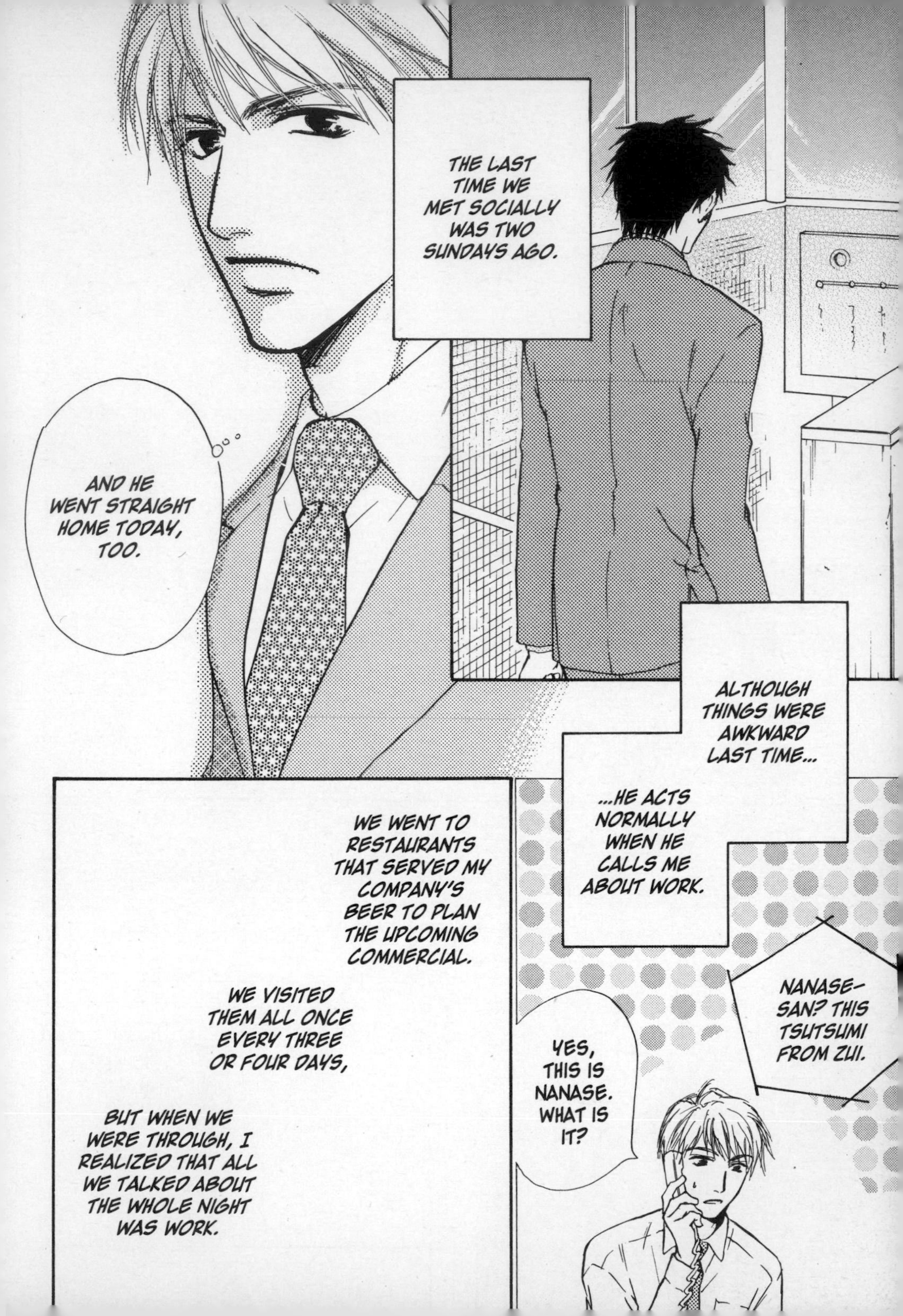
THE LAST TIME WE MET SOCIALLY WAS TWO SUNDAYS AGO.
AND HE WENT STRAIGHT HOME TODAY, TOO.
ALTHOUGH THINGS WERE AWKWARD LAST TIME...
...HE ACTS NORMALLY WHEN HE CALLS ME ABOUT WORK.
NANASE-SAN? THIS TSUTSUMI FROM ZUI.
YES, THIS IS NANASE. WHAT IS IT?
WE WENT TO RESTAURANTS THAT SERVED MY COMPANY'S BEER TO PLAN THE UPCOMING COMMERCIAL.
WE VISITED THEM ALL ONCE EVERY THREE OR FOUR DAYS,
BUT WHEN WE WERE THROUGH, I REALIZED THAT ALL WE TALKED ABOUT THE WHOLE NIGHT WAS WORK.

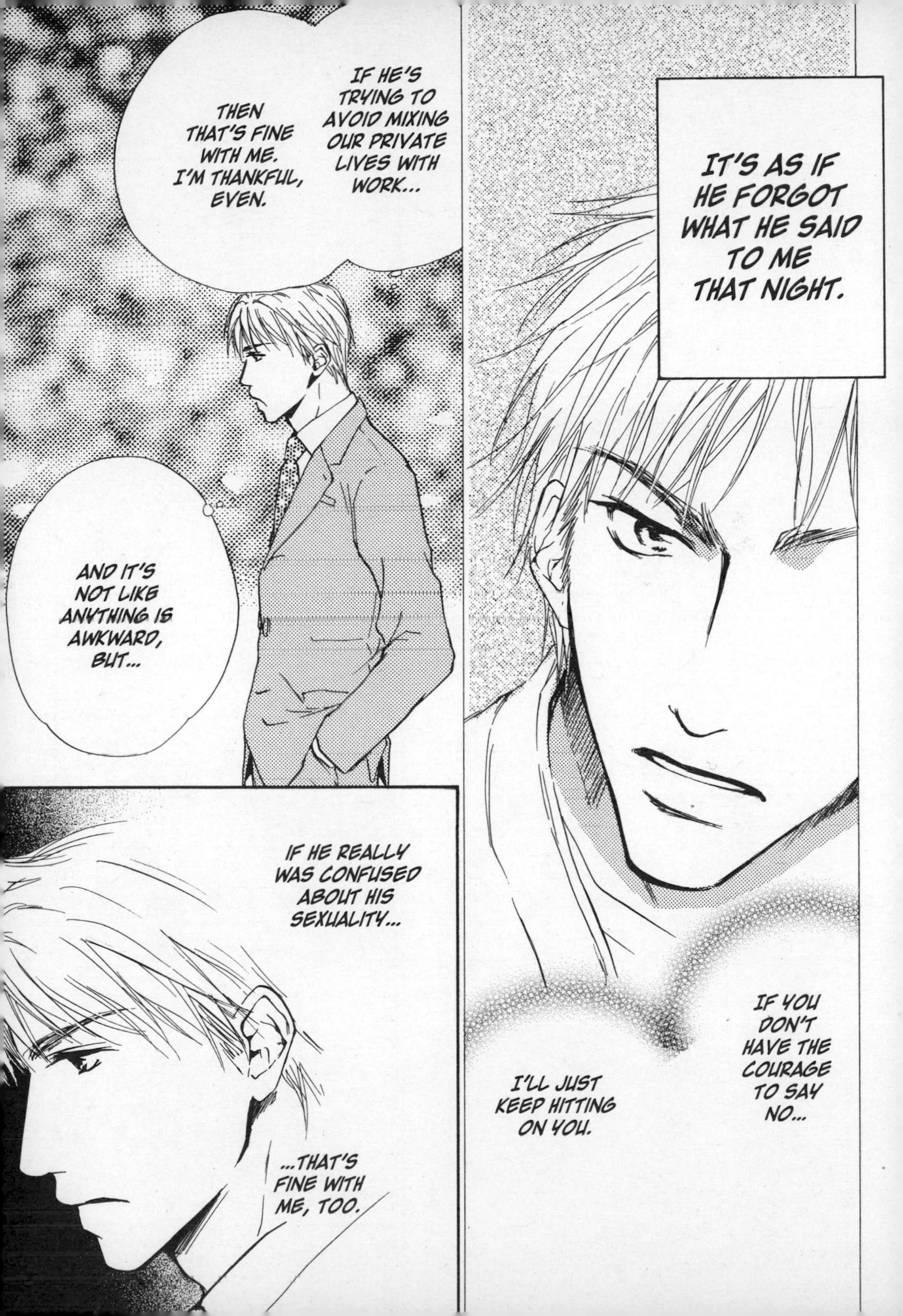
IT'S AS IF HE FORGOT WHAT HE SAID TO ME THAT NIGHT.
IF YOU DON'T HAVE THE COURAGE TO SAY NO...
I'LL JUST KEEP HITTING ON YOU.
IF HE'S TRYING TO AVOID MIXING OUR PRIVATE LIVES WITH WORK...
THEN THAT'S FINE WITH ME. I'M THANKFUL, EVEN.
AND IT'S NOT LIKE ANYTHING IS AWKWARD, BUT...
IF HE REALLY WAS CONFUSED ABOUT HIS SEXUALITY...
...THAT'S FINE WITH ME, TOO.

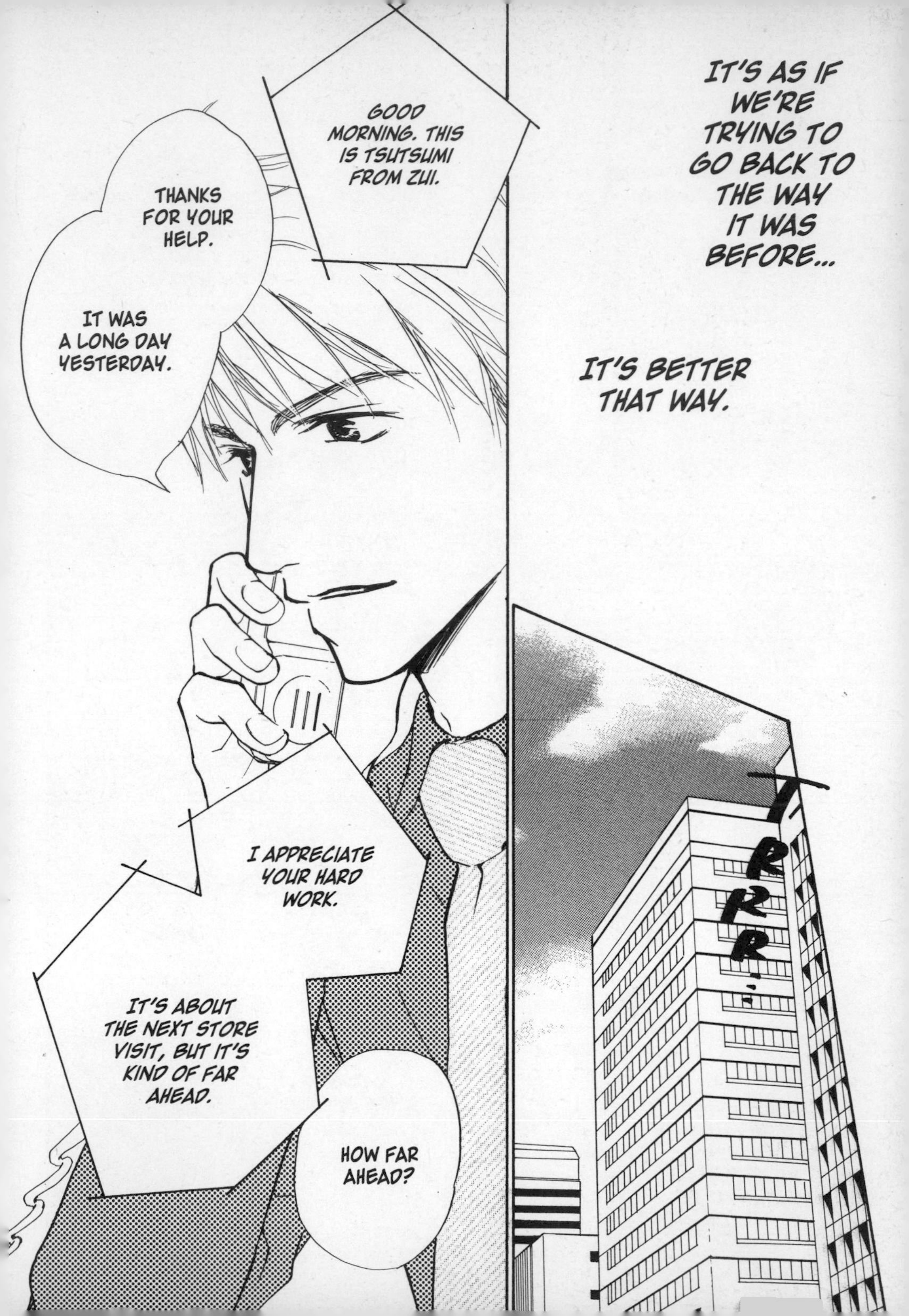
IT'S AS IF WE'RE TRYING TO GO BACK TO THE WAY IT WAS BEFORE...
IT'S BETTER THAT WAY.
TRRR...
GOOD MORNING. THIS IS TSUTSUMI FROM ZUI.
THANKS FOR YOUR HELP.
IT WAS A LONG DAY YESTERDAY.
I APPRECIATE YOUR HARD WORK.
IT'S ABOUT THE NEXT STORE VISIT, BUT IT'S KIND OF FAR AHEAD.
HOW FAR AHEAD?

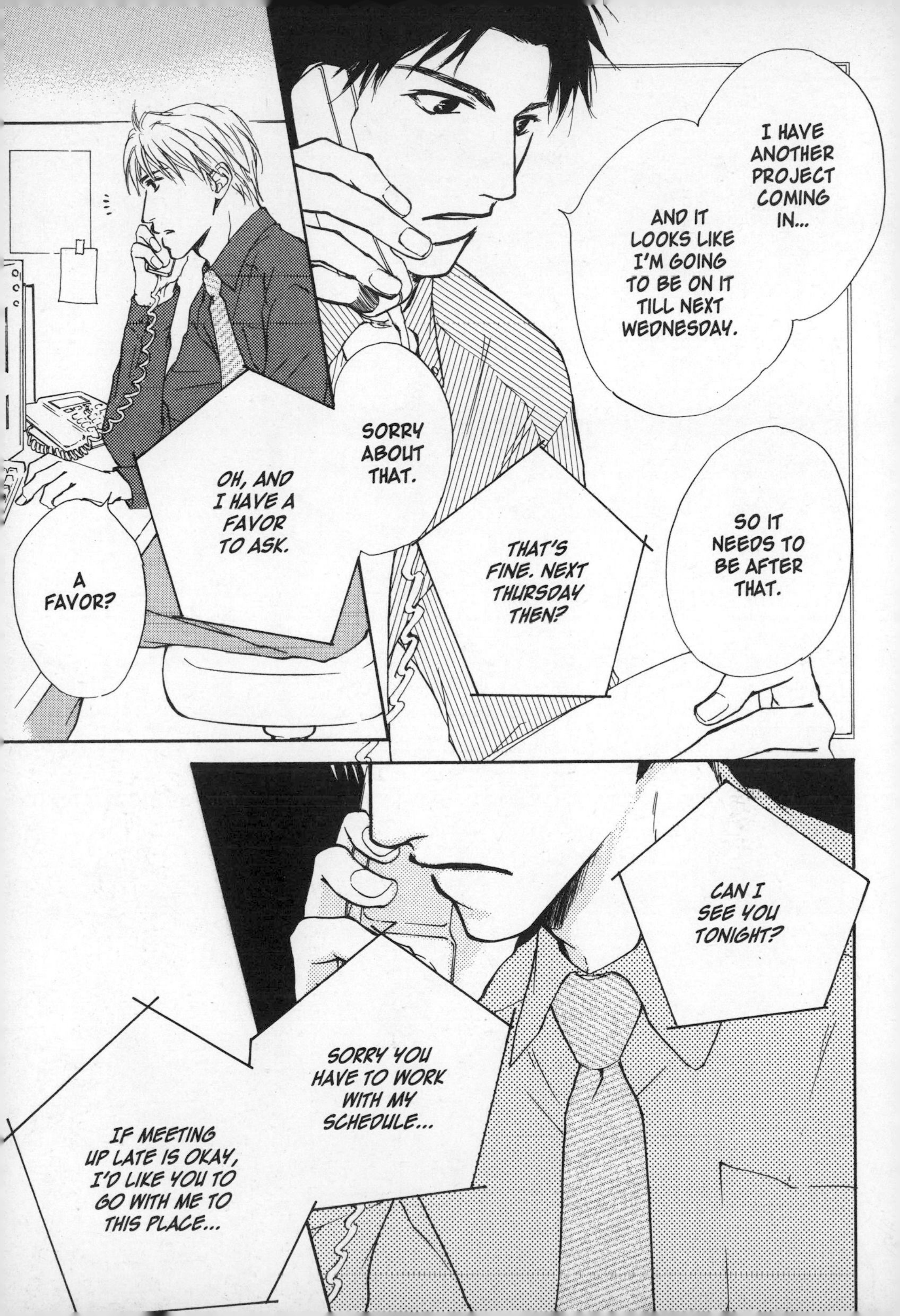
I HAVE ANOTHER PROJECT COMING IN...
AND IT LOOKS LIKE I'M GOING TO BE ON IT TILL NEXT WEDNESDAY.
SO IT NEEDS TO BE AFTER THAT.
SORRY ABOUT THAT.
THAT'S FINE. NEXT THURSDAY THEN?
OH, AND I HAVE A FAVOR TO ASK.
A FAVOR?
CAN I SEE YOU TONIGHT?
SORRY YOU HAVE TO WORK WITH MY SCHEDULE...
IF MEETING UP LATE IS OKAY, I'D LIKE YOU TO GO WITH ME TO THIS PLACE...

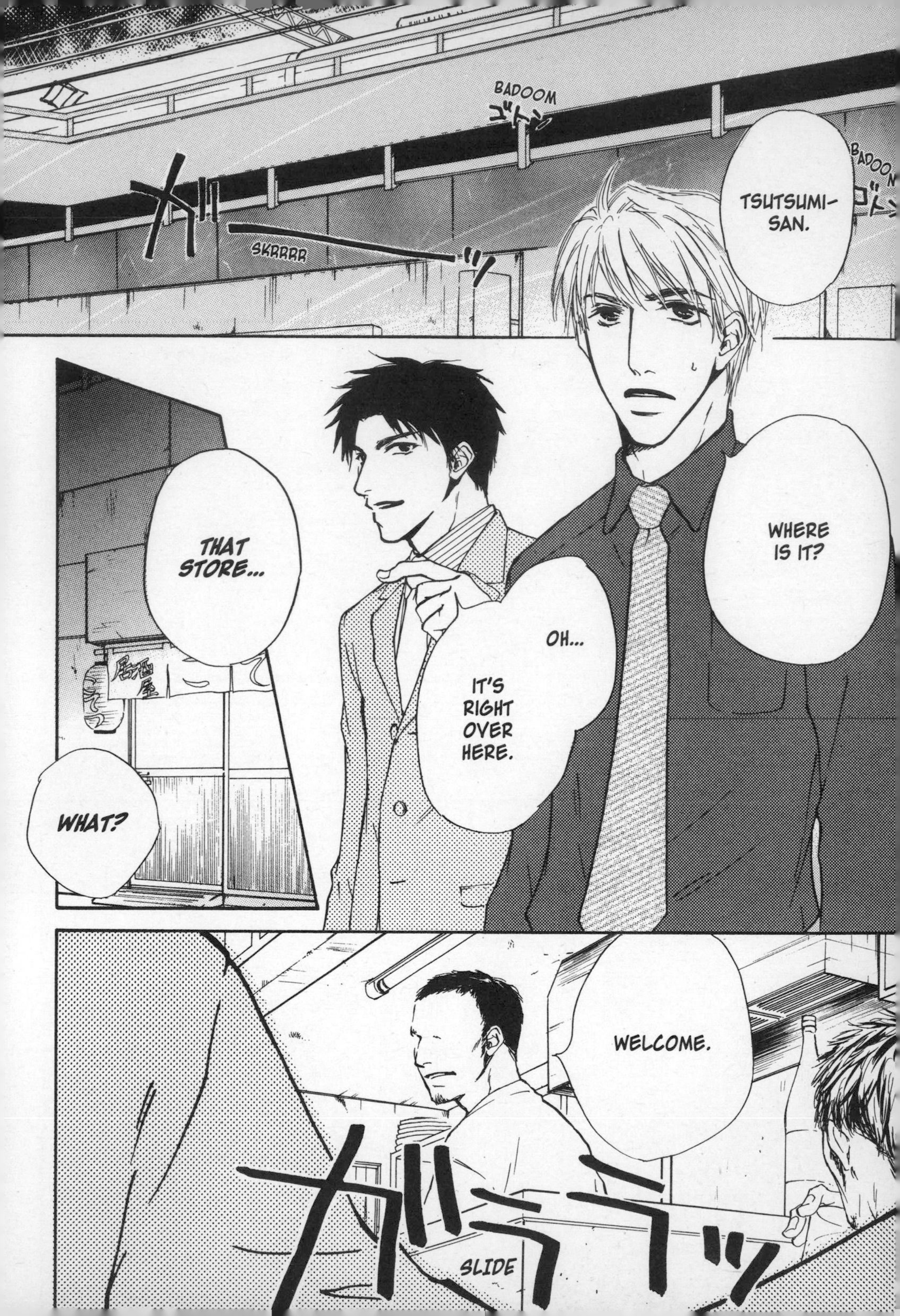
BADOON
ゴトン
TSUTSUMI-SAN.
BADOOM
ゴトン
SKRRRR
WHERE IS IT?
OH...
IT'S RIGHT OVER HERE.
THAT STORE...
居酒屋
WHAT?
WELCOME.
ガラララッ
SLIDE

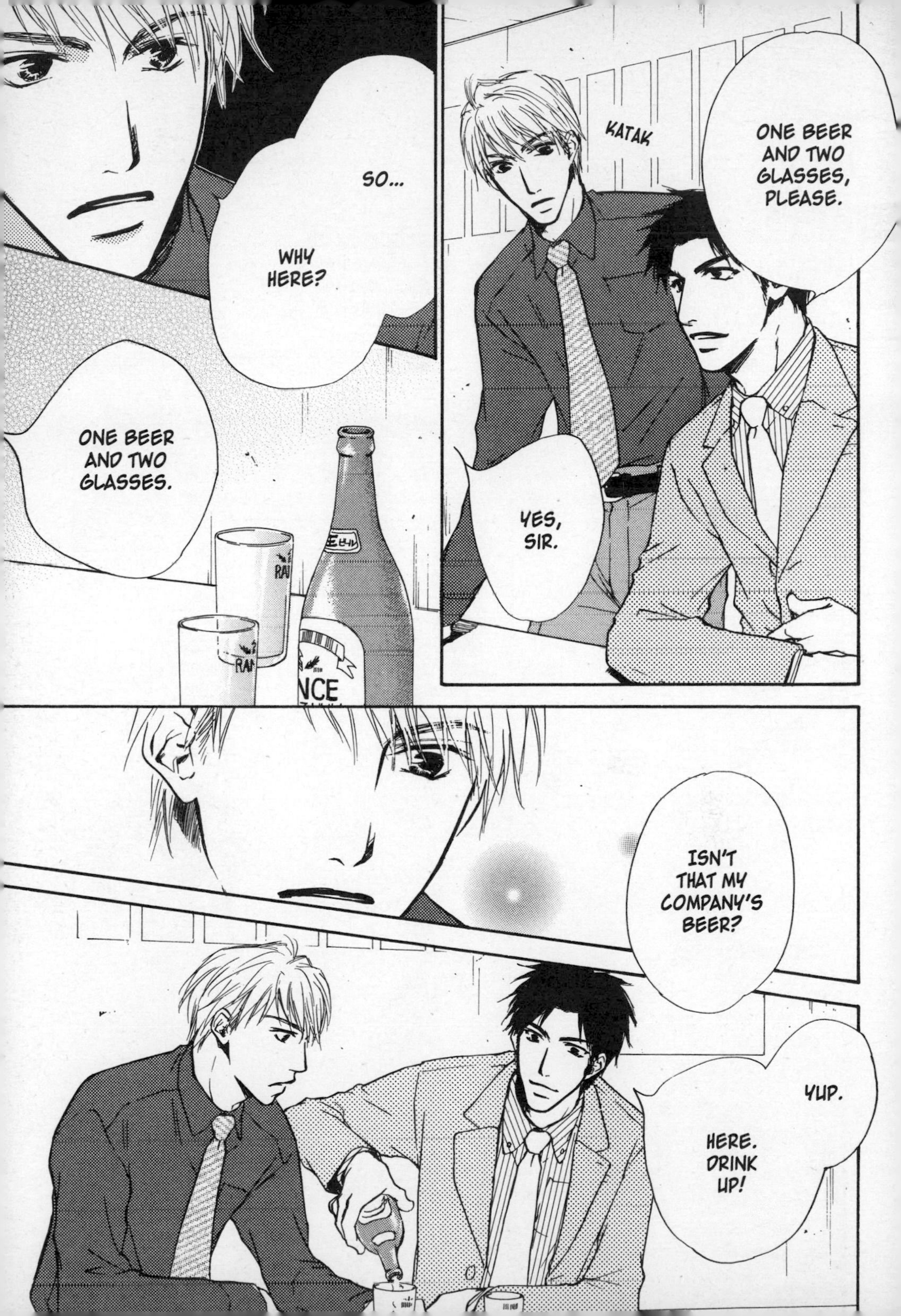
ONE BEER AND TWO GLASSES, PLEASE.
KATAK
YES, SIR.
SO...
WHY HERE?
ONE BEER AND TWO GLASSES.
ISN'T THAT MY COMPANY'S BEER?
YUP.
HERE. DRINK UP!

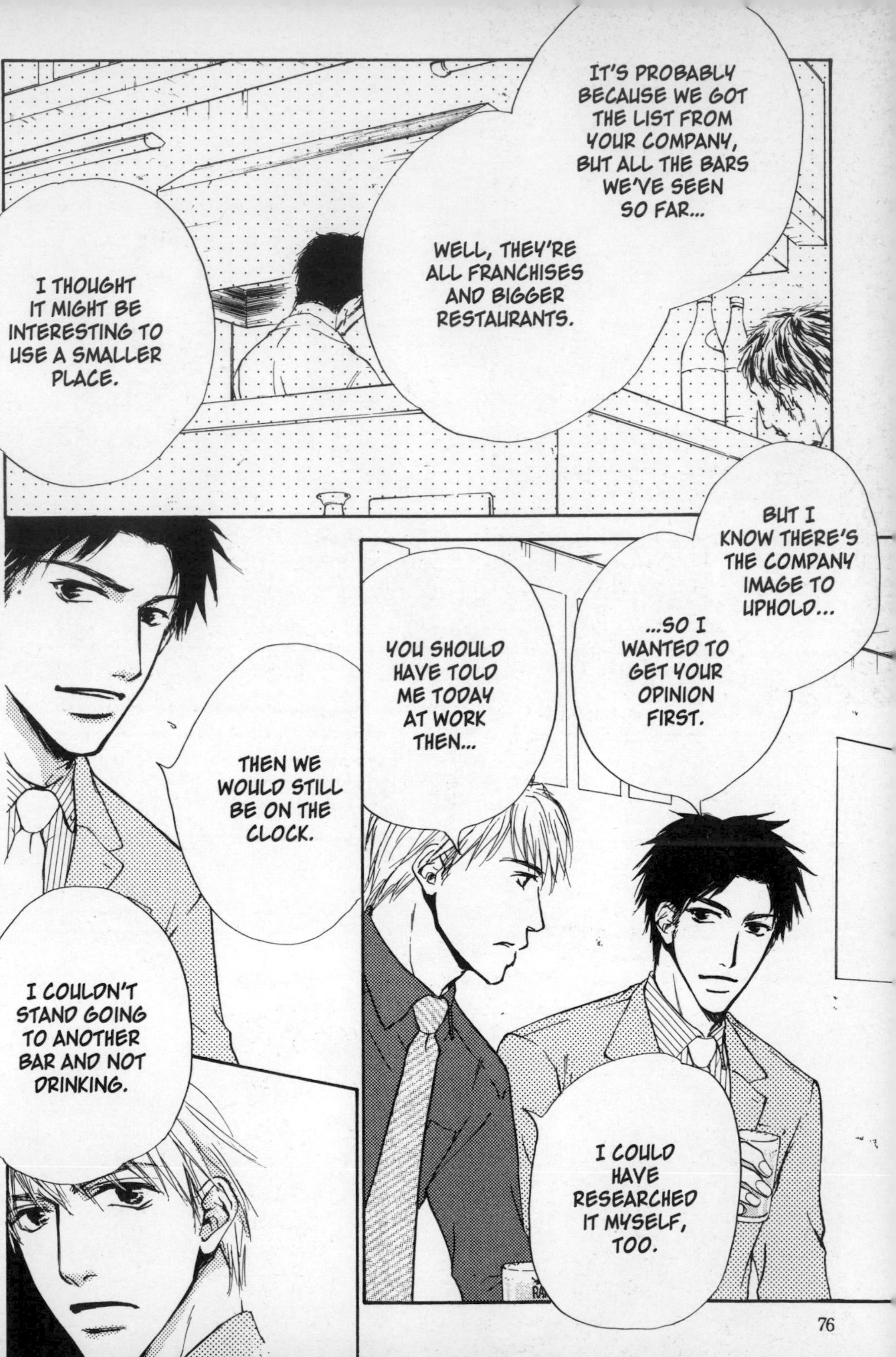
IT'S PROBABLY BECAUSE WE GOT THE LIST FROM YOUR COMPANY, BUT ALL THE BARS WE'VE SEEN SO FAR...
WELL, THEY'RE ALL FRANCHISES AND BIGGER RESTAURANTS.
I THOUGHT IT MIGHT BE INTERESTING TO USE A SMALLER PLACE.
BUT I KNOW THERE'S THE COMPANY IMAGE TO UPHOLD...
...SO I WANTED TO GET YOUR OPINION FIRST.
YOU SHOULD HAVE TOLD ME TODAY AT WORK THEN...
I COULD HAVE RESEARCHED IT MYSELF, TOO.
THEN WE WOULD STILL BE ON THE CLOCK.
I COULDN'T STAND GOING TO ANOTHER BAR AND NOT DRINKING.

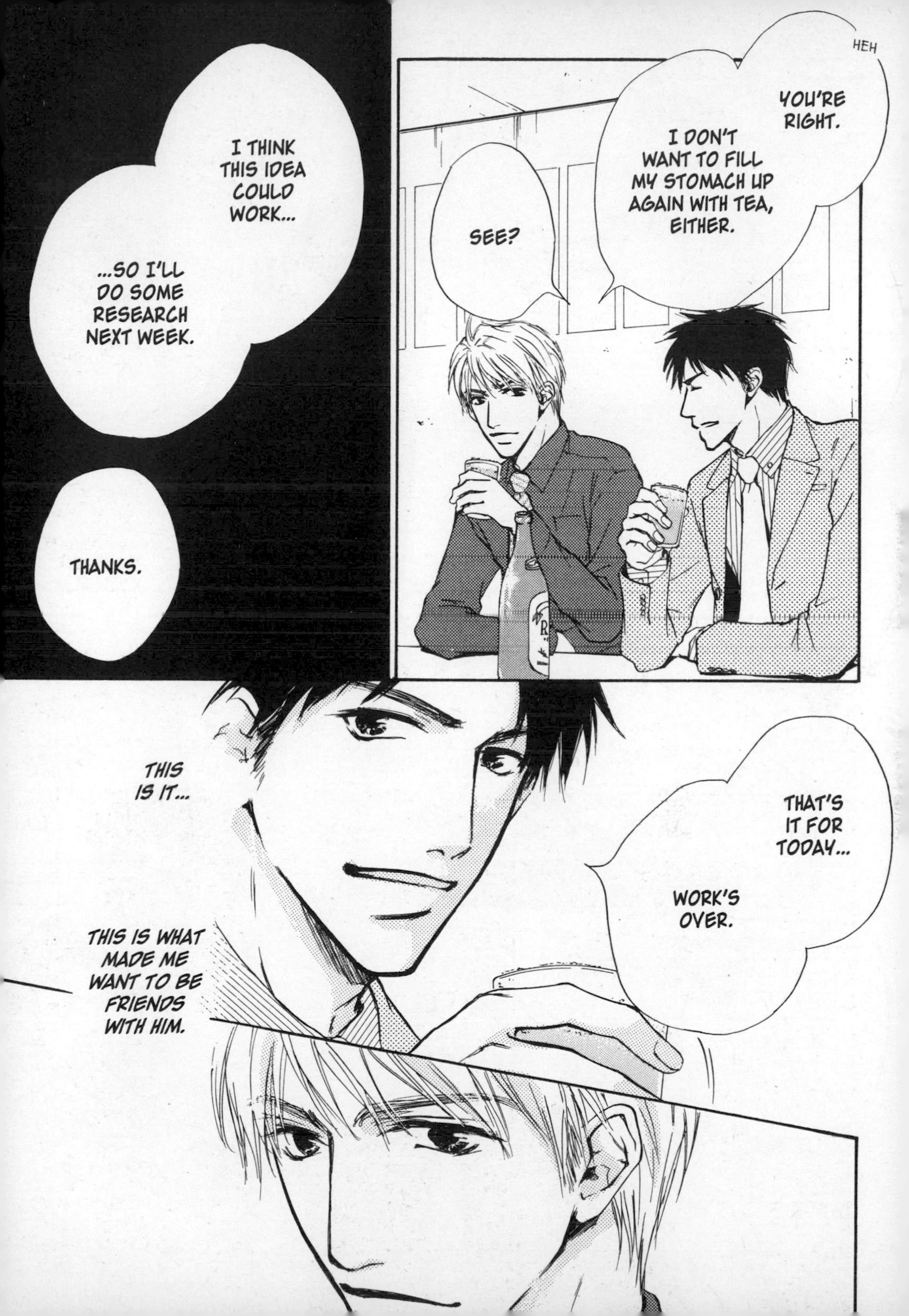
HEH
YOU'RE RIGHT.
I DON'T WANT TO FILL MY STOMACH UP AGAIN WITH TEA, EITHER.
SEE?
I THINK THIS IDEA COULD WORK...
...SO I'LL DO SOME RESEARCH NEXT WEEK.
THANKS.
THAT'S IT FOR TODAY...
WORK'S OVER.
THIS IS IT...
THIS IS WHAT MADE ME WANT TO BE FRIENDS WITH HIM.

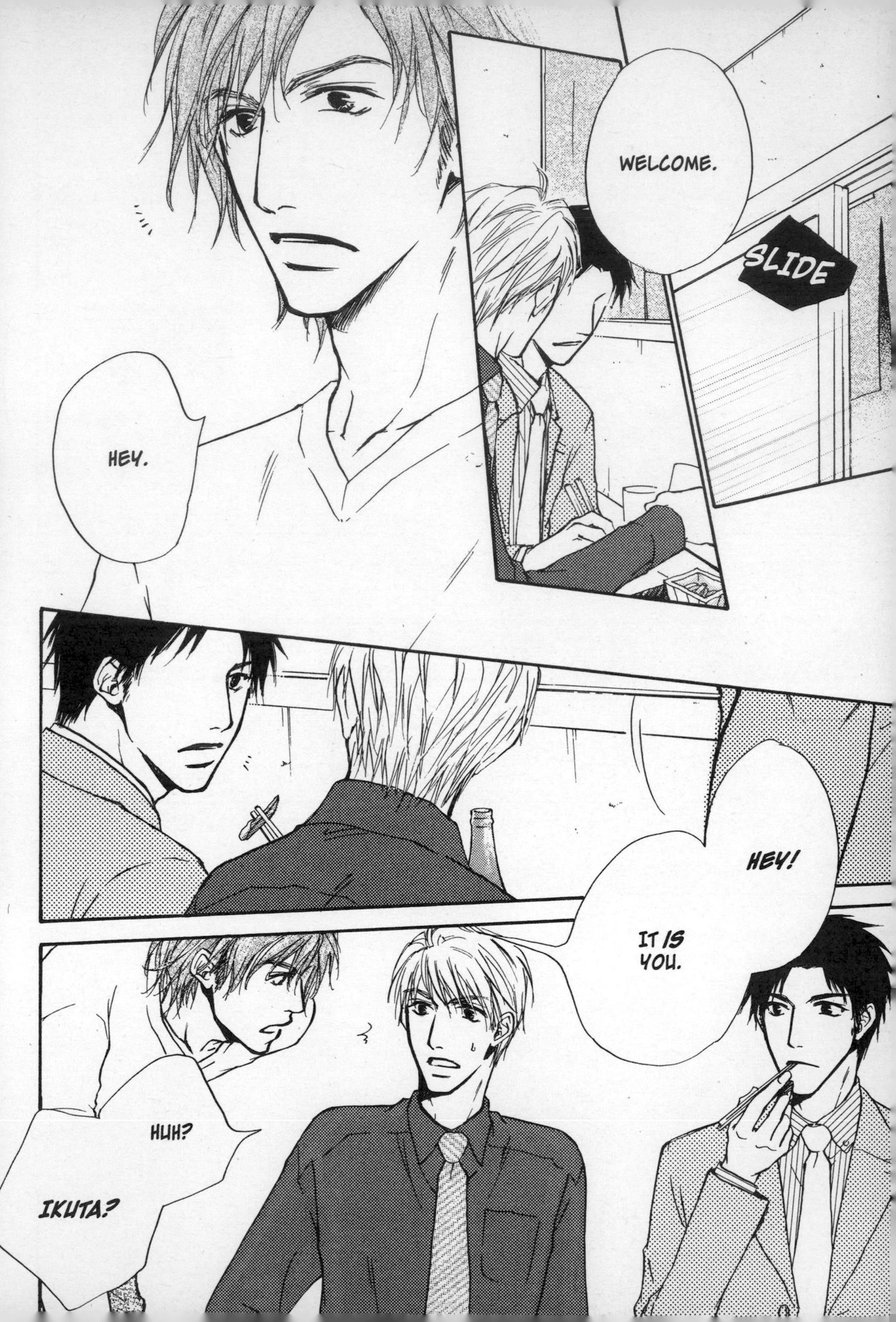
WELCOME.
SLIDE
HEY.
HEY!
IT IS YOU.
HUH?
IKUTA?

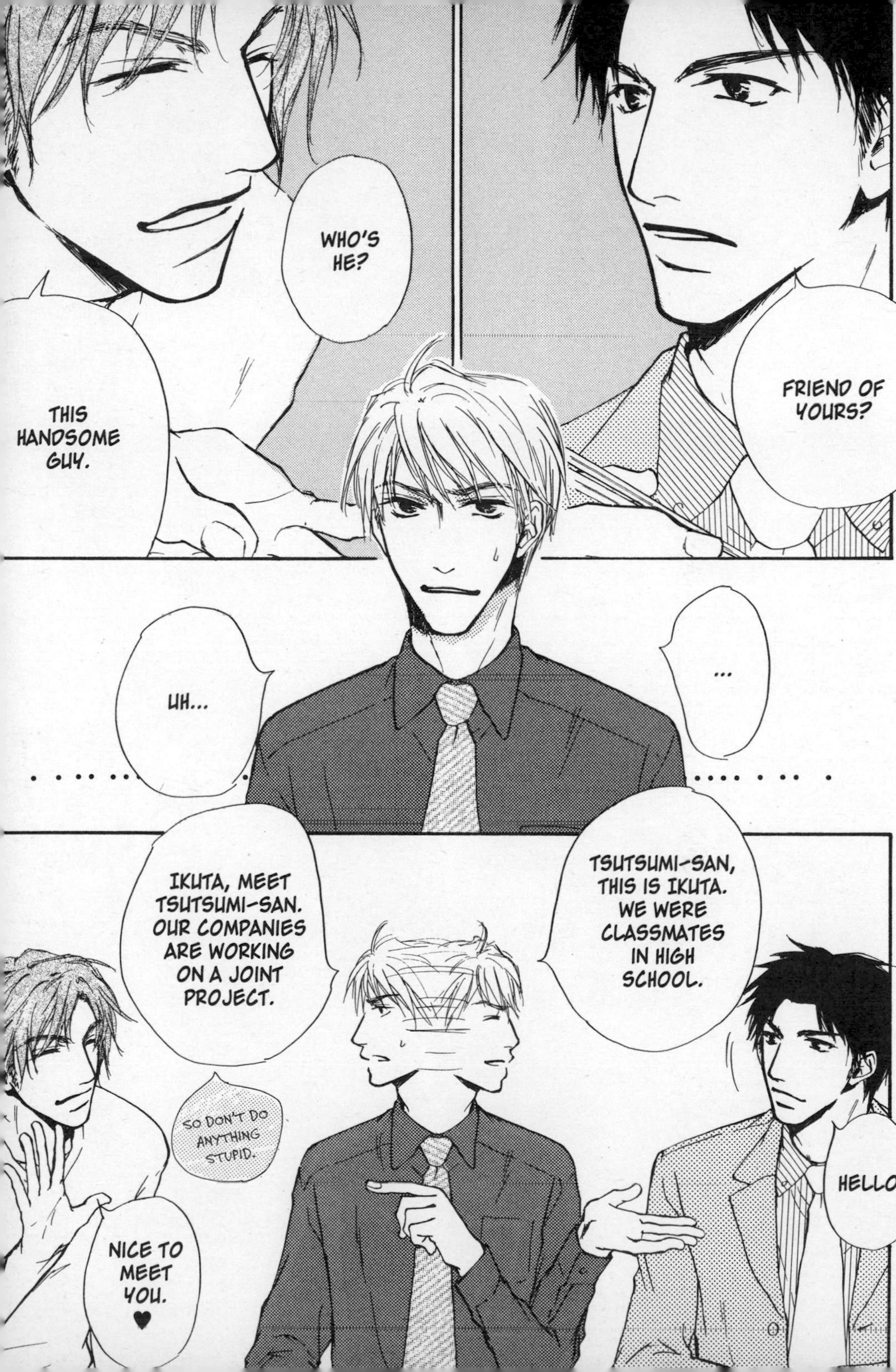
FRIEND OF YOURS?
WHO'S HE?
THIS HANDSOME GUY.
...
UH...
TSUTSUMI-SAN, THIS IS IKUTA. WE WERE CLASSMATES IN HIGH SCHOOL.
IKUTA, MEET TSUTSUMI-SAN. OUR COMPANIES ARE WORKING ON A JOINT PROJECT.
HELLO.
SO DON'T DO ANYTHING STUPID.
NICE TO MEET YOU. ♥

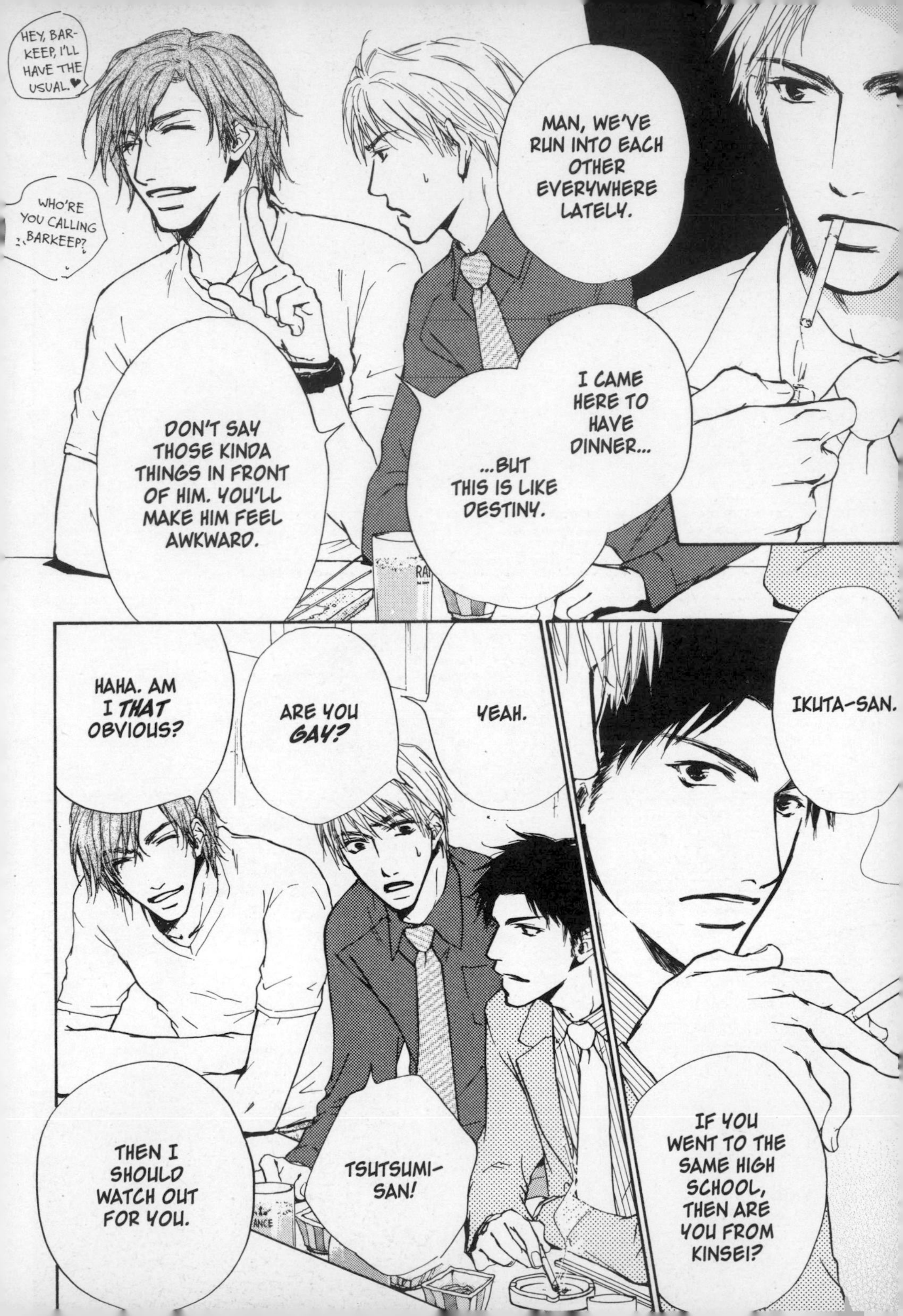
MAN, WE'VE RUN INTO EACH OTHER EVERYWHERE LATELY.
I CAME HERE TO HAVE DINNER...
...BUT THIS IS LIKE DESTINY.
DON'T SAY THOSE KINDA THINGS IN FRONT OF HIM. YOU'LL MAKE HIM FEEL AWKWARD.
HEY, BARKEEP, I'LL HAVE THE USUAL.♥
WHO'RE YOU CALLING BARKEEP?
IKUTA-SAN.
IF YOU WENT TO THE SAME HIGH SCHOOL, THEN ARE YOU FROM KINSEI?
YEAH.
ARE YOU *GAY?*
HAHA. AM I *THAT* OBVIOUS?
TSUTSUMI-SAN!
THEN I SHOULD WATCH OUT FOR YOU.

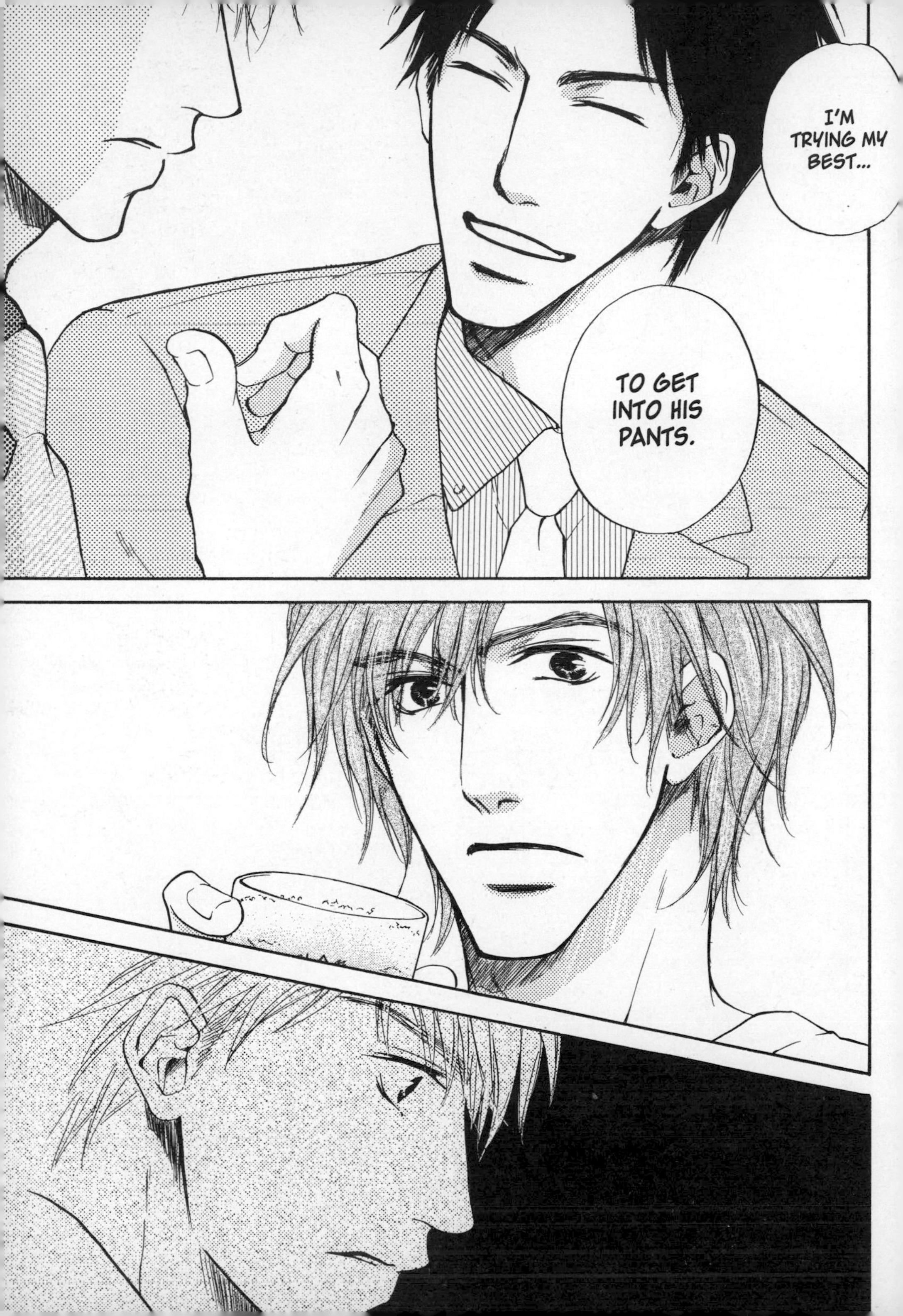
I'M TRYING MY BEST...
TO GET INTO HIS PANTS.

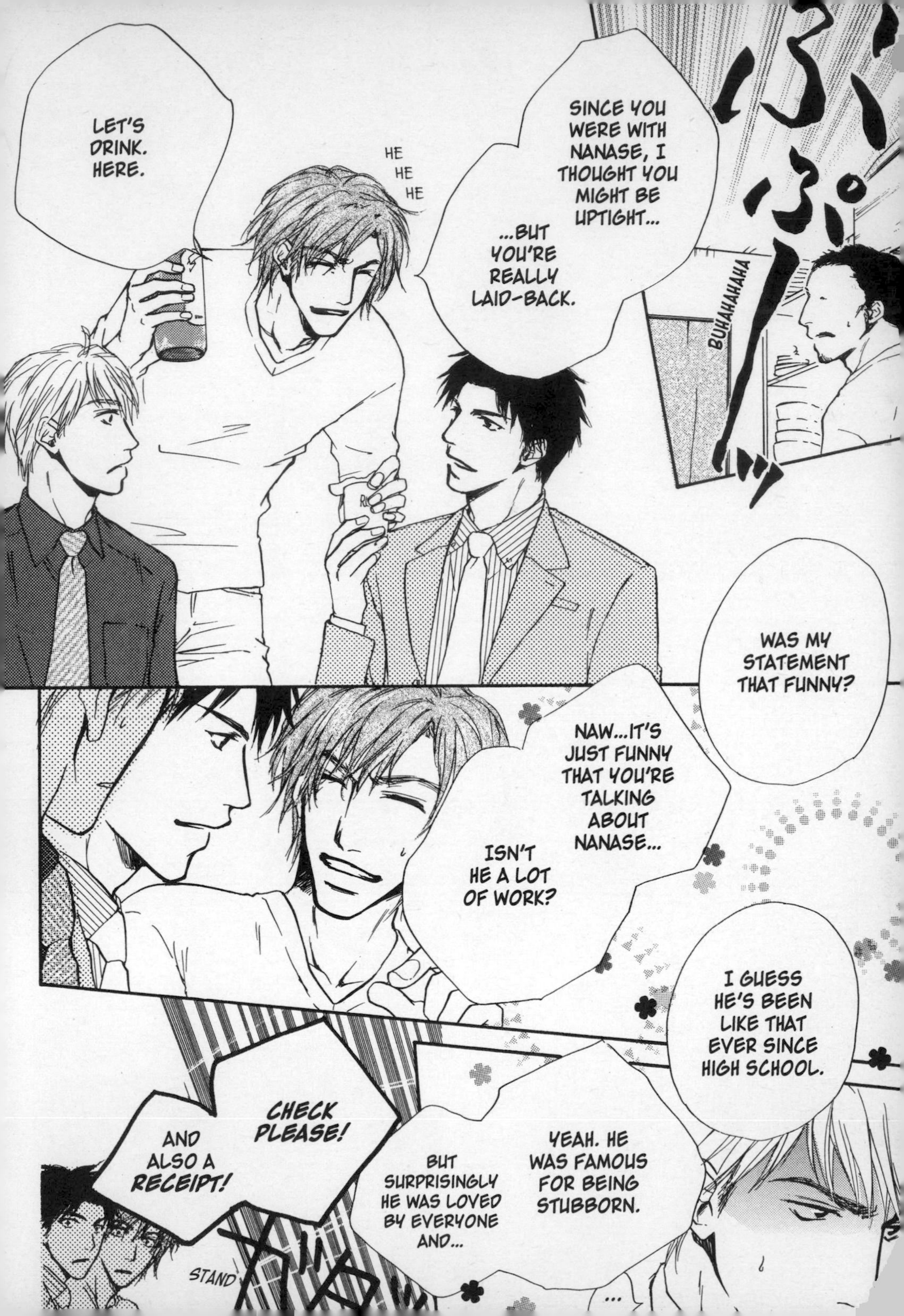
BUHAHAHAHA
SINCE YOU WERE WITH NANASE, I THOUGHT YOU MIGHT BE UPTIGHT...
...BUT YOU'RE REALLY LAID-BACK.
HE HE HE
LET'S DRINK. HERE.
WAS MY STATEMENT THAT FUNNY?
NAW...IT'S JUST FUNNY THAT YOU'RE TALKING ABOUT NANASE...
ISN'T HE A LOT OF WORK?
I GUESS HE'S BEEN LIKE THAT EVER SINCE HIGH SCHOOL.
YEAH. HE WAS FAMOUS FOR BEING STUBBORN.
...
BUT SURPRISINGLY HE WAS LOVED BY EVERYONE AND...
CHECK PLEASE!
AND ALSO A RECEIPT!
STAND

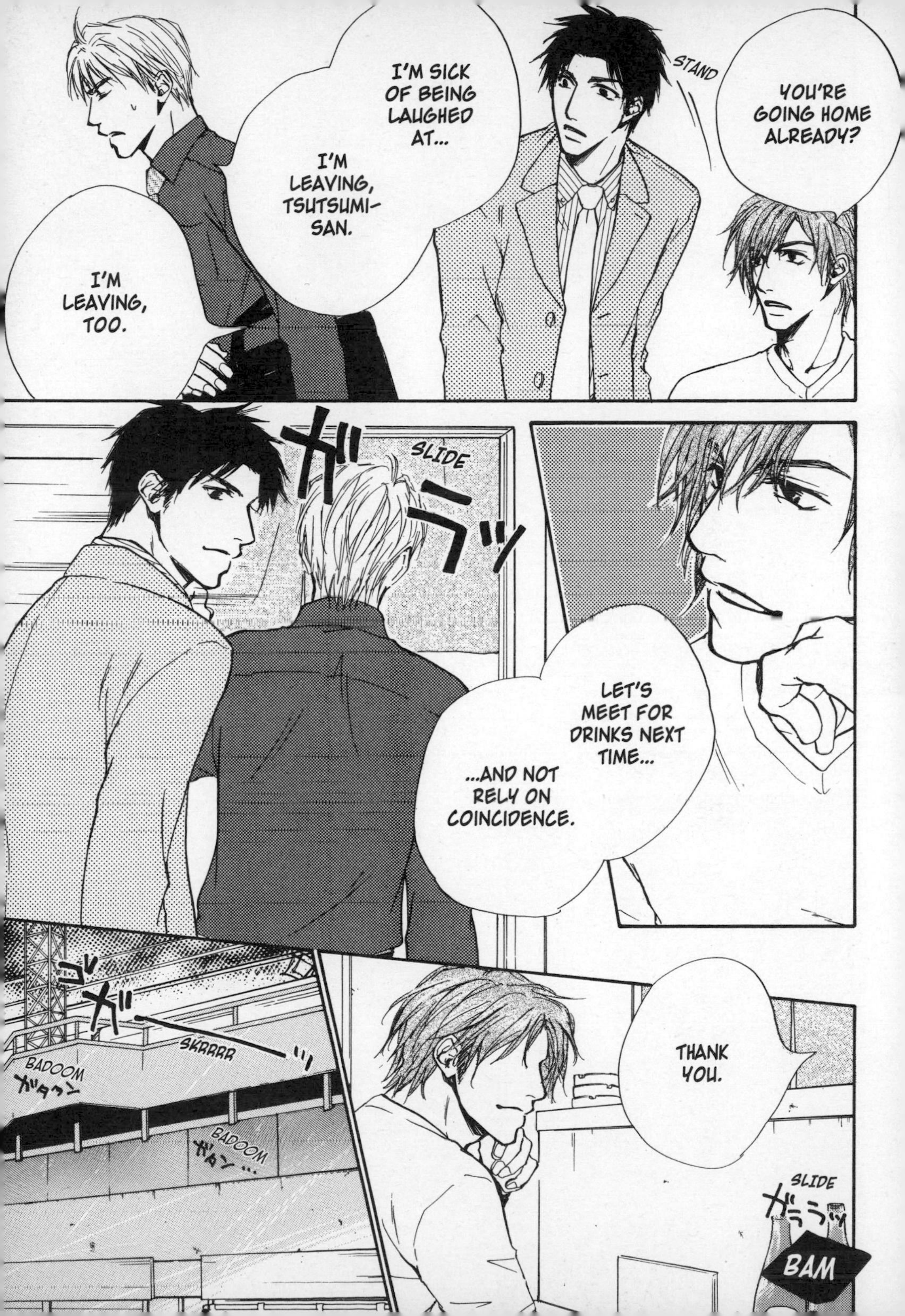
STAND
YOU'RE GOING HOME ALREADY?
I'M SICK OF BEING LAUGHED AT...
I'M LEAVING, TSUTSUMI-SAN.
I'M LEAVING, TOO.
LET'S MEET FOR DRINKS NEXT TIME...
...AND NOT RELY ON COINCIDENCE.
ガラッ
SLIDE
THANK YOU.
SLIDE
ガラッ
BAM
ゴガー
SKRRRR
BADOOM
ガタン
BADOOM
ガタン…

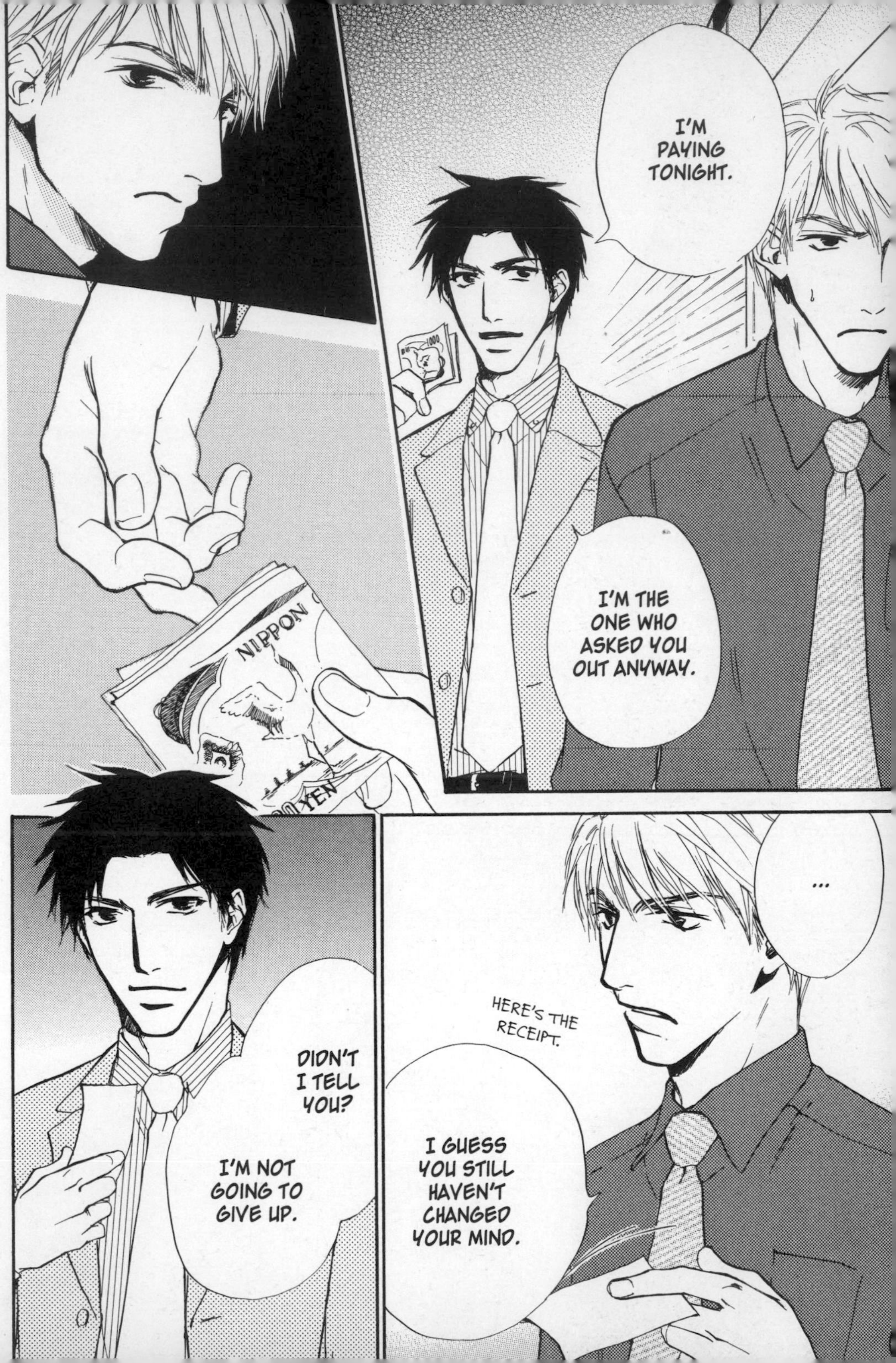

I'M PAYING TONIGHT.
I'M THE ONE WHO ASKED YOU OUT ANYWAY.
NIPPON
...
HERE'S THE RECEIPT.
I GUESS YOU STILL HAVEN'T CHANGED YOUR MIND.
DIDN'T I TELL YOU?
I'M NOT GOING TO GIVE UP.

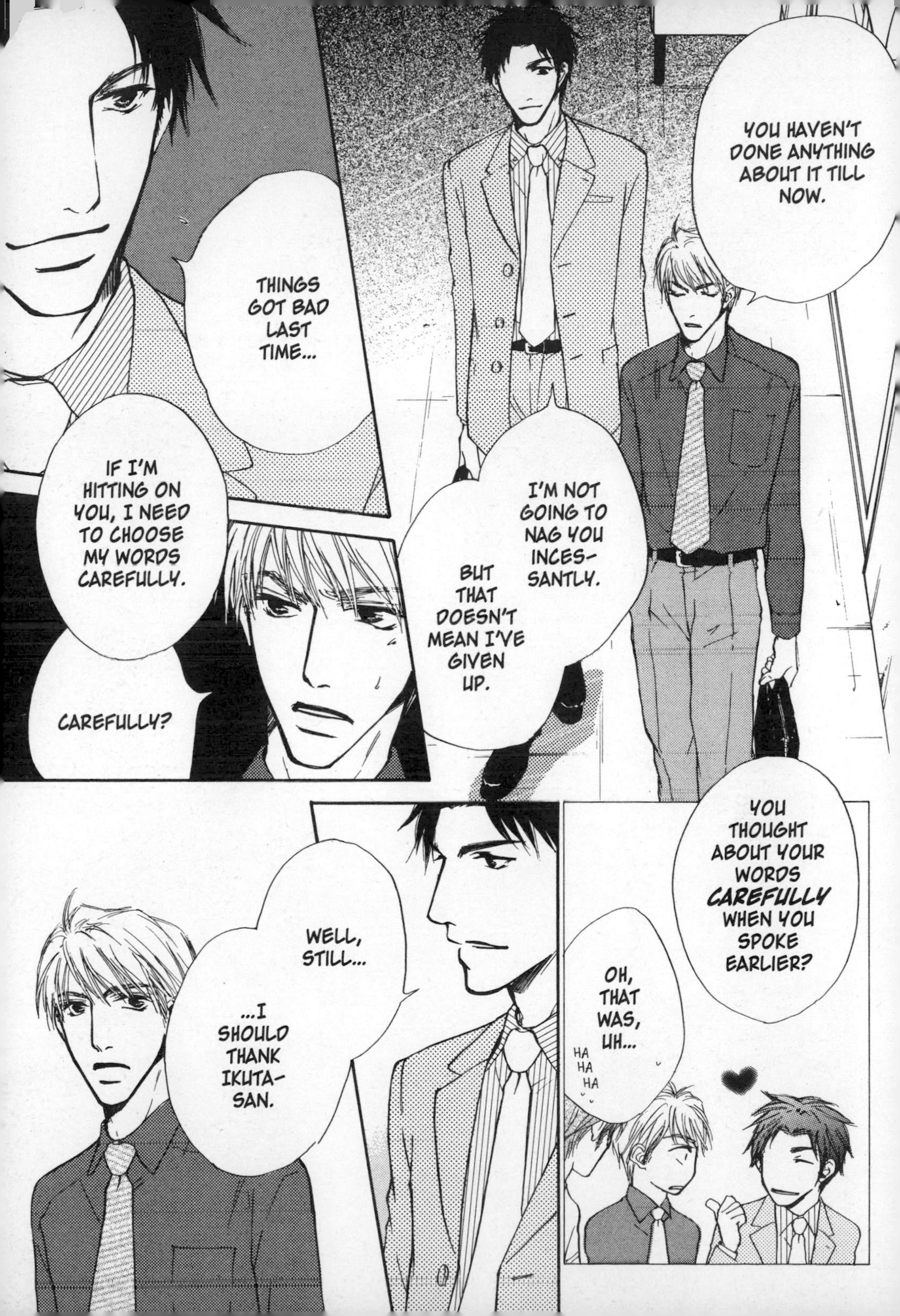
YOU HAVEN'T DONE ANYTHING ABOUT IT TILL NOW.
I'M NOT GOING TO NAG YOU INCES-SANTLY.
BUT THAT DOESN'T MEAN I'VE GIVEN UP.
THINGS GOT BAD LAST TIME...
IF I'M HITTING ON YOU, I NEED TO CHOOSE MY WORDS CAREFULLY.
CAREFULLY?
YOU THOUGHT ABOUT YOUR WORDS **CAREFULLY** WHEN YOU SPOKE EARLIER?
OH, THAT WAS, UH...
HA HA HA
WELL, STILL...
...I SHOULD THANK IKUTA-SAN.

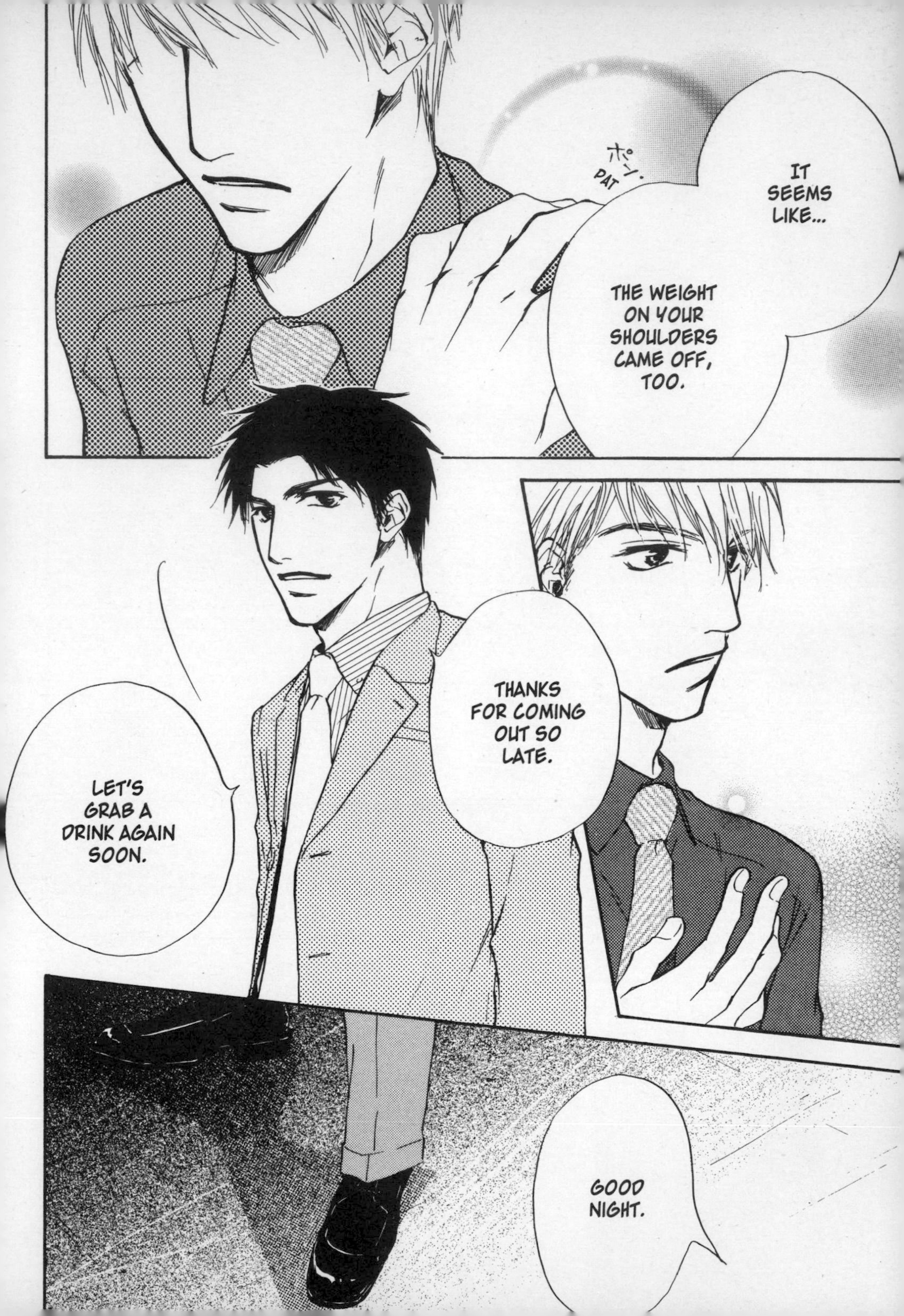
ポン
PAT
IT SEEMS LIKE...
THE WEIGHT ON YOUR SHOULDERS CAME OFF, TOO.
THANKS FOR COMING OUT SO LATE.
LET'S GRAB A DRINK AGAIN SOON.
GOOD NIGHT.

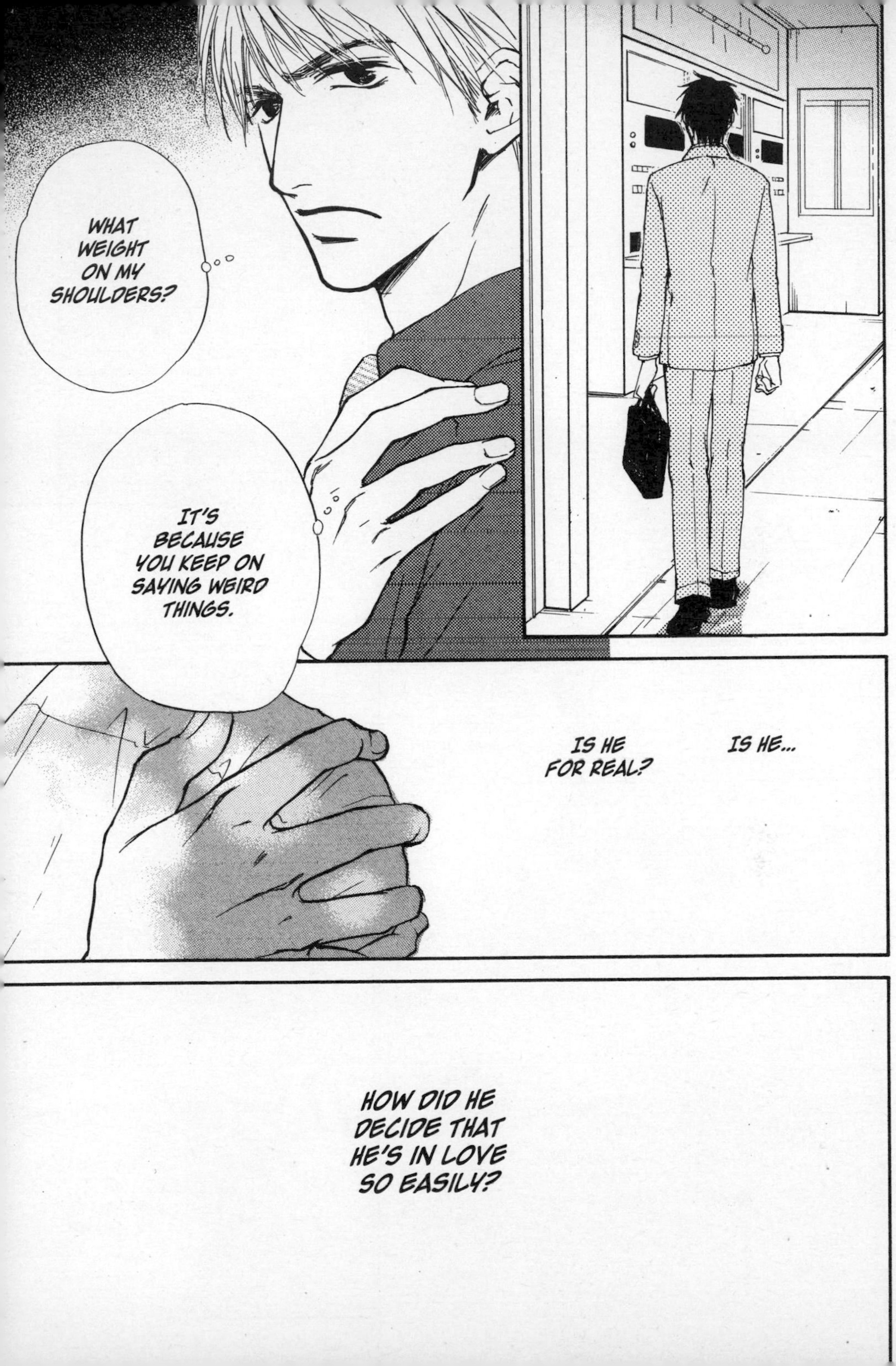
WHAT WEIGHT ON MY SHOULDERS?
IT'S BECAUSE YOU KEEP ON SAYING WEIRD THINGS.
IS HE...
IS HE FOR REAL?
HOW DID HE DECIDE THAT HE'S IN LOVE SO EASILY?

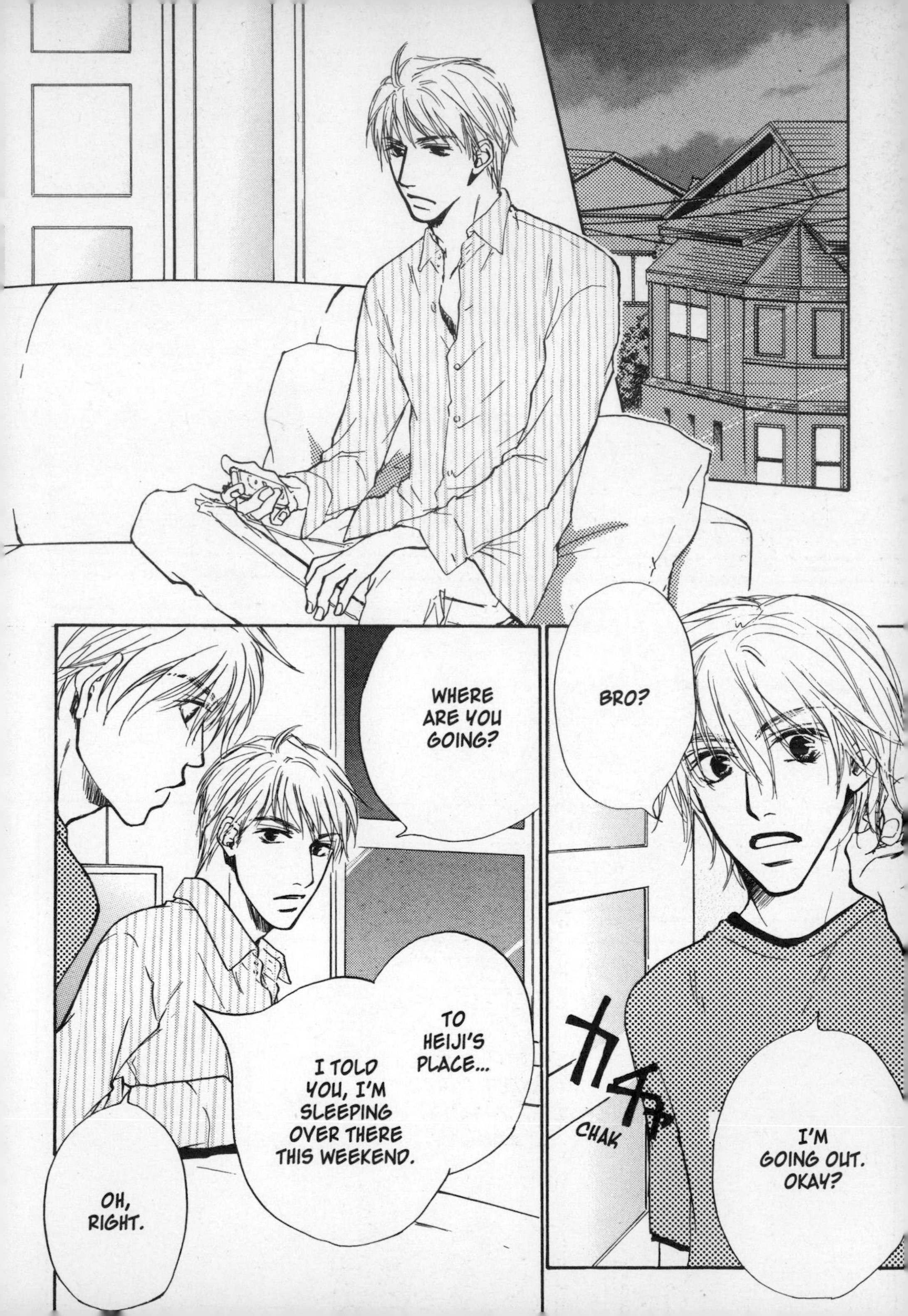
BRO?
CHAK
I'M GOING OUT. OKAY?
WHERE ARE YOU GOING?
TO HEIJI'S PLACE...
I TOLD YOU, I'M SLEEPING OVER THERE THIS WEEKEND.
OH, RIGHT.

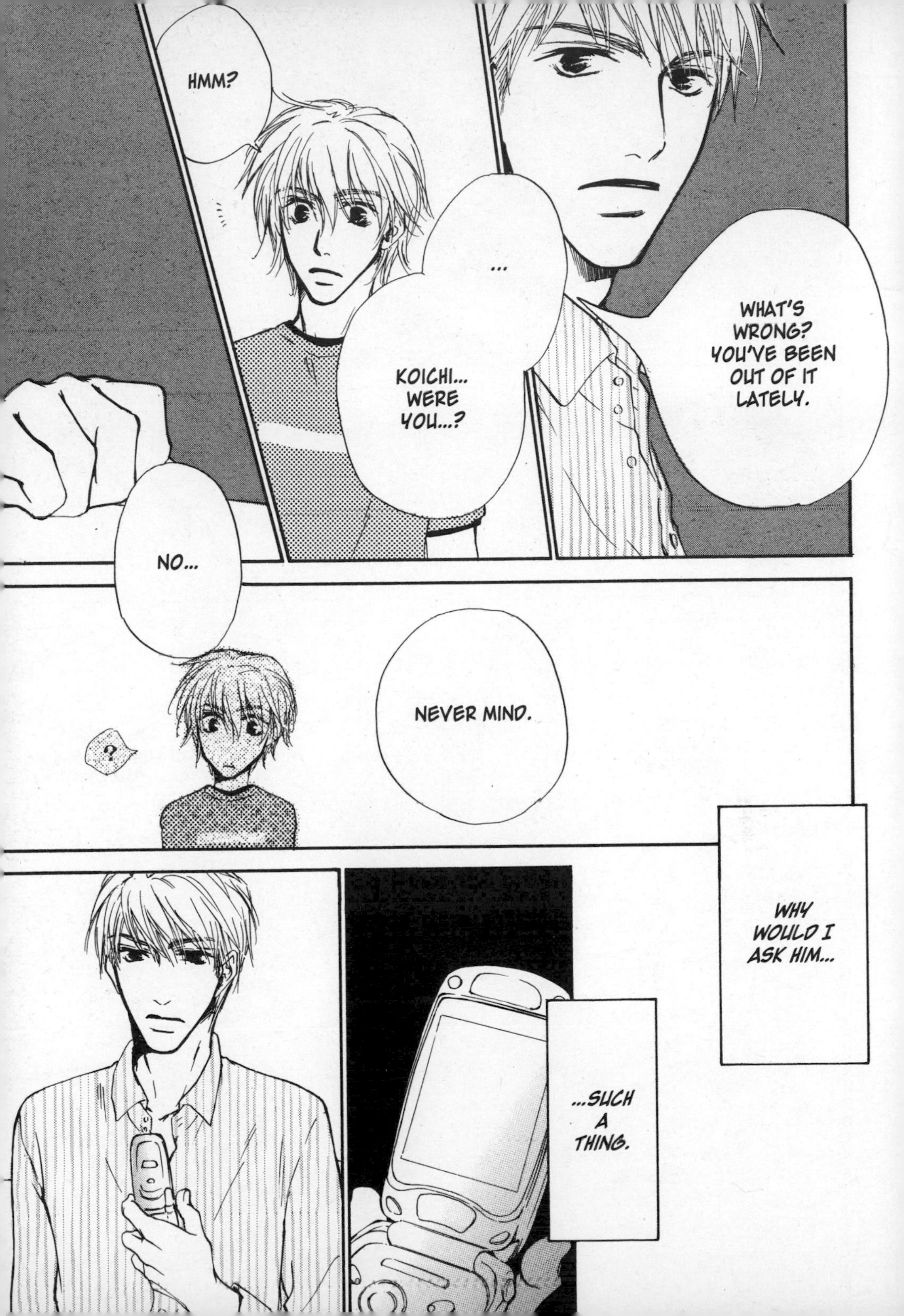
WHAT'S WRONG? YOU'VE BEEN OUT OF IT LATELY.
...
KOICHI... WERE YOU...?
HMM?
NO...
NEVER MIND.
?
WHY WOULD I ASK HIM...
...SUCH A THING.

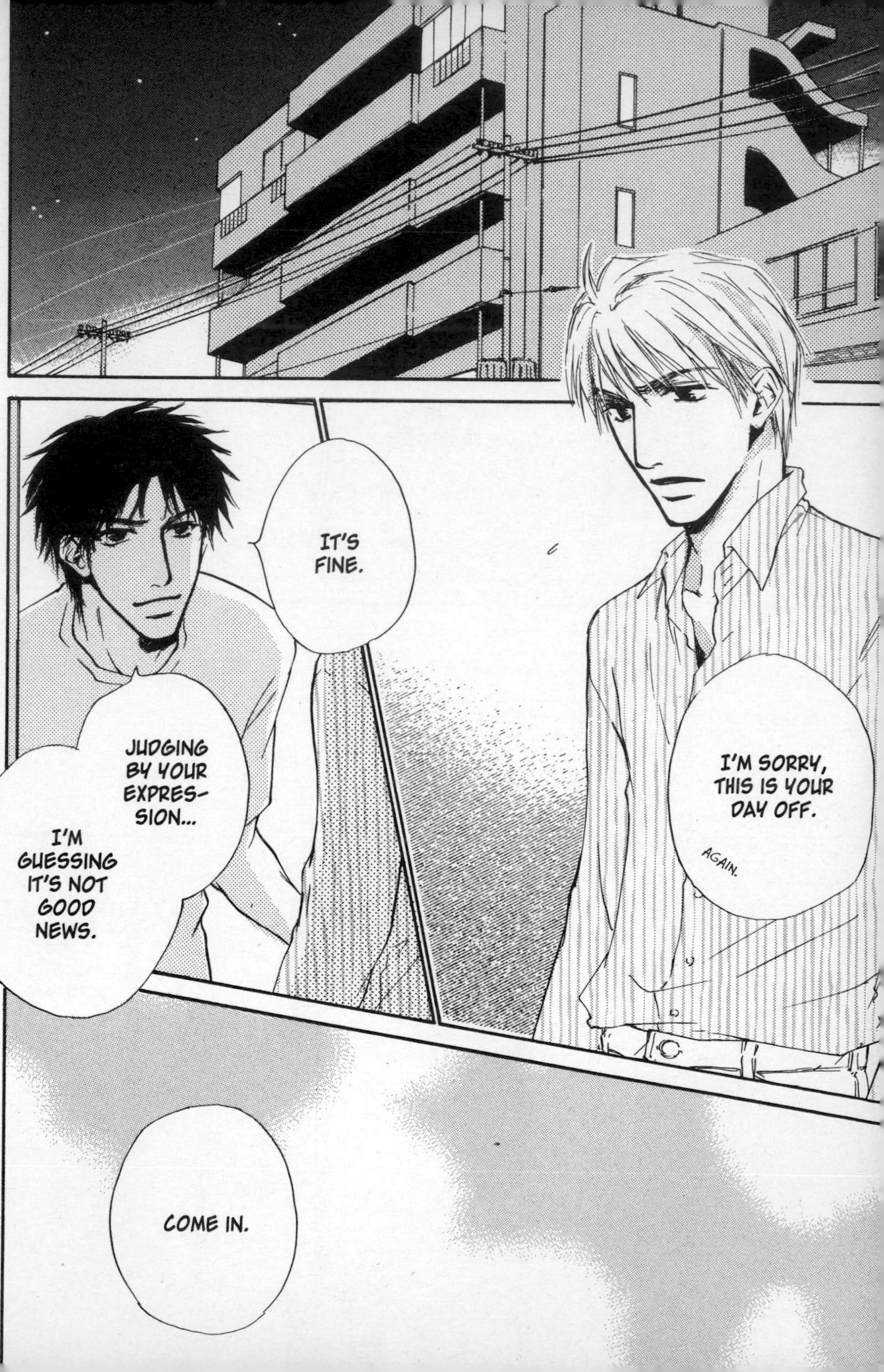
I'M SORRY, THIS IS YOUR DAY OFF.
AGAIN.
IT'S FINE.
JUDGING BY YOUR EXPRES-SION...
I'M GUESSING IT'S NOT GOOD NEWS.
COME IN.

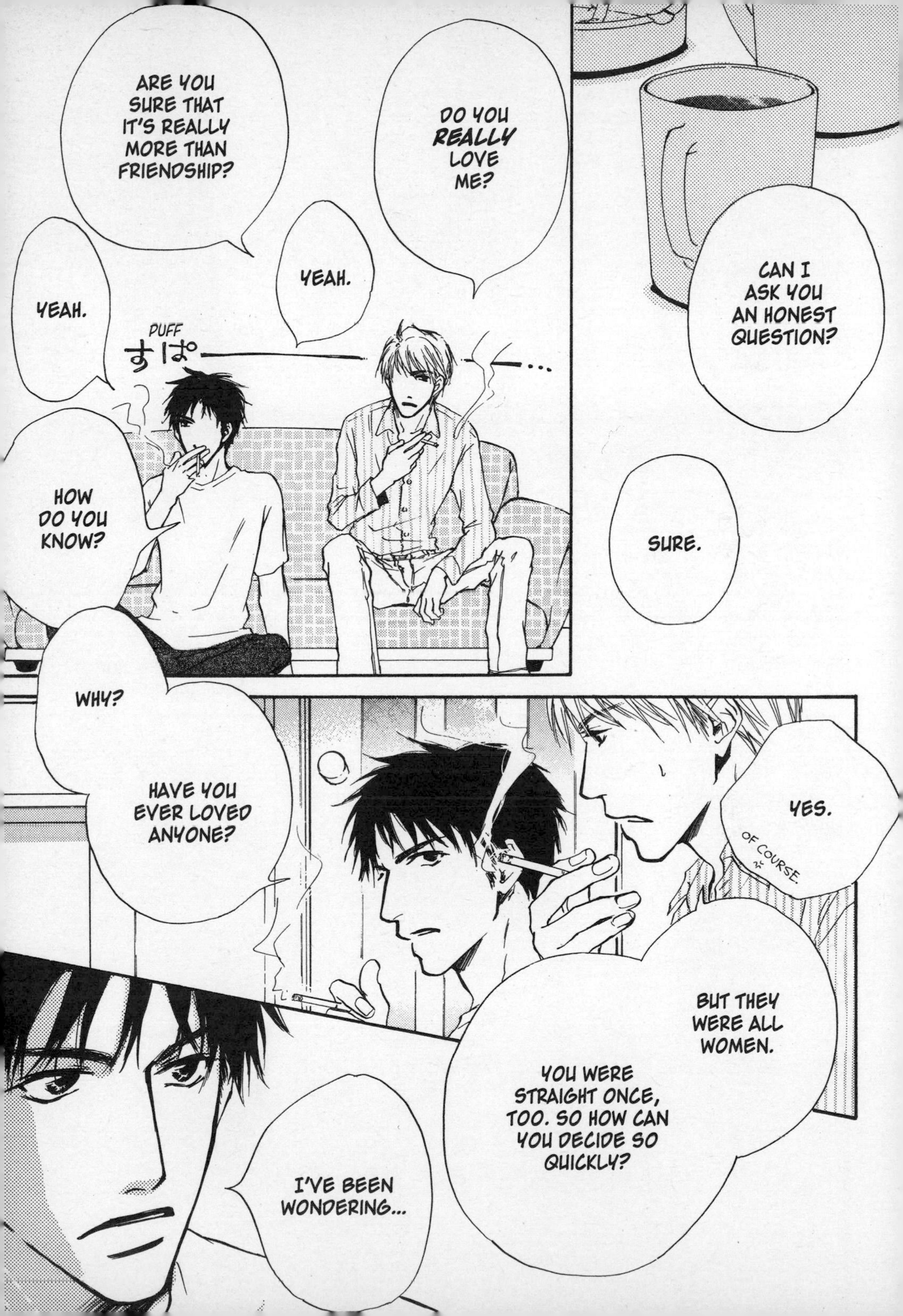

CAN I ASK YOU AN HONEST QUESTION?
SURE.
DO YOU REALLY LOVE ME?
YEAH.
ARE YOU SURE THAT IT'S REALLY MORE THAN FRIENDSHIP?
YEAH.
PUFF
すぱー…
HOW DO YOU KNOW?
WHY?
HAVE YOU EVER LOVED ANYONE?
YES.
OF COURSE.
BUT THEY WERE ALL WOMEN.
YOU WERE STRAIGHT ONCE, TOO. SO HOW CAN YOU DECIDE SO QUICKLY?
I'VE BEEN WONDERING...

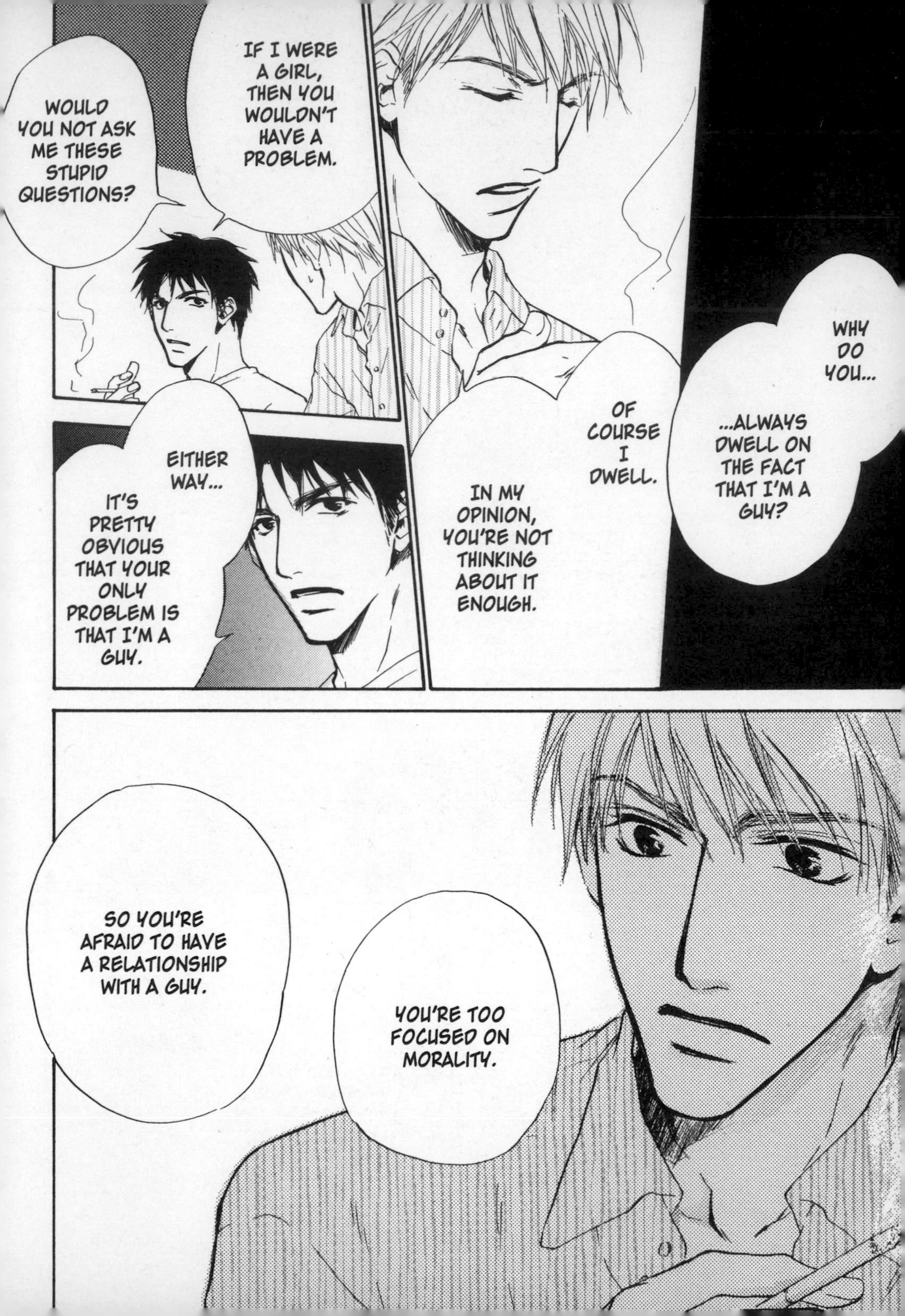
WHY DO YOU...
...ALWAYS DWELL ON THE FACT THAT I'M A GUY?
OF COURSE I DWELL.
IN MY OPINION, YOU'RE NOT THINKING ABOUT IT ENOUGH.
IF I WERE A GIRL, THEN YOU WOULDN'T HAVE A PROBLEM.
WOULD YOU NOT ASK ME THESE STUPID QUESTIONS?
EITHER WAY...
IT'S PRETTY OBVIOUS THAT YOUR ONLY PROBLEM IS THAT I'M A GUY.
YOU'RE TOO FOCUSED ON MORALITY.
SO YOU'RE AFRAID TO HAVE A RELATIONSHIP WITH A GUY.

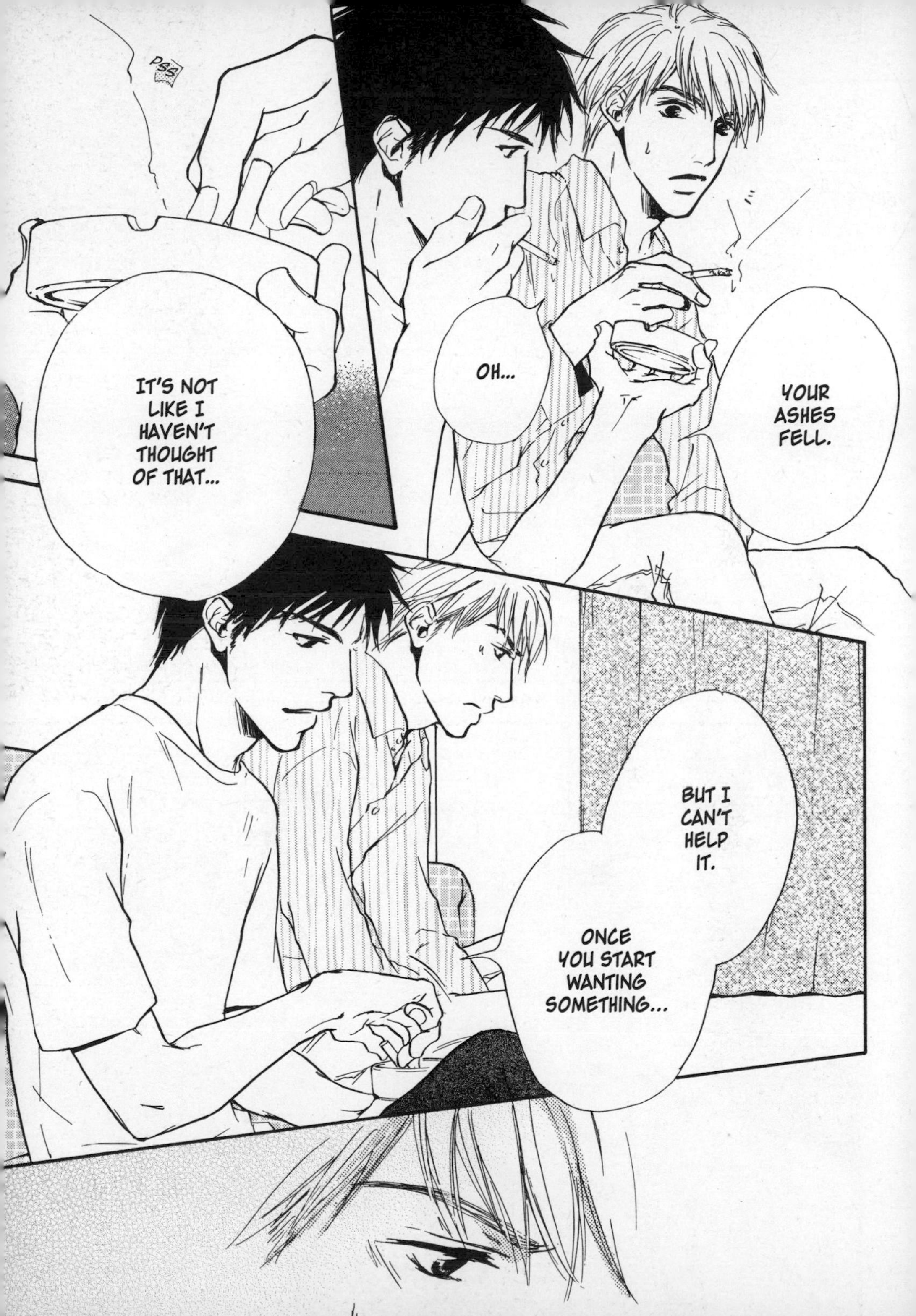
YOUR ASHES FELL.
OH...
PSS
IT'S NOT LIKE I HAVEN'T THOUGHT OF THAT...
BUT I CAN'T HELP IT.
ONCE YOU START WANTING SOMETHING...

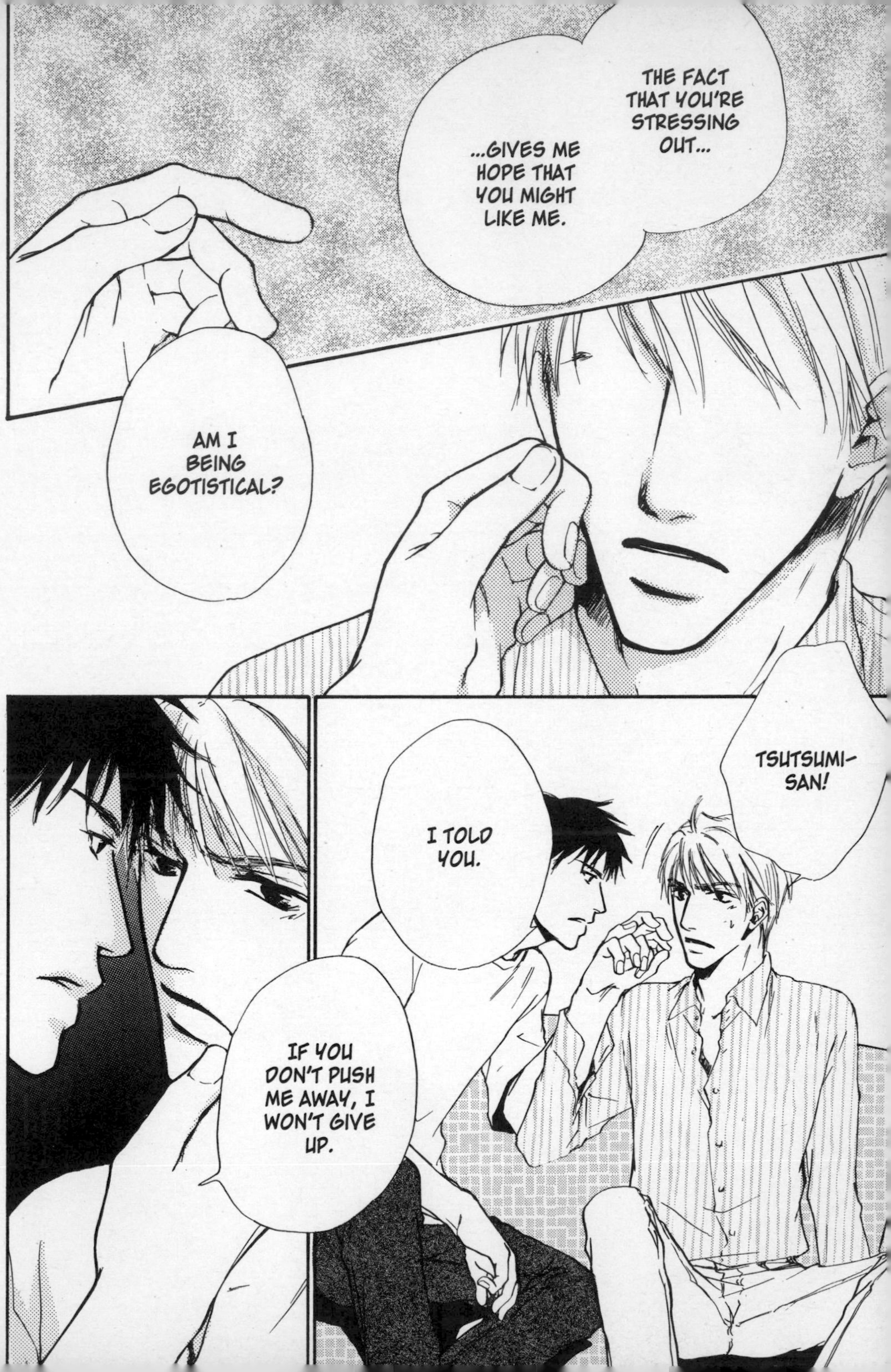
THE FACT THAT YOU'RE STRESSING OUT...
...GIVES ME HOPE THAT YOU MIGHT LIKE ME.
AM I BEING EGOTISTICAL?
TSUTSUMI-SAN!
I TOLD YOU.
IF YOU DON'T PUSH ME AWAY, I WON'T GIVE UP.

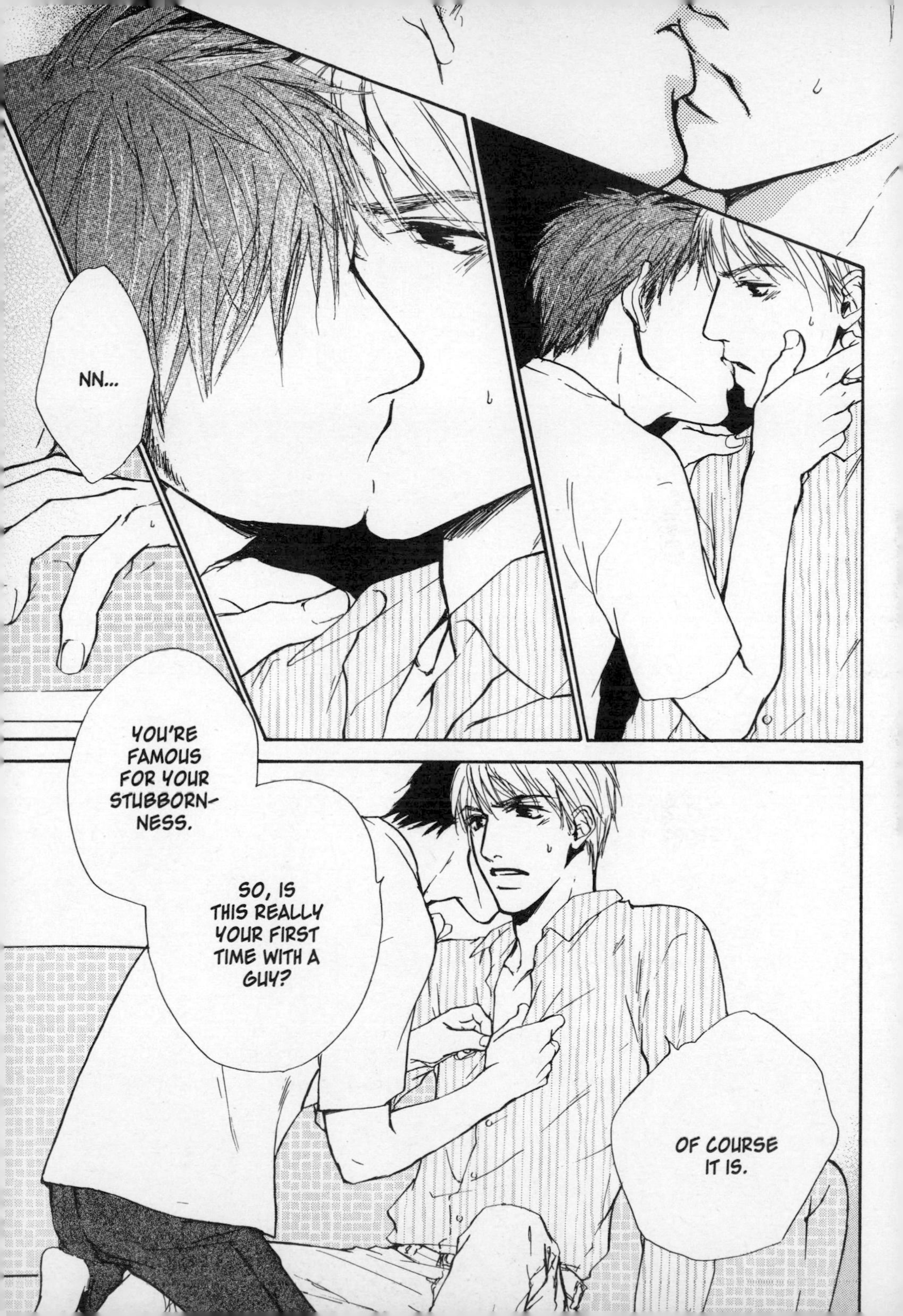
NN...
YOU'RE FAMOUS FOR YOUR STUBBORN-NESS.
SO, IS THIS REALLY YOUR FIRST TIME WITH A GUY?
OF COURSE IT IS.

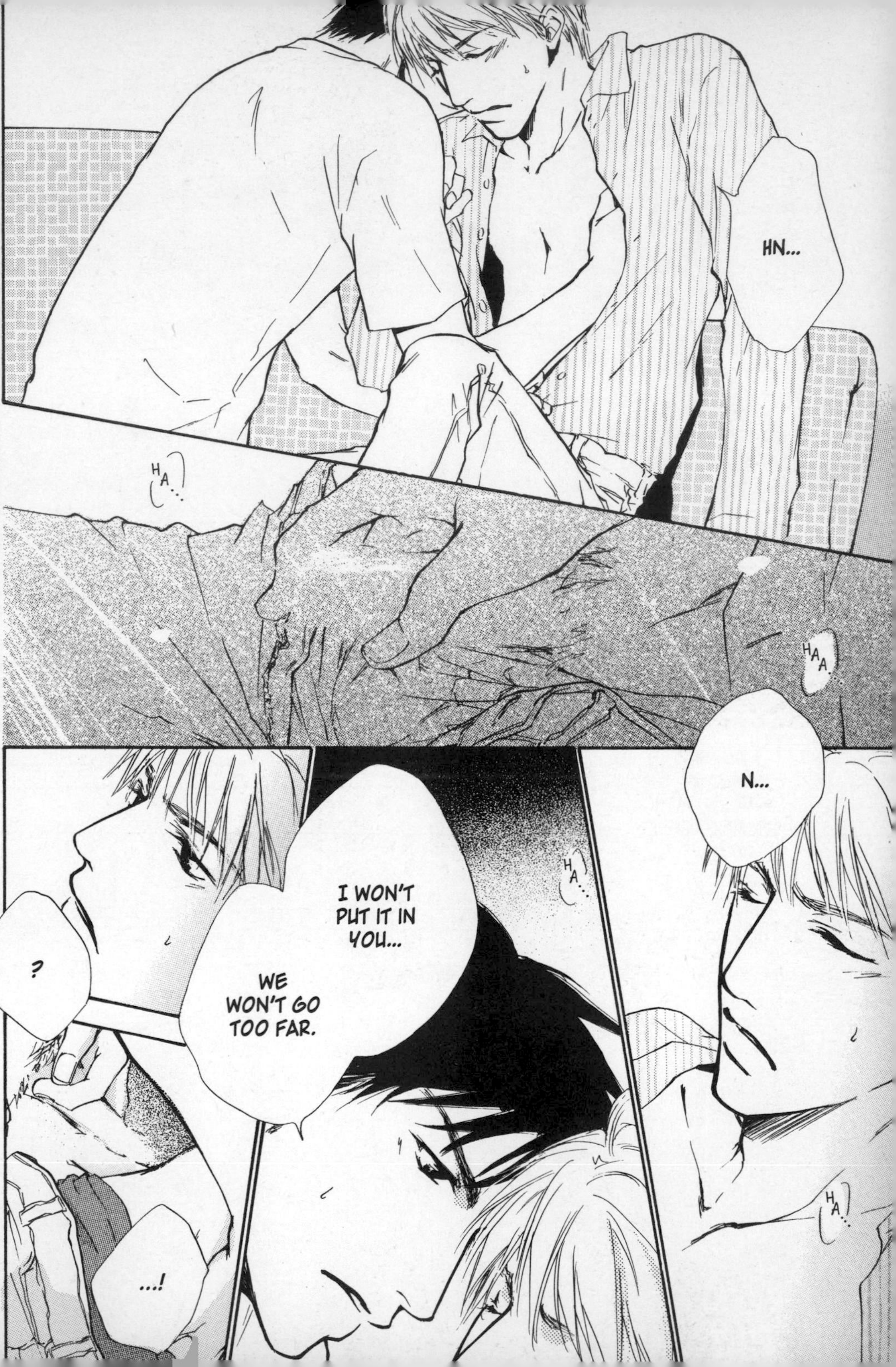
HN...
HAA...
HA...
N...
HA...
HA...
I WON'T PUT IT IN YOU...
WE WON'T GO TOO FAR.
?
...!

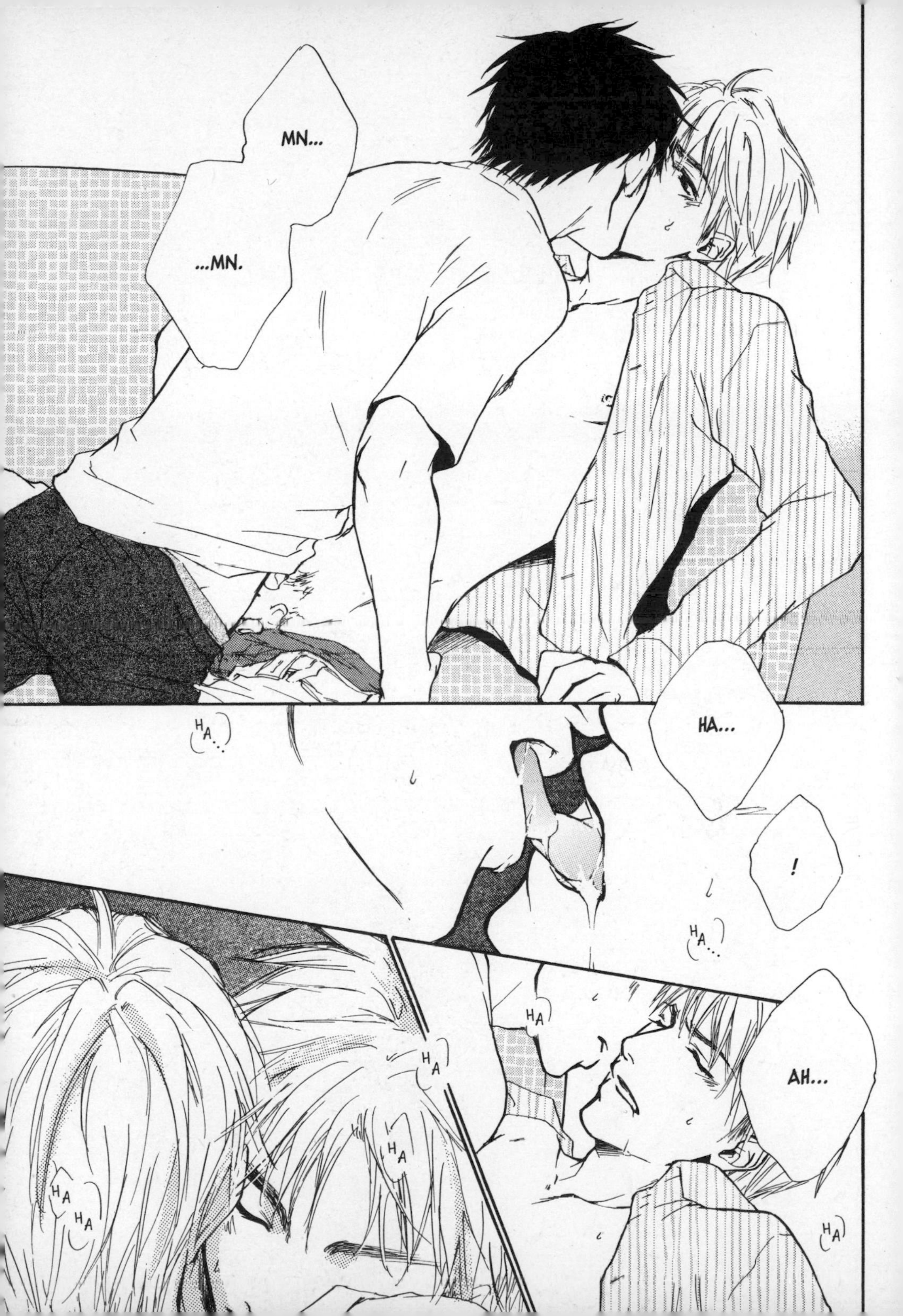
MN...
...MN.
HA...
!
HA...
HA...
HA...
AH...
HA
HA
HA
HA
HA HA

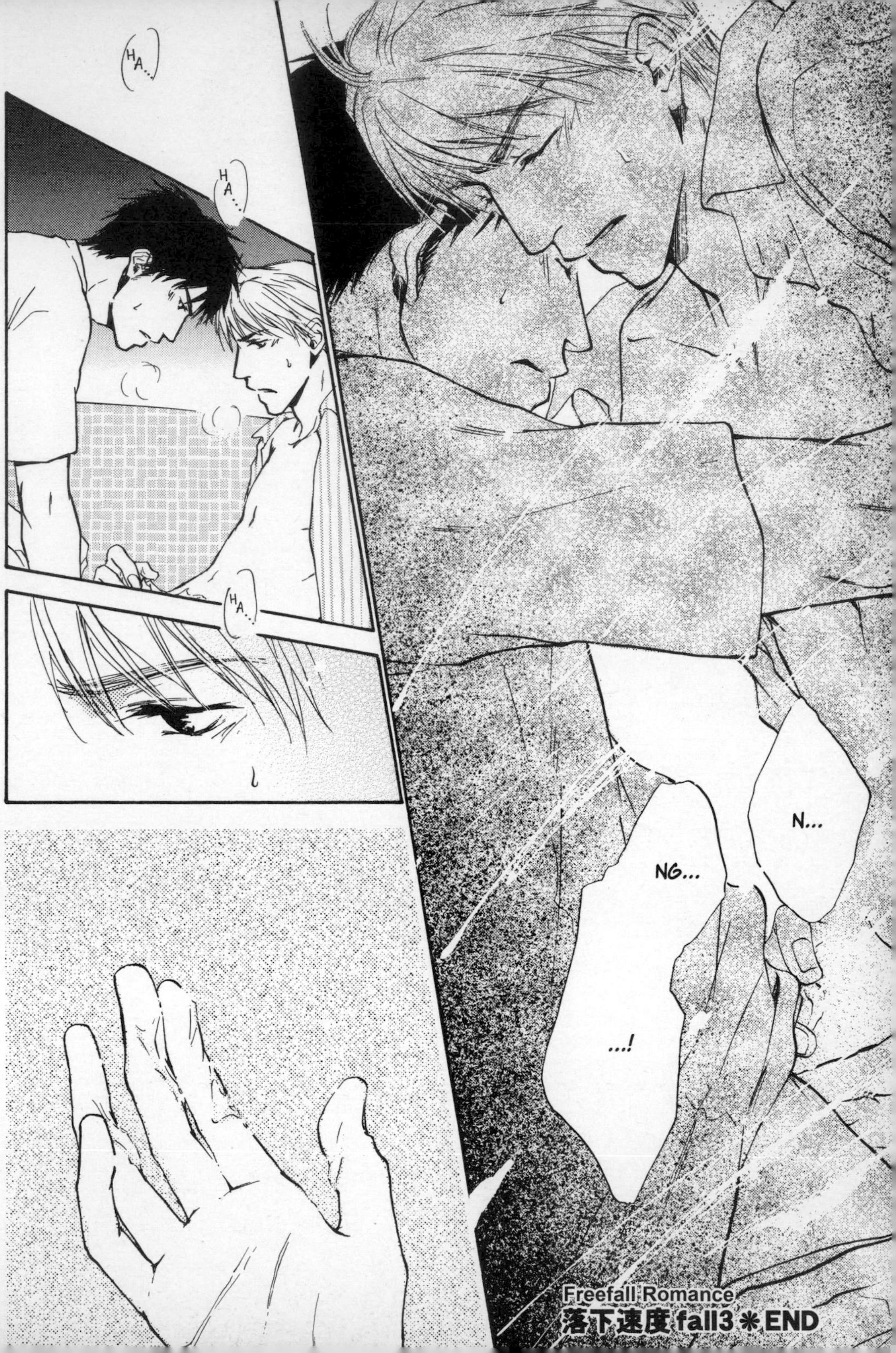

N...
NG...
...!
HA...
HA...
HA...
Freefall Romance
落下速度 fall3 * END

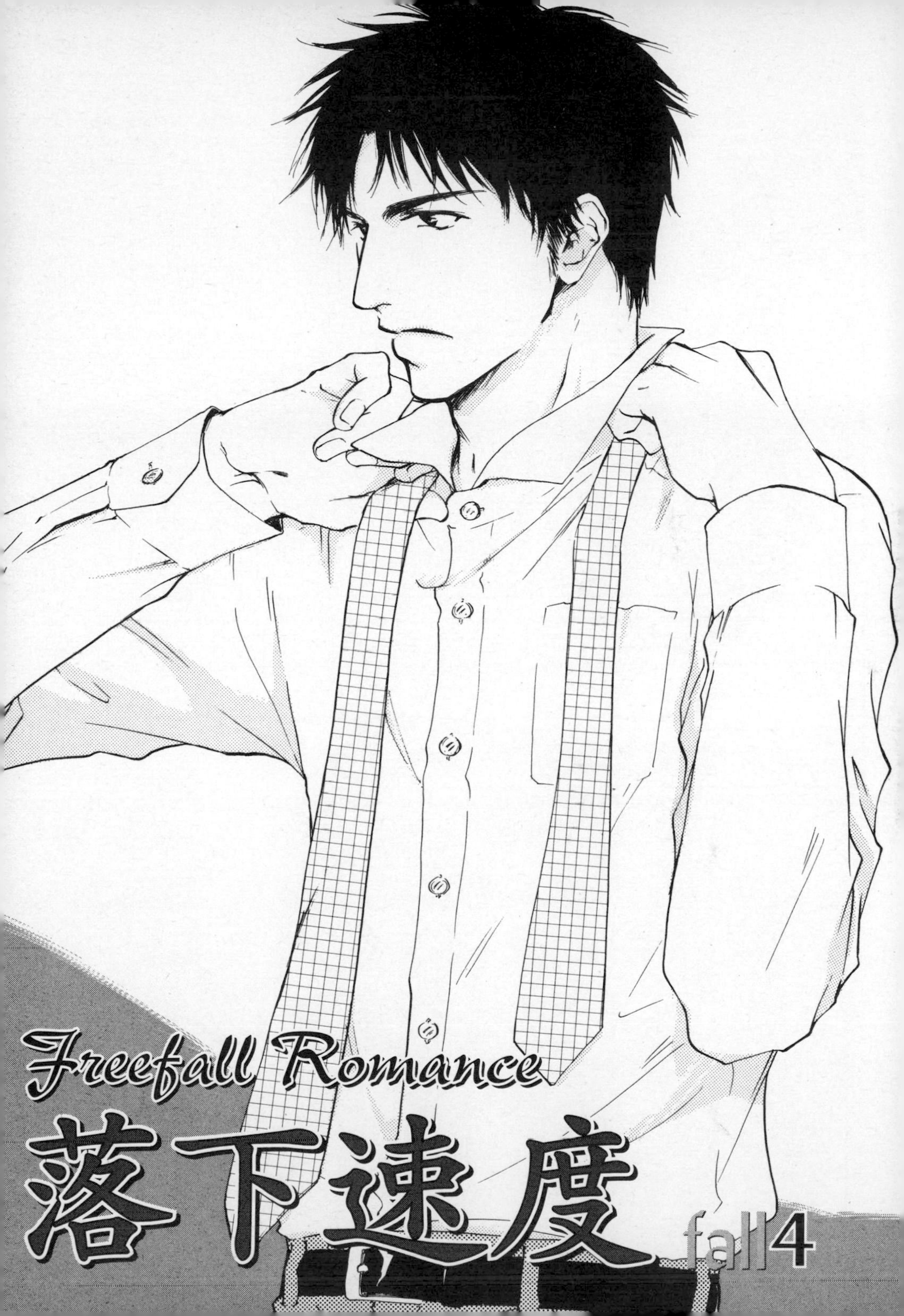
Freefall Romance
落下速度
fall4

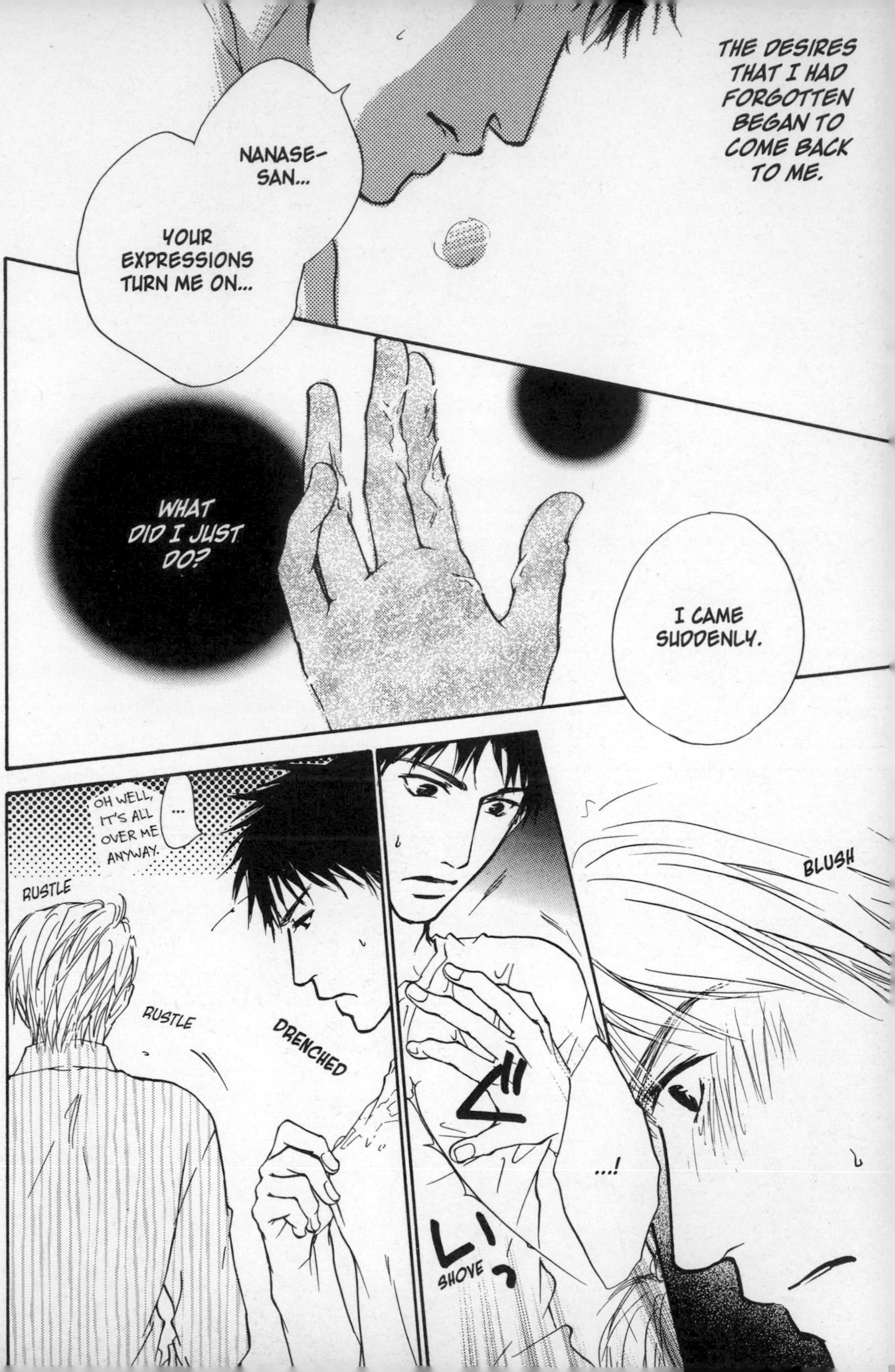
THE DESIRES THAT I HAD FORGOTTEN BEGAN TO COME BACK TO ME.
NANASE-SAN...
YOUR EXPRESSIONS TURN ME ON...
I CAME SUDDENLY.
WHAT DID I JUST DO?
BLUSH
...!
SHOVE
...
OH WELL, IT'S ALL OVER ME ANYWAY.
RUSTLE
RUSTLE
DRENCHED

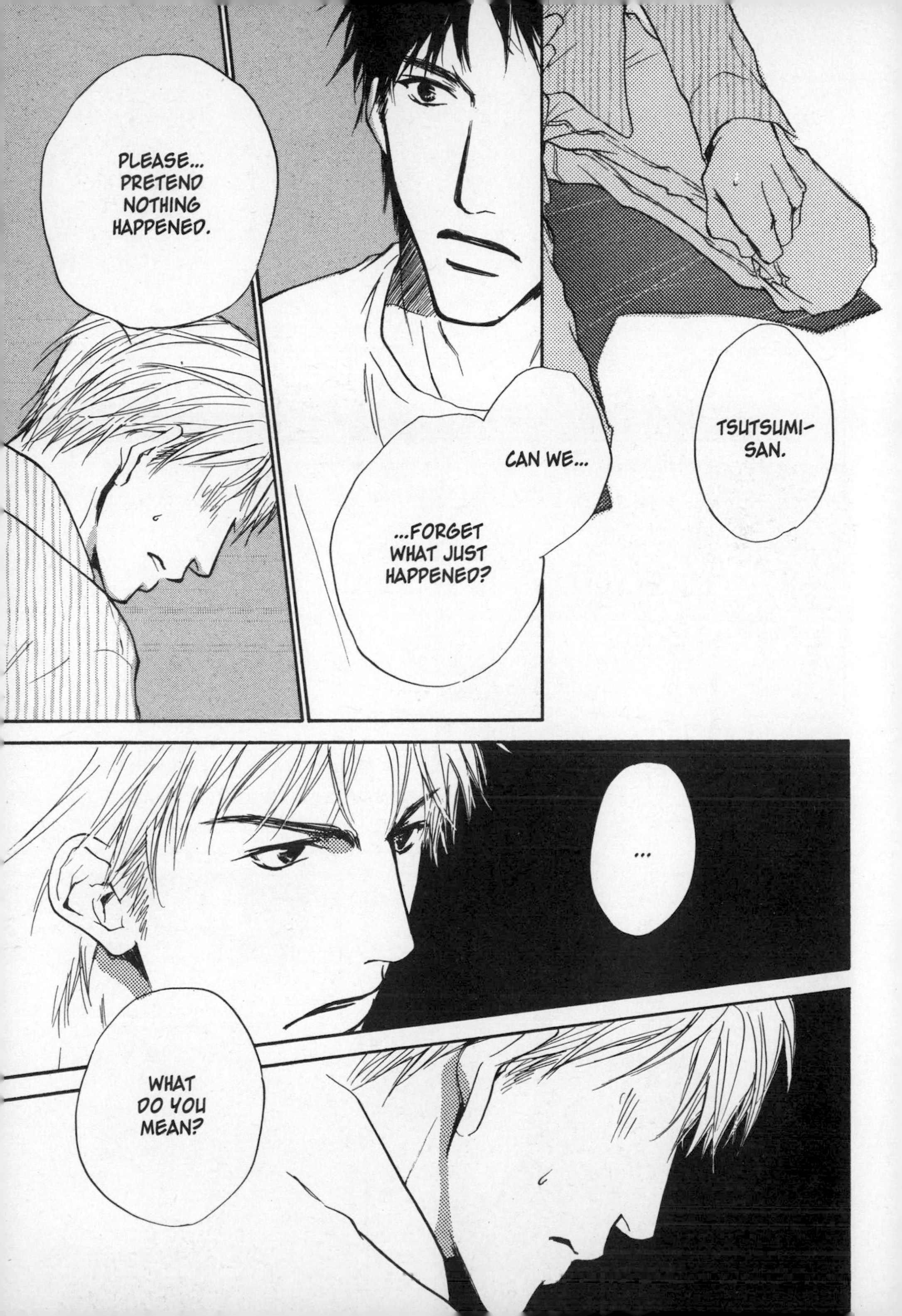
TSUTSUMI-SAN.
CAN WE...
...FORGET WHAT JUST HAPPENED?
PLEASE... PRETEND NOTHING HAPPENED.
...
WHAT DO YOU MEAN?

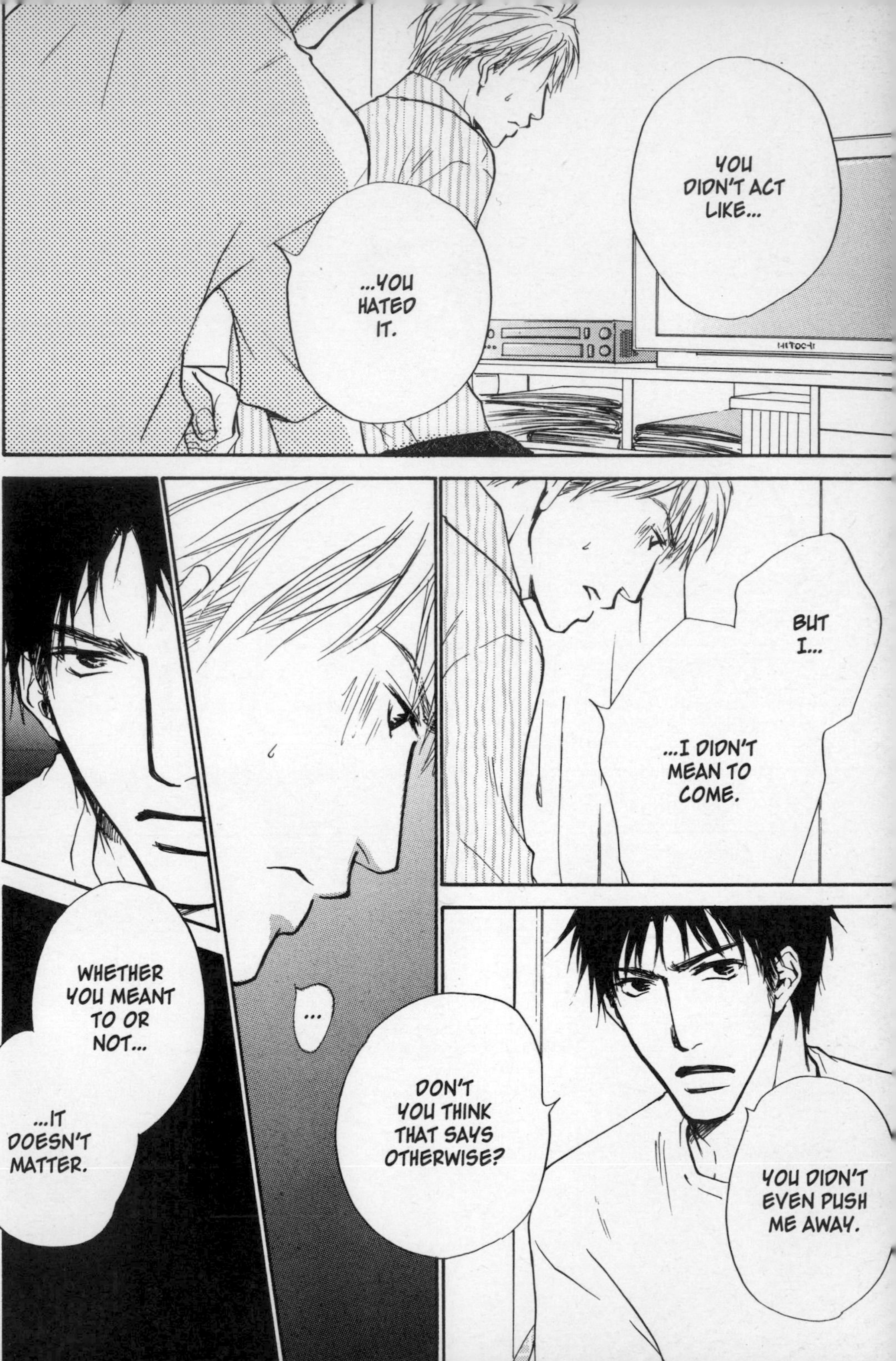
YOU DIDN'T ACT LIKE...
...YOU HATED IT.
BUT I...
...I DIDN'T MEAN TO COME.
YOU DIDN'T EVEN PUSH ME AWAY.
DON'T YOU THINK THAT SAYS OTHERWISE?
...
WHETHER YOU MEANT TO OR NOT...
...IT DOESN'T MATTER.

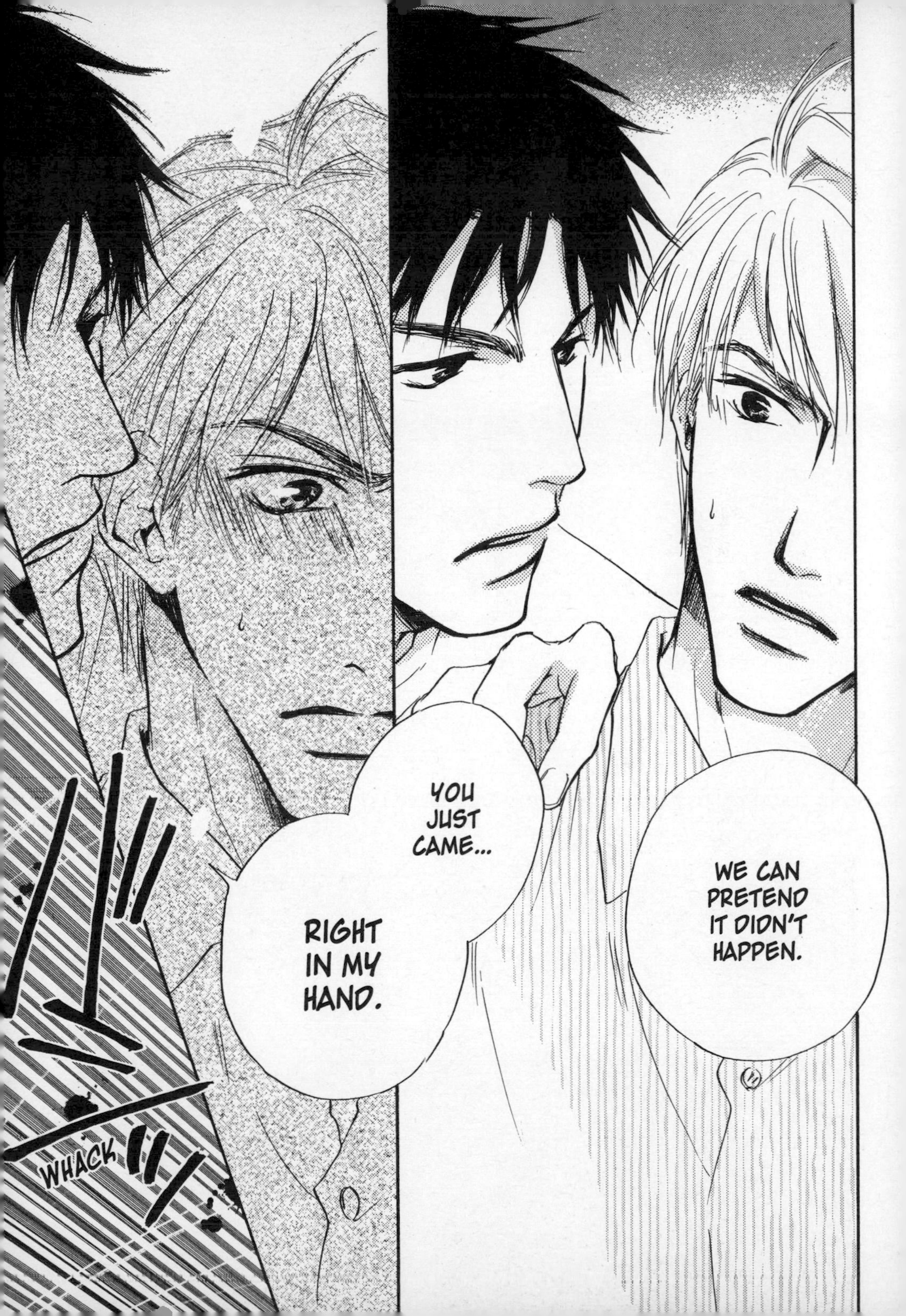
WE CAN PRETEND IT DIDN'T HAPPEN.
YOU JUST CAME...
RIGHT IN MY HAND.
WHACK

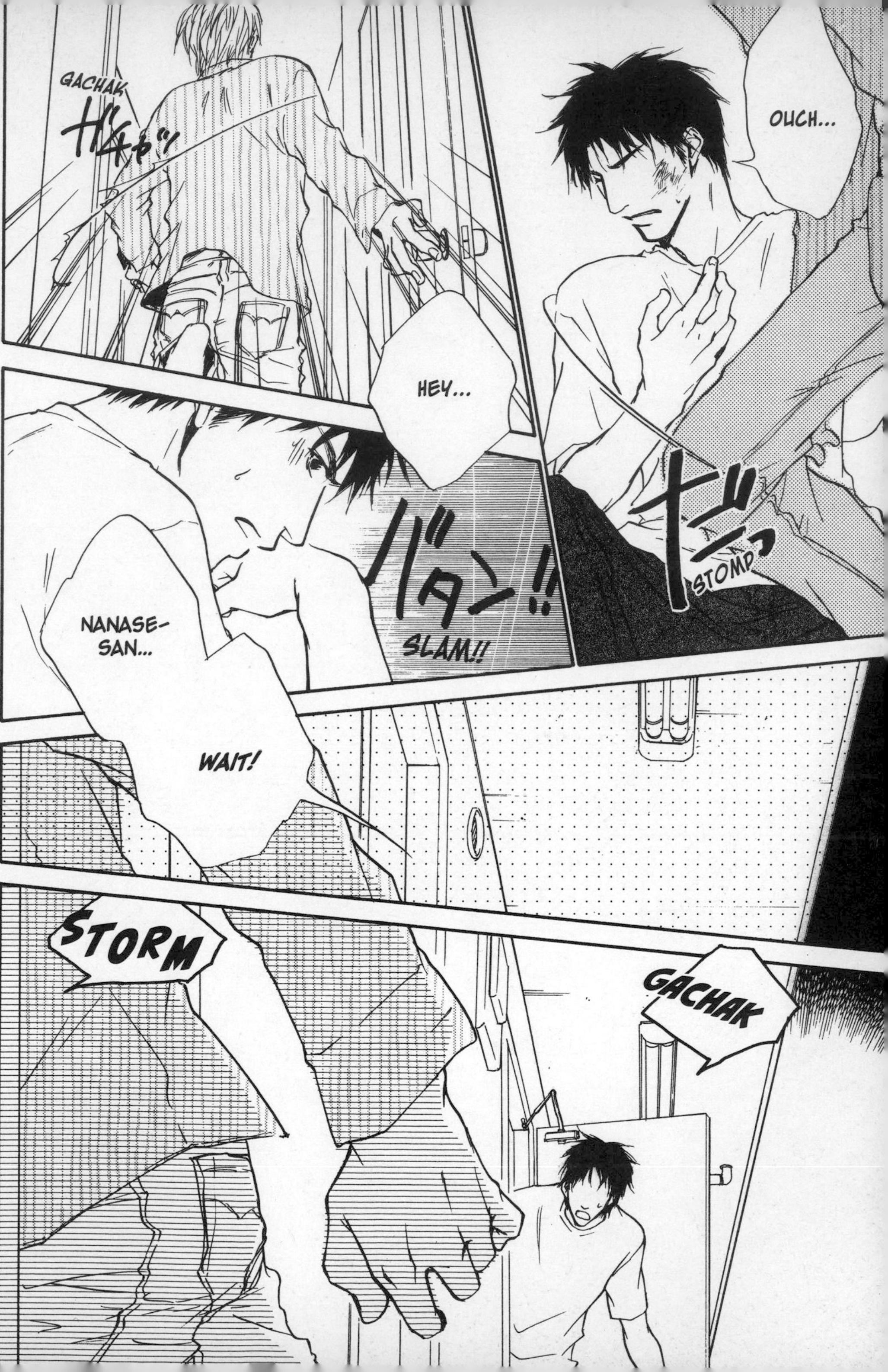
OUCH...
ズッ
STOMP
GACHAK
ガチャッ
HEY...
バタン!!
SLAM!!
NANASE-SAN...
WAIT!
GACHAK
STORM

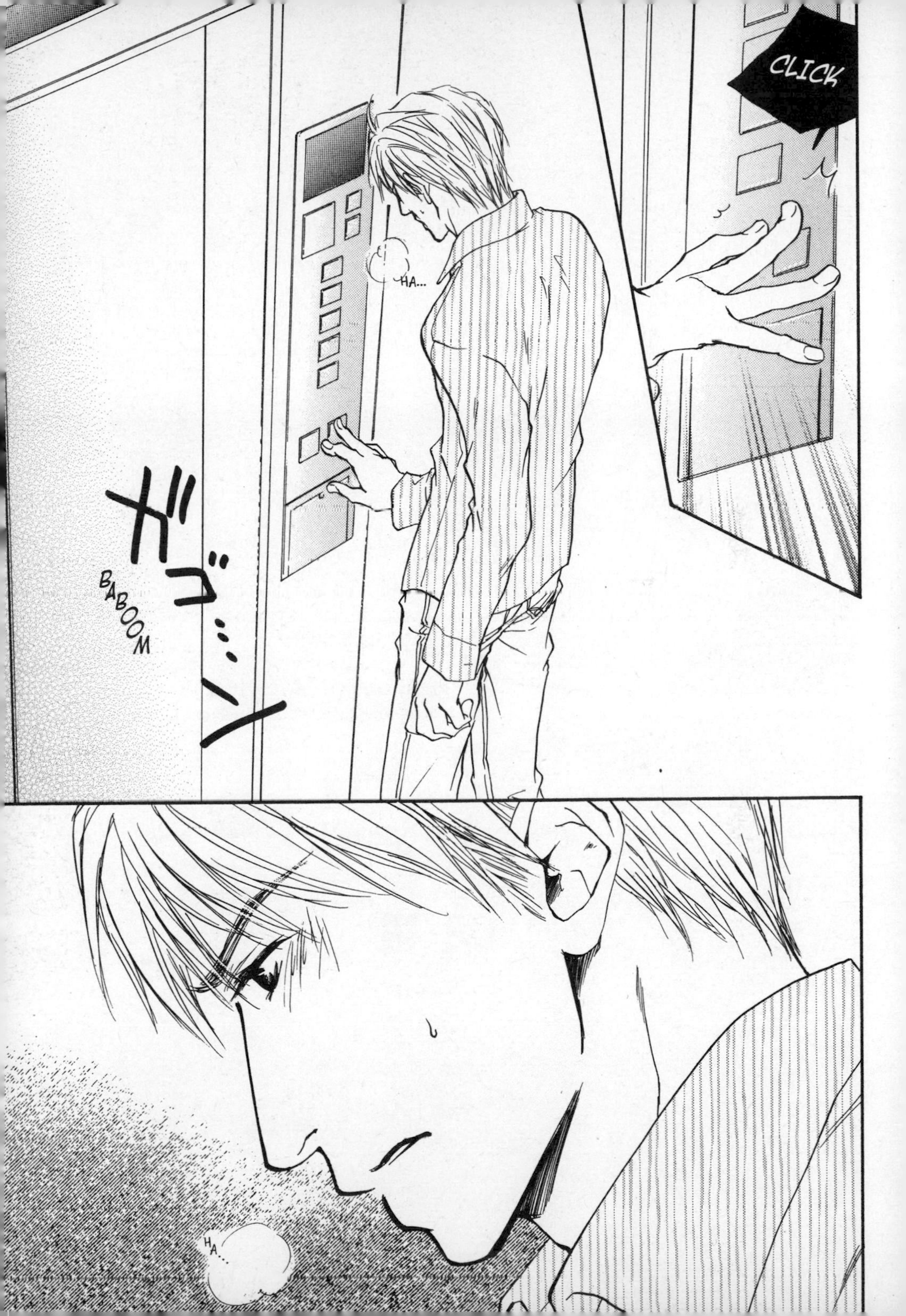
CLICK
HA...
ガゴン
BABOOM
HA...

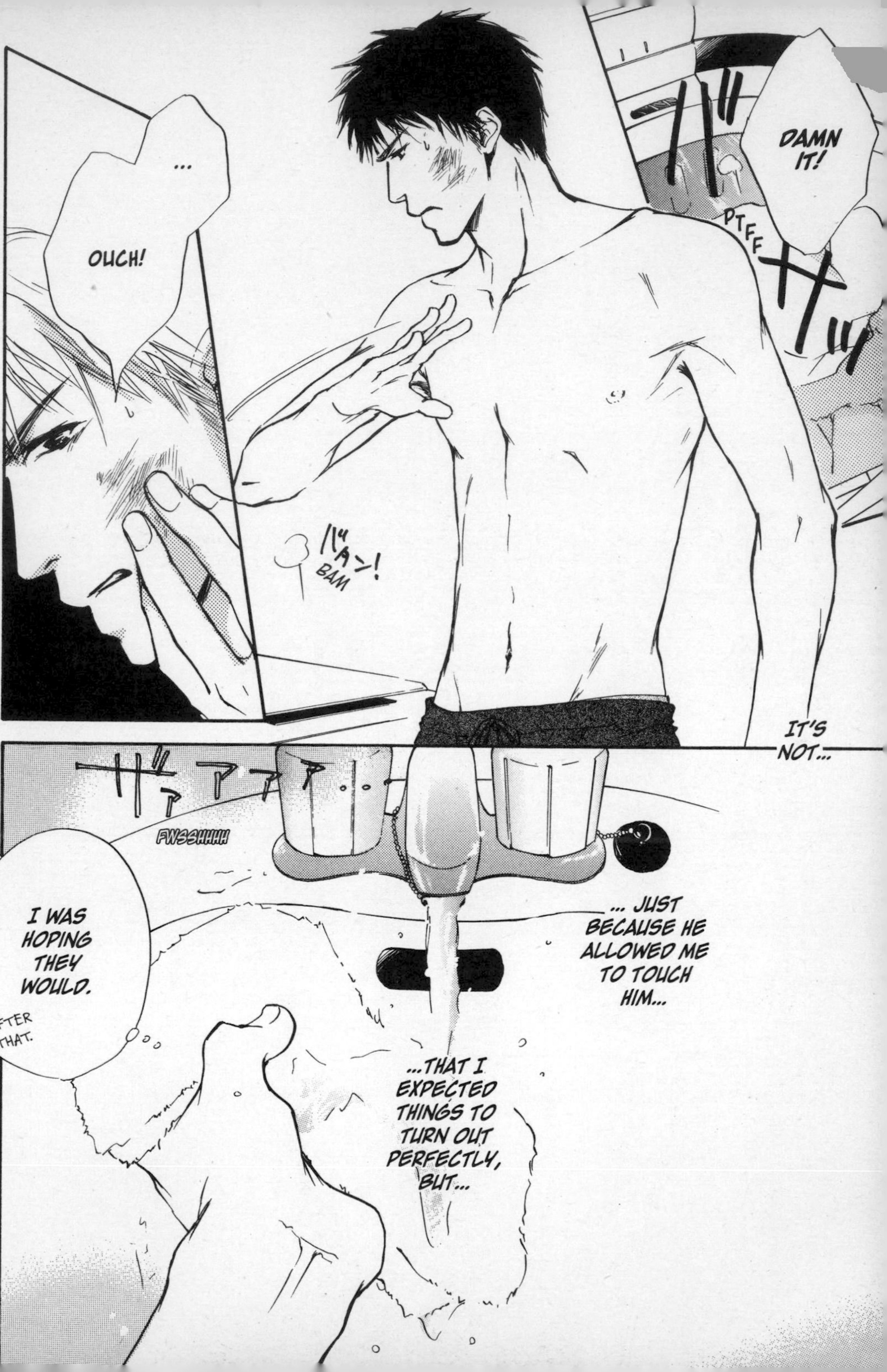
DAMN IT!
PTFF
BAM
...
OUCH!
IT'S NOT...
FWSSHHHH
... JUST BECAUSE HE ALLOWED ME TO TOUCH HIM...
...THAT I EXPECTED THINGS TO TURN OUT PERFECTLY, BUT...
I WAS HOPING THEY WOULD.
AFTER THAT.

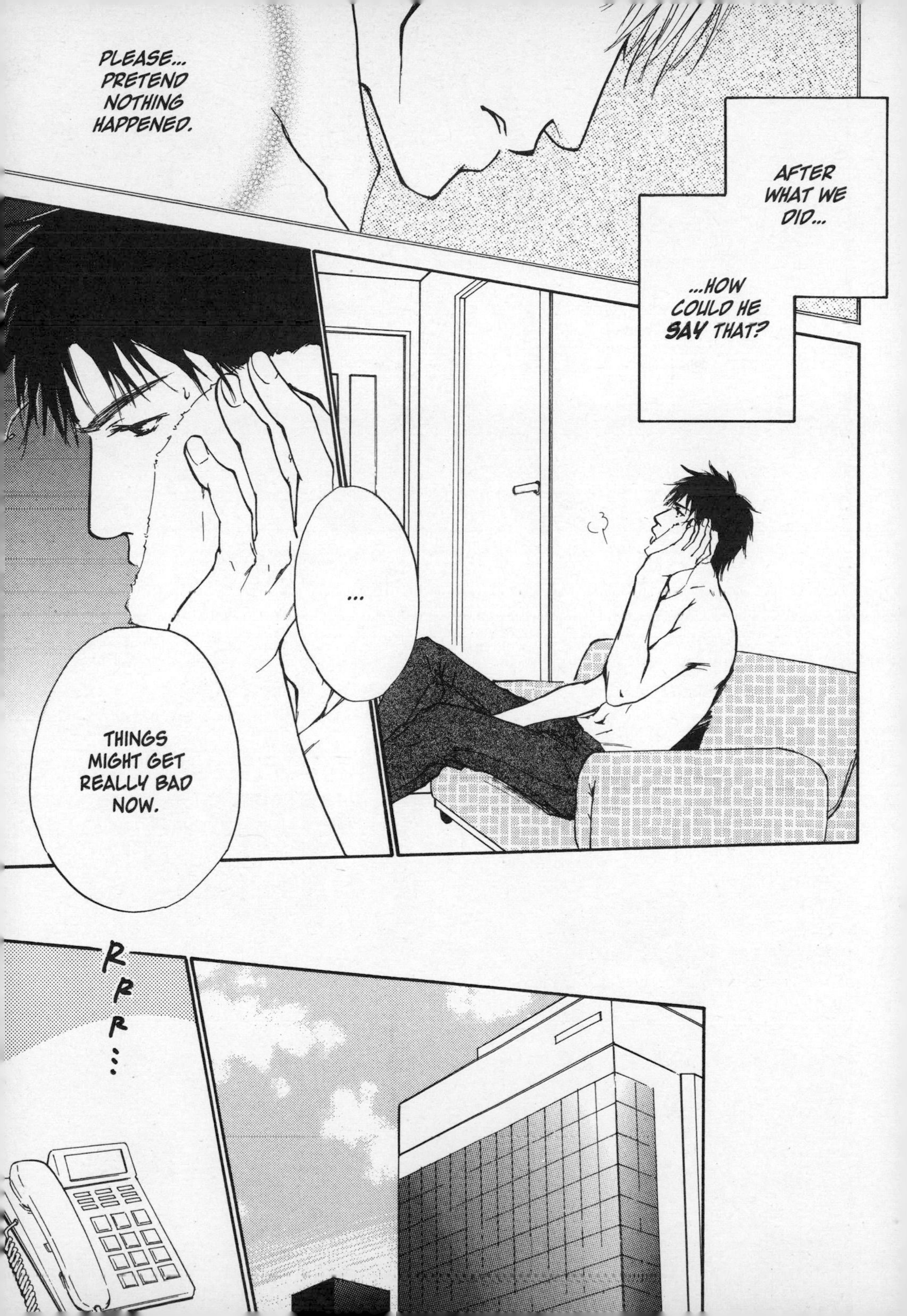

PLEASE... PRETEND NOTHING HAPPENED.
AFTER WHAT WE DID...
...HOW COULD HE SAY THAT?
...
THINGS MIGHT GET REALLY BAD NOW.
RRR...

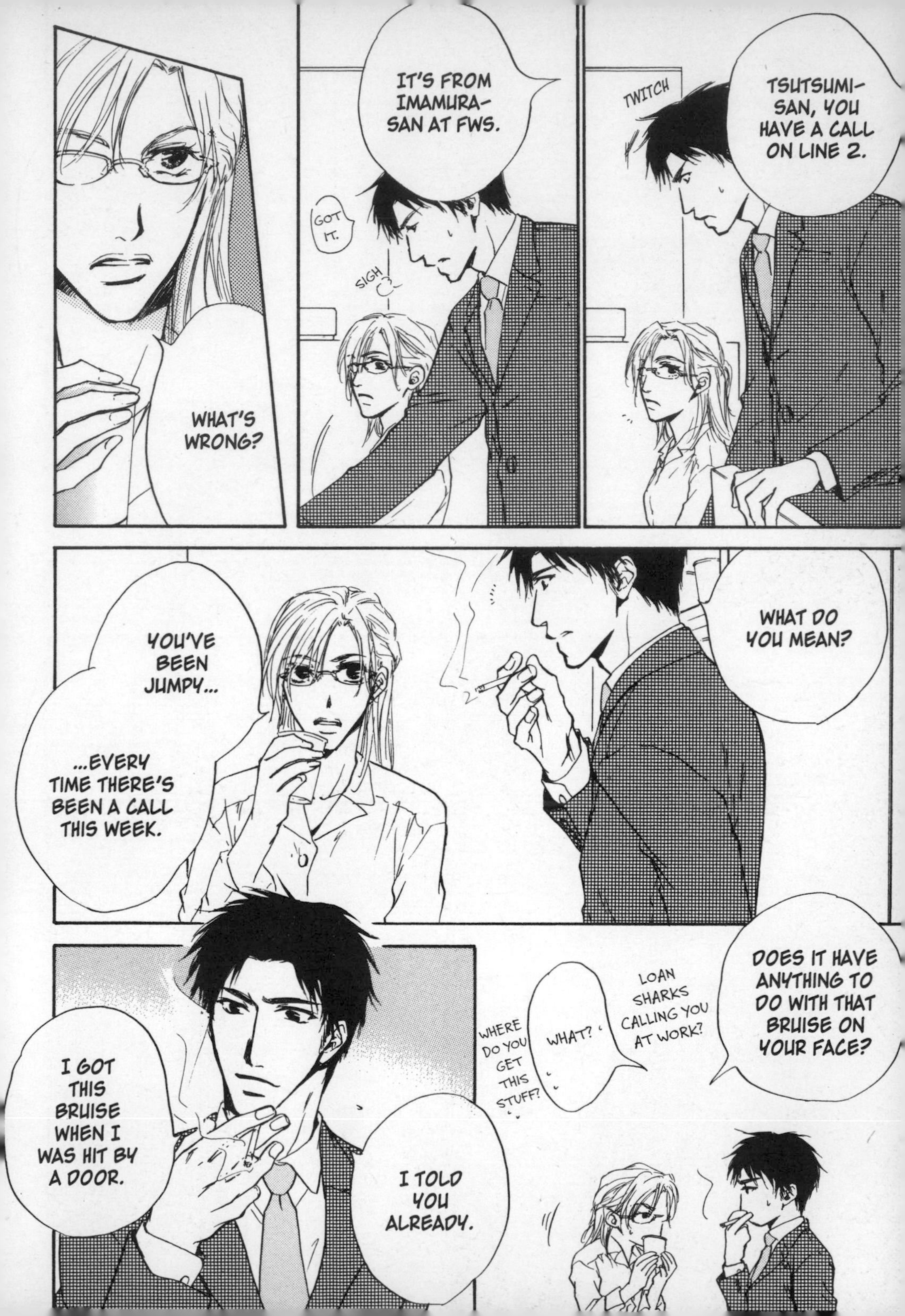
TWITCH
TSUTSUMI-SAN, YOU HAVE A CALL ON LINE 2.
IT'S FROM IMAMURA-SAN AT FWS.
GOT IT.
SIGH
WHAT'S WRONG?
WHAT DO YOU MEAN?
YOU'VE BEEN JUMPY...
...EVERY TIME THERE'S BEEN A CALL THIS WEEK.
DOES IT HAVE ANYTHING TO DO WITH THAT BRUISE ON YOUR FACE?
LOAN SHARKS CALLING YOU AT WORK?
WHAT?
WHERE DO YOU GET THIS STUFF?
I TOLD YOU ALREADY.
I GOT THIS BRUISE WHEN I WAS HIT BY A DOOR.

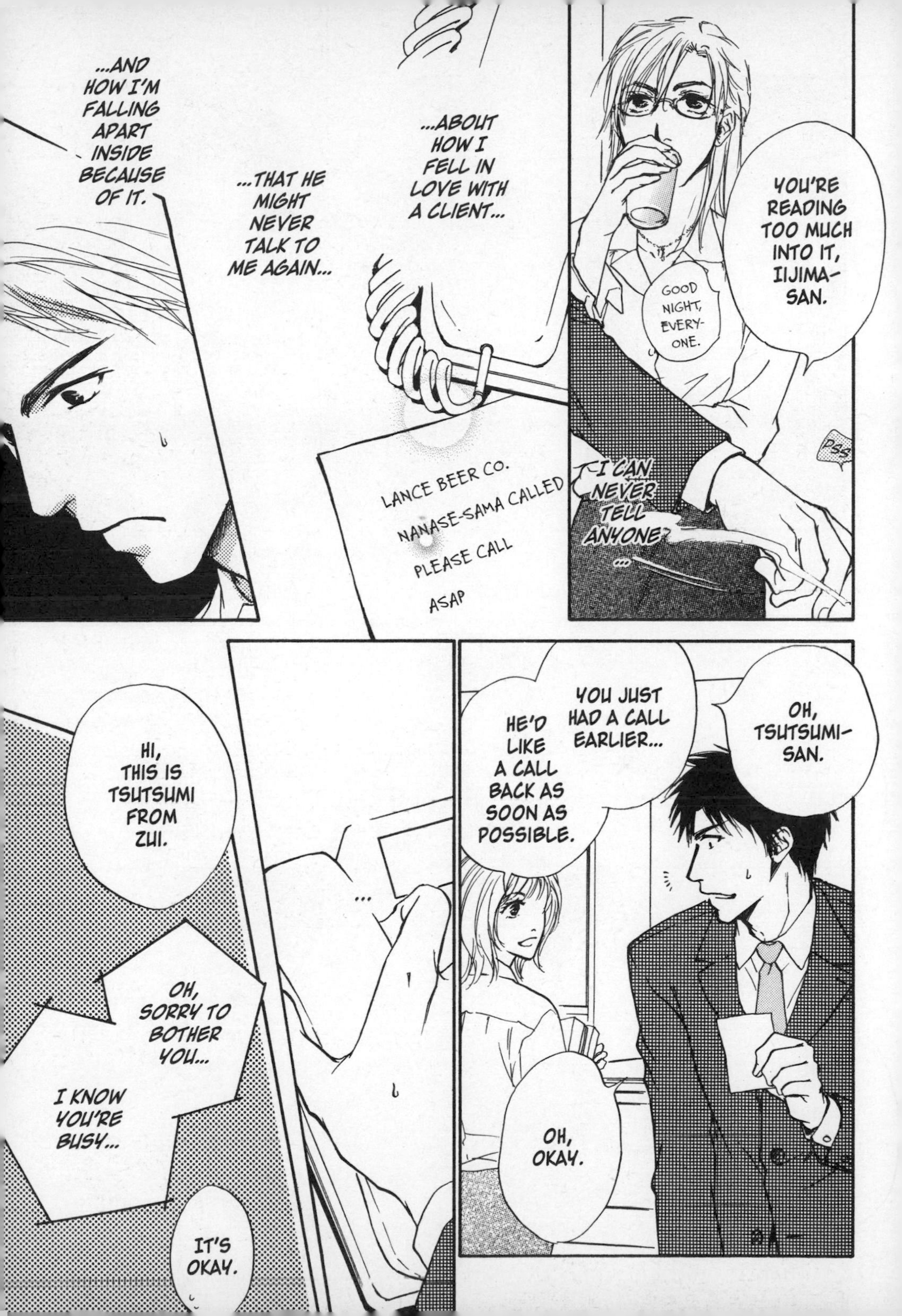
YOU'RE READING TOO MUCH INTO IT, IIJIMA-SAN.
GOOD NIGHT, EVERY-ONE.
PSS
I CAN NEVER TELL ANYONE...
...ABOUT HOW I FELL IN LOVE WITH A CLIENT...
...THAT HE MIGHT NEVER TALK TO ME AGAIN...
LANCE BEER CO.
NANASE-SAMA CALLED
PLEASE CALL
ASAP
...AND HOW I'M FALLING APART INSIDE BECAUSE OF IT.
OH, TSUTSUMI-SAN.
YOU JUST HAD A CALL EARLIER...
HE'D LIKE A CALL BACK AS SOON AS POSSIBLE.
OH, OKAY.
...
HI, THIS IS TSUTSUMI FROM ZUI.
OH, SORRY TO BOTHER YOU...
I KNOW YOU'RE BUSY...
IT'S OKAY.

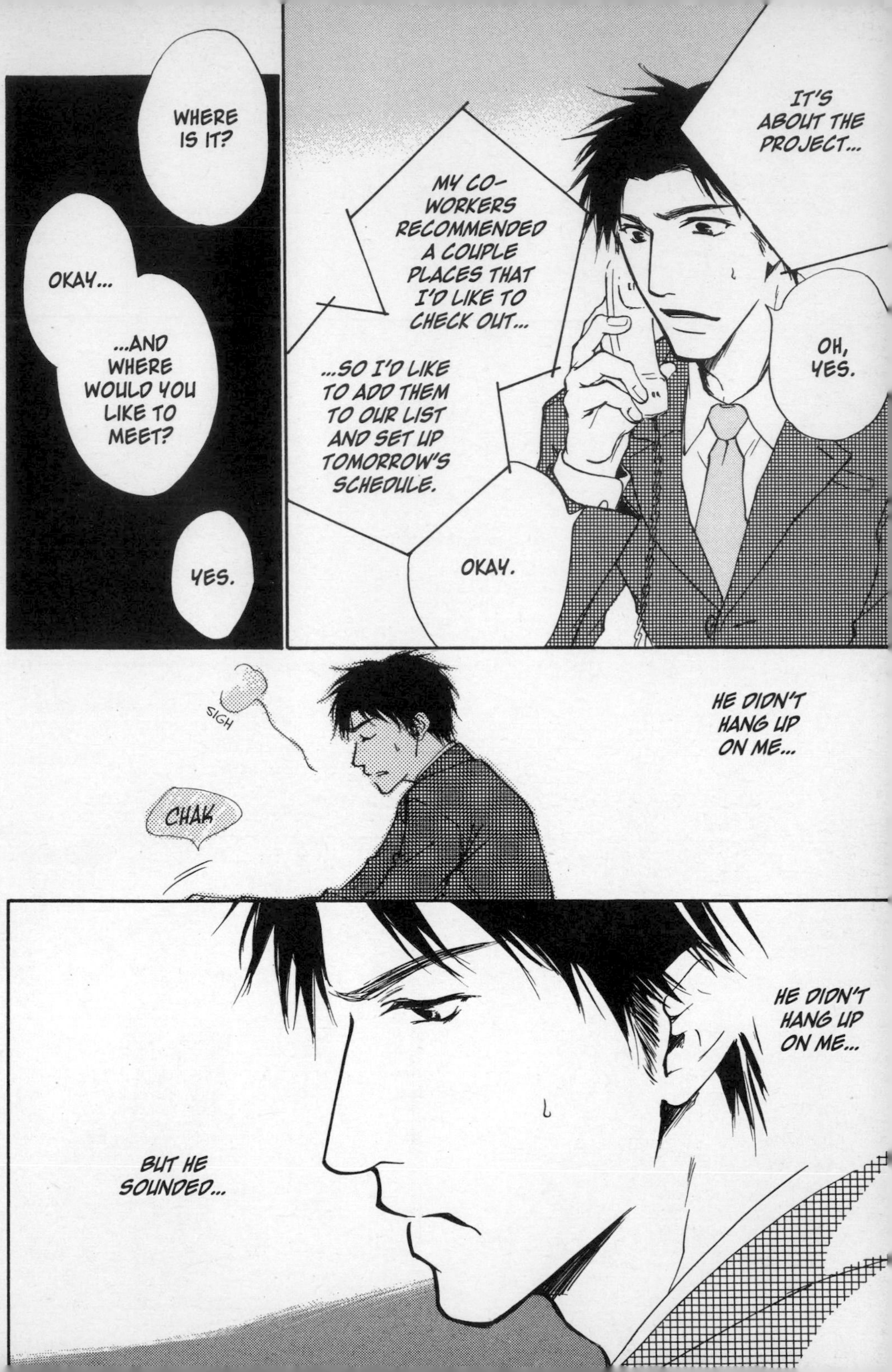
IT'S ABOUT THE PROJECT...
OH, YES.
MY CO-WORKERS RECOMMENDED A COUPLE PLACES THAT I'D LIKE TO CHECK OUT...
...SO I'D LIKE TO ADD THEM TO OUR LIST AND SET UP TOMORROW'S SCHEDULE.
OKAY.
WHERE IS IT?
OKAY...
...AND WHERE WOULD YOU LIKE TO MEET?
YES.
HE DIDN'T HANG UP ON ME...
SIGH
CHAK
HE DIDN'T HANG UP ON ME...
BUT HE SOUNDED...

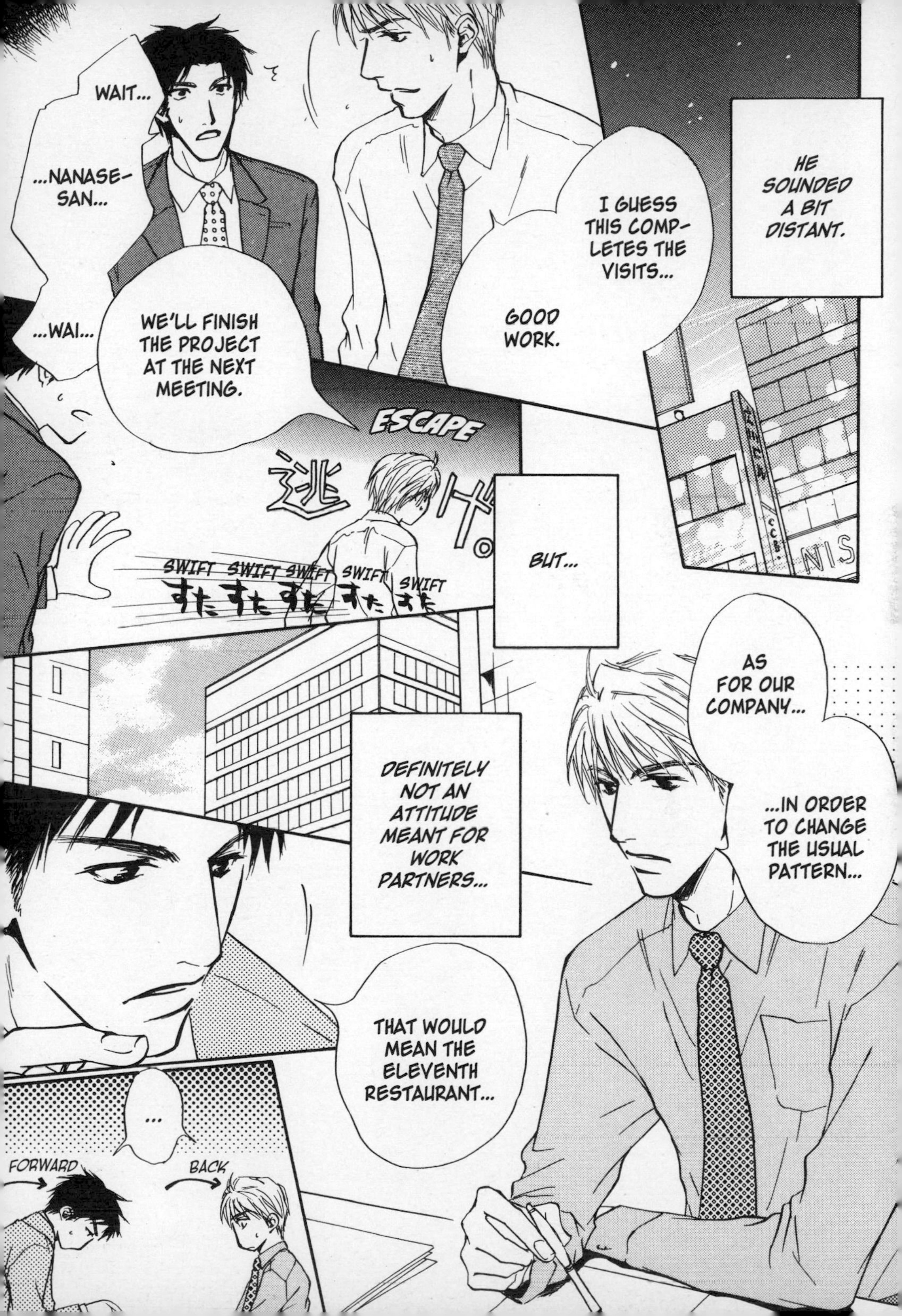
HE SOUNDED A BIT DISTANT.
I GUESS THIS COMPLETES THE VISITS...
GOOD WORK.
WAIT...
...NANASE-SAN...
WE'LL FINISH THE PROJECT AT THE NEXT MEETING.
...WAI...
ESCAPE
逃げ。
SWIFT SWIFT SWIFT SWIFT SWIFT
すたすたすたすたすた
BUT...
AS FOR OUR COMPANY...
...IN ORDER TO CHANGE THE USUAL PATTERN...
DEFINITELY NOT AN ATTITUDE MEANT FOR WORK PARTNERS...
THAT WOULD MEAN THE ELEVENTH RESTAURANT...
...
BACK
FORWARD

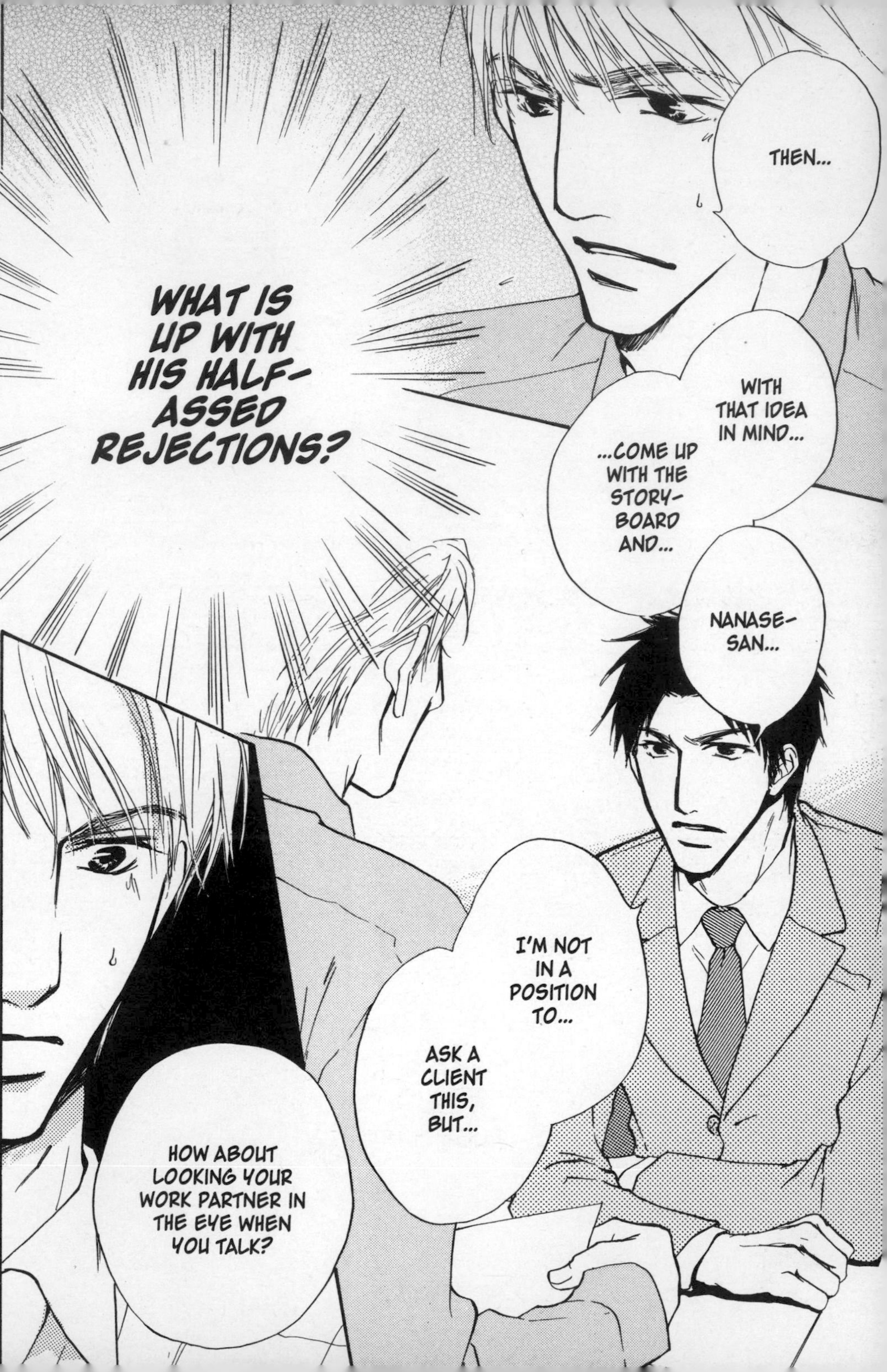
THEN...
WITH THAT IDEA IN MIND...
...COME UP WITH THE STORY-BOARD AND...
WHAT IS UP WITH HIS HALF-ASSED REJECTIONS?
NANASE-SAN...
I'M NOT IN A POSITION TO...
ASK A CLIENT THIS, BUT...
HOW ABOUT LOOKING YOUR WORK PARTNER IN THE EYE WHEN YOU TALK?

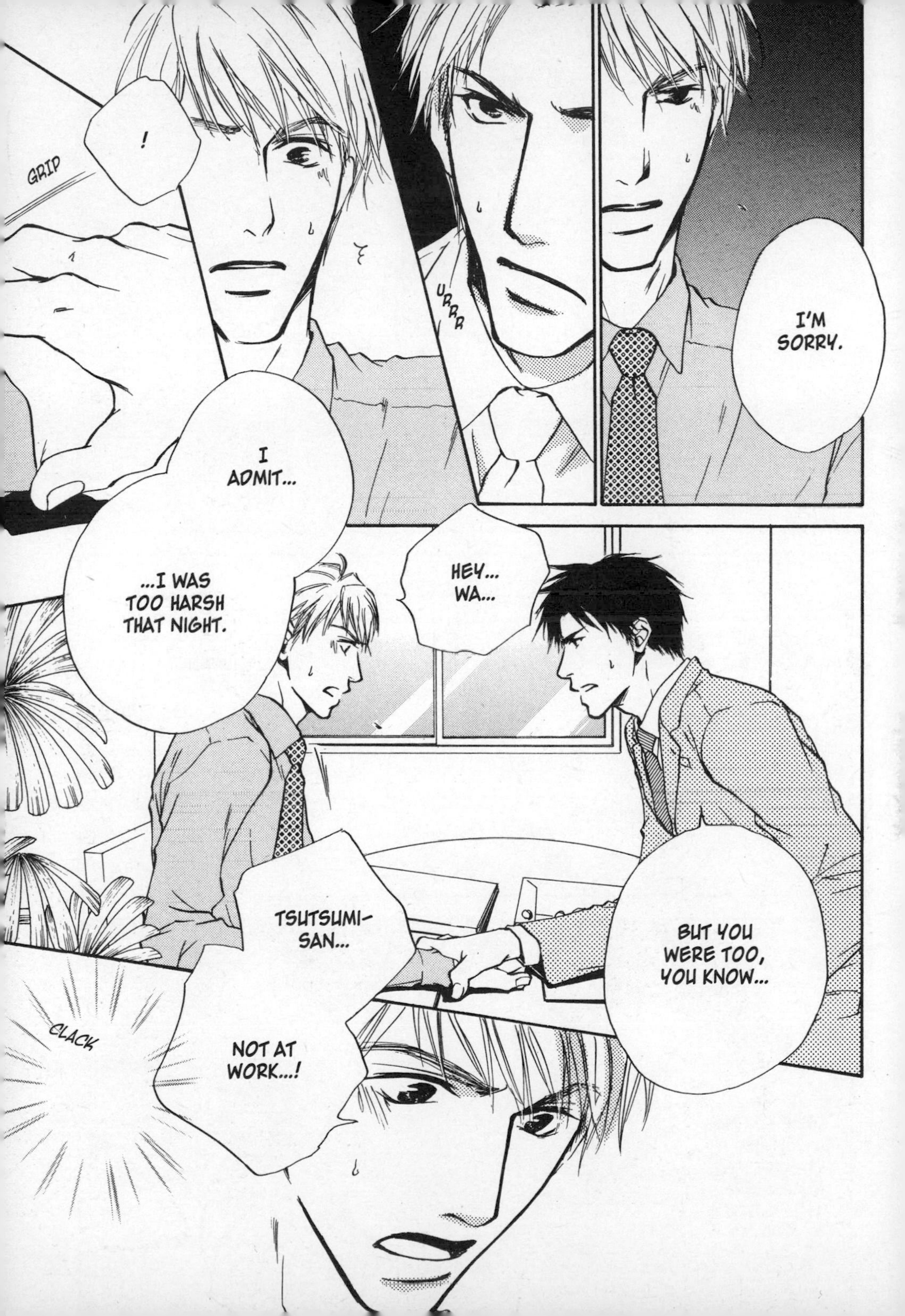
I'M SORRY.
URRR
!
GRIP
I ADMIT...
...I WAS TOO HARSH THAT NIGHT.
BUT YOU WERE TOO, YOU KNOW...
HEY... WA...
TSUTSUMI-SAN...
CLACK
NOT AT WORK...!

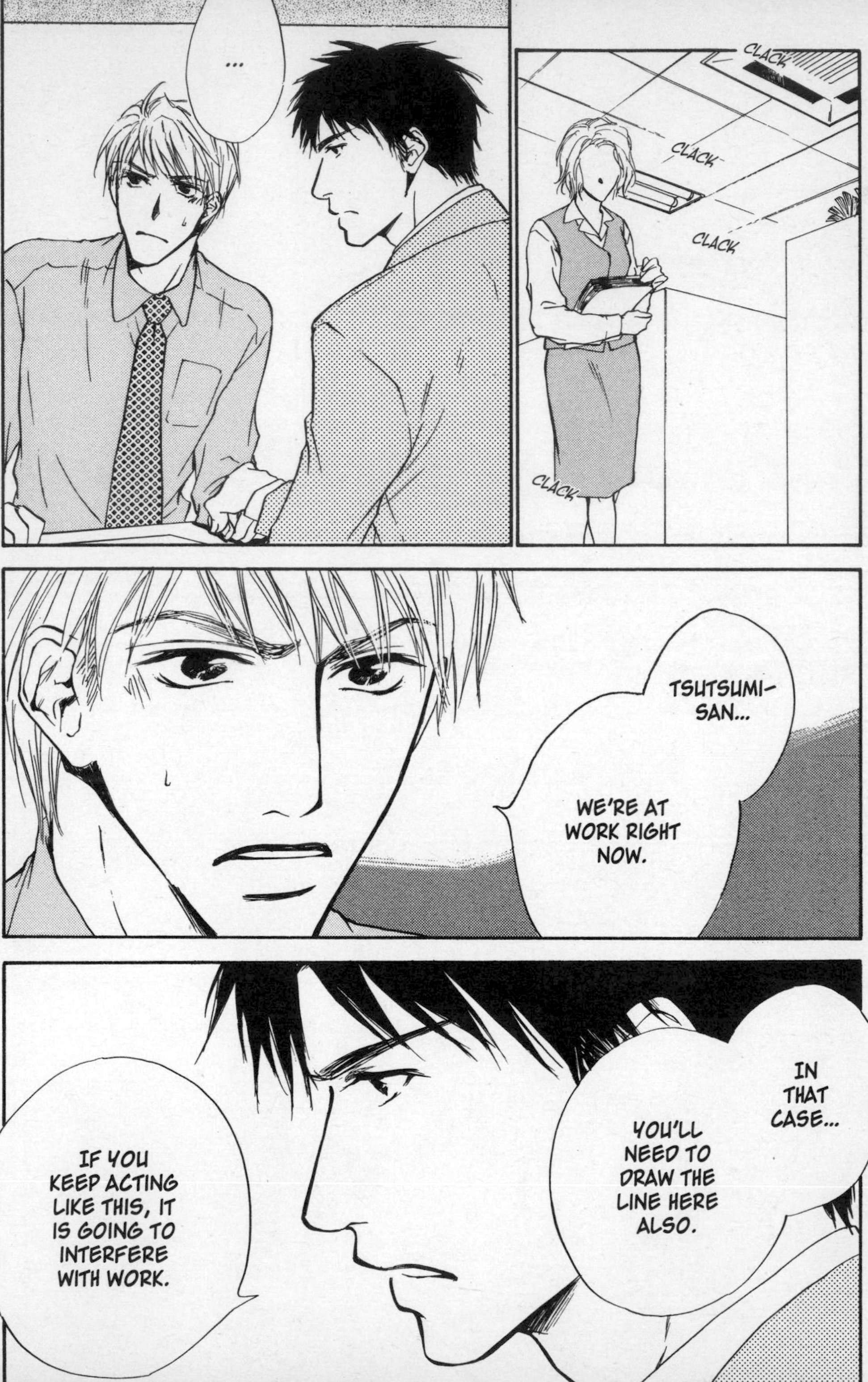
CLACK
CLACK
CLACK
CLACK
...
TSUTSUMI-SAN...
WE'RE AT WORK RIGHT NOW.
IN THAT CASE...
YOU'LL NEED TO DRAW THE LINE HERE ALSO.
IF YOU KEEP ACTING LIKE THIS, IT IS GOING TO INTERFERE WITH WORK.

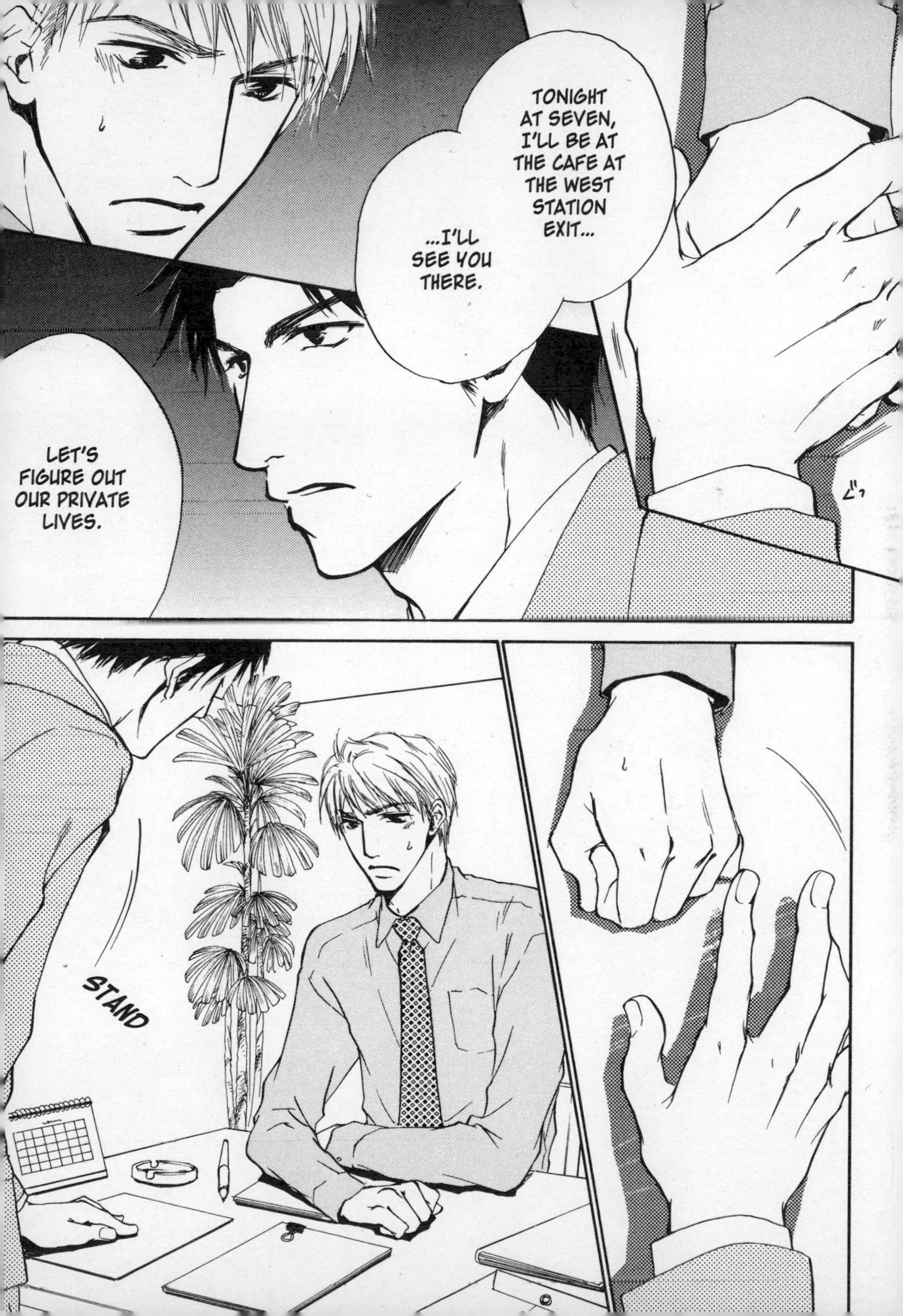
TONIGHT AT SEVEN, I'LL BE AT THE CAFE AT THE WEST STATION EXIT...
...I'LL SEE YOU THERE.
LET'S FIGURE OUT OUR PRIVATE LIVES.
ぐっ
STAND

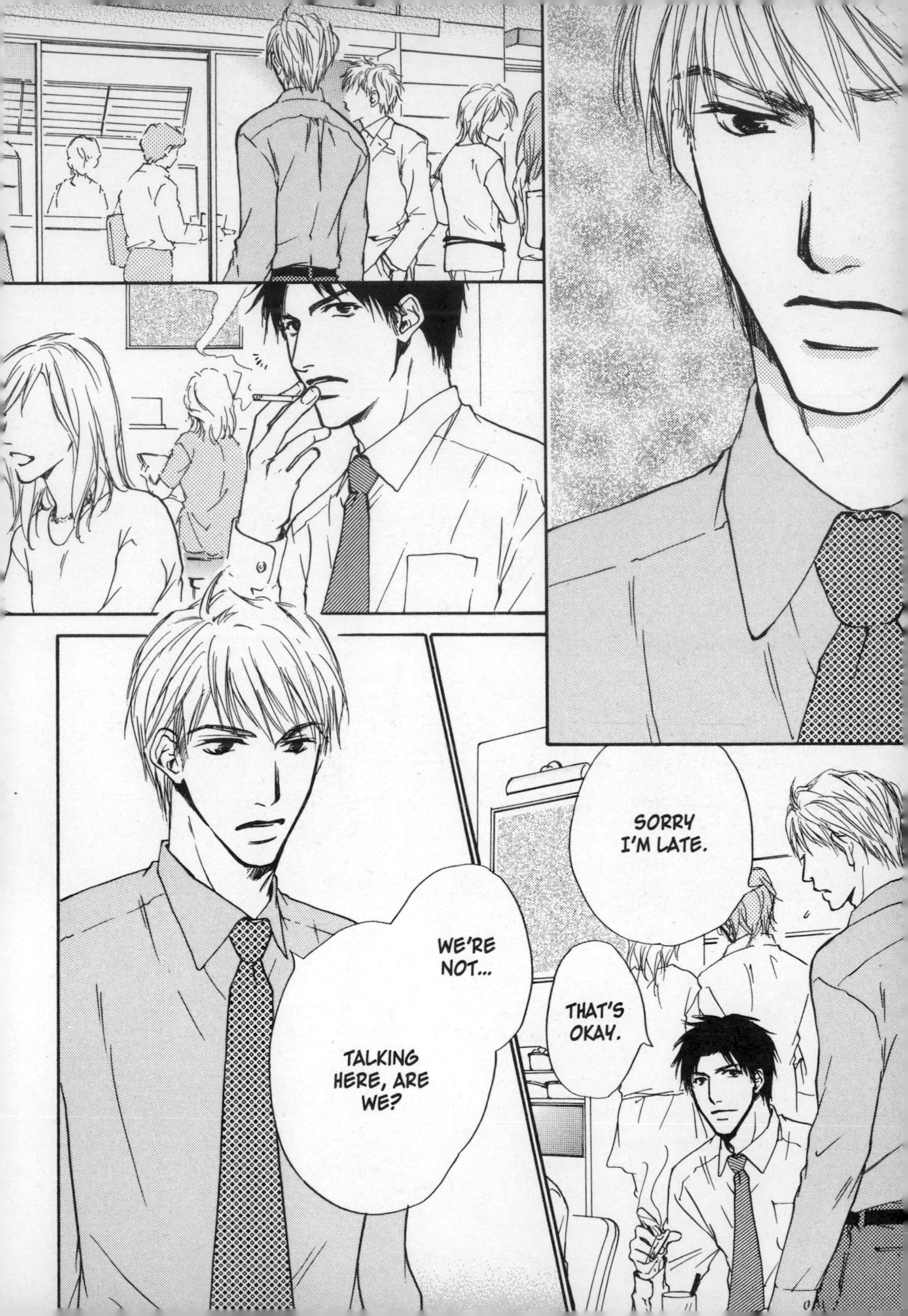
SORRY I'M LATE.
THAT'S OKAY.
WE'RE NOT...
TALKING HERE, ARE WE?

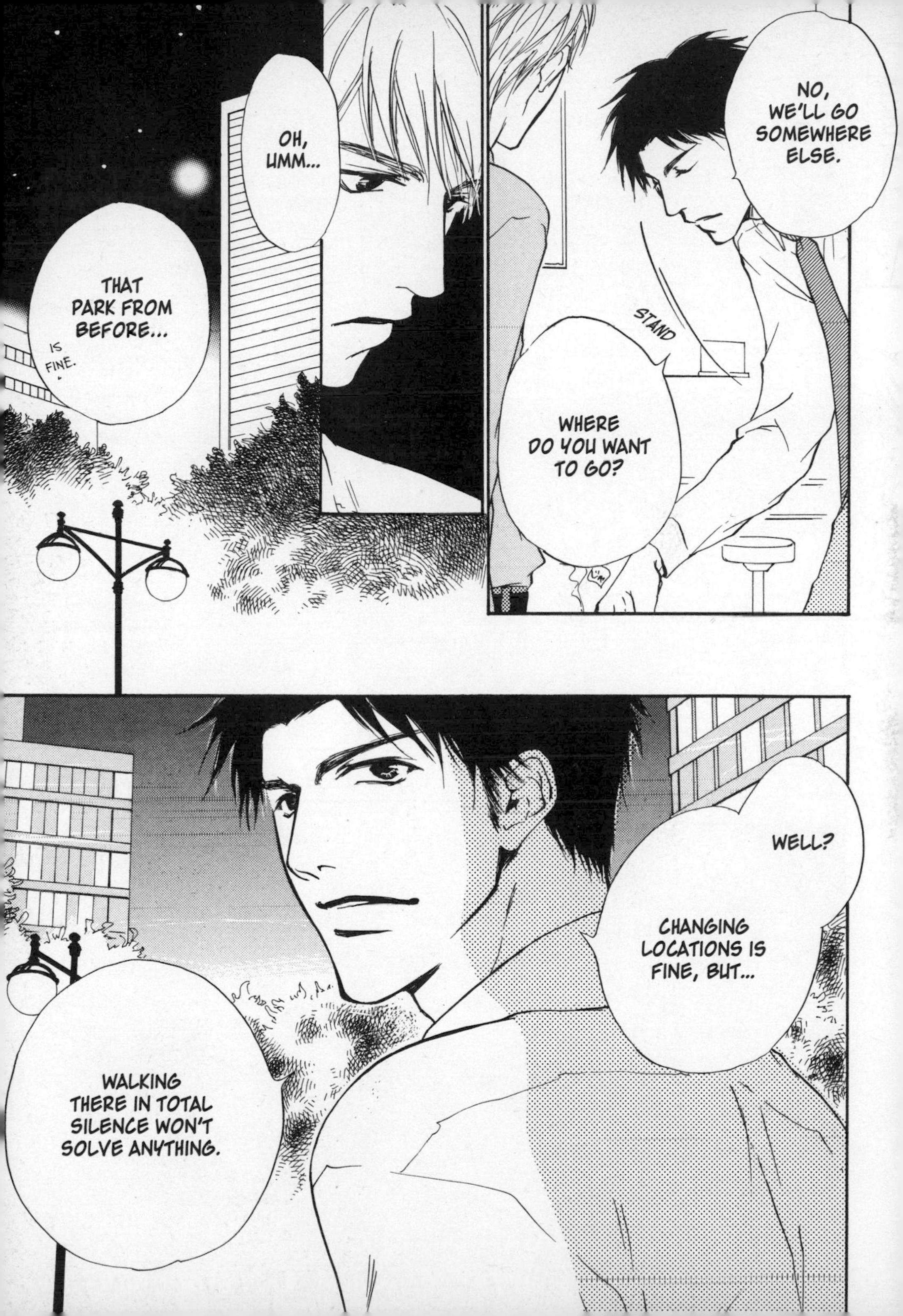
NO, WE'LL GO SOMEWHERE ELSE.
STAND
WHERE DO YOU WANT TO GO?
OH, UMM...
THAT PARK FROM BEFORE...
IS FINE.
WELL?
CHANGING LOCATIONS IS FINE, BUT...
WALKING THERE IN TOTAL SILENCE WON'T SOLVE ANYTHING.

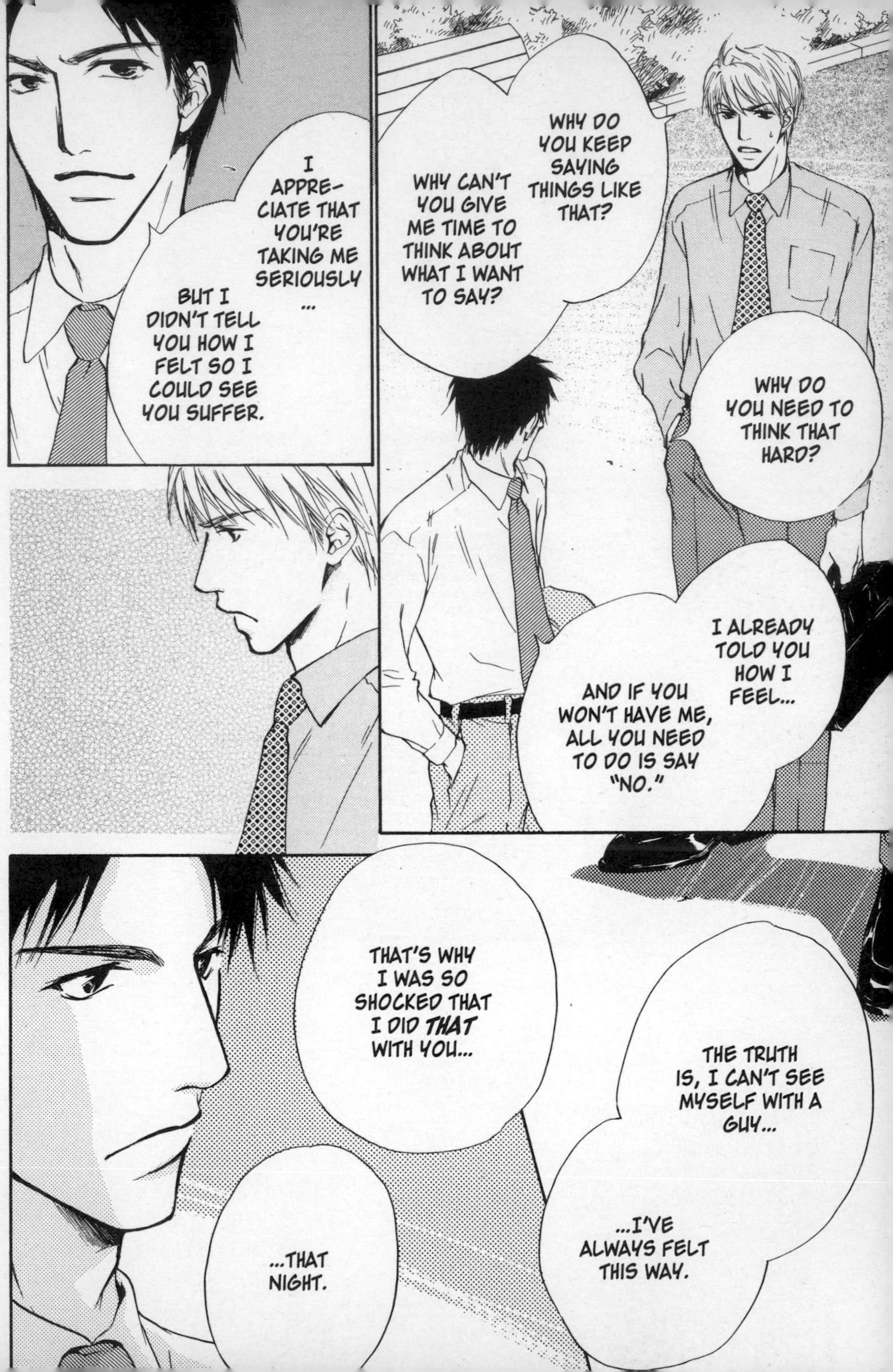
WHY DO YOU KEEP SAYING THINGS LIKE THAT?
WHY CAN'T YOU GIVE ME TIME TO THINK ABOUT WHAT I WANT TO SAY?
WHY DO YOU NEED TO THINK THAT HARD?
I ALREADY TOLD YOU HOW I FEEL...
AND IF YOU WON'T HAVE ME, ALL YOU NEED TO DO IS SAY "NO."
I APPRE-CIATE THAT YOU'RE TAKING ME SERIOUSLY...
BUT I DIDN'T TELL YOU HOW I FELT SO I COULD SEE YOU SUFFER.
THE TRUTH IS, I CAN'T SEE MYSELF WITH A GUY...
...I'VE ALWAYS FELT THIS WAY.
THAT'S WHY I WAS SO SHOCKED THAT I DID *THAT* WITH YOU...
...THAT NIGHT.

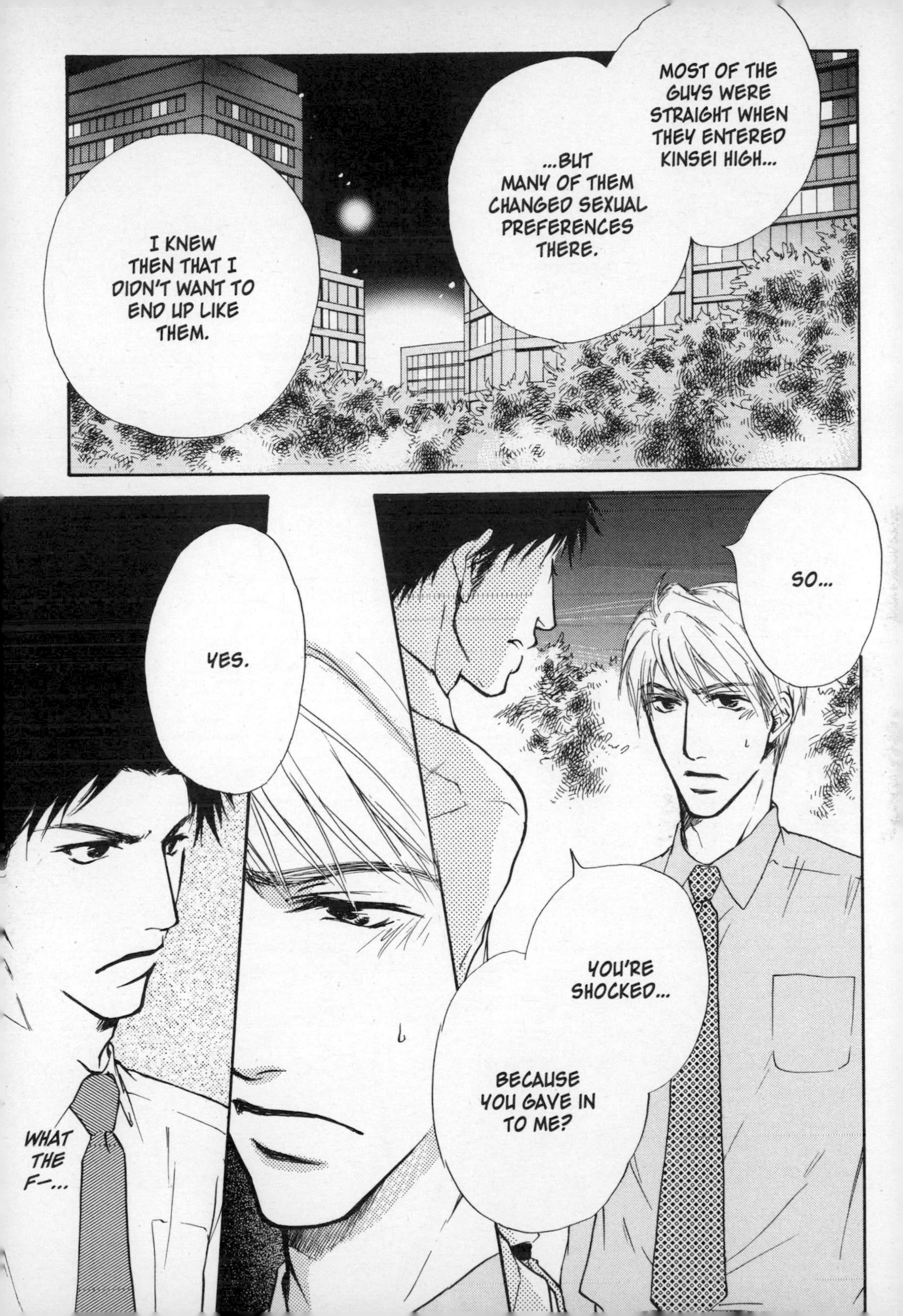
MOST OF THE GUYS WERE STRAIGHT WHEN THEY ENTERED KINSEI HIGH...
...BUT MANY OF THEM CHANGED SEXUAL PREFERENCES THERE.
I KNEW THEN THAT I DIDN'T WANT TO END UP LIKE THEM.
SO...
YOU'RE SHOCKED...
BECAUSE YOU GAVE IN TO ME?
YES.
WHAT THE F—...

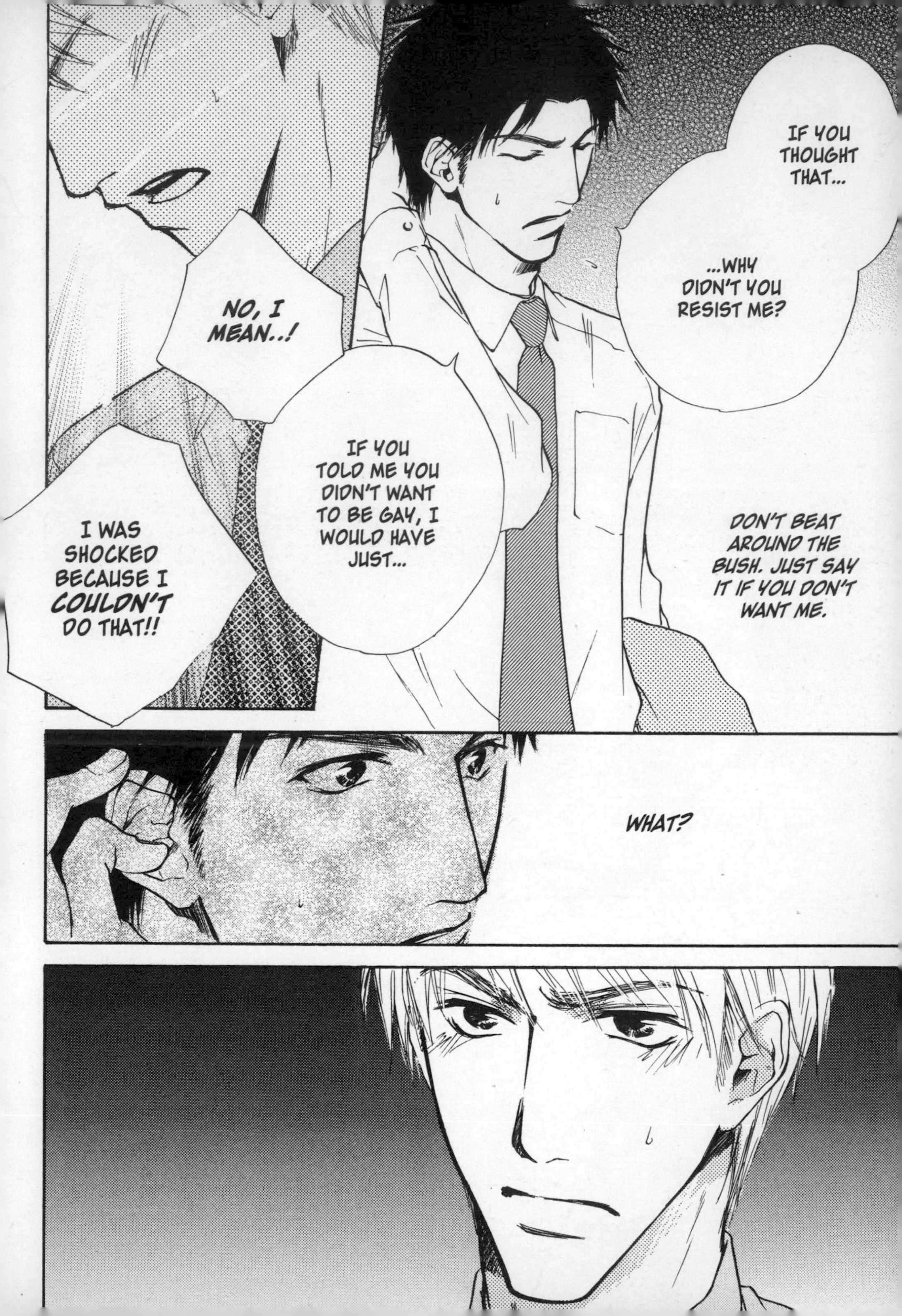
IF YOU THOUGHT THAT...
...WHY DIDN'T YOU RESIST ME?
IF YOU TOLD ME YOU DIDN'T WANT TO BE GAY, I WOULD HAVE JUST...
DON'T BEAT AROUND THE BUSH. JUST SAY IT IF YOU DON'T WANT ME.
NO, I MEAN..!
I WAS SHOCKED BECAUSE I COULDN'T DO THAT!!
WHAT?

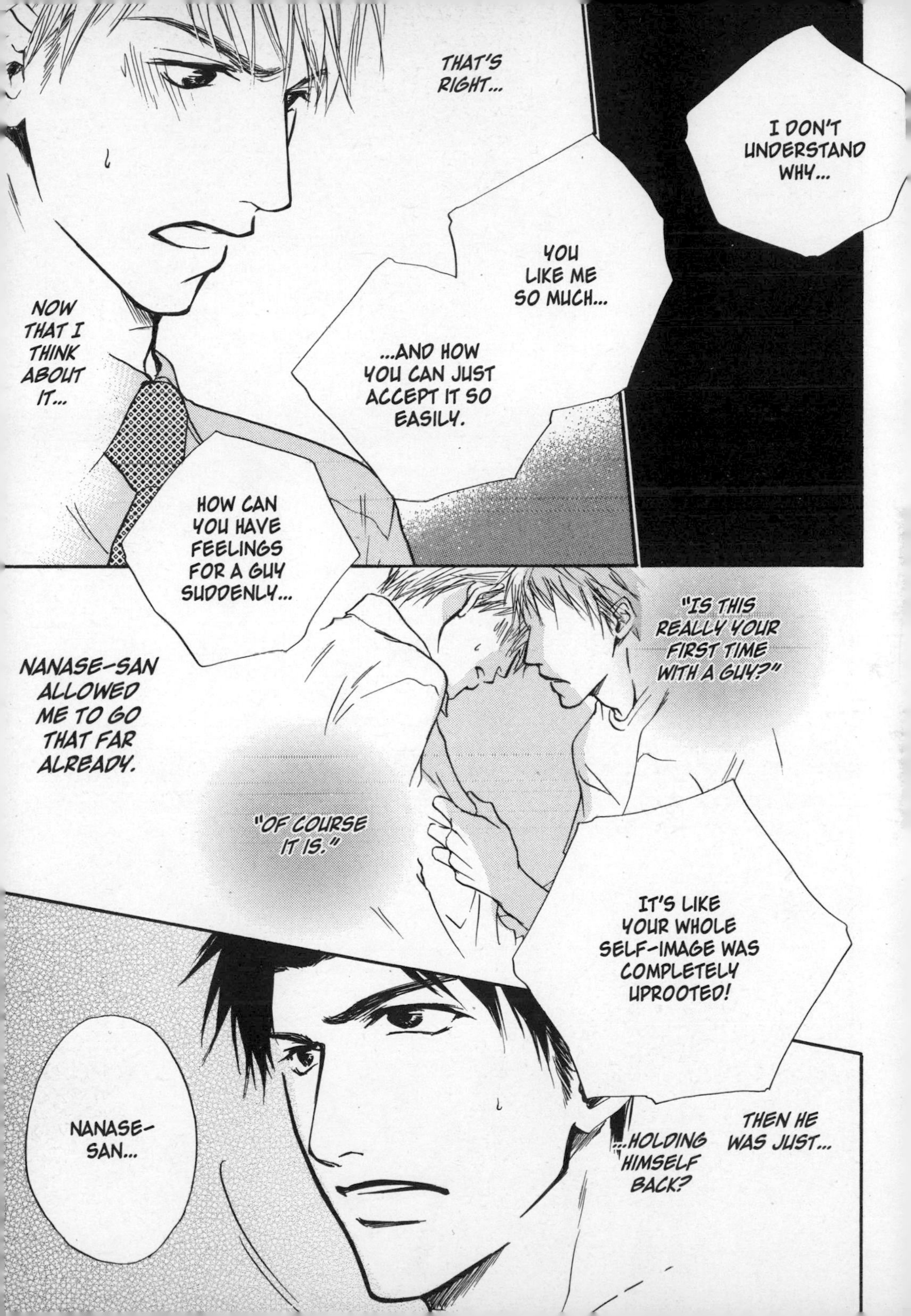
THAT'S RIGHT...
NOW THAT I THINK ABOUT IT...
I DON'T UNDERSTAND WHY...
YOU LIKE ME SO MUCH...
...AND HOW YOU CAN JUST ACCEPT IT SO EASILY.
HOW CAN YOU HAVE FEELINGS FOR A GUY SUDDENLY...
"IS THIS REALLY YOUR FIRST TIME WITH A GUY?"
"OF COURSE IT IS."
NANASE-SAN ALLOWED ME TO GO THAT FAR ALREADY.
IT'S LIKE YOUR WHOLE SELF-IMAGE WAS COMPLETELY UPROOTED!
THEN HE WAS JUST...
...HOLDING HIMSELF BACK?
NANASE-SAN...

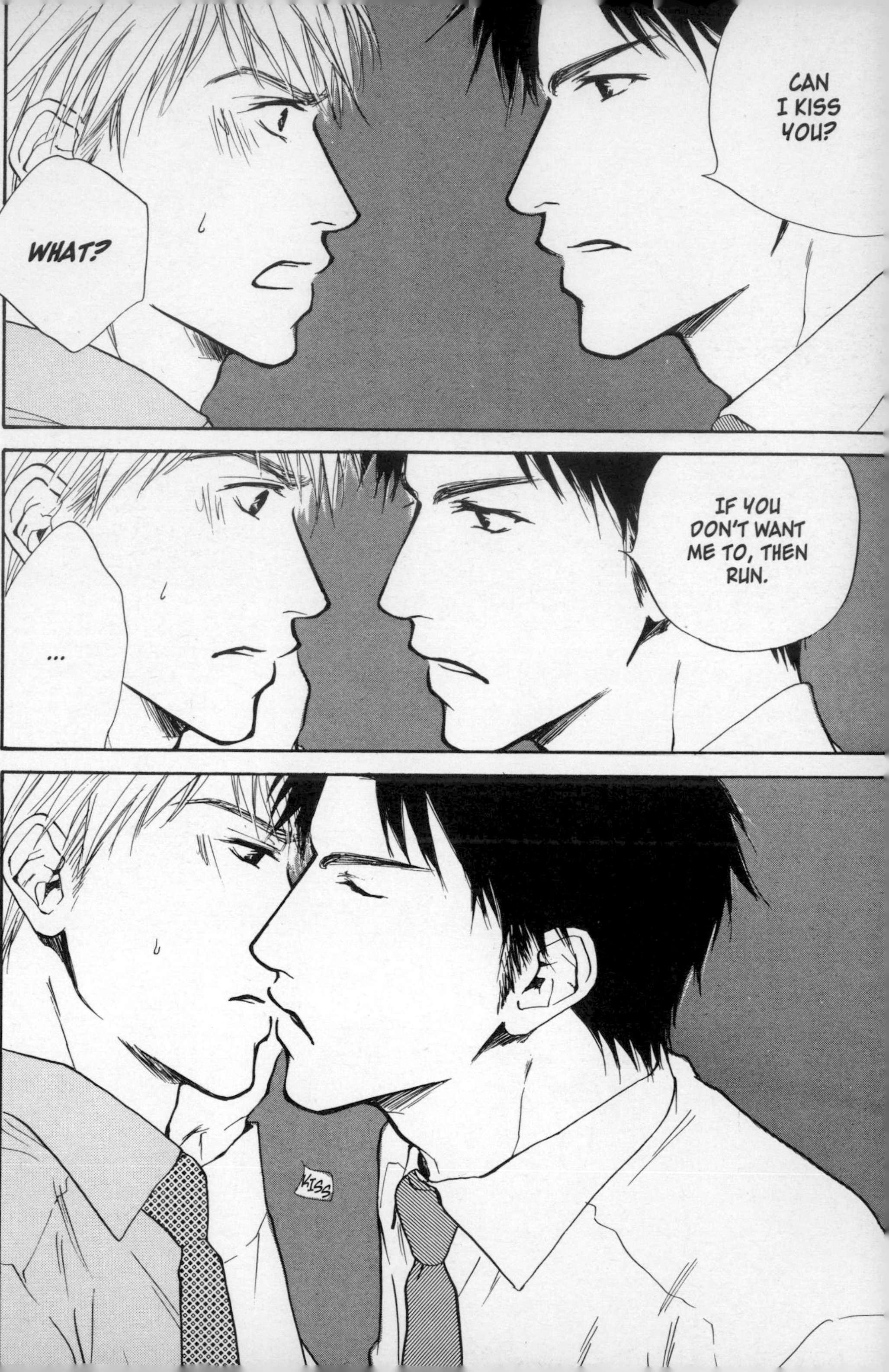
CAN I KISS YOU?
WHAT?
IF YOU DON'T WANT ME TO, THEN RUN.
...
KISS

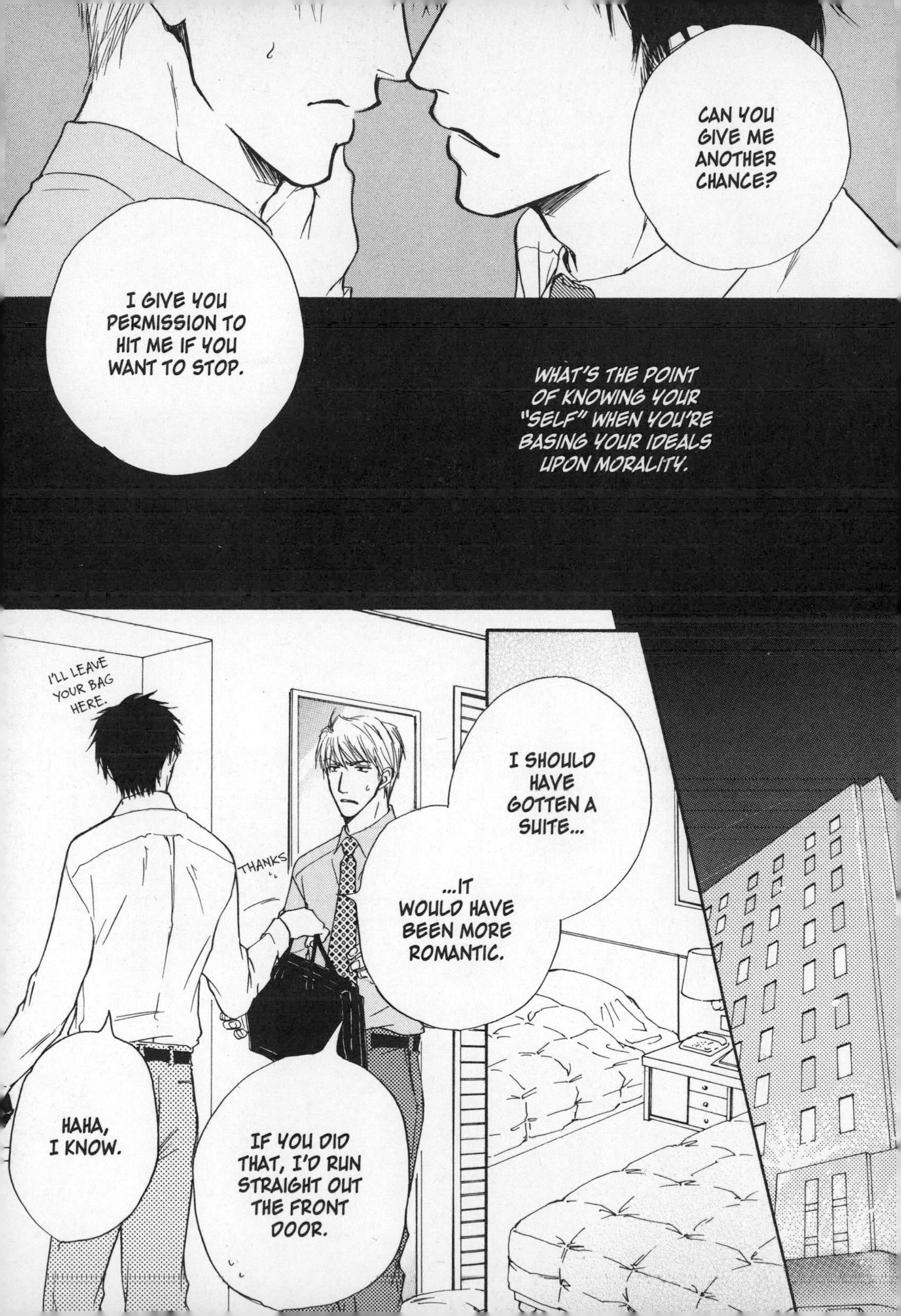
CAN YOU GIVE ME ANOTHER CHANCE?
I GIVE YOU PERMISSION TO HIT ME IF YOU WANT TO STOP.
WHAT'S THE POINT OF KNOWING YOUR "SELF" WHEN YOU'RE BASING YOUR IDEALS UPON MORALITY.
I SHOULD HAVE GOTTEN A SUITE...
...IT WOULD HAVE BEEN MORE ROMANTIC.
I'LL LEAVE YOUR BAG HERE.
THANKS
IF YOU DID THAT, I'D RUN STRAIGHT OUT THE FRONT DOOR.
HAHA, I KNOW.

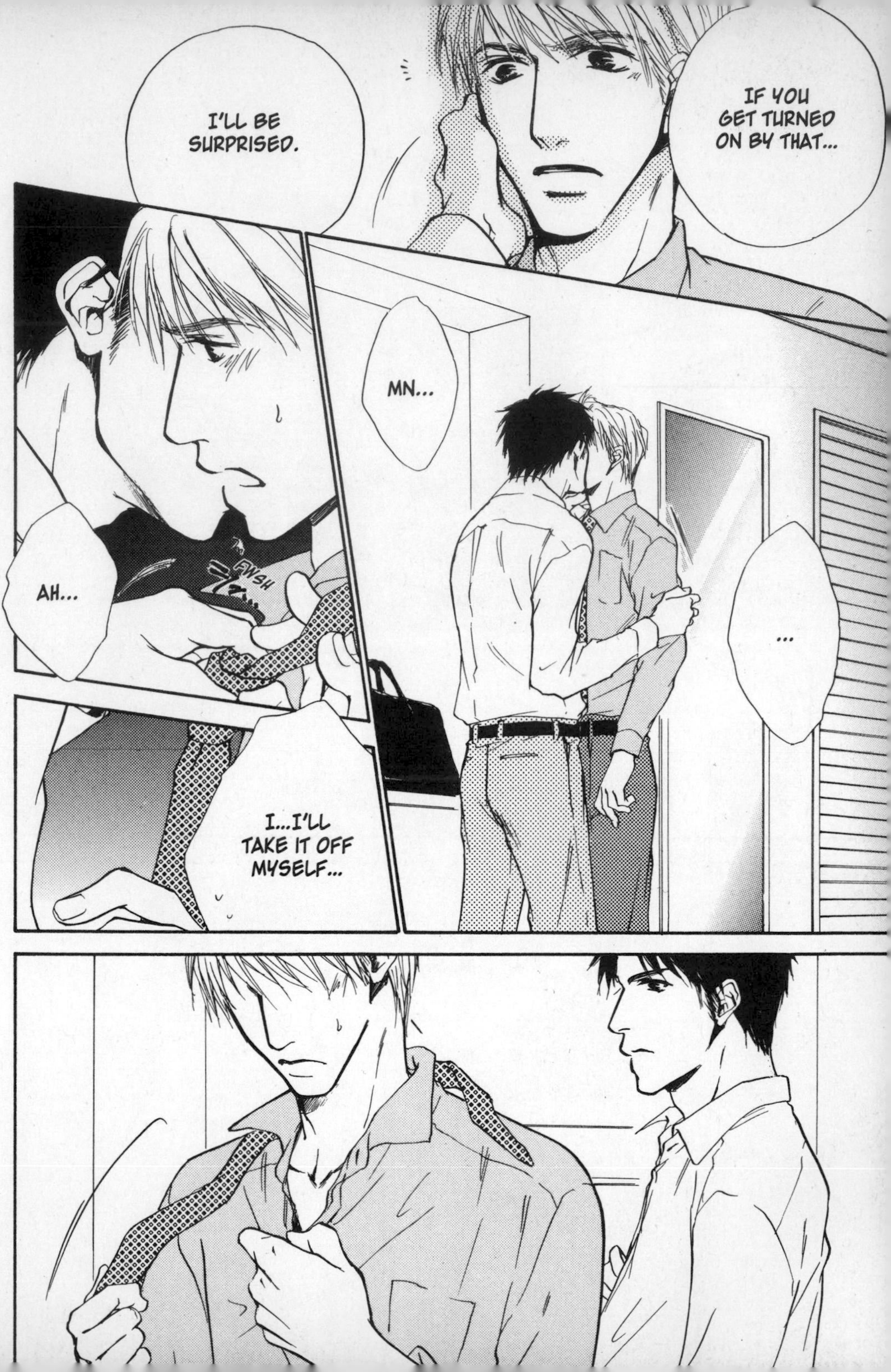
IF YOU GET TURNED ON BY THAT...
I'LL BE SURPRISED.
MN...
...
AH...
FWSH
I...I'LL TAKE IT OFF MYSELF...

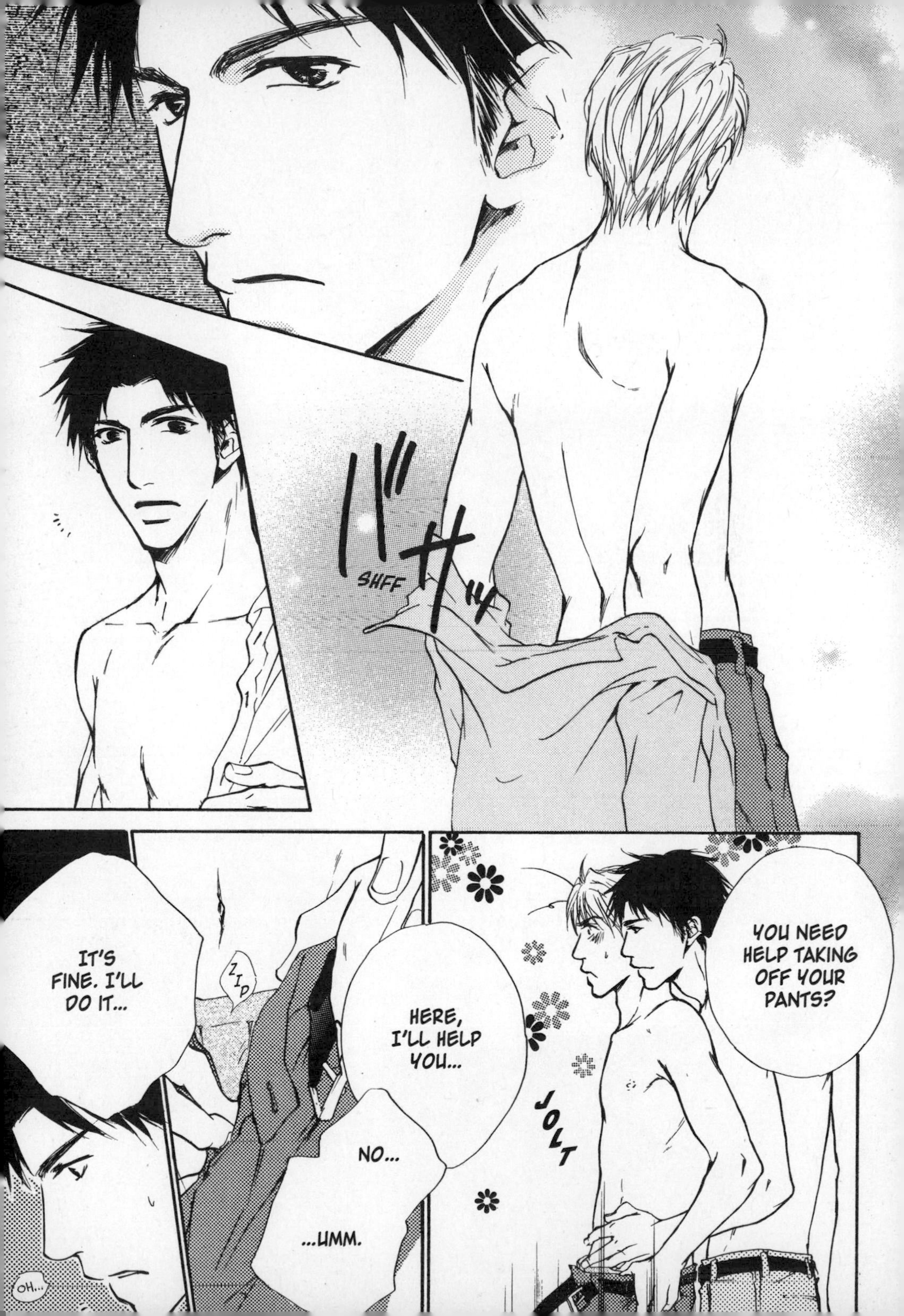
バサッ
SHFF
YOU NEED HELP TAKING OFF YOUR PANTS?
JOLT
HERE, I'LL HELP YOU...
NO...
...UMM.
IT'S FINE. I'LL DO IT...
ZIP
OH...

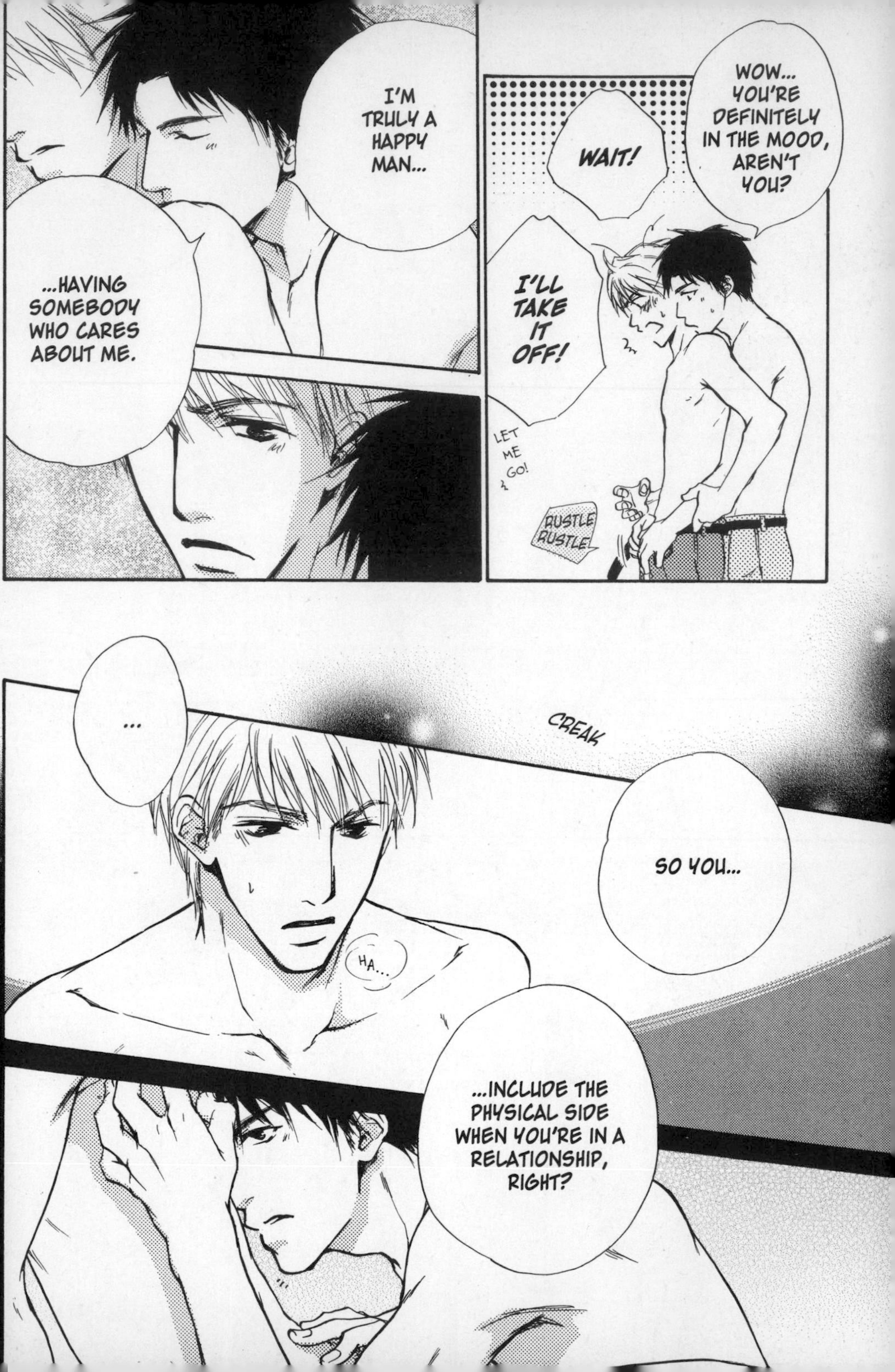
WOW... YOU'RE DEFINITELY IN THE MOOD, AREN'T YOU?
WAIT!
I'LL TAKE IT OFF!
LET ME GO!
RUSTLE RUSTLE
I'M TRULY A HAPPY MAN...
...HAVING SOMEBODY WHO CARES ABOUT ME.
CREAK
...
SO YOU...
HA...
...INCLUDE THE PHYSICAL SIDE WHEN YOU'RE IN A RELATIONSHIP, RIGHT?

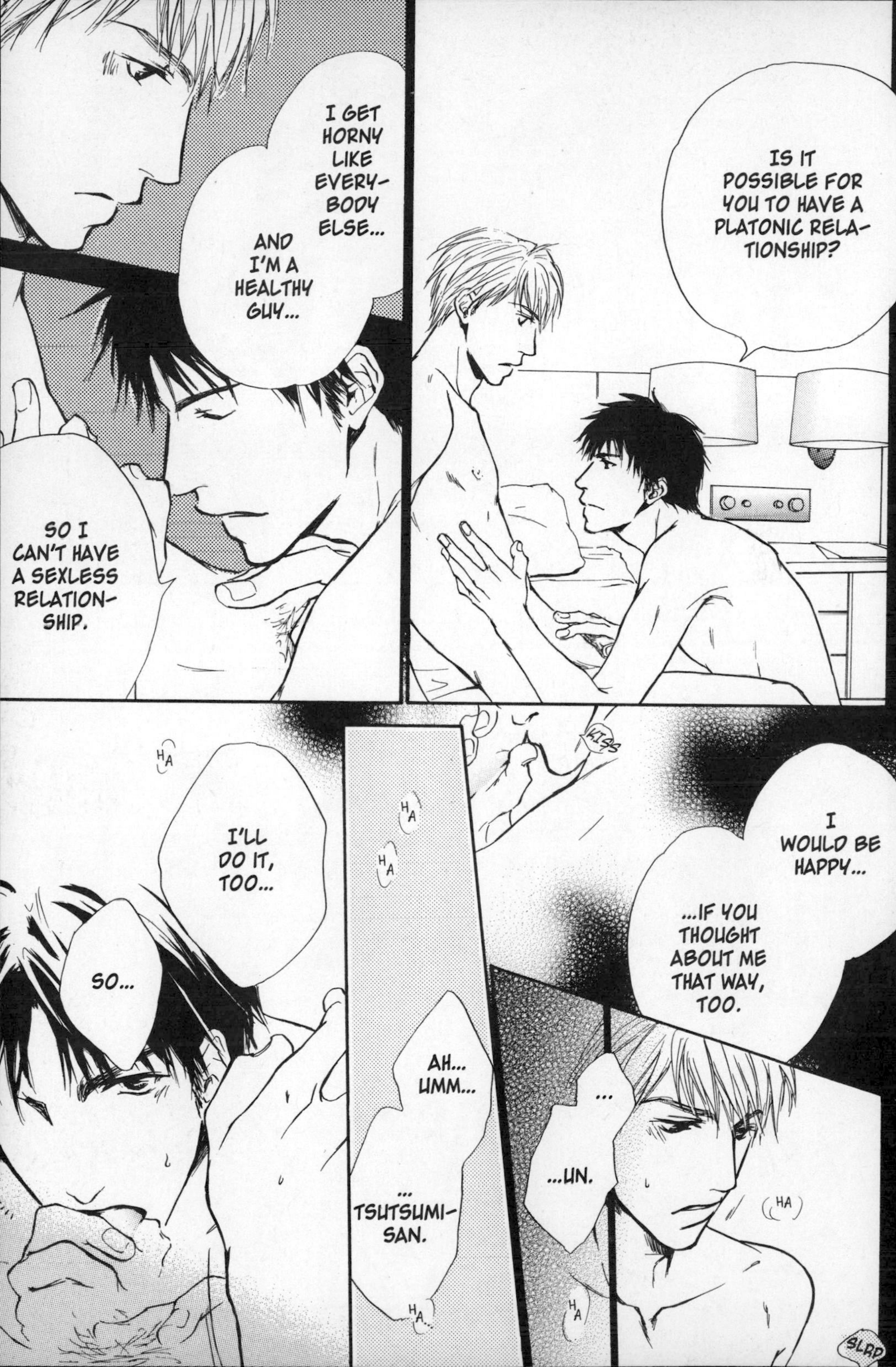
IS IT POSSIBLE FOR YOU TO HAVE A PLATONIC RELATIONSHIP?
I GET HORNY LIKE EVERYBODY ELSE...
AND I'M A HEALTHY GUY...
SO I CAN'T HAVE A SEXLESS RELATIONSHIP.
KISS
I WOULD BE HAPPY...
...IF YOU THOUGHT ABOUT ME THAT WAY, TOO.
...
...UN.
HA
HA
SLRP
HA
HA
AH... UMM...
...TSUTSUMI-SAN.
HA...
HA
I'LL DO IT, TOO...
SO...

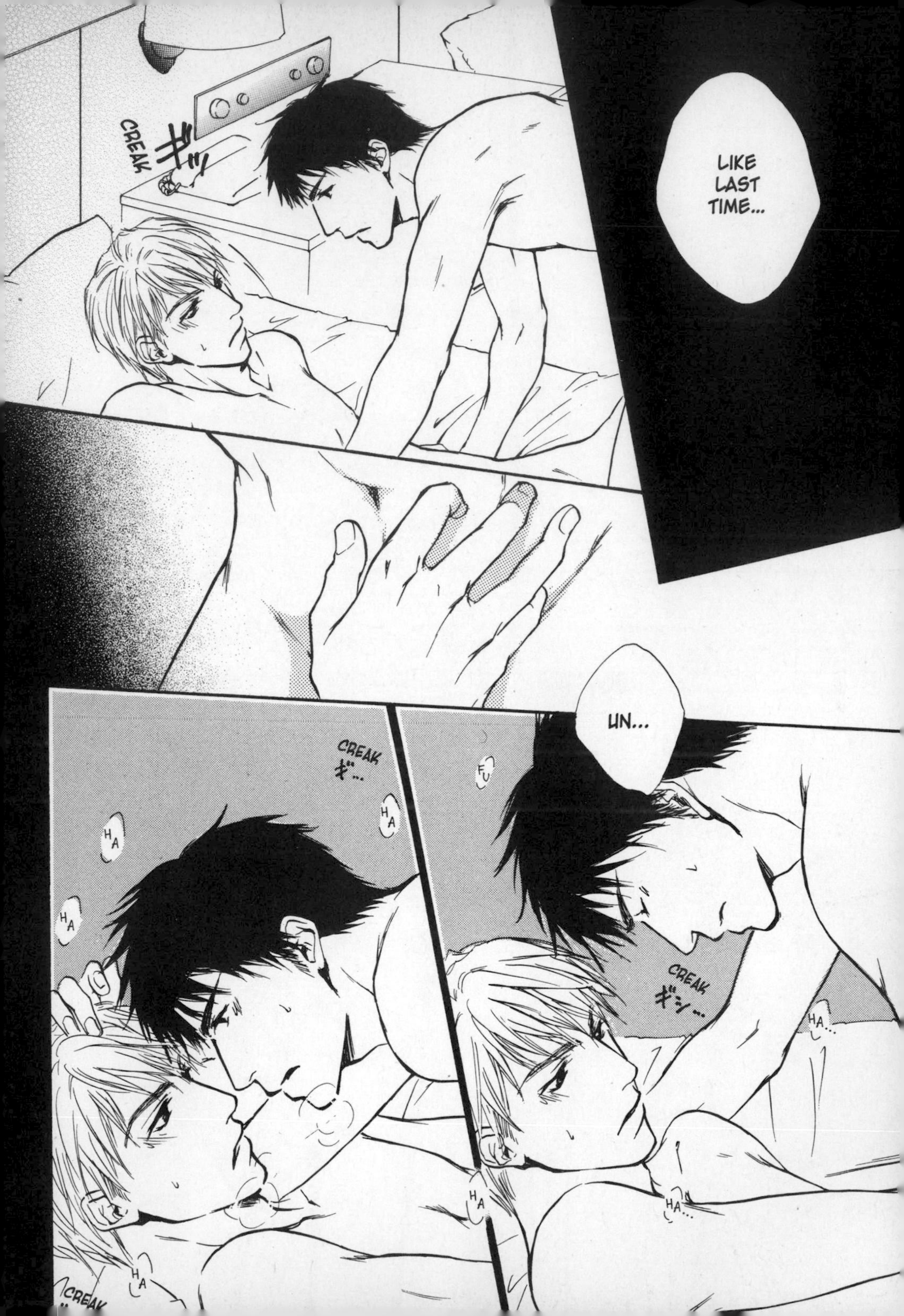
LIKE LAST TIME...
CREAK
ギッ
UN...
FU
CREAK
ギシ...
HA...
HA...
HA
CREAK
ギ...
HA
HA
HA
HA
CREAK

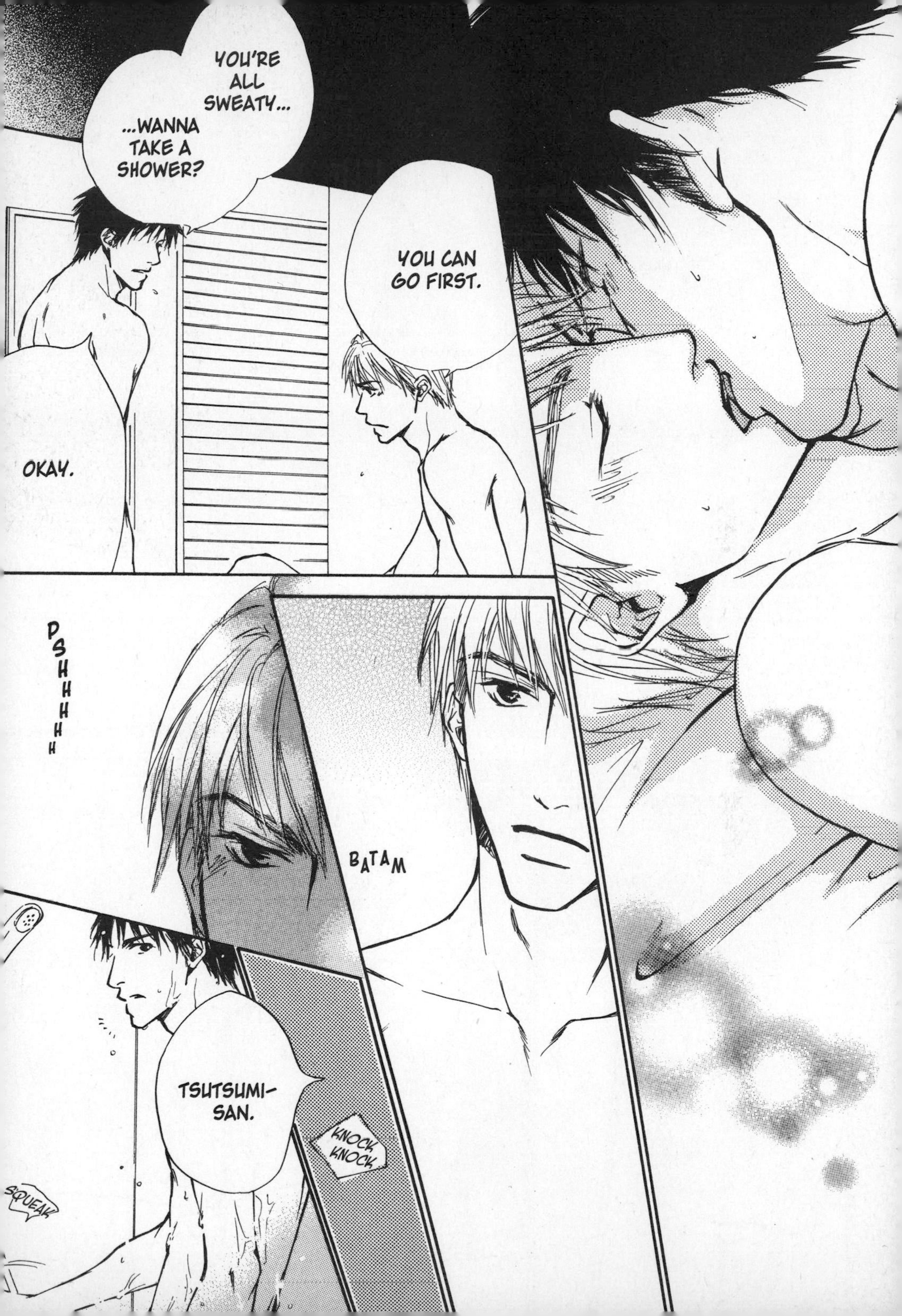
YOU'RE ALL SWEATY...
...WANNA TAKE A SHOWER?
YOU CAN GO FIRST.
OKAY.
BATAM
PSHHHHH
TSUTSUMI-SAN.
KNOCK KNOCK
SQUEAK

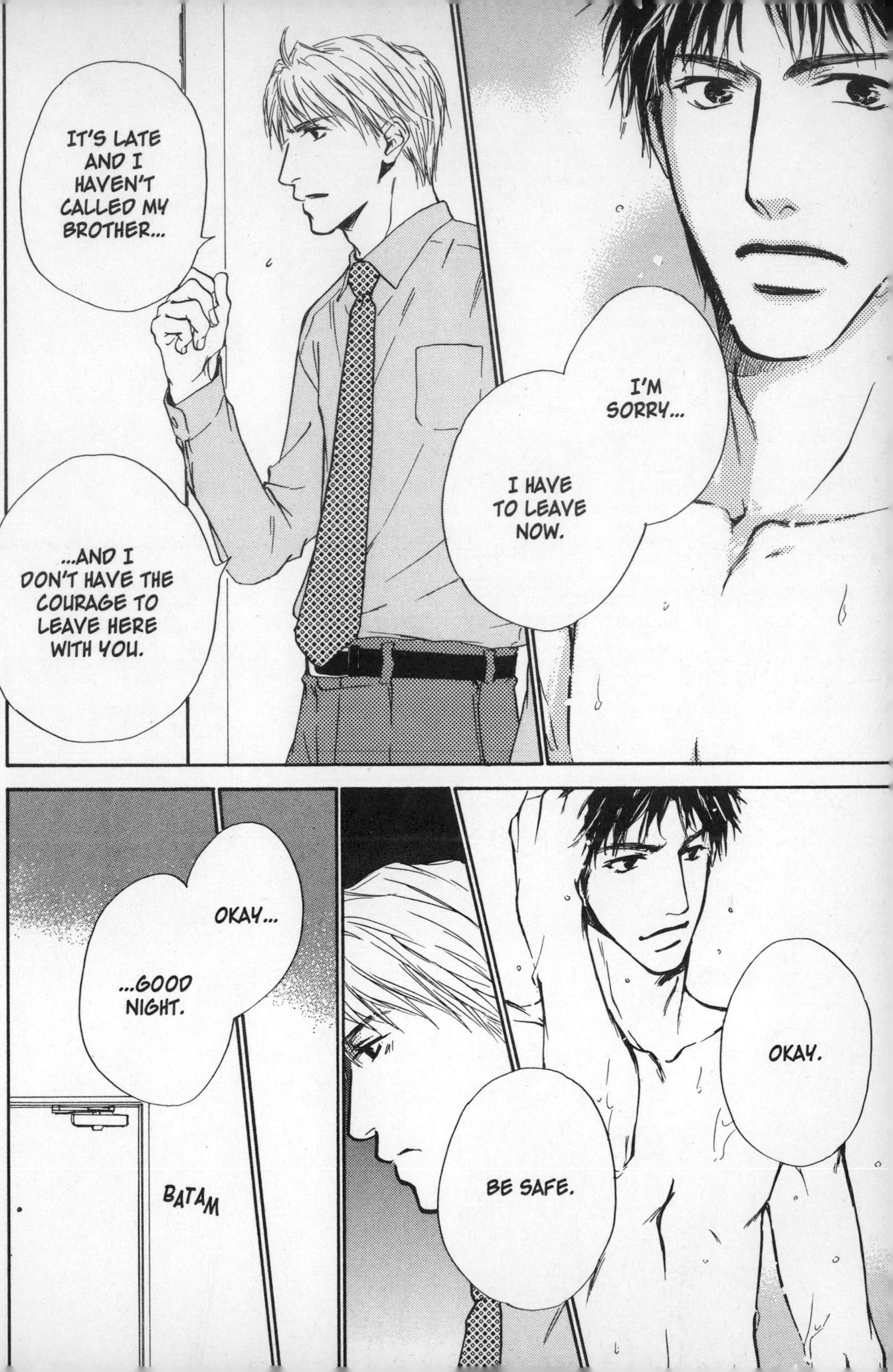
I'M SORRY...
I HAVE TO LEAVE NOW.
IT'S LATE AND I HAVEN'T CALLED MY BROTHER...
...AND I DON'T HAVE THE COURAGE TO LEAVE HERE WITH YOU.
OKAY.
BE SAFE.
OKAY...
...GOOD NIGHT.
BATAM

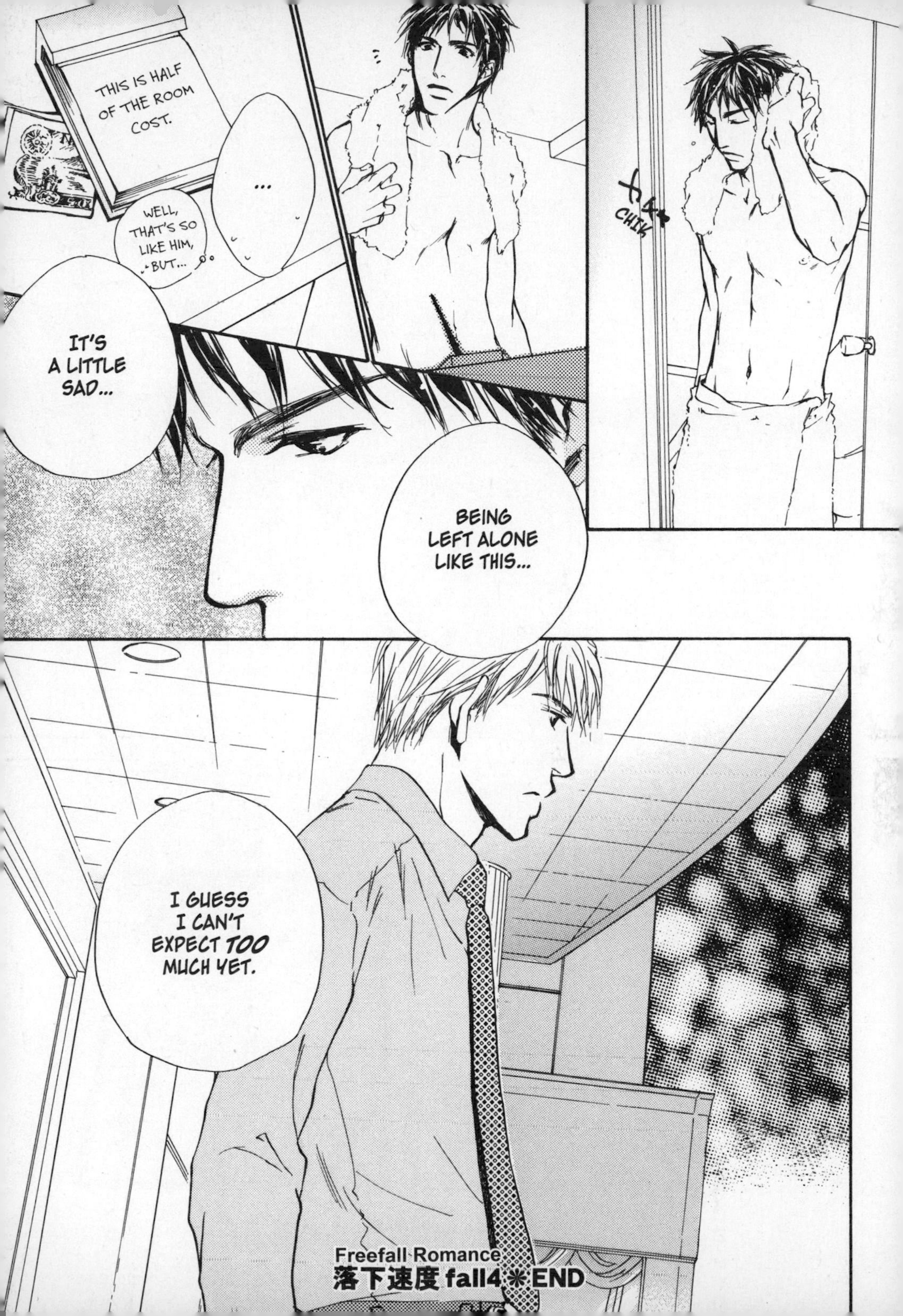
CHIK
THIS IS HALF OF THE ROOM COST.
...
WELL, THAT'S SO LIKE HIM, BUT...
IT'S A LITTLE SAD...
BEING LEFT ALONE LIKE THIS...
I GUESS I CAN'T EXPECT *TOO* MUCH YET.

Freefall Romance
落下速度 fall4＊END

Freefall Romance

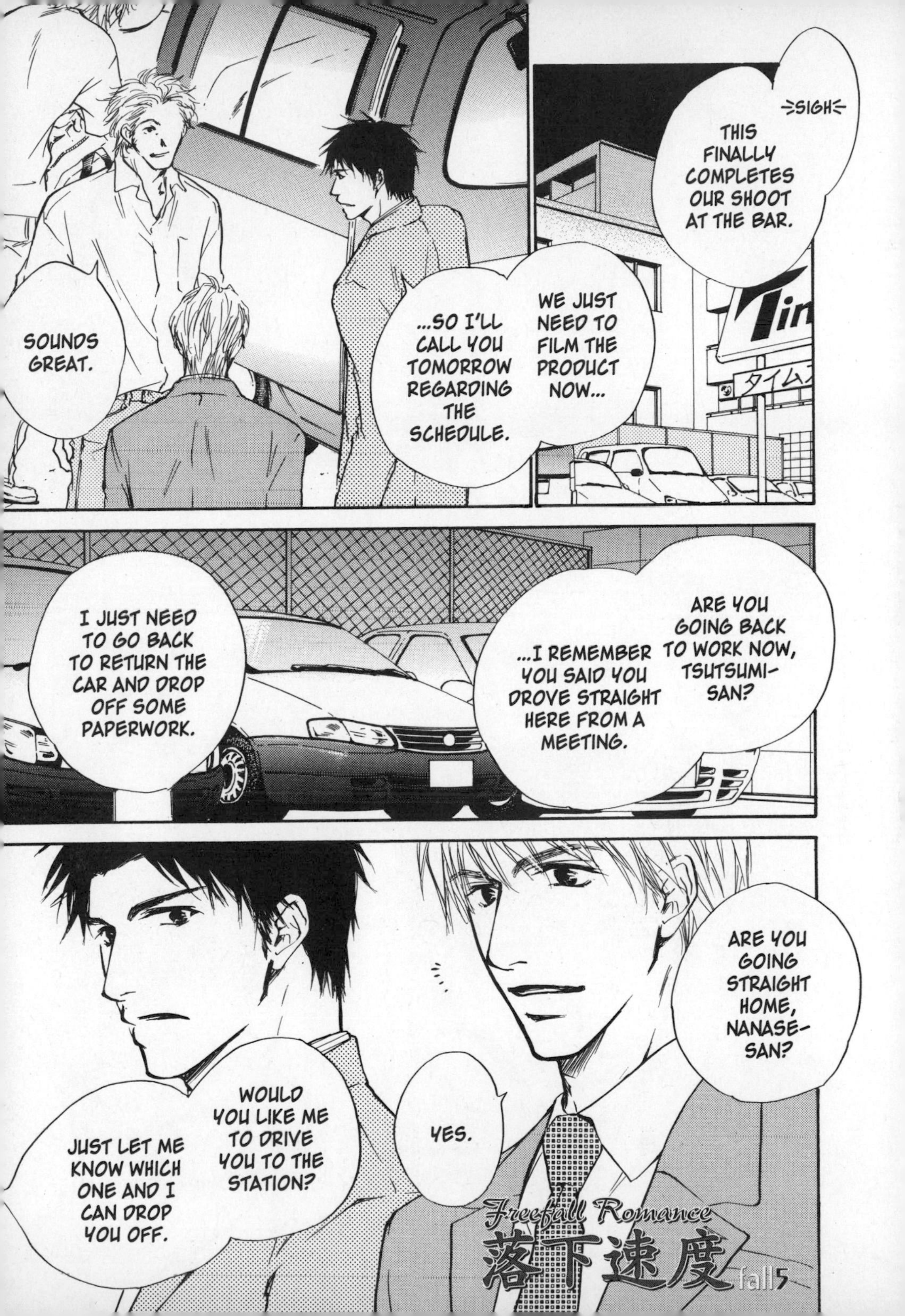
=SIGH=
THIS FINALLY COMPLETES OUR SHOOT AT THE BAR.
WE JUST NEED TO FILM THE PRODUCT NOW...
...SO I'LL CALL YOU TOMORROW REGARDING THE SCHEDULE.
SOUNDS GREAT.
ARE YOU GOING BACK TO WORK NOW, TSUTSUMI-SAN?
...I REMEMBER YOU SAID YOU DROVE STRAIGHT HERE FROM A MEETING.
I JUST NEED TO GO BACK TO RETURN THE CAR AND DROP OFF SOME PAPERWORK.
ARE YOU GOING STRAIGHT HOME, NANASE-SAN?
YES.
WOULD YOU LIKE ME TO DRIVE YOU TO THE STATION?
JUST LET ME KNOW WHICH ONE AND I CAN DROP YOU OFF.
Freefall Romance
落下速度
fall5

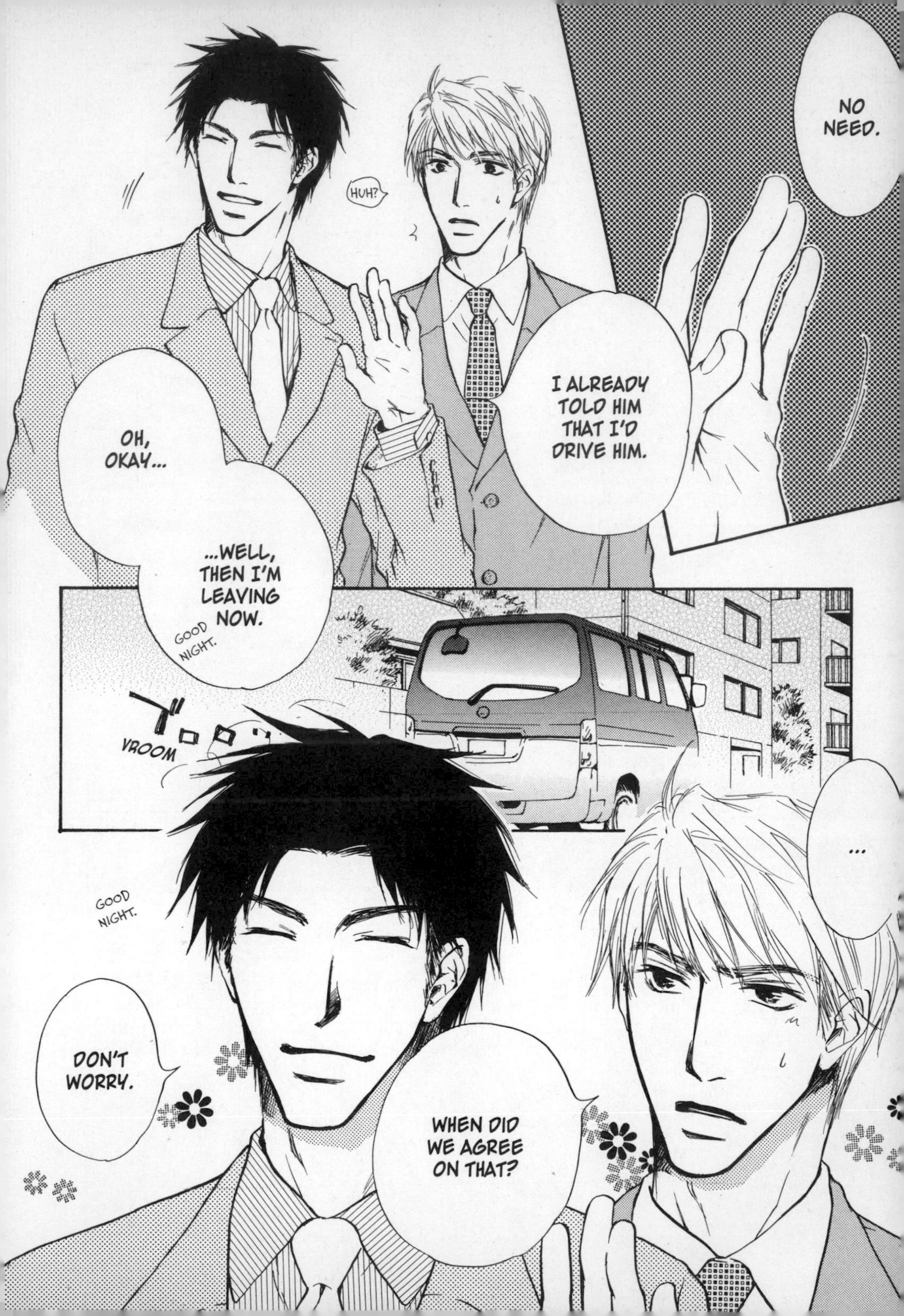
NO NEED.
I ALREADY TOLD HIM THAT I'D DRIVE HIM.
HUH?
OH, OKAY...
...WELL, THEN I'M LEAVING NOW.
GOOD NIGHT.
VROOM
...
WHEN DID WE AGREE ON THAT?
GOOD NIGHT.
DON'T WORRY.

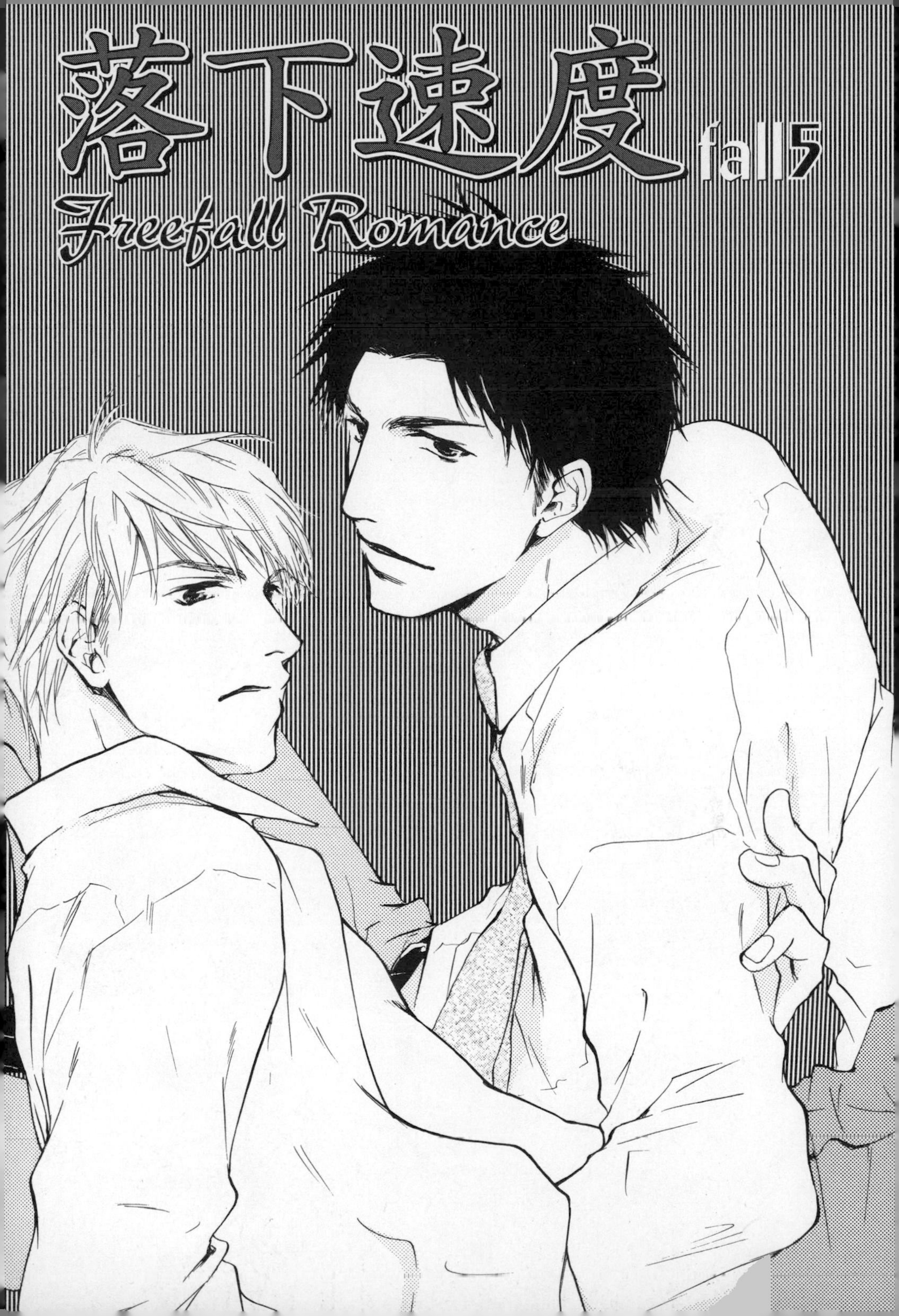
落下速度
fall5
Freefall Romance

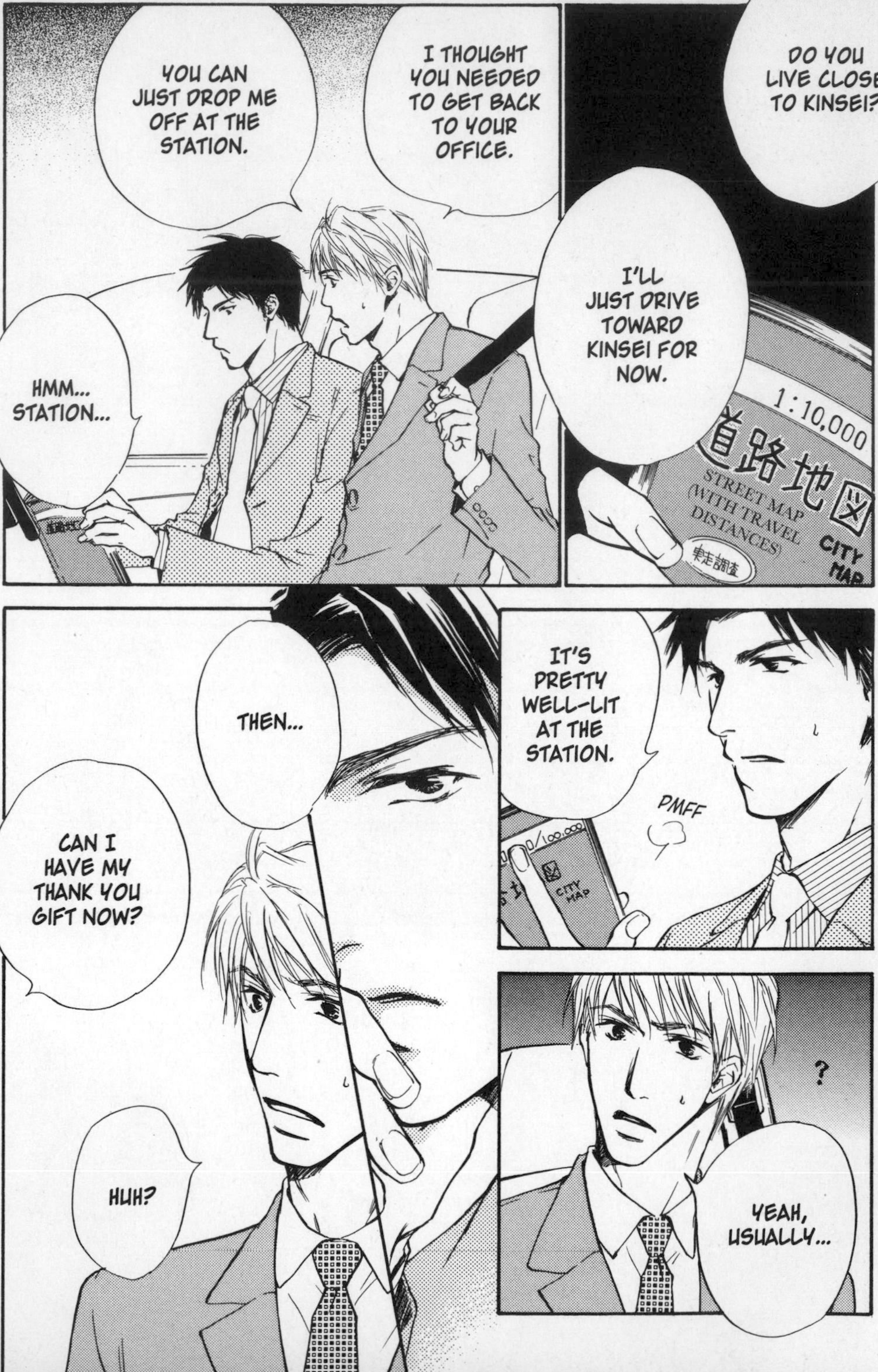
DO YOU LIVE CLOSE TO KINSEI?
I'LL JUST DRIVE TOWARD KINSEI FOR NOW.
1:10,000
道路地図
STREET MAP (WITH TRAVEL DISTANCES)
CITY MAP
I THOUGHT YOU NEEDED TO GET BACK TO YOUR OFFICE.
YOU CAN JUST DROP ME OFF AT THE STATION.
HMM... STATION...
IT'S PRETTY WELL-LIT AT THE STATION.
PMFF
CITY MAP
?
YEAH, USUALLY...
THEN...
CAN I HAVE MY THANK YOU GIFT NOW?
HUH?

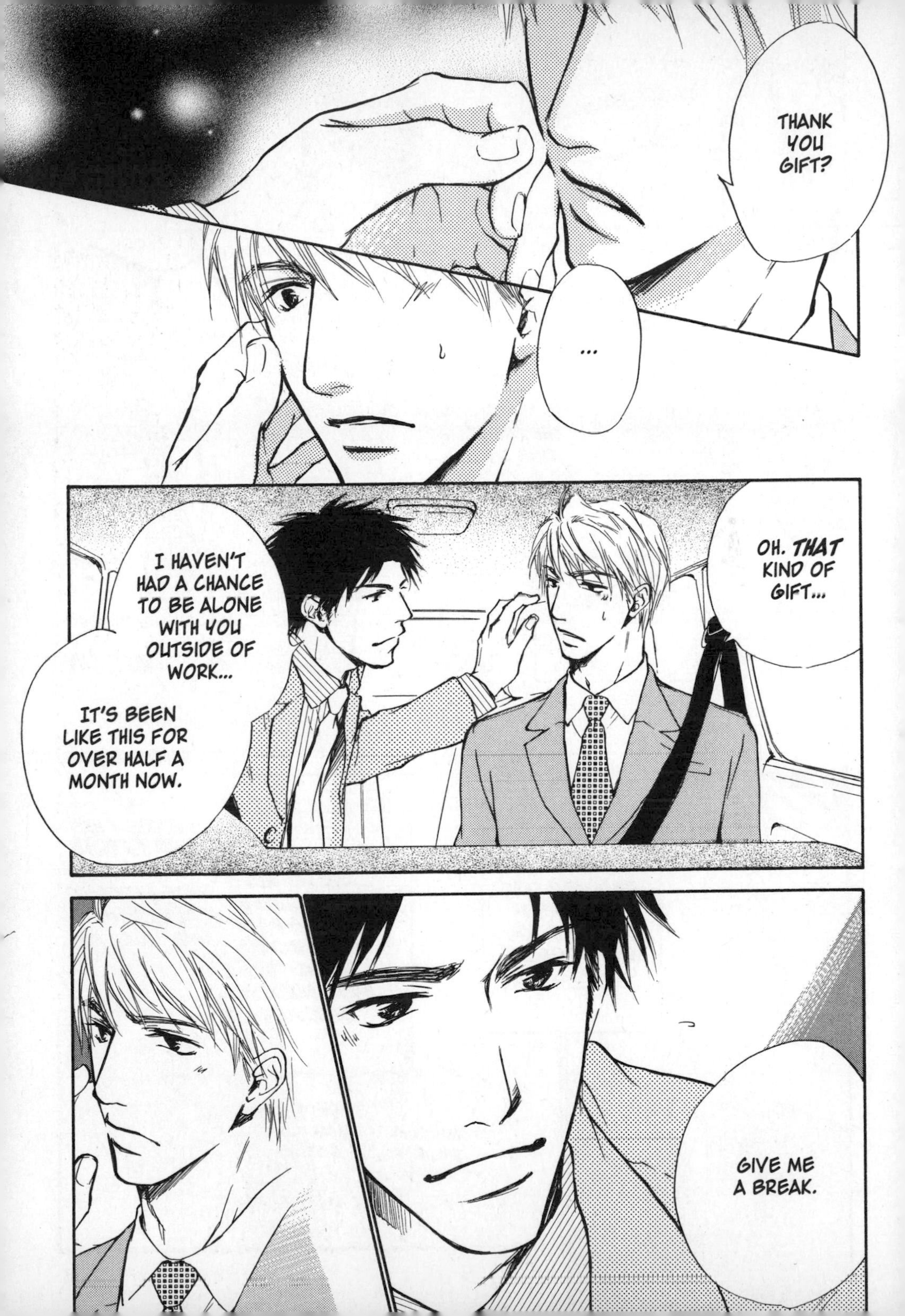
THANK YOU GIFT?
...
OH. *THAT* KIND OF GIFT...
I HAVEN'T HAD A CHANCE TO BE ALONE WITH YOU OUTSIDE OF WORK...
IT'S BEEN LIKE THIS FOR OVER HALF A MONTH NOW.
GIVE ME A BREAK.

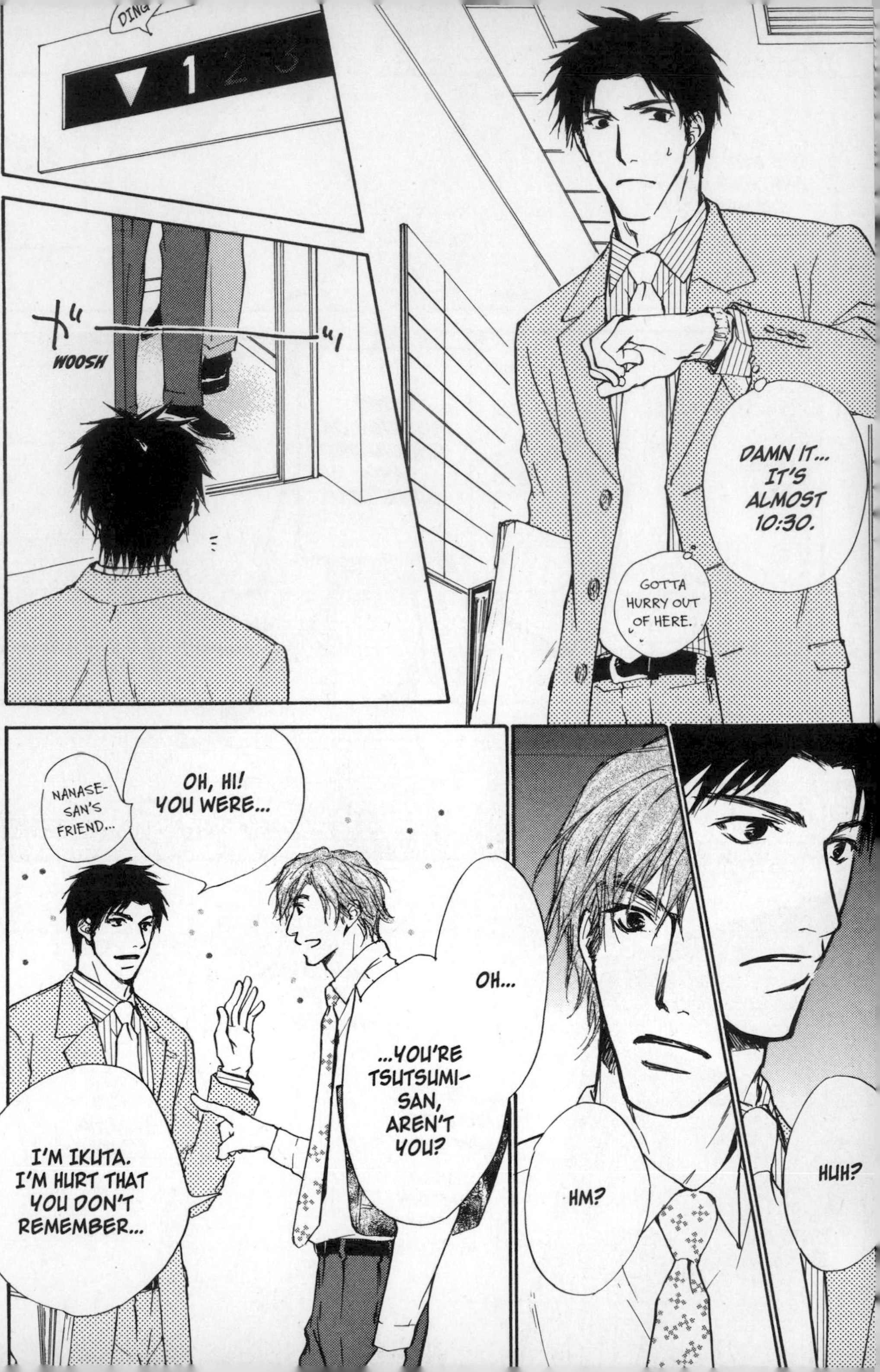
DAMN IT... IT'S ALMOST 10:30.
GOTTA HURRY OUT OF HERE.
DING
WOOSH
HUH?
HM?
OH...
...YOU'RE TSUTSUMI-SAN, AREN'T YOU?
OH, HI! YOU WERE...
NANASE-SAN'S FRIEND...
I'M IKUTA. I'M HURT THAT YOU DON'T REMEMBER...

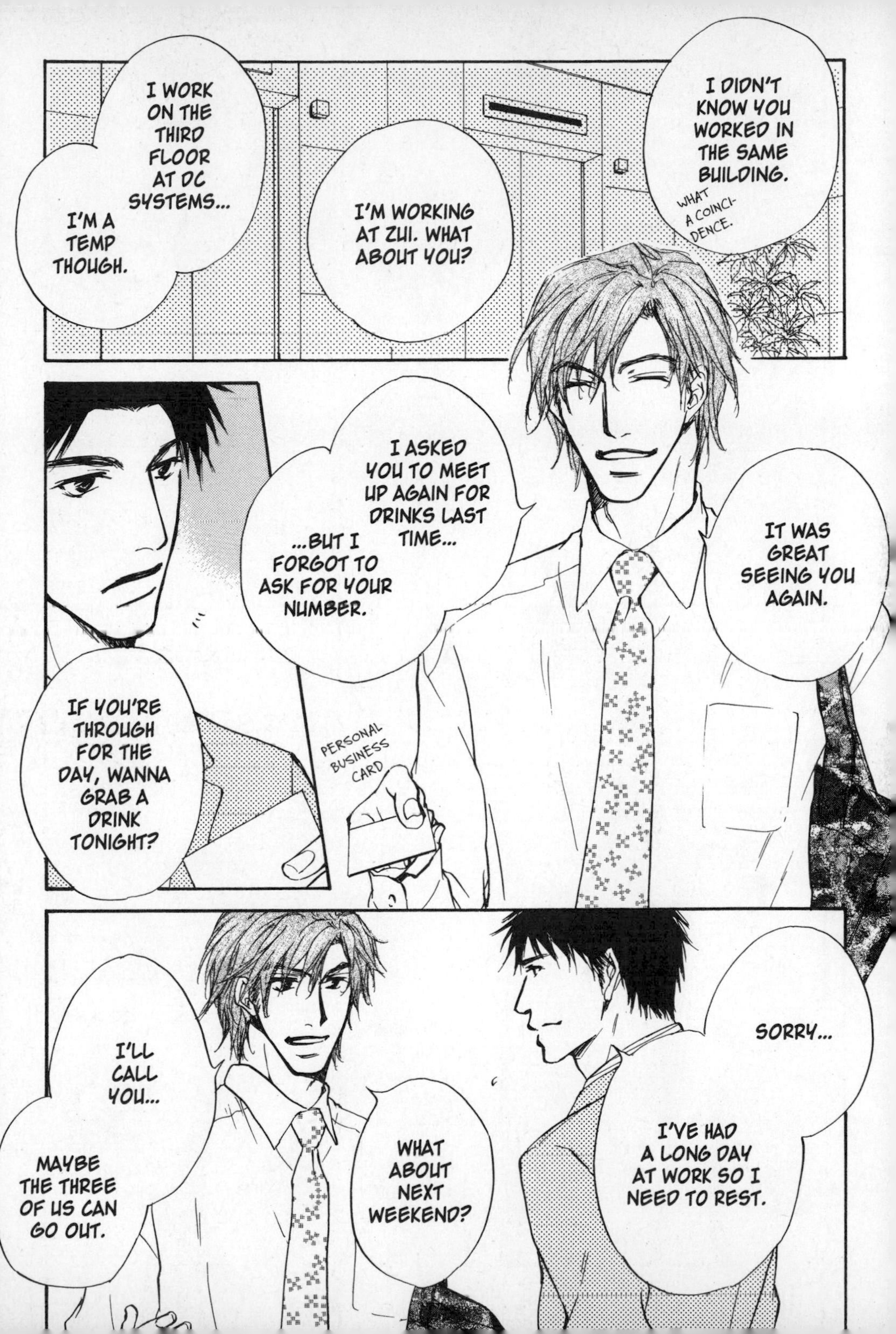
I DIDN'T KNOW YOU WORKED IN THE SAME BUILDING.
WHAT A COINCI-DENCE.
I'M WORKING AT ZUI. WHAT ABOUT YOU?
I WORK ON THE THIRD FLOOR AT DC SYSTEMS...
I'M A TEMP THOUGH.
IT WAS GREAT SEEING YOU AGAIN.
I ASKED YOU TO MEET UP AGAIN FOR DRINKS LAST TIME...
...BUT I FORGOT TO ASK FOR YOUR NUMBER.
PERSONAL BUSINESS CARD
IF YOU'RE THROUGH FOR THE DAY, WANNA GRAB A DRINK TONIGHT?
SORRY...
I'VE HAD A LONG DAY AT WORK SO I NEED TO REST.
WHAT ABOUT NEXT WEEKEND?
I'LL CALL YOU...
MAYBE THE THREE OF US CAN GO OUT.

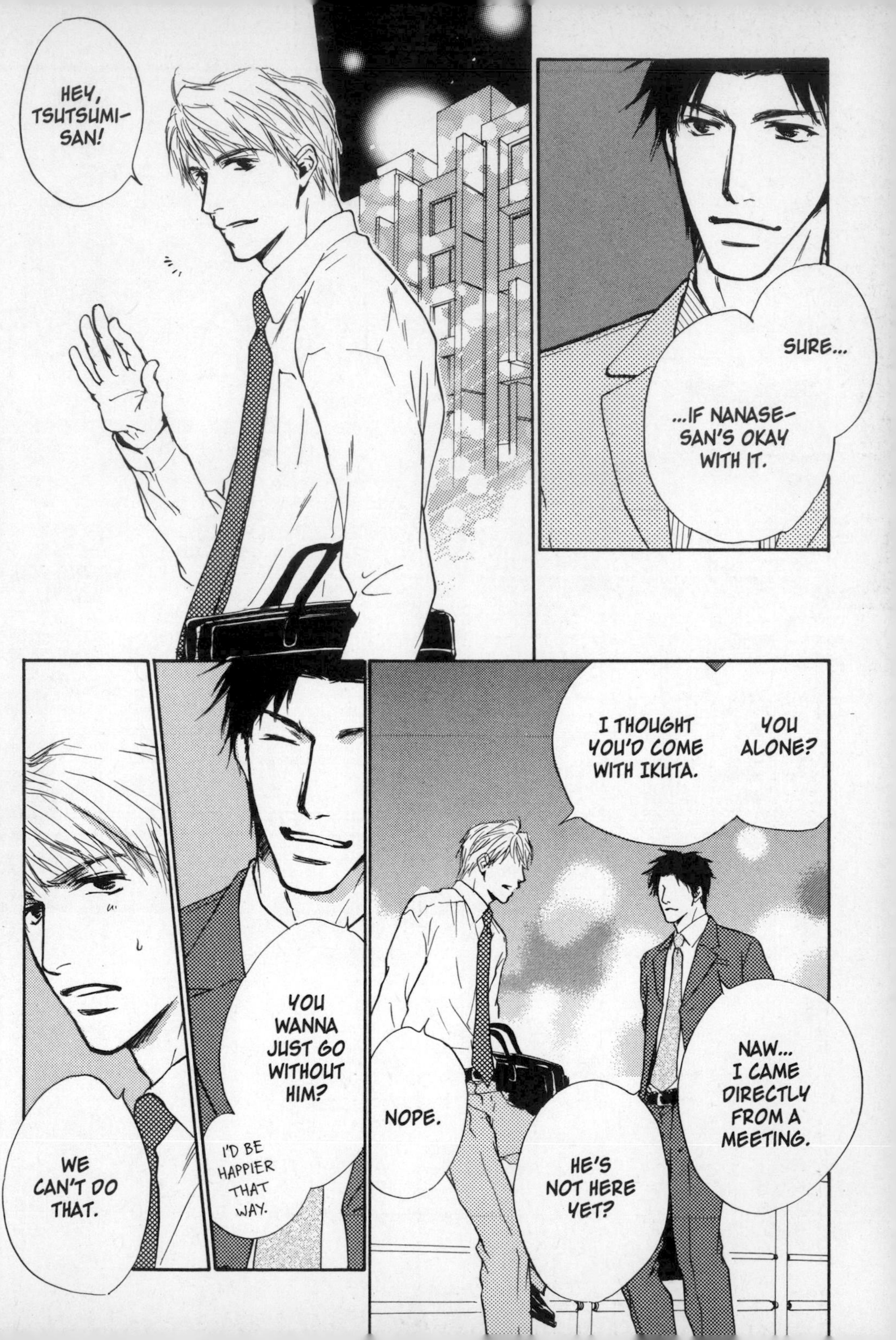
SURE...
...IF NANASE-SAN'S OKAY WITH IT.
HEY, TSUTSUMI-SAN!
YOU ALONE?
I THOUGHT YOU'D COME WITH IKUTA.
NAW... I CAME DIRECTLY FROM A MEETING.
HE'S NOT HERE YET?
NOPE.
YOU WANNA JUST GO WITHOUT HIM?
I'D BE HAPPIER THAT WAY.
WE CAN'T DO THAT.

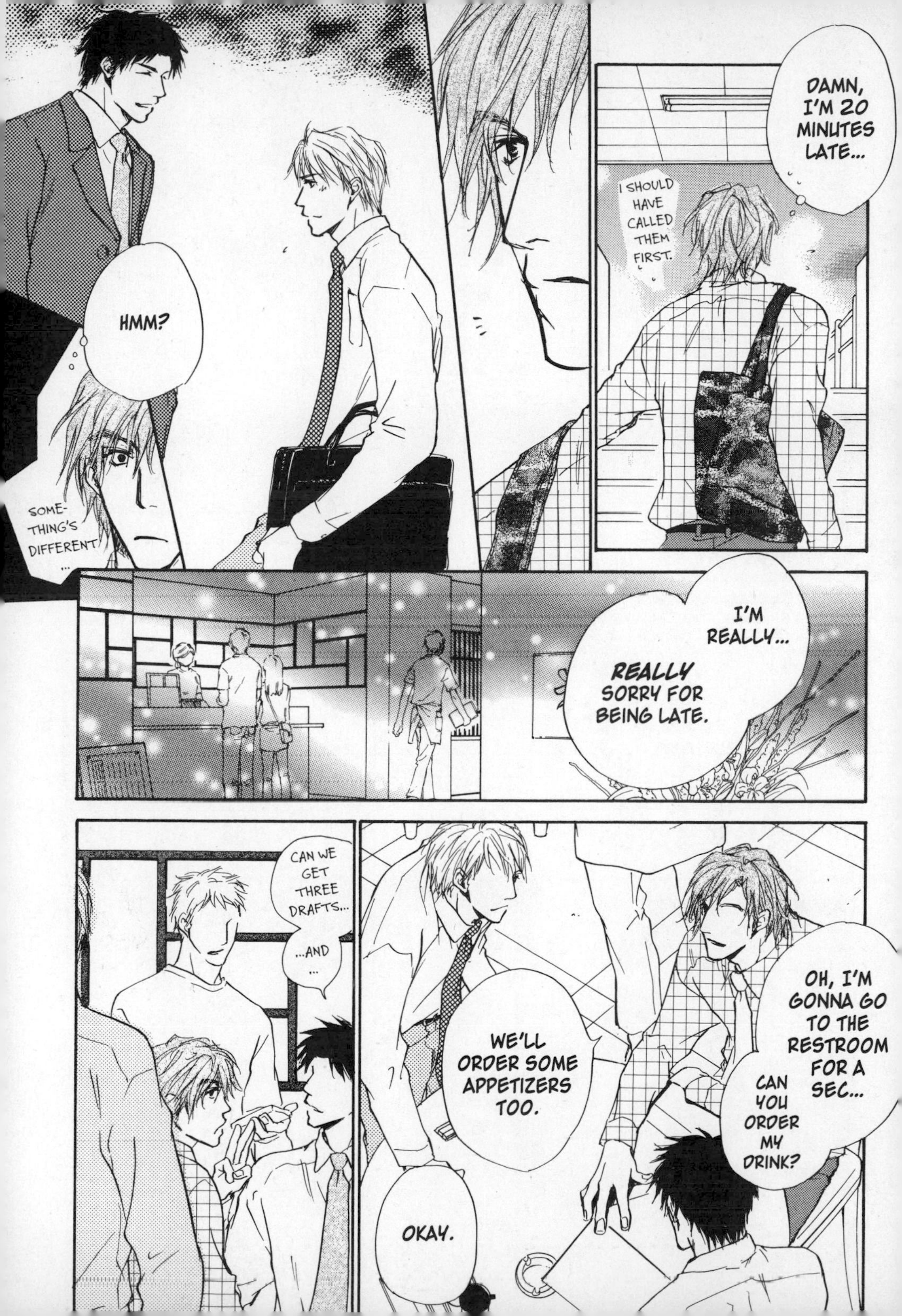
DAMN, I'M 20 MINUTES LATE...
I SHOULD HAVE CALLED THEM FIRST.
HMM?
SOME-THING'S DIFFERENT ...
I'M REALLY... REALLY SORRY FOR BEING LATE.
OH, I'M GONNA GO TO THE RESTROOM FOR A SEC...
CAN YOU ORDER MY DRINK?
WE'LL ORDER SOME APPETIZERS TOO.
OKAY.
CAN WE GET THREE DRAFTS...
...AND ...

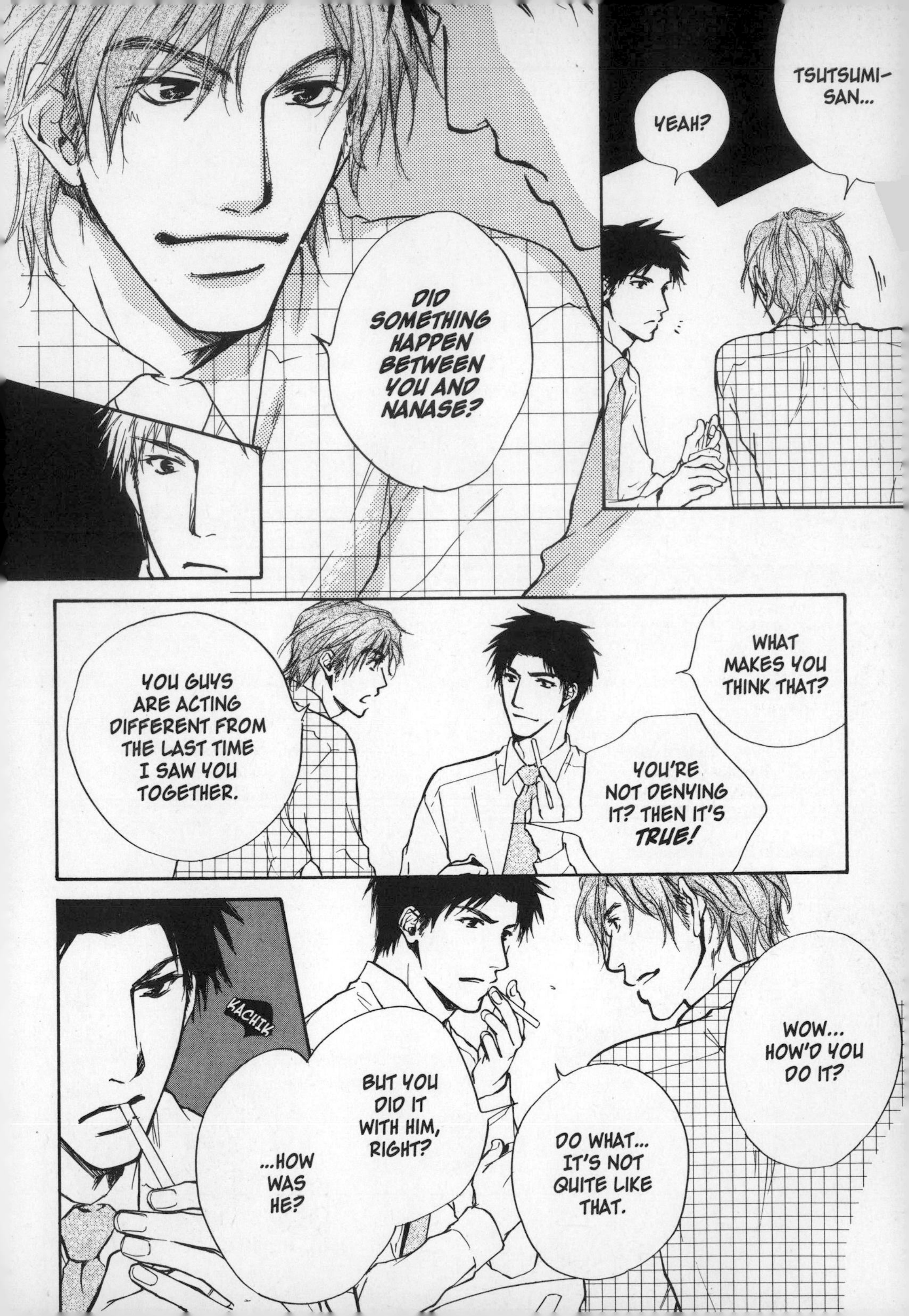
TSUTSUMI-SAN...
YEAH?
DID SOMETHING HAPPEN BETWEEN YOU AND NANASE?
WHAT MAKES YOU THINK THAT?
YOU'RE NOT DENYING IT? THEN IT'S *TRUE!*
YOU GUYS ARE ACTING DIFFERENT FROM THE LAST TIME I SAW YOU TOGETHER.
WOW... HOW'D YOU DO IT?
DO WHAT... IT'S NOT QUITE LIKE THAT.
BUT YOU DID IT WITH HIM, RIGHT?
...HOW WAS HE?
KACHIK

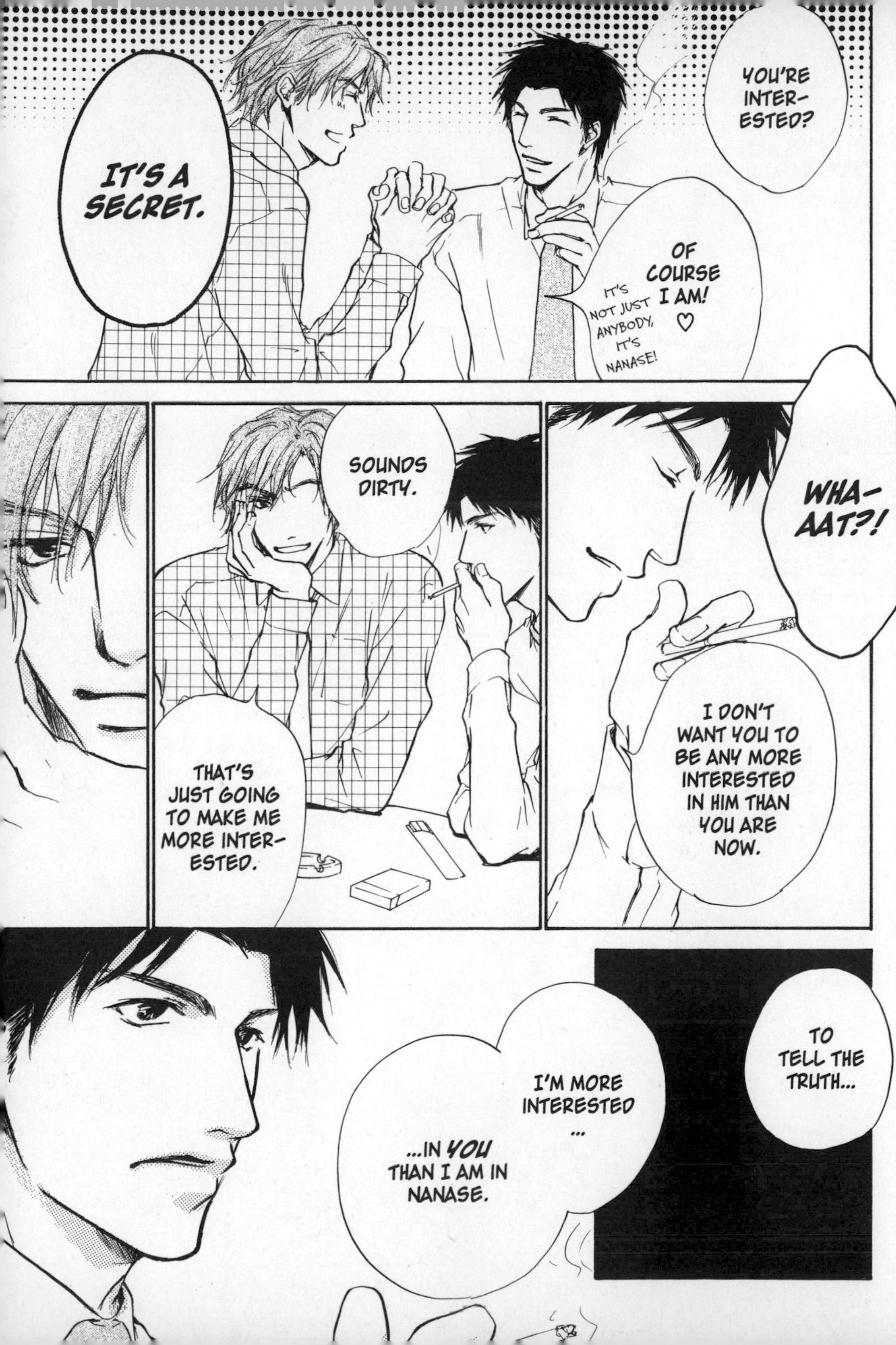
YOU'RE INTER-ESTED?
OF COURSE I AM! ♡
IT'S NOT JUST ANYBODY, IT'S NANASE!
IT'S A SECRET.
WHA-AAT?!
I DON'T WANT YOU TO BE ANY MORE INTERESTED IN HIM THAN YOU ARE NOW.
SOUNDS DIRTY.
THAT'S JUST GOING TO MAKE ME MORE INTER-ESTED.
TO TELL THE TRUTH...
I'M MORE INTERESTED ...
...IN YOU THAN I AM IN NANASE.

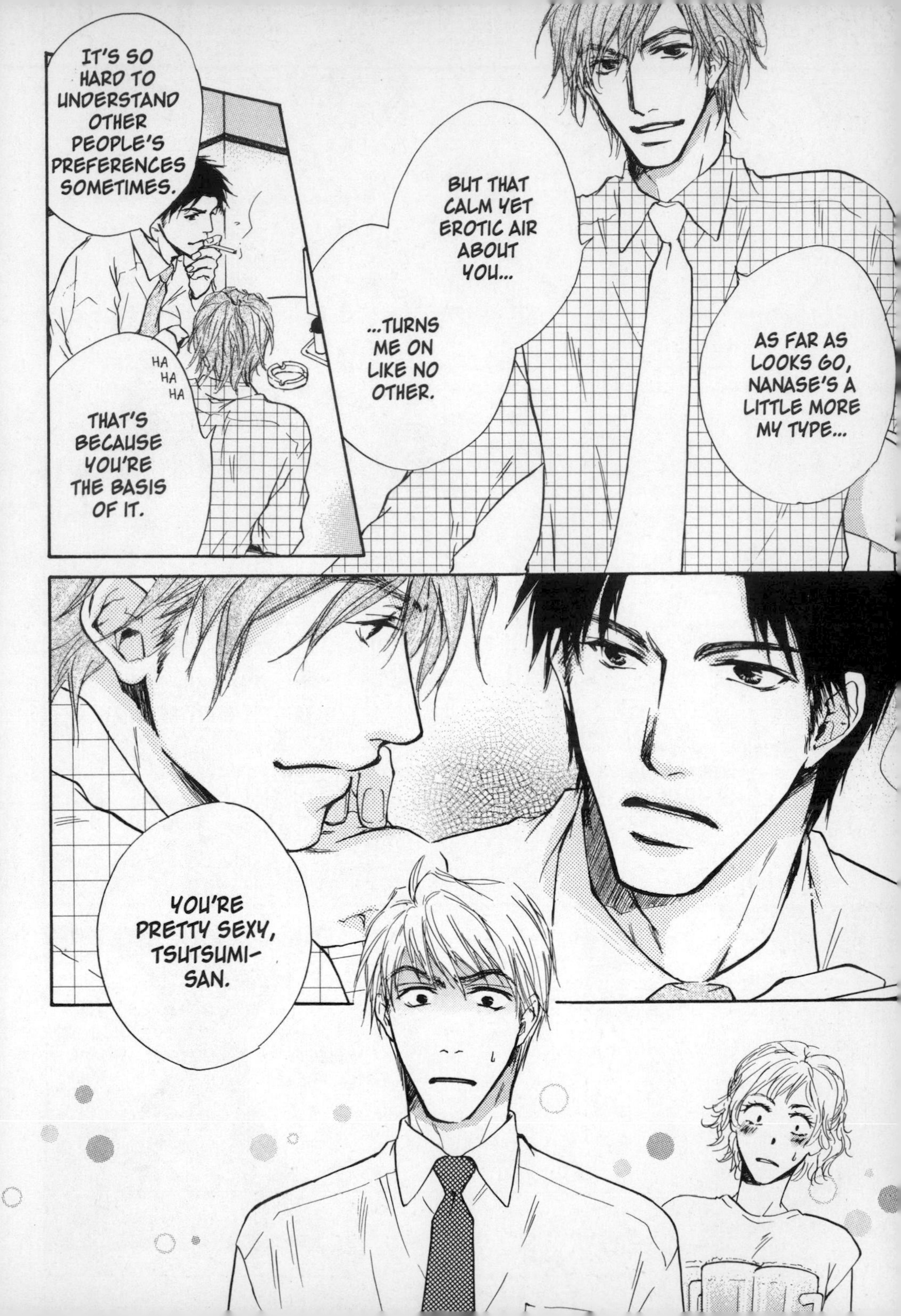
AS FAR AS LOOKS GO, NANASE'S A LITTLE MORE MY TYPE...
BUT THAT CALM YET EROTIC AIR ABOUT YOU...
...TURNS ME ON LIKE NO OTHER.
IT'S SO HARD TO UNDERSTAND OTHER PEOPLE'S PREFERENCES SOMETIMES.
HA HA HA
THAT'S BECAUSE YOU'RE THE BASIS OF IT.
YOU'RE PRETTY SEXY, TSUTSUMI-SAN.

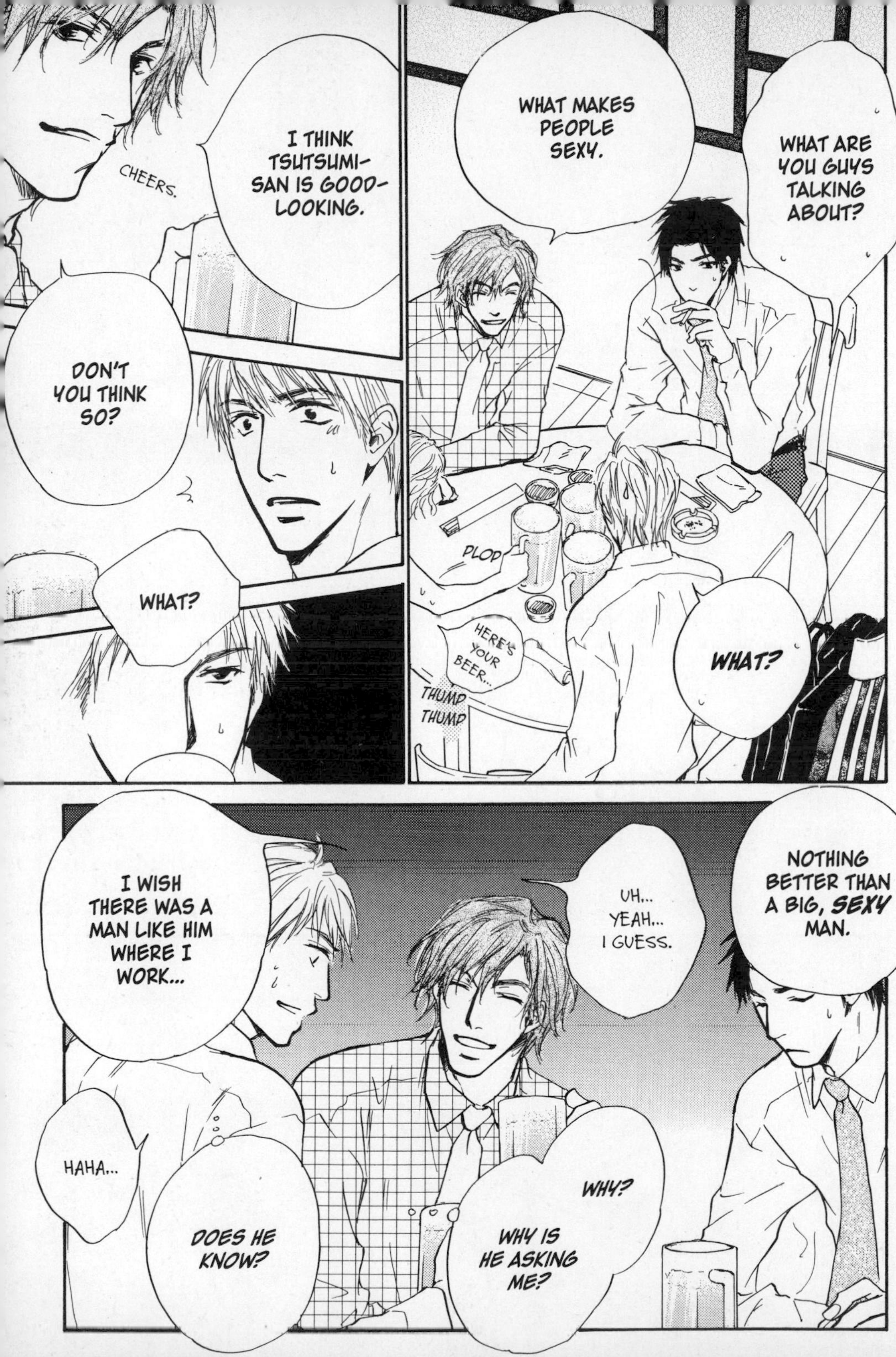
WHAT ARE YOU GUYS TALKING ABOUT?
WHAT MAKES PEOPLE SEXY.
PLOP
WHAT?
HERE'S YOUR BEER...
THUMP THUMP
CHEERS.
I THINK TSUTSUMI-SAN IS GOOD-LOOKING.
DON'T YOU THINK SO?
WHAT?
NOTHING BETTER THAN A BIG, SEXY MAN.
UH... YEAH... I GUESS.
I WISH THERE WAS A MAN LIKE HIM WHERE I WORK...
WHY?
WHY IS HE ASKING ME?
DOES HE KNOW?
HAHA...

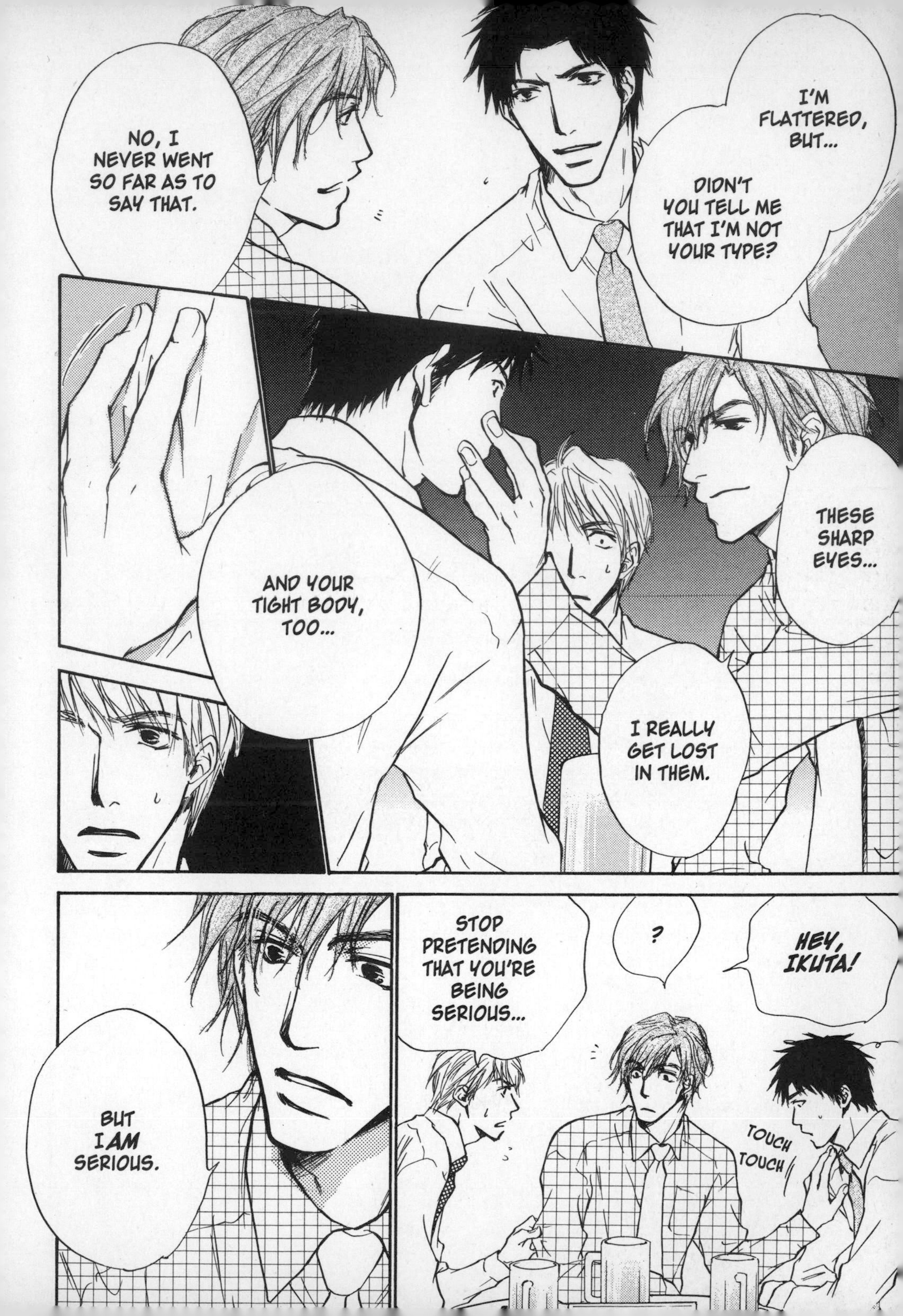
I'M FLATTERED, BUT...
DIDN'T YOU TELL ME THAT I'M NOT YOUR TYPE?
NO, I NEVER WENT SO FAR AS TO SAY THAT.
THESE SHARP EYES...
AND YOUR TIGHT BODY, TOO...
I REALLY GET LOST IN THEM.
HEY, IKUTA!
?
STOP PRETENDING THAT YOU'RE BEING SERIOUS...
TOUCH TOUCH
BUT I AM SERIOUS.

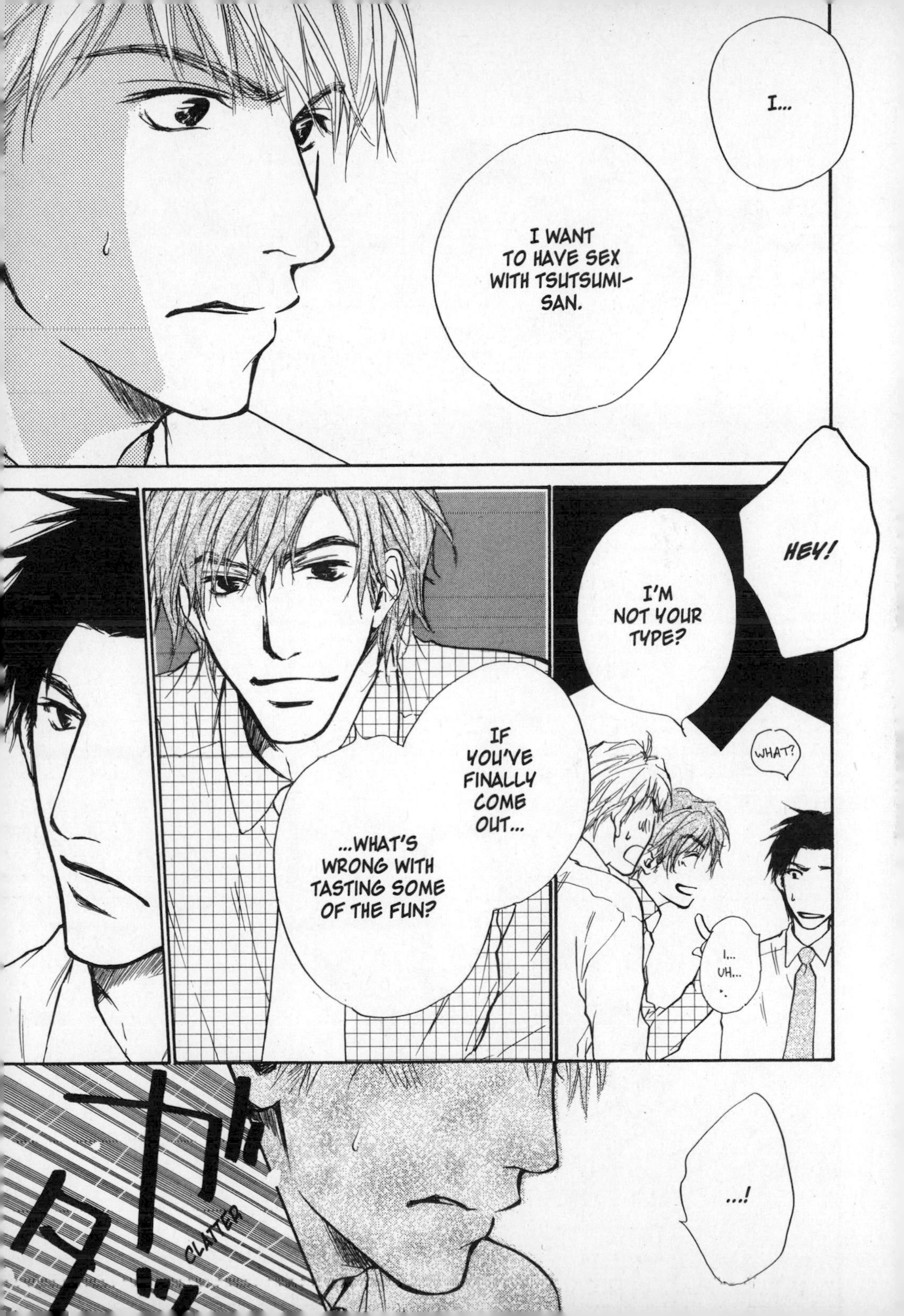
I...
I WANT TO HAVE SEX WITH TSUTSUMI-SAN.
HEY!
I'M NOT YOUR TYPE?
WHAT?
I... UH...
IF YOU'VE FINALLY COME OUT...
...WHAT'S WRONG WITH TASTING SOME OF THE FUN?
...!
CLATER

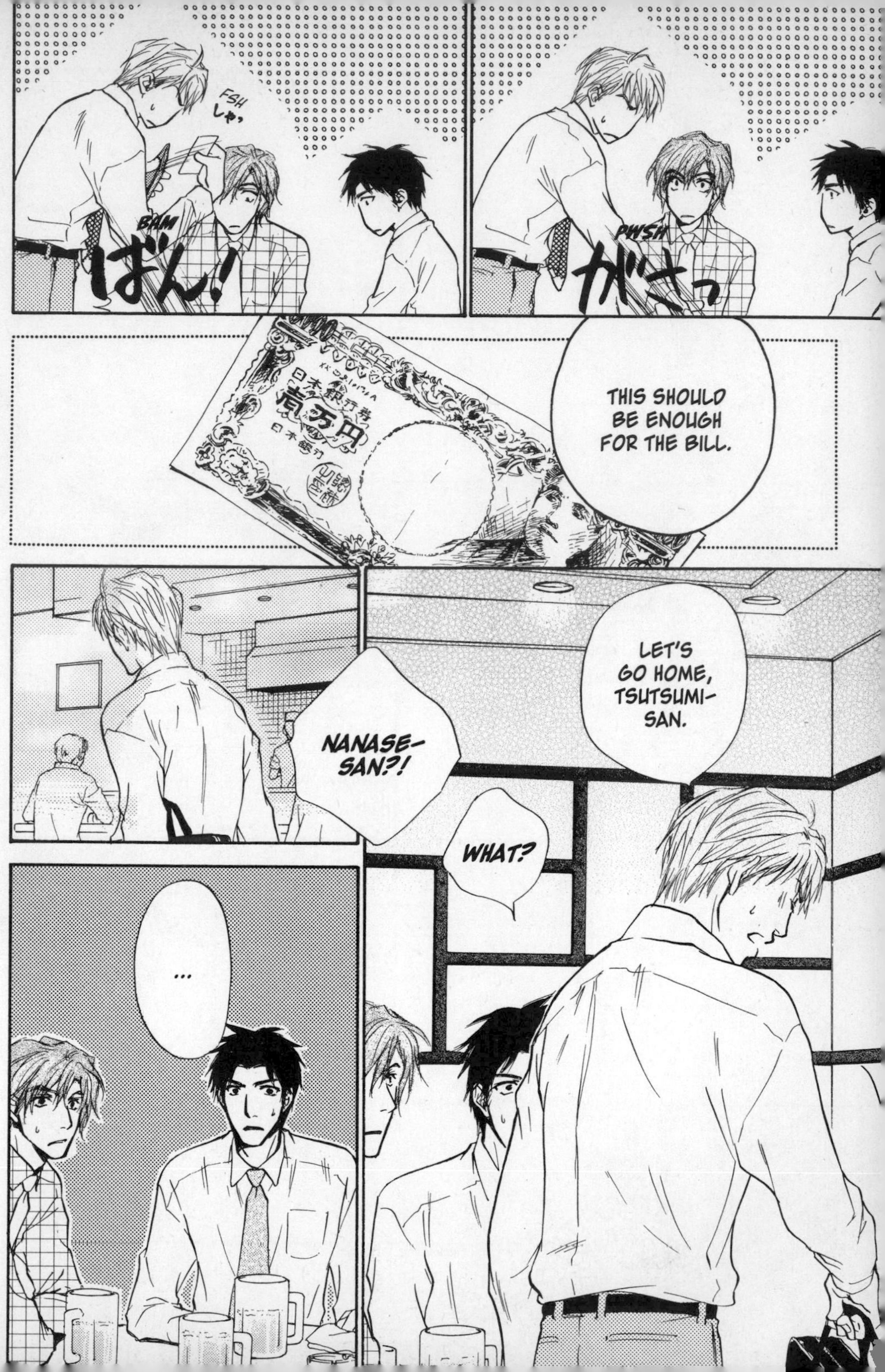
PWSH
がさっ
FSH
しゃっ
BAM
ばん!
THIS SHOULD BE ENOUGH FOR THE BILL.
LET'S GO HOME, TSUTSUMI-SAN.
NANASE-SAN?!
WHAT?
...

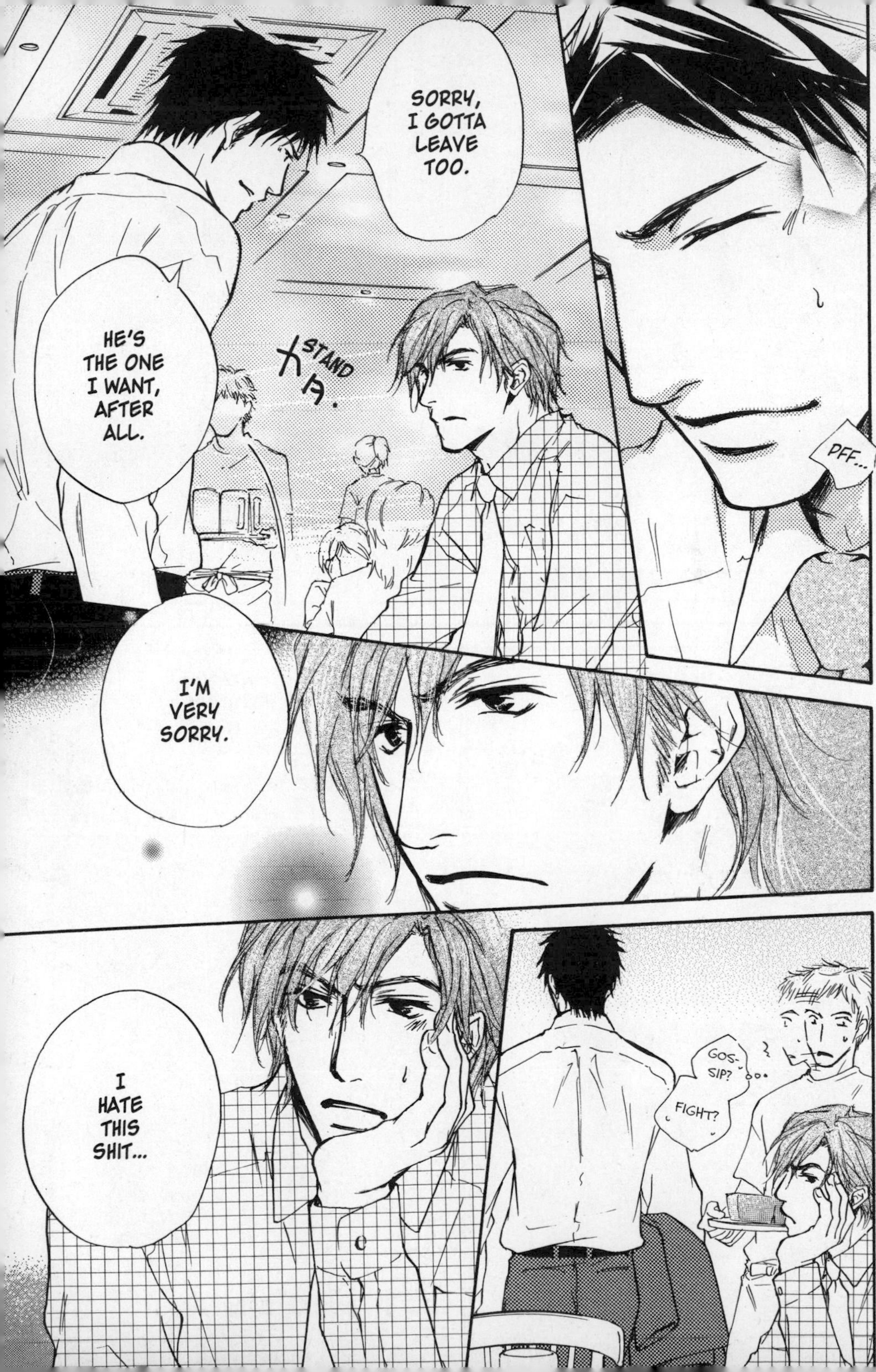
PFF...
SORRY, I GOTTA LEAVE TOO.
STAND
HE'S THE ONE I WANT, AFTER ALL.
I'M VERY SORRY.
GOS-SIP?
FIGHT?
I HATE THIS SHIT...

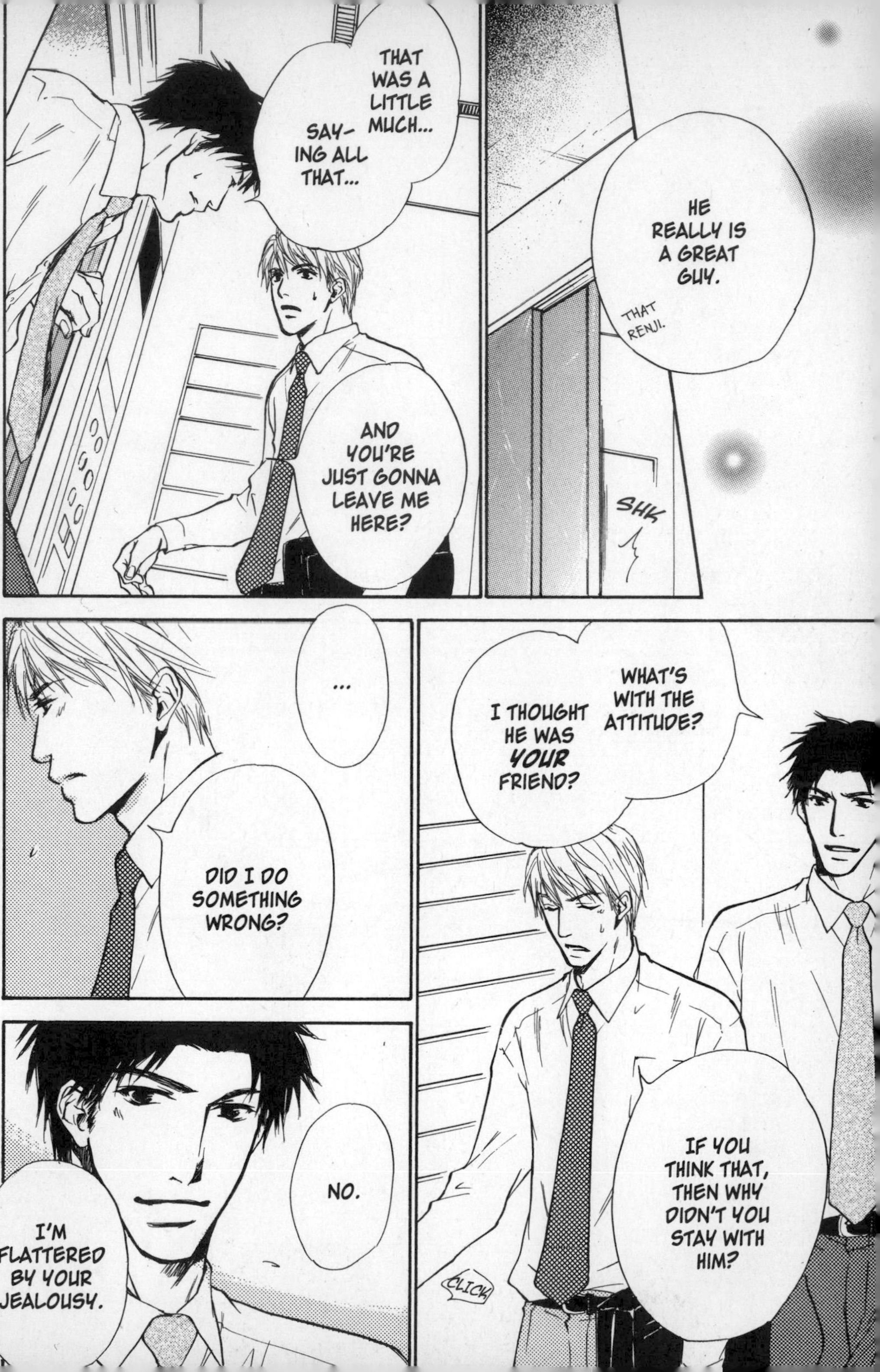
HE REALLY IS A GREAT GUY.
THAT RENJI.
SHK
THAT WAS A LITTLE MUCH...
SAY-ING ALL THAT...
AND YOU'RE JUST GONNA LEAVE ME HERE?
WHAT'S WITH THE ATTITUDE?
I THOUGHT HE WAS *YOUR* FRIEND?
IF YOU THINK THAT, THEN WHY DIDN'T YOU STAY WITH HIM?
CLICK
...
DID I DO SOMETHING WRONG?
NO.
I'M FLATTERED BY YOUR JEALOUSY.

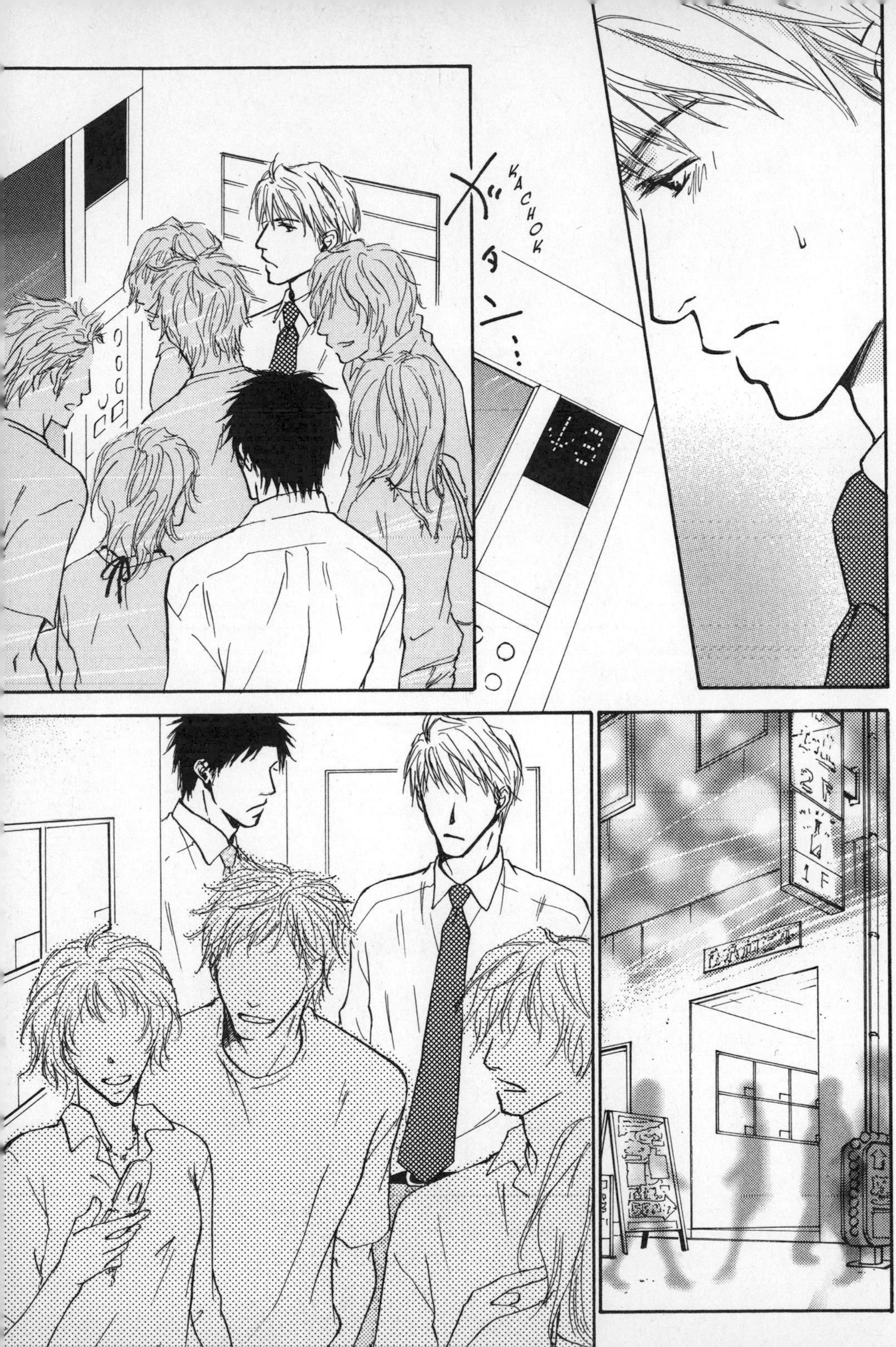
KACHOK
2F
1F

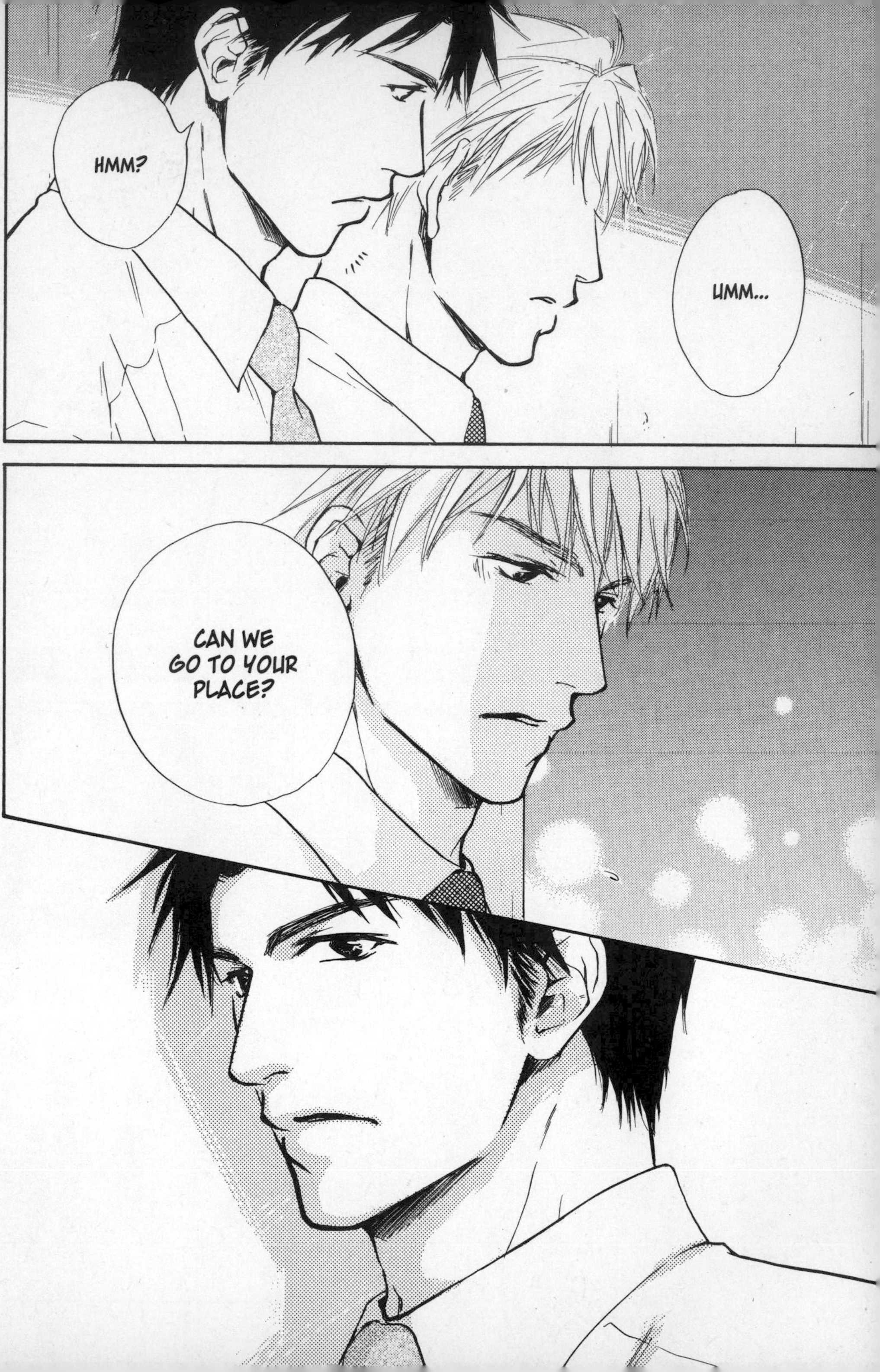
UMM...
HMM?
CAN WE GO TO YOUR PLACE?

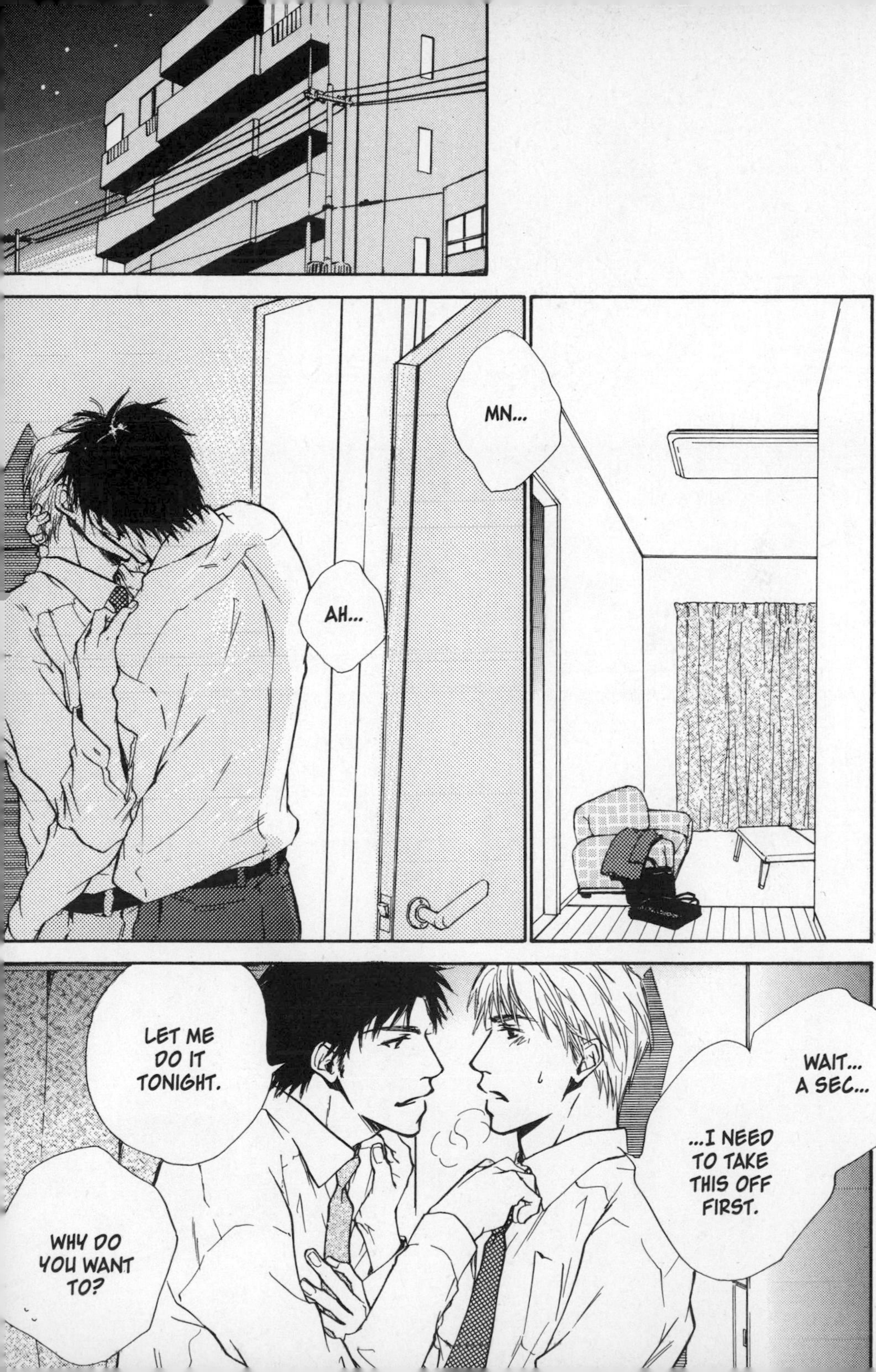
MN...
AH...
AH...
WAIT... A SEC...
...I NEED TO TAKE THIS OFF FIRST.
LET ME DO IT TONIGHT.
WHY DO YOU WANT TO?

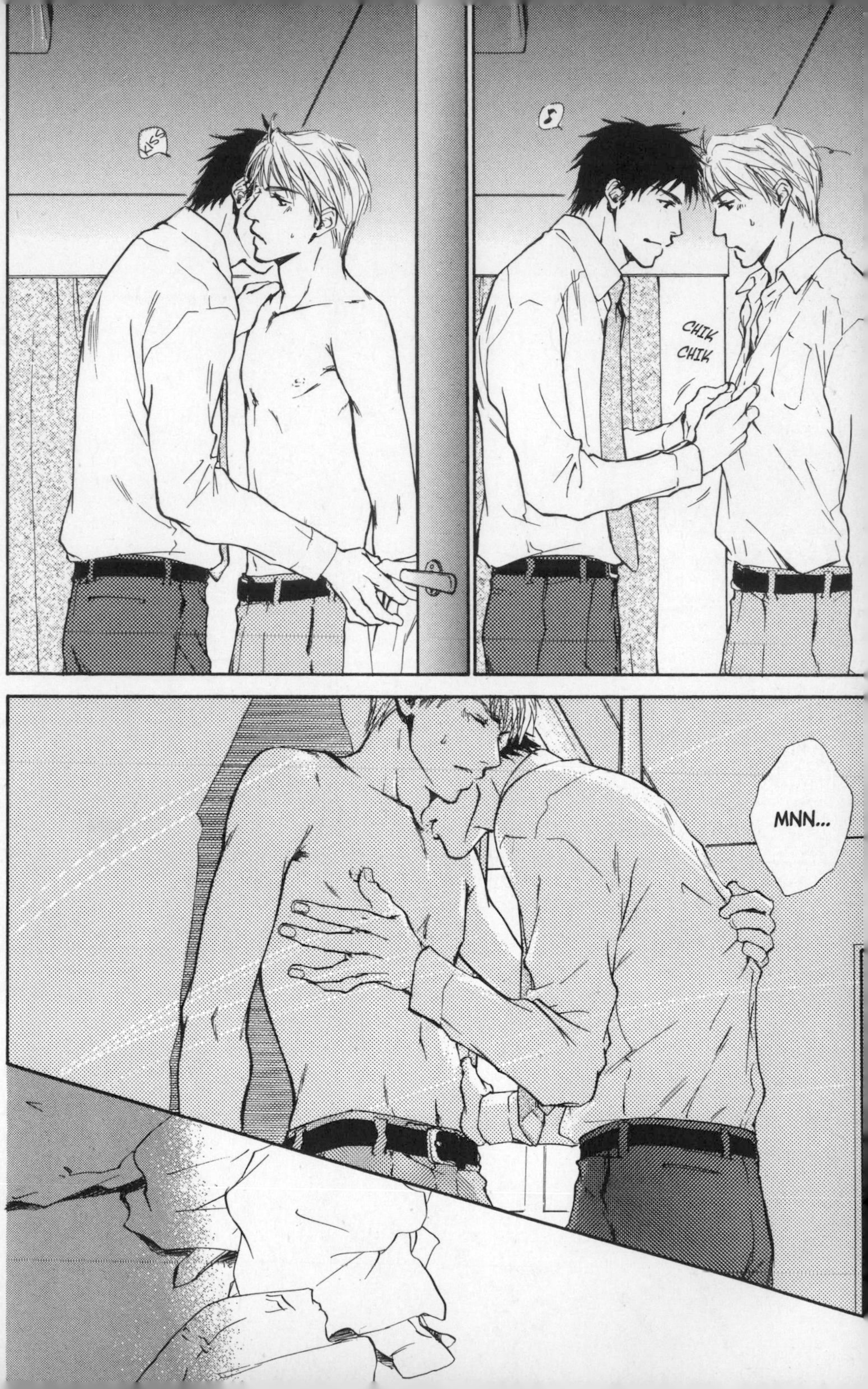
♪
CHIK CHIK
KISS
MNN...

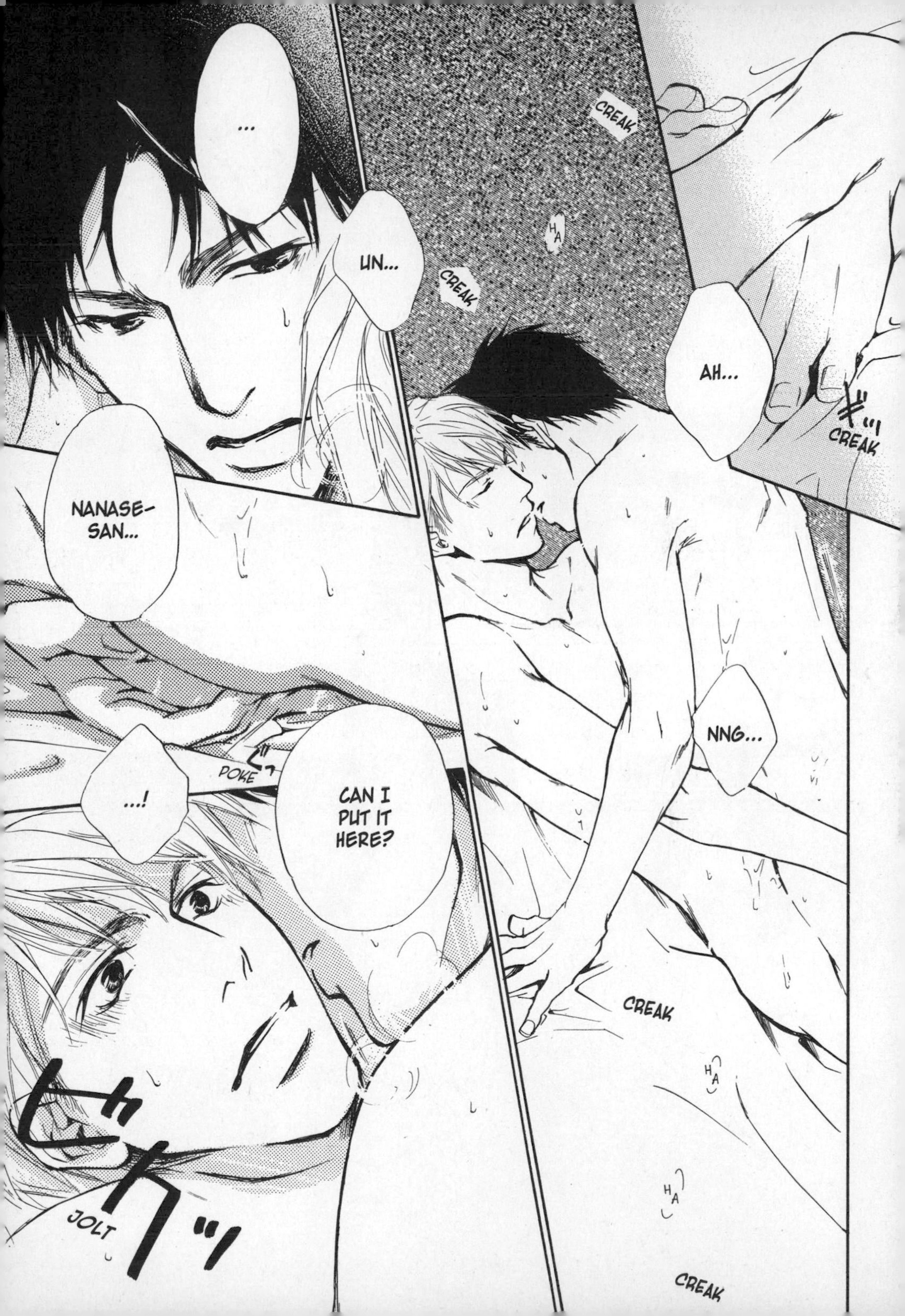
AH...
CREAK
CREAK
HA
CREAK
...
UN...
NNG...
CREAK
HA
HA
CREAK
NANASE-SAN...
CAN I PUT IT HERE?
POKE
...!
JOLT

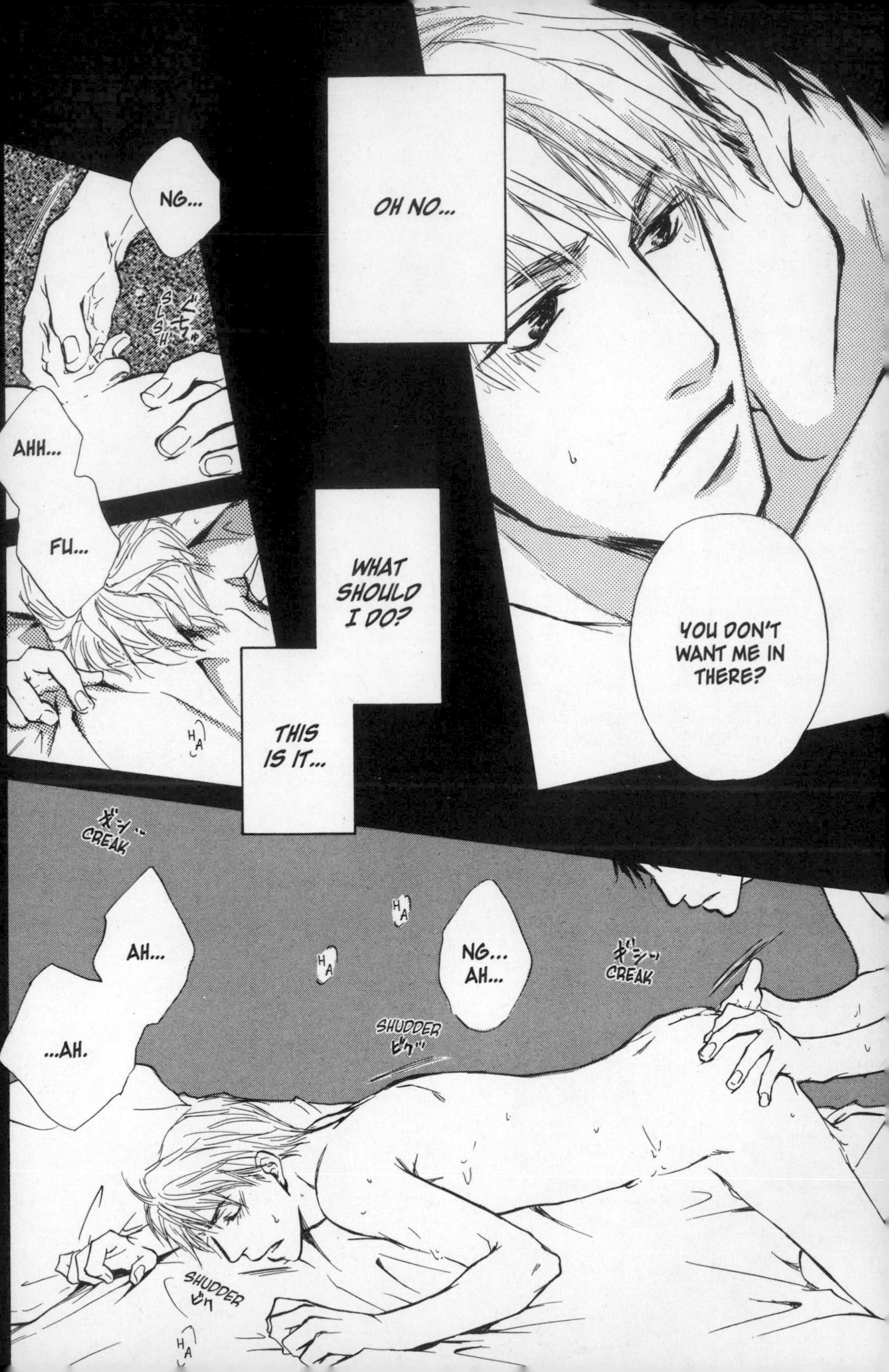
OH NO...
YOU DON'T WANT ME IN THERE?
NG...
SLSH
AHH...
WHAT SHOULD I DO?
FU...
HA
THIS IS IT...
CREAK
CREAK
HA
NG... AH...
HA
AH...
SHUDDER
...AH.
SHUDDER
HA

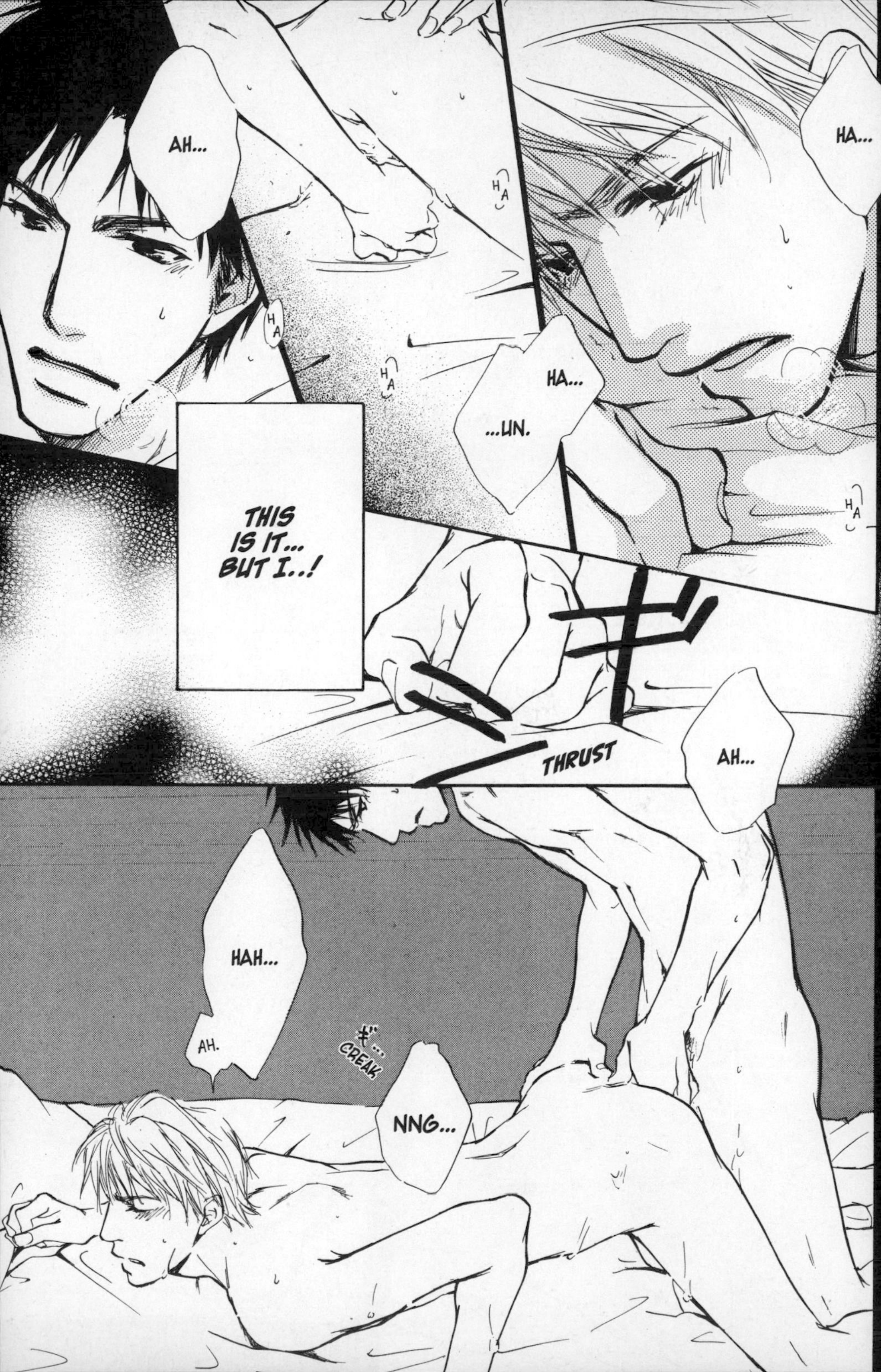
HA...
HA...
...UN.
HA
HA
HA
AH...
HA
THRUST
AH...
THIS IS IT... BUT I..!
HAH...
AH.
ギ... CREAK
NNG...

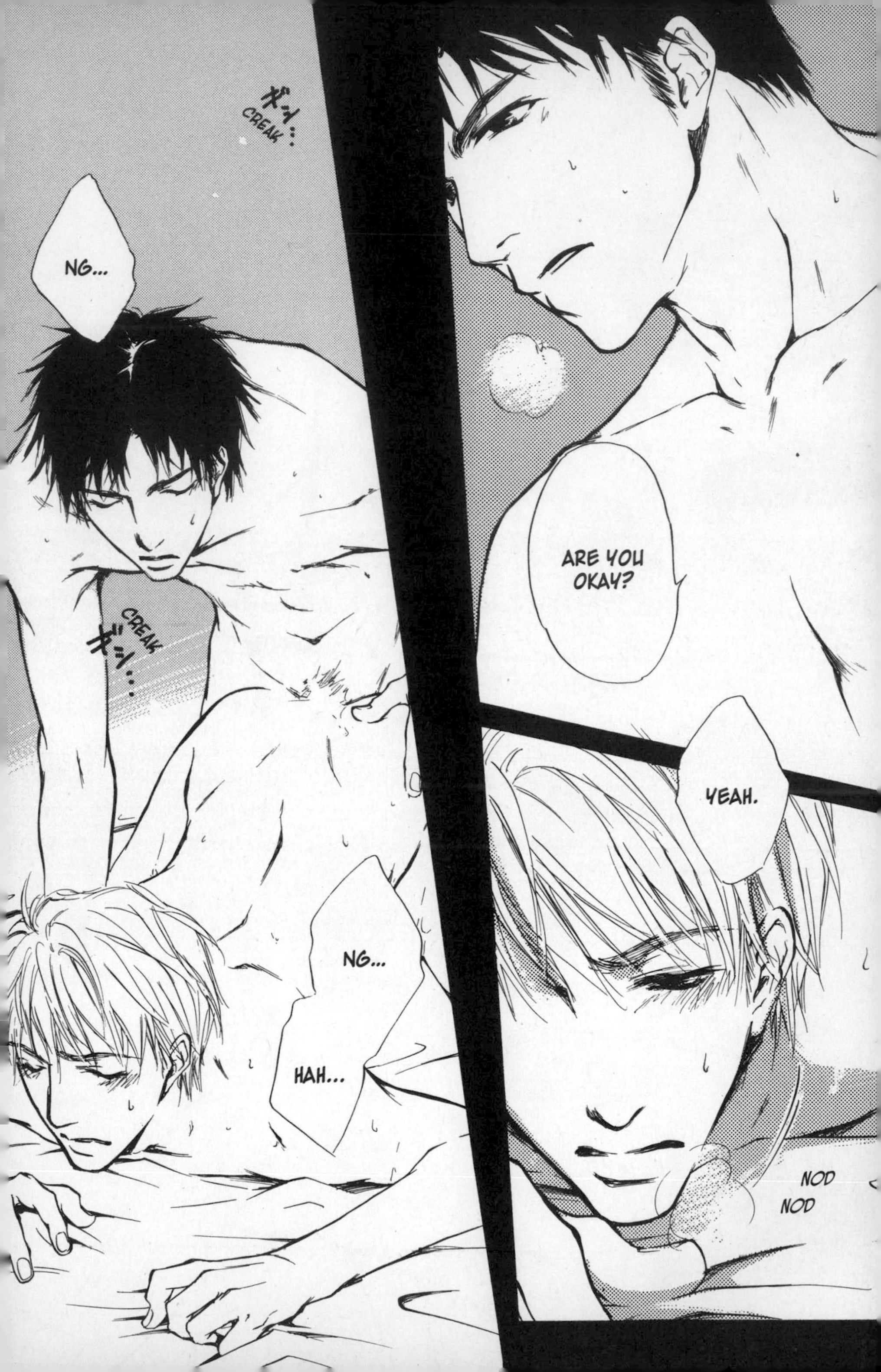
ARE YOU OKAY?
YEAH.
NOD NOD
ギシ…
CREAK
NG...
CREAK
ギシ…
NG...
HAH...

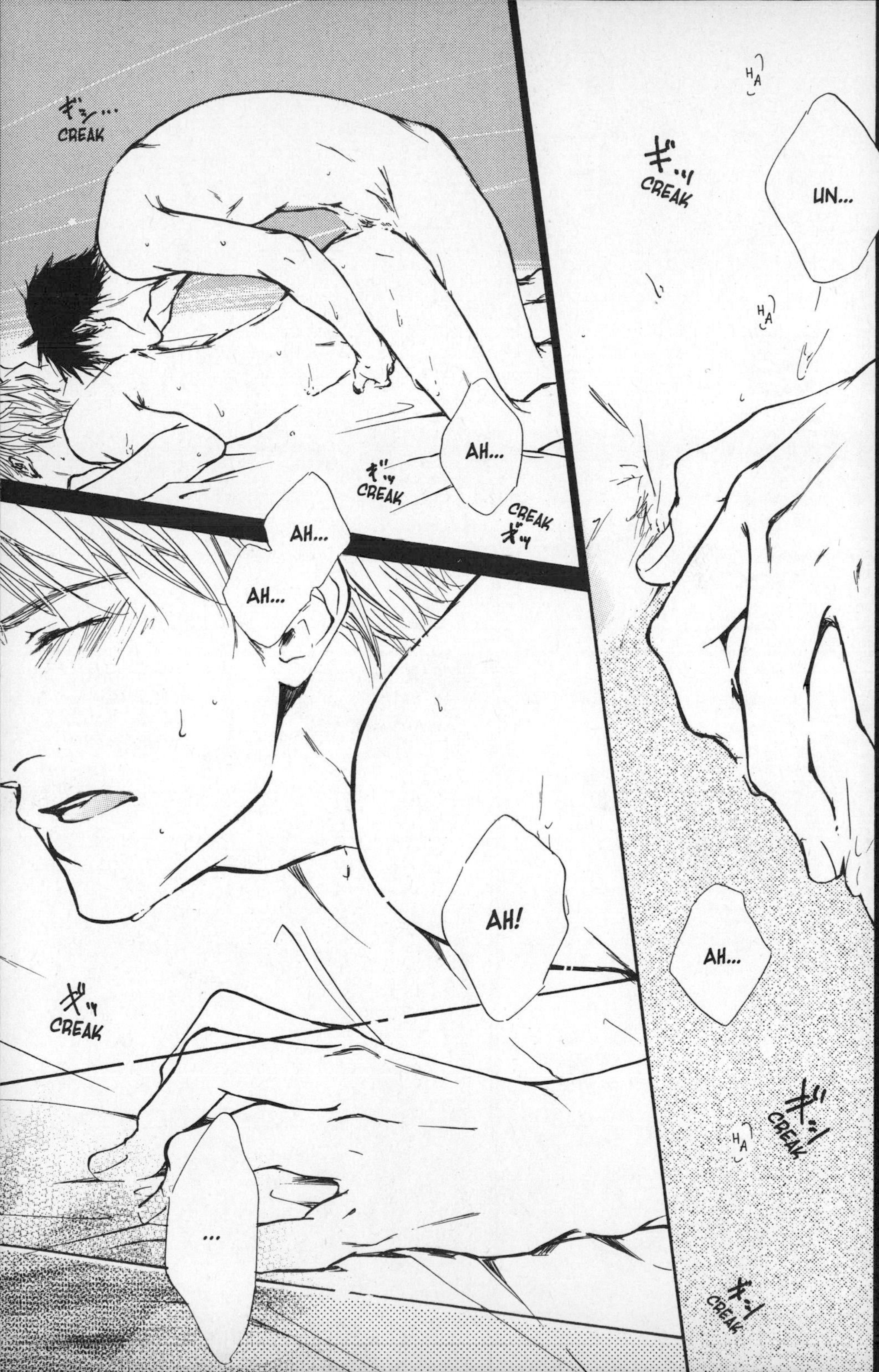
HA
ギッ
CREAK
UN...
HA
AH...
ギッ
CREAK
HA
ギッ
CREAK
ギシ…
CREAK
CREAK
ギッ
AH...
ギッ
CREAK
AH...
AH...
AH!
ギッ
CREAK
...

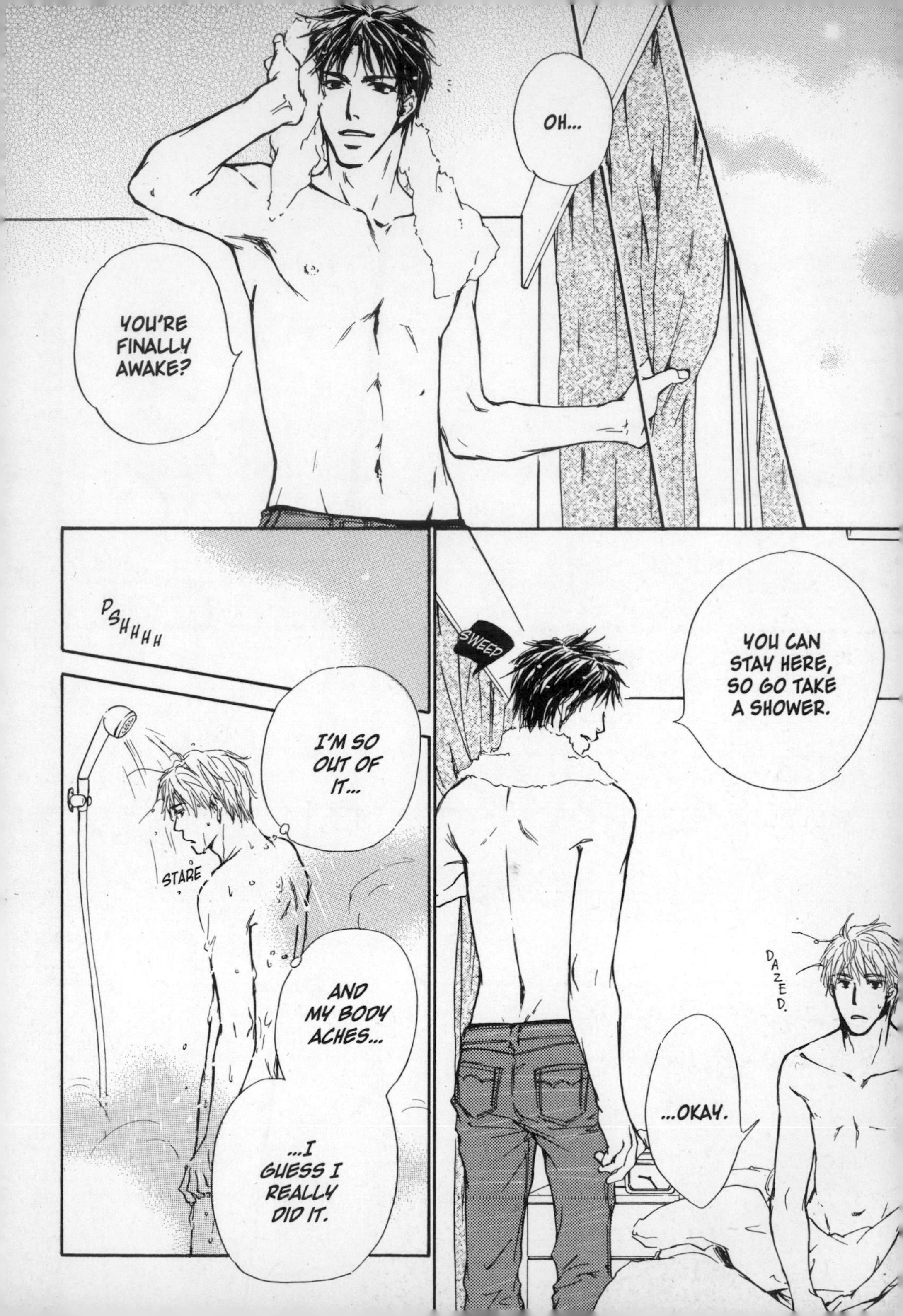
OH...
YOU'RE FINALLY AWAKE?
SWEEP
YOU CAN STAY HERE, SO GO TAKE A SHOWER.
DAZED.
...OKAY.
PSHHHHH
I'M SO OUT OF IT...
STARE
AND MY BODY ACHES...
...I GUESS I REALLY DID IT.

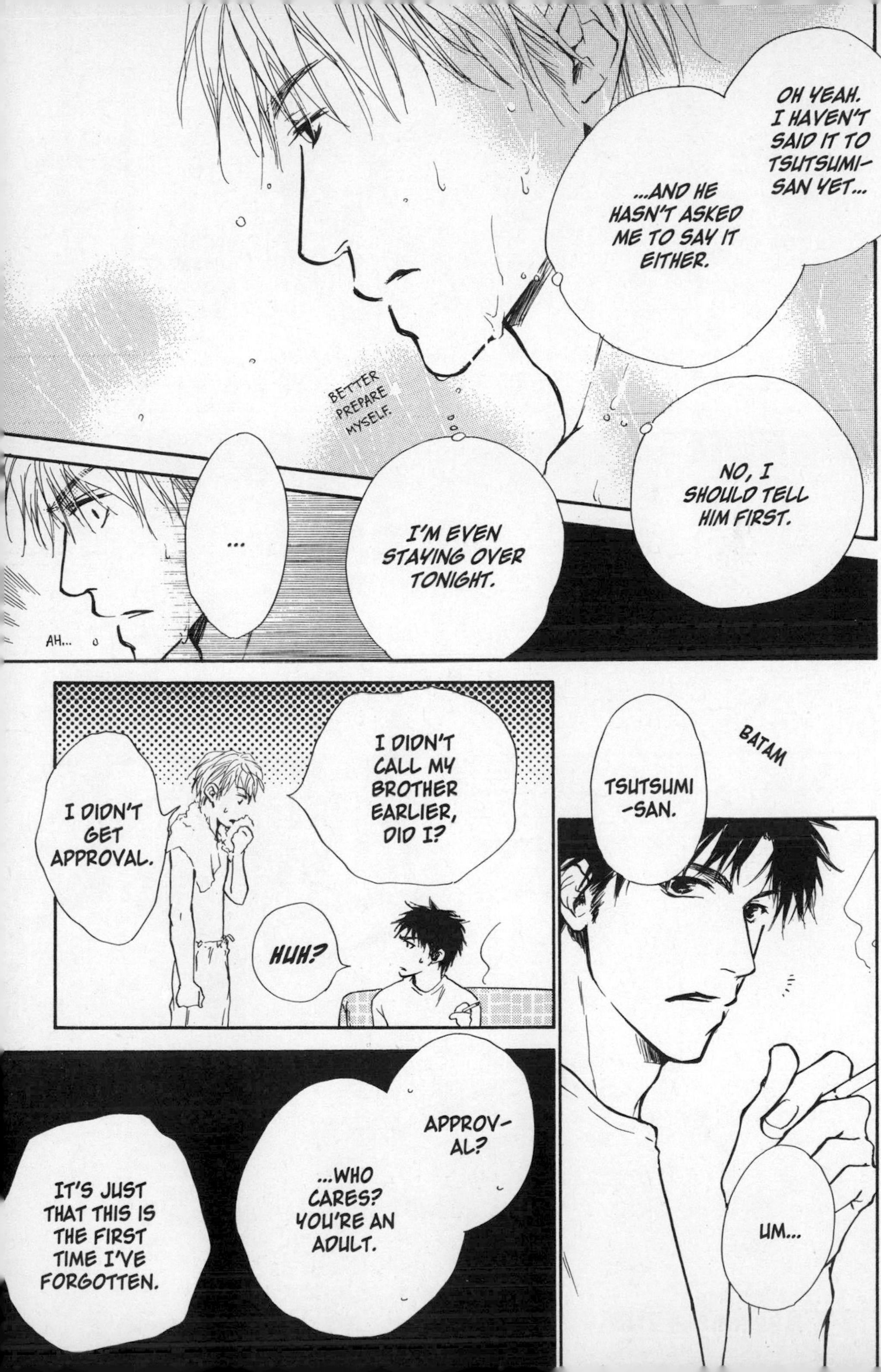
OH YEAH. I HAVEN'T SAID IT TO TSUTSUMI-SAN YET...
...AND HE HASN'T ASKED ME TO SAY IT EITHER.
BETTER PREPARE MYSELF.
NO, I SHOULD TELL HIM FIRST.
I'M EVEN STAYING OVER TONIGHT.
...
AH...
BATAM
TSUTSUMI-SAN.
UM...
I DIDN'T CALL MY BROTHER EARLIER, DID I?
I DIDN'T GET APPROVAL.
HUH?
APPROVAL?
...WHO CARES? YOU'RE AN ADULT.
IT'S JUST THAT THIS IS THE FIRST TIME I'VE FORGOTTEN.

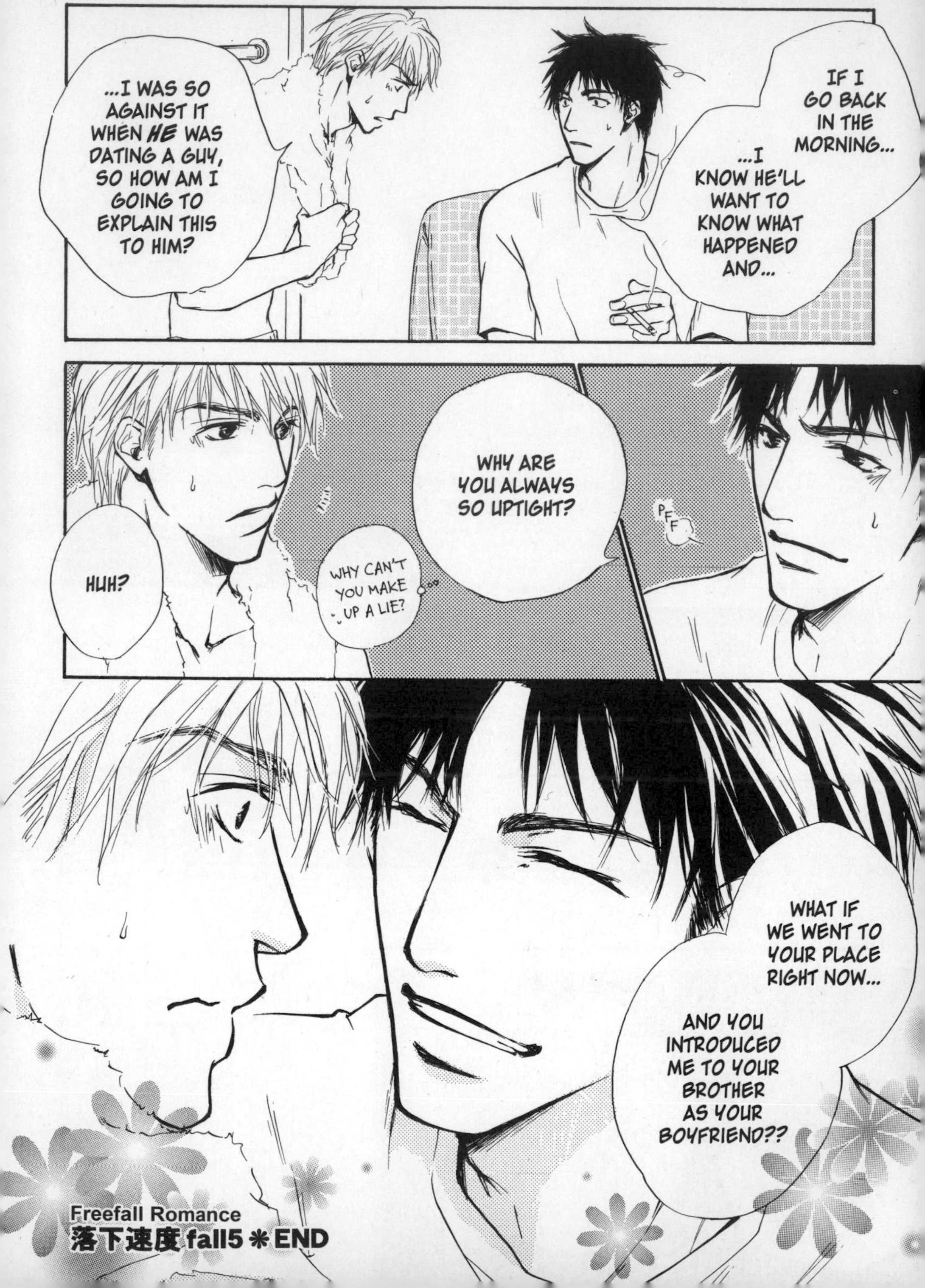
IF I GO BACK IN THE MORNING...
...I KNOW HE'LL WANT TO KNOW WHAT HAPPENED AND...
...I WAS SO AGAINST IT WHEN HE WAS DATING A GUY, SO HOW AM I GOING TO EXPLAIN THIS TO HIM?
PFF
WHY ARE YOU ALWAYS SO UPTIGHT?
WHY CAN'T YOU MAKE UP A LIE?
HUH?
WHAT IF WE WENT TO YOUR PLACE RIGHT NOW...
AND YOU INTRODUCED ME TO YOUR BROTHER AS YOUR BOYFRIEND??

Freefall Romance
落下速度 fall5 * END

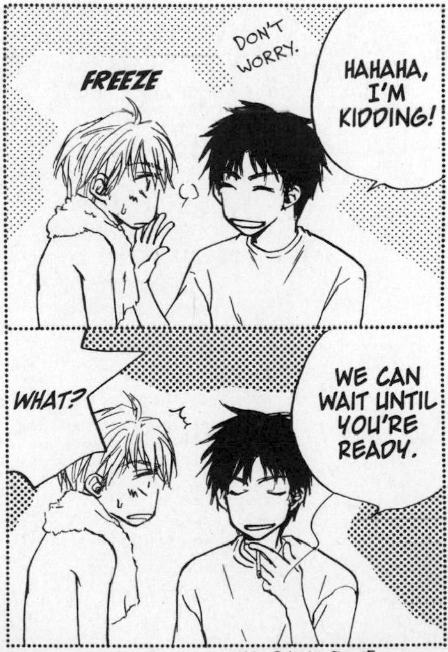
HAHAHA, I'M KIDDING!
DON'T WORRY.
FREEZE
WE CAN WAIT UNTIL YOU'RE READY.
WHAT?
THAT DAY IS CLOSE...

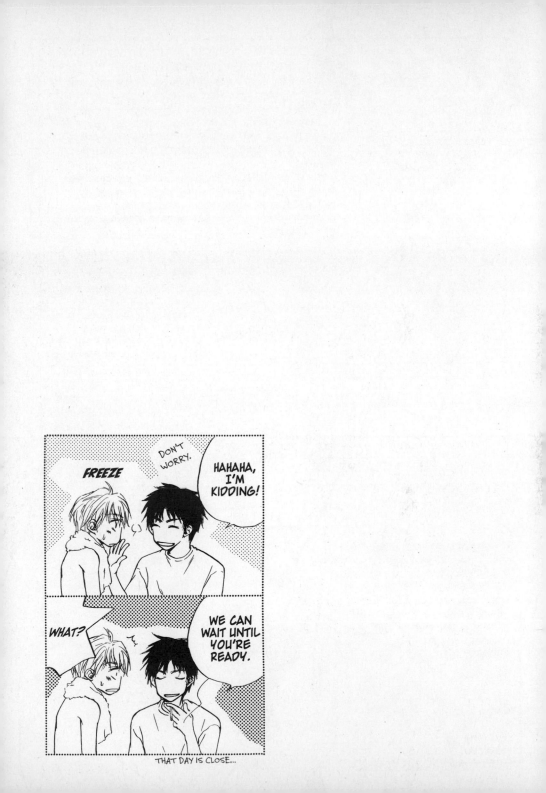

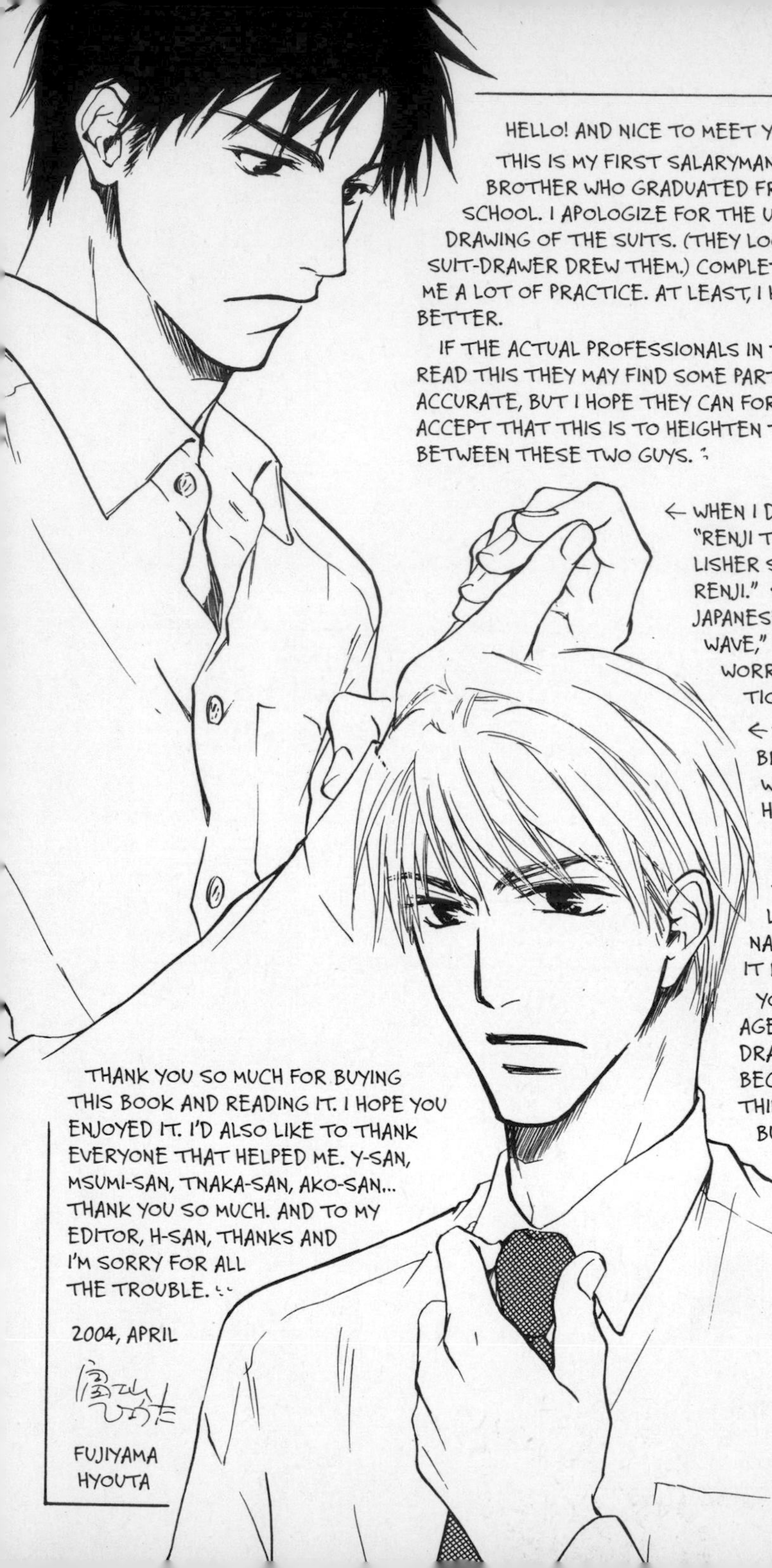

AFTERWORD

HELLO! AND NICE TO MEET YOU!!

THIS IS MY FIRST SALARYMAN STORY, ABOUT A BROTHER WHO GRADUATED FROM AN ALL-BOYS SCHOOL. I APOLOGIZE FOR THE UNPROFESSIONAL DRAWING OF THE SUITS. (THEY LOOK LIKE A FIRST-TIME SUIT-DRAWER DREW THEM.) COMPLETING THIS WORK GAVE ME A LOT OF PRACTICE. AT LEAST, I HOPE I GOT A LOT BETTER.

IF THE ACTUAL PROFESSIONALS IN THE WORKING FIELD READ THIS THEY MAY FIND SOME PARTS THAT AREN'T ACCURATE, BUT I HOPE THEY CAN FORGIVE ME. PLEASE ACCEPT THAT THIS IS TO HEIGHTEN THE ROMANTIC MOOD BETWEEN THESE TWO GUYS.

← WHEN I DECIDED TO NAME HIM "RENJI TSUTSUMI," THE PUBLISHER SAID, "HEAT IT UP WITH RENJI." SINCE "RENJI" IN JAPANESE ALSO MEANS "MICROWAVE," I WAS A LITTLE WORRIED, BUT NO ONE MENTIONED IT AFTER THAT.

← THE ELDER NANASE BROTHER. WHEN HE WAS AT HIS ALL-BOYS HIGH SCHOOL HE NEVER INTENDED TO END UP LIKE THIS. BUT FOR THIS STORY HE GOT A LITTLE MORE UKE. THE NANASE FAMILY SURE HAS IT ROUGH.

YOUICHI WAS A GOOD AGE, SO IT WAS FUN TO DRAW HIM. IT'S HARD BECAUSE HE'S ALWAYS THINKING ABOUT WORK, BUT I'D LIKE TO HAVE THE CHANCE TO DRAW HIM AGAIN.

THANK YOU SO MUCH FOR BUYING THIS BOOK AND READING IT. I HOPE YOU ENJOYED IT. I'D ALSO LIKE TO THANK EVERYONE THAT HELPED ME. Y-SAN, MSUMI-SAN, TNAKA-SAN, AKO-SAN... THANK YOU SO MUCH. AND TO MY EDITOR, H-SAN, THANKS AND I'M SORRY FOR ALL THE TROUBLE.

2004, APRIL

FUJIYAMA HYOUTA

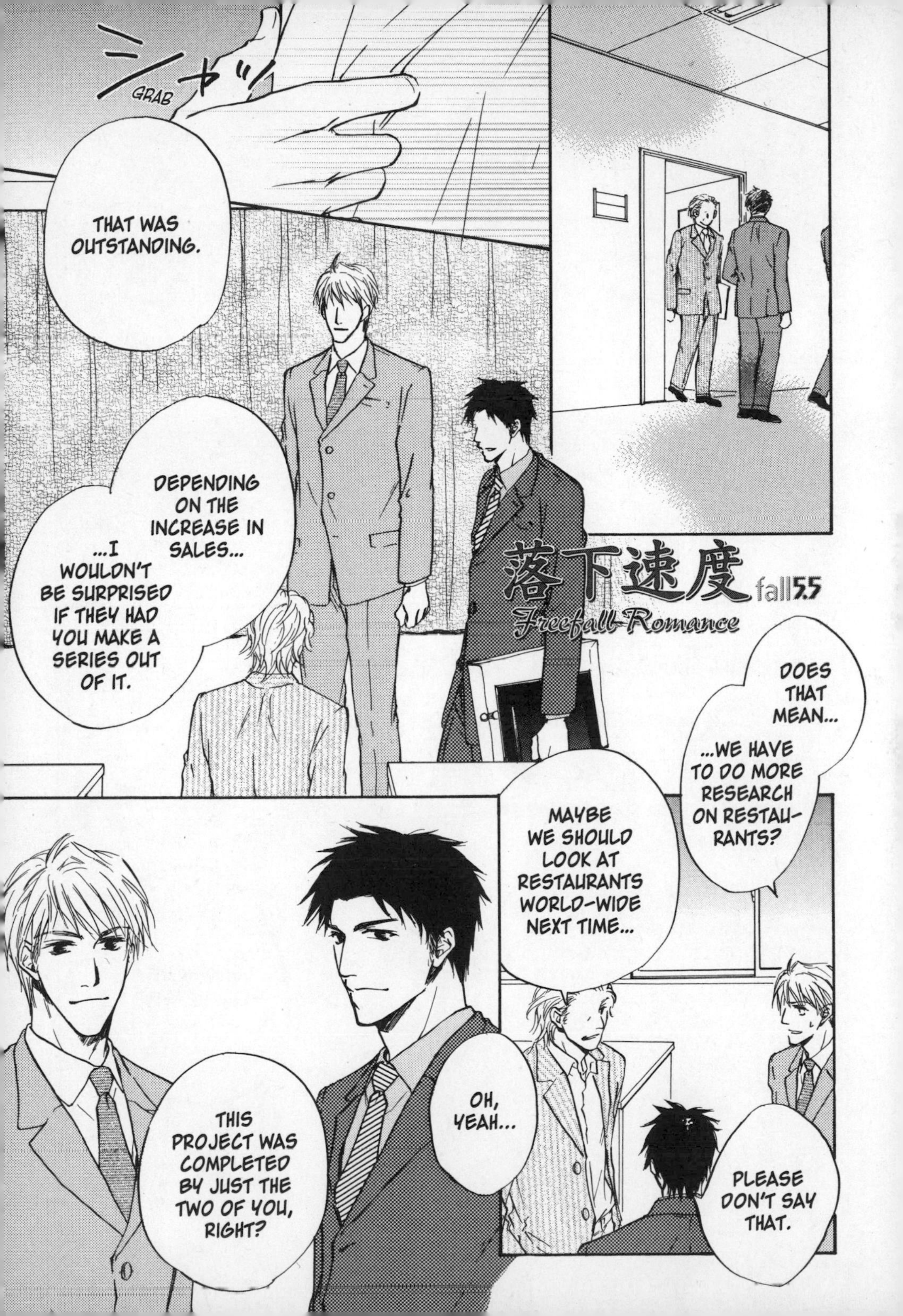
GRAB
THAT WAS OUTSTANDING.
DEPENDING ON THE INCREASE IN SALES...
...I WOULDN'T BE SURPRISED IF THEY HAD YOU MAKE A SERIES OUT OF IT.
落下速度 fall 5.5
Freefall Romance
DOES THAT MEAN...
...WE HAVE TO DO MORE RESEARCH ON RESTAU-RANTS?
MAYBE WE SHOULD LOOK AT RESTAURANTS WORLD-WIDE NEXT TIME...
PLEASE DON'T SAY THAT.
OH, YEAH...
THIS PROJECT WAS COMPLETED BY JUST THE TWO OF YOU, RIGHT?

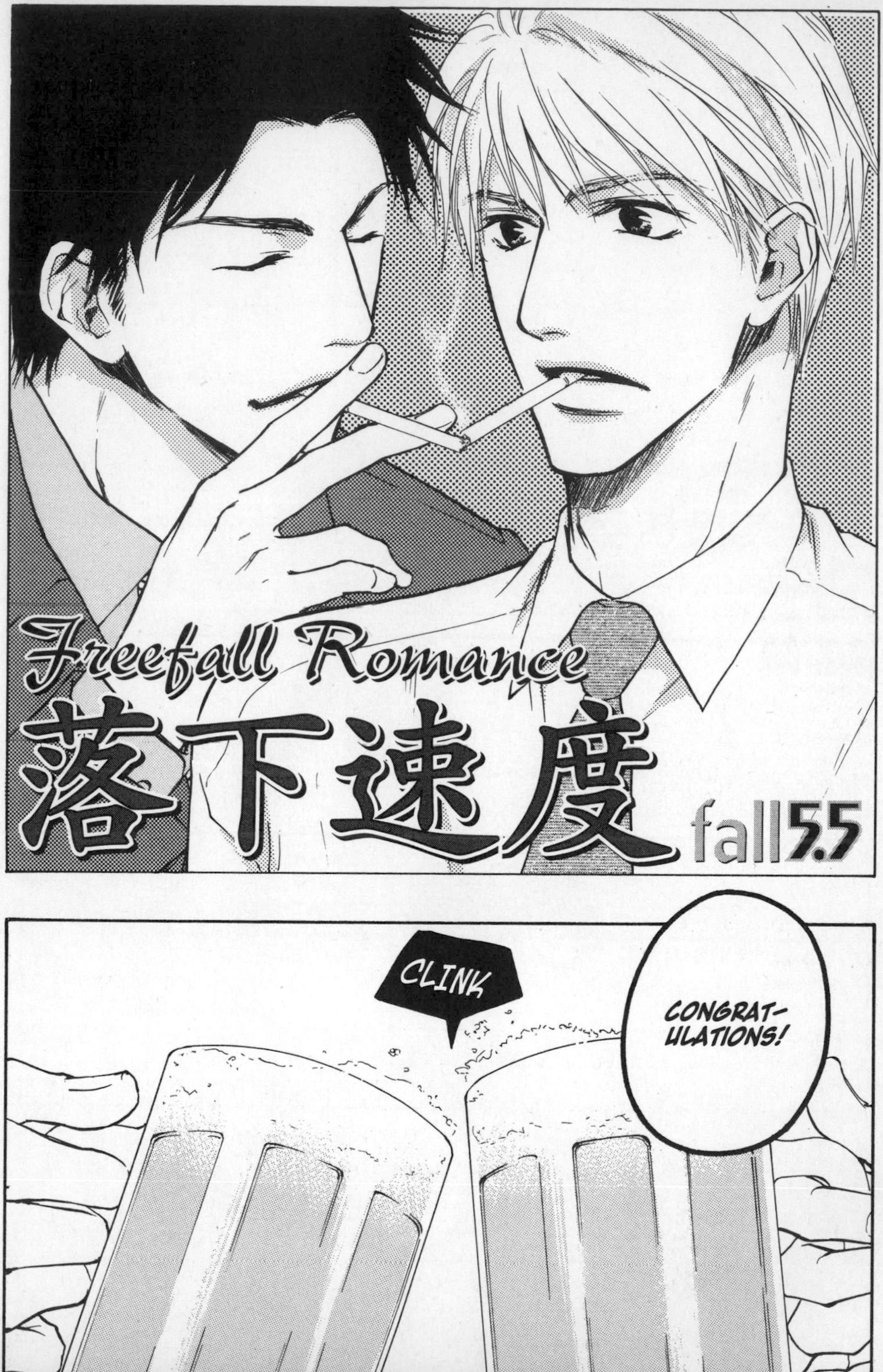
Freefall Romance
落下速度
fall 5.5
CONGRAT-
ULATIONS!
CLINK

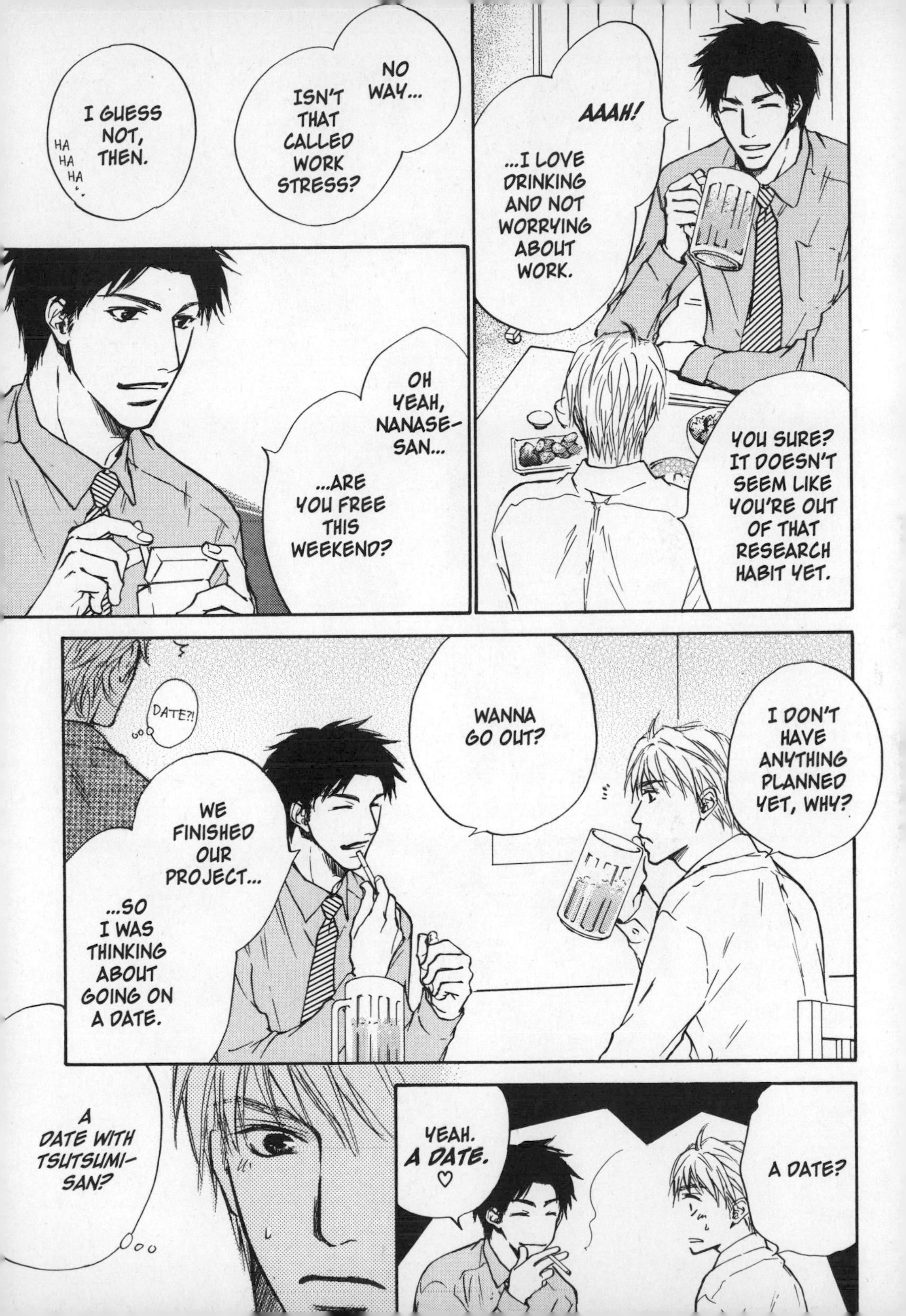
AAAH!
...I LOVE DRINKING AND NOT WORRYING ABOUT WORK.
YOU SURE? IT DOESN'T SEEM LIKE YOU'RE OUT OF THAT RESEARCH HABIT YET.
NO WAY... ISN'T THAT CALLED WORK STRESS?
I GUESS NOT, THEN.
HA HA HA
OH YEAH, NANASE-SAN...
...ARE YOU FREE THIS WEEKEND?
I DON'T HAVE ANYTHING PLANNED YET, WHY?
WANNA GO OUT?
DATE?!
WE FINISHED OUR PROJECT...
...SO I WAS THINKING ABOUT GOING ON A DATE.
A DATE?
YEAH. A DATE. ♡
A DATE WITH TSUTSUMI-SAN?

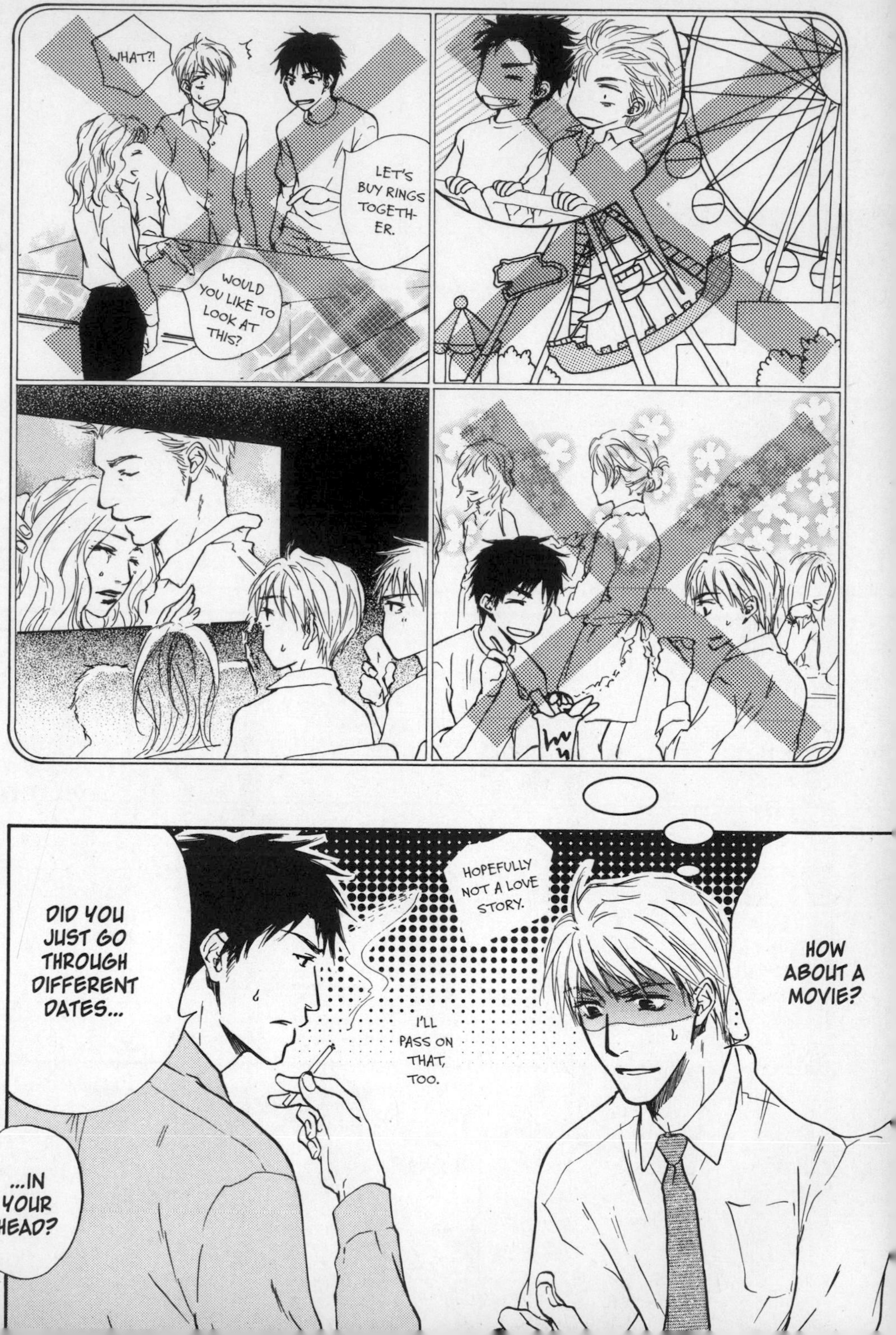
LET'S BUY RINGS TOGETH-ER.
WHAT?!
WOULD YOU LIKE TO LOOK AT THIS?
HOW ABOUT A MOVIE?
HOPEFULLY NOT A LOVE STORY.
I'LL PASS ON THAT, TOO.
DID YOU JUST GO THROUGH DIFFERENT DATES...
...IN YOUR HEAD?

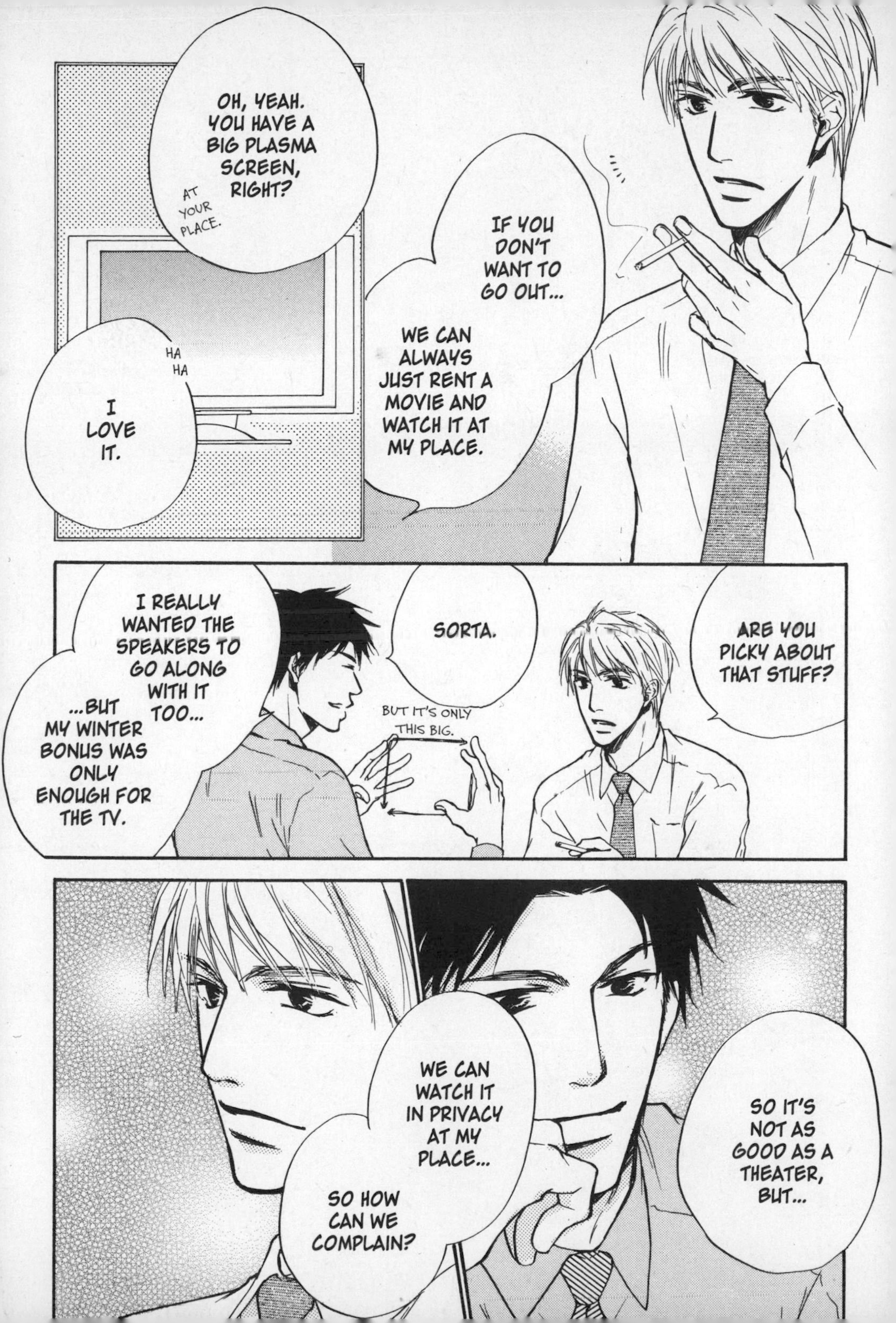
IF YOU DON'T WANT TO GO OUT...
WE CAN ALWAYS JUST RENT A MOVIE AND WATCH IT AT MY PLACE.
OH, YEAH. YOU HAVE A BIG PLASMA SCREEN, RIGHT?
AT YOUR PLACE.
HA HA
I LOVE IT.
ARE YOU PICKY ABOUT THAT STUFF?
SORTA.
BUT IT'S ONLY THIS BIG.
I REALLY WANTED THE SPEAKERS TO GO ALONG WITH IT TOO...
...BUT MY WINTER BONUS WAS ONLY ENOUGH FOR THE TV.
SO IT'S NOT AS GOOD AS A THEATER, BUT...
WE CAN WATCH IT IN PRIVACY AT MY PLACE...
SO HOW CAN WE COMPLAIN?

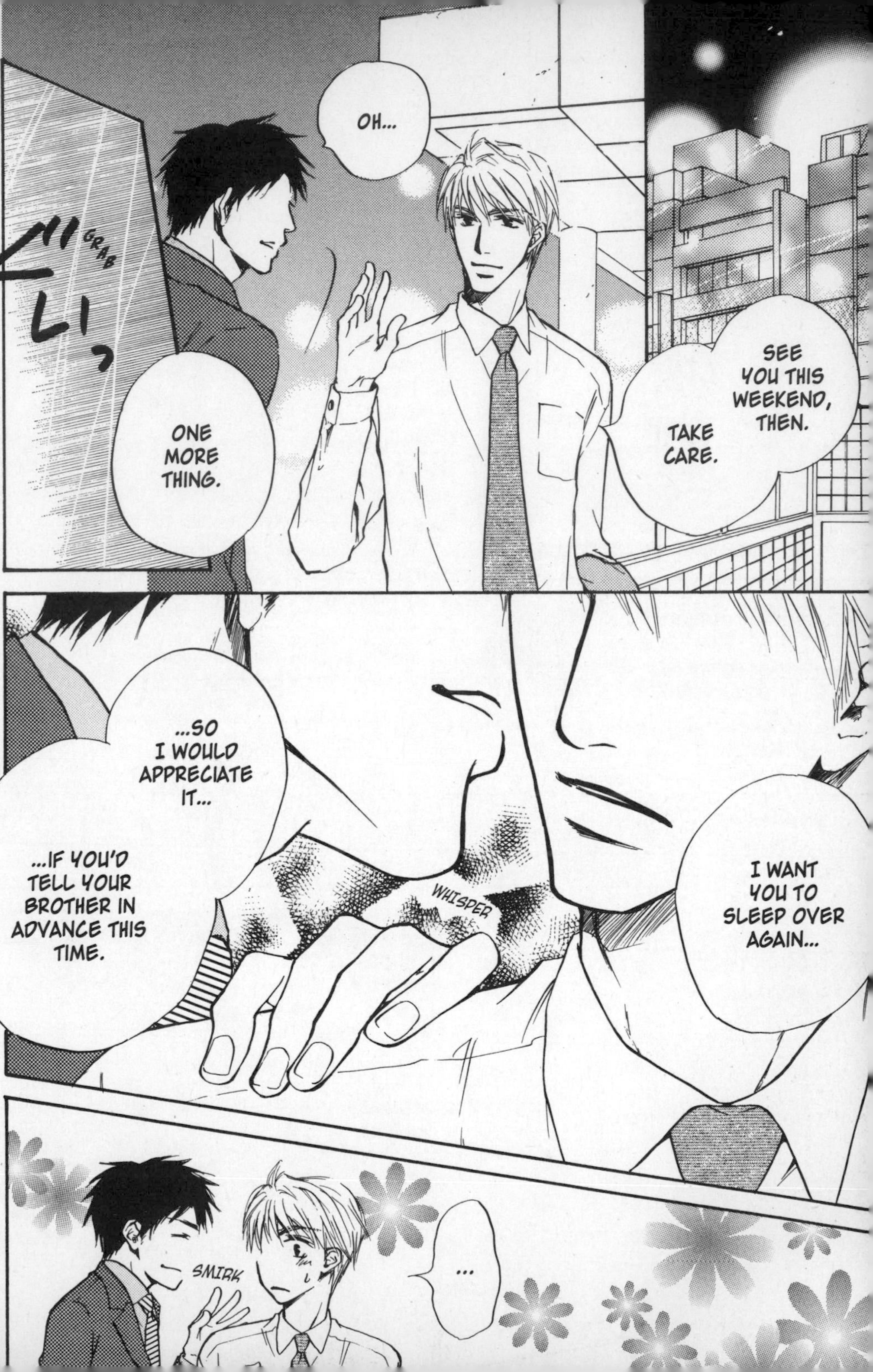
SEE YOU THIS WEEKEND, THEN.
TAKE CARE.
OH...
ぐいっ
GRAB
ONE MORE THING.
I WANT YOU TO SLEEP OVER AGAIN...
WHISPER
...SO I WOULD APPRECIATE IT...
...IF YOU'D TELL YOUR BROTHER IN ADVANCE THIS TIME.
...
SMIRK

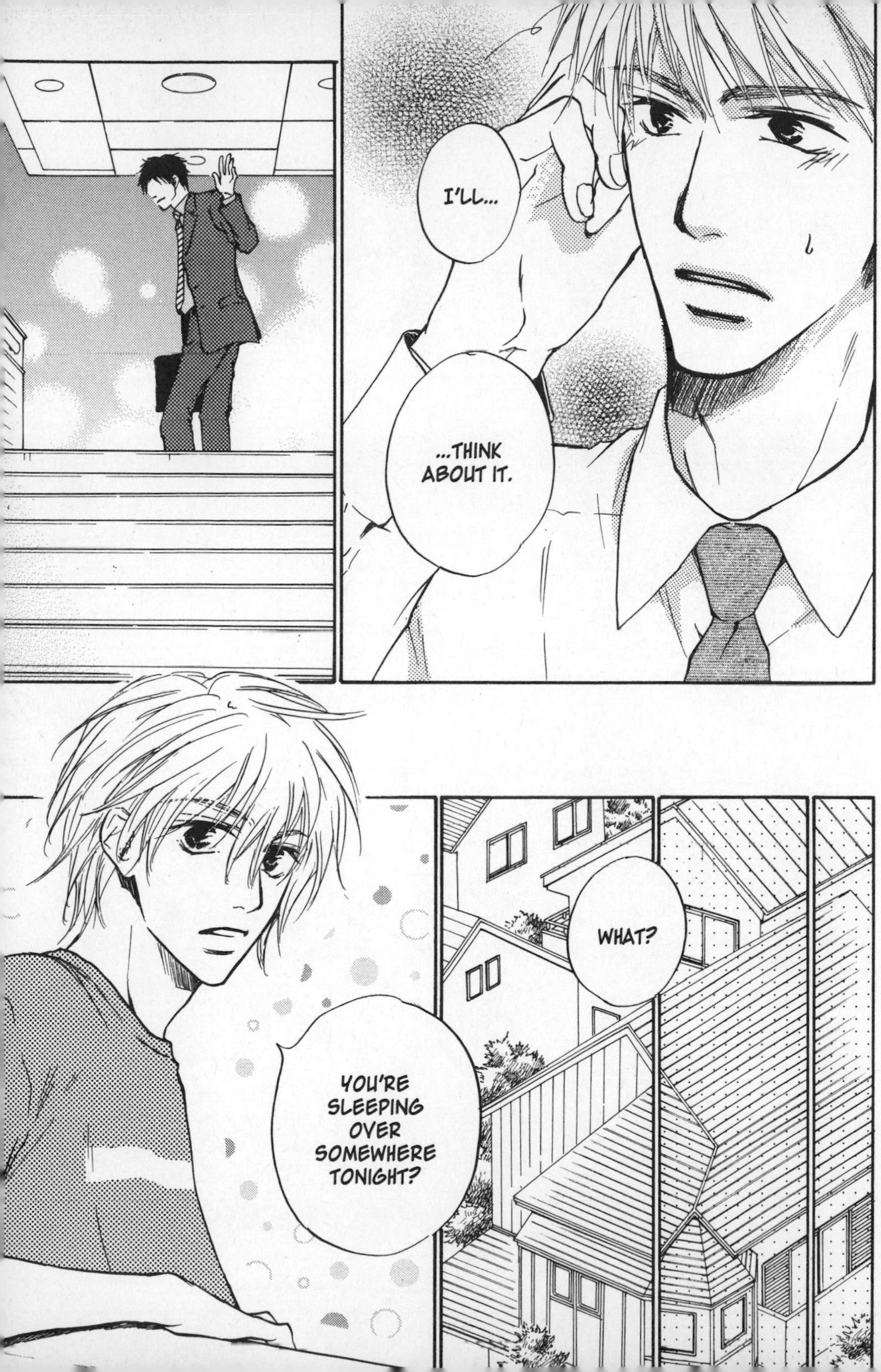
I'LL...
...THINK ABOUT IT.
WHAT?
YOU'RE SLEEPING OVER SOMEWHERE TONIGHT?

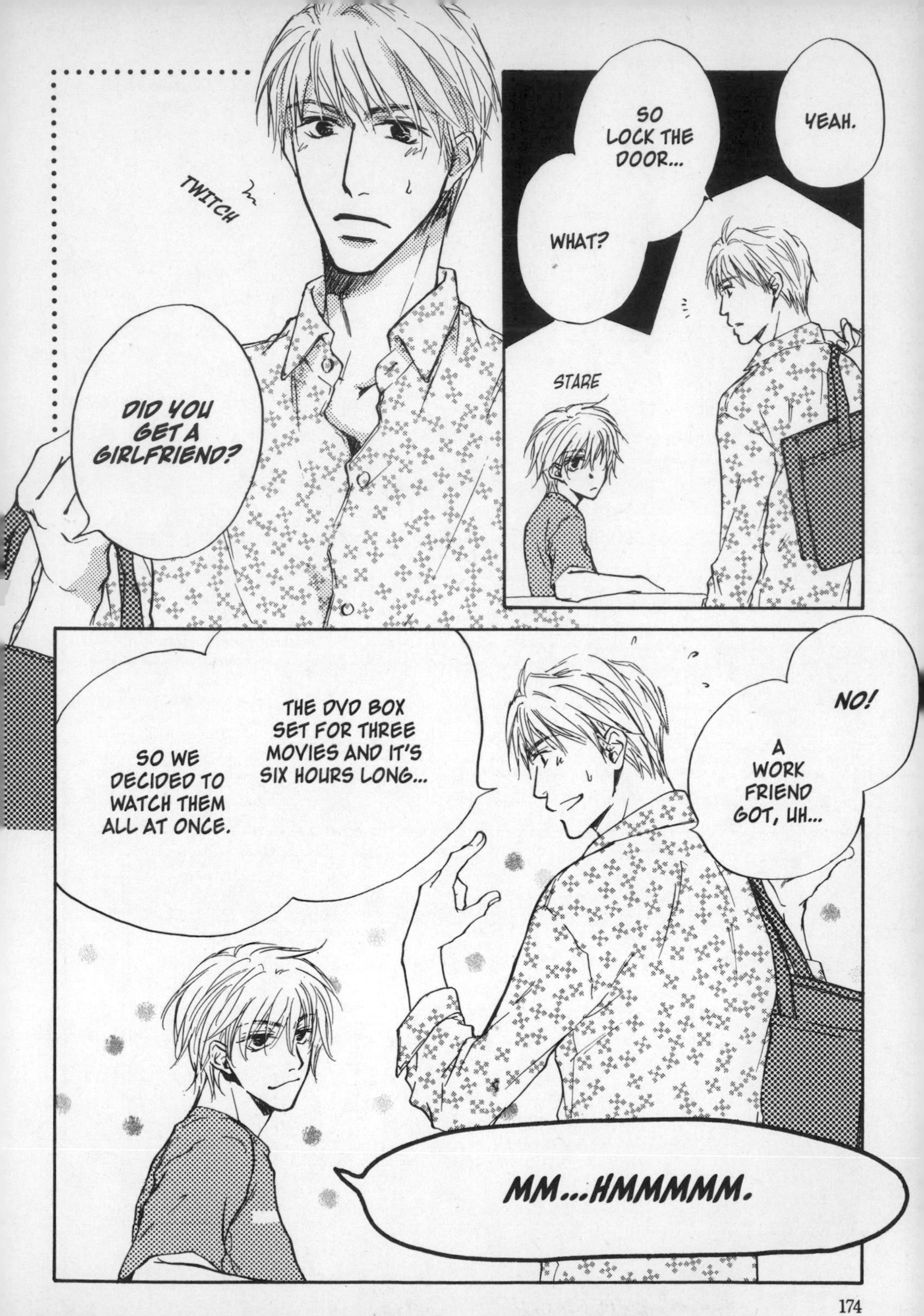
YEAH.
SO LOCK THE DOOR...
WHAT?
STARE
TWITCH
DID YOU GET A GIRLFRIEND?
NO!
A WORK FRIEND GOT, UH...
THE DVD BOX SET FOR THREE MOVIES AND IT'S SIX HOURS LONG...
SO WE DECIDED TO WATCH THEM ALL AT ONCE.
MM...HMMMMM.

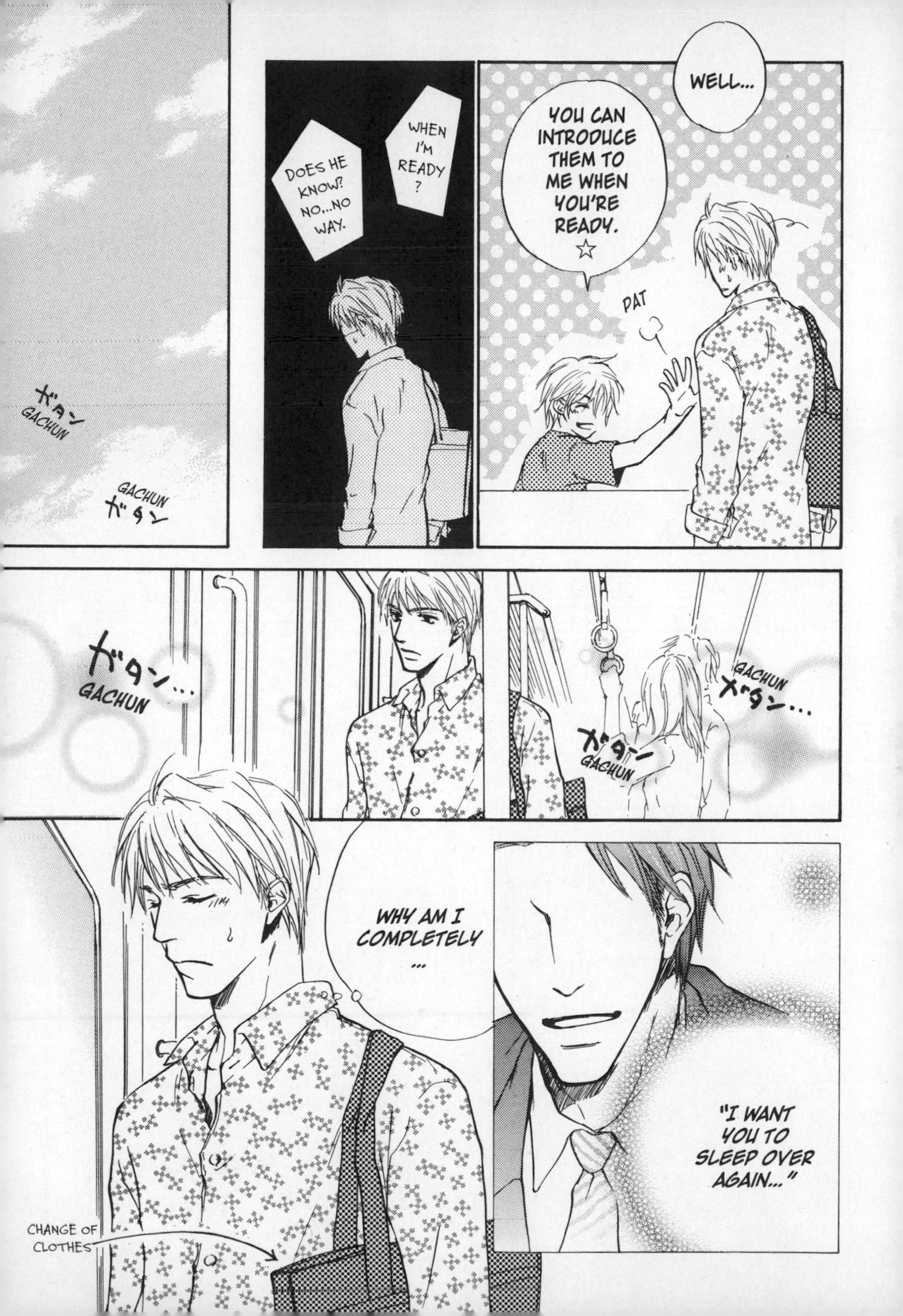
WELL...
YOU CAN INTRODUCE THEM TO ME WHEN YOU'RE READY. ☆
PAT
WHEN I'M READY?
DOES HE KNOW? NO...NO WAY.
ガタン GACHUN
GACHUN ガタン
GACHUN ガタン...
ガタン GACHUN
ガタン... GACHUN
"I WANT YOU TO SLEEP OVER AGAIN..."
WHY AM I COMPLETELY ...
CHANGE OF CLOTHES

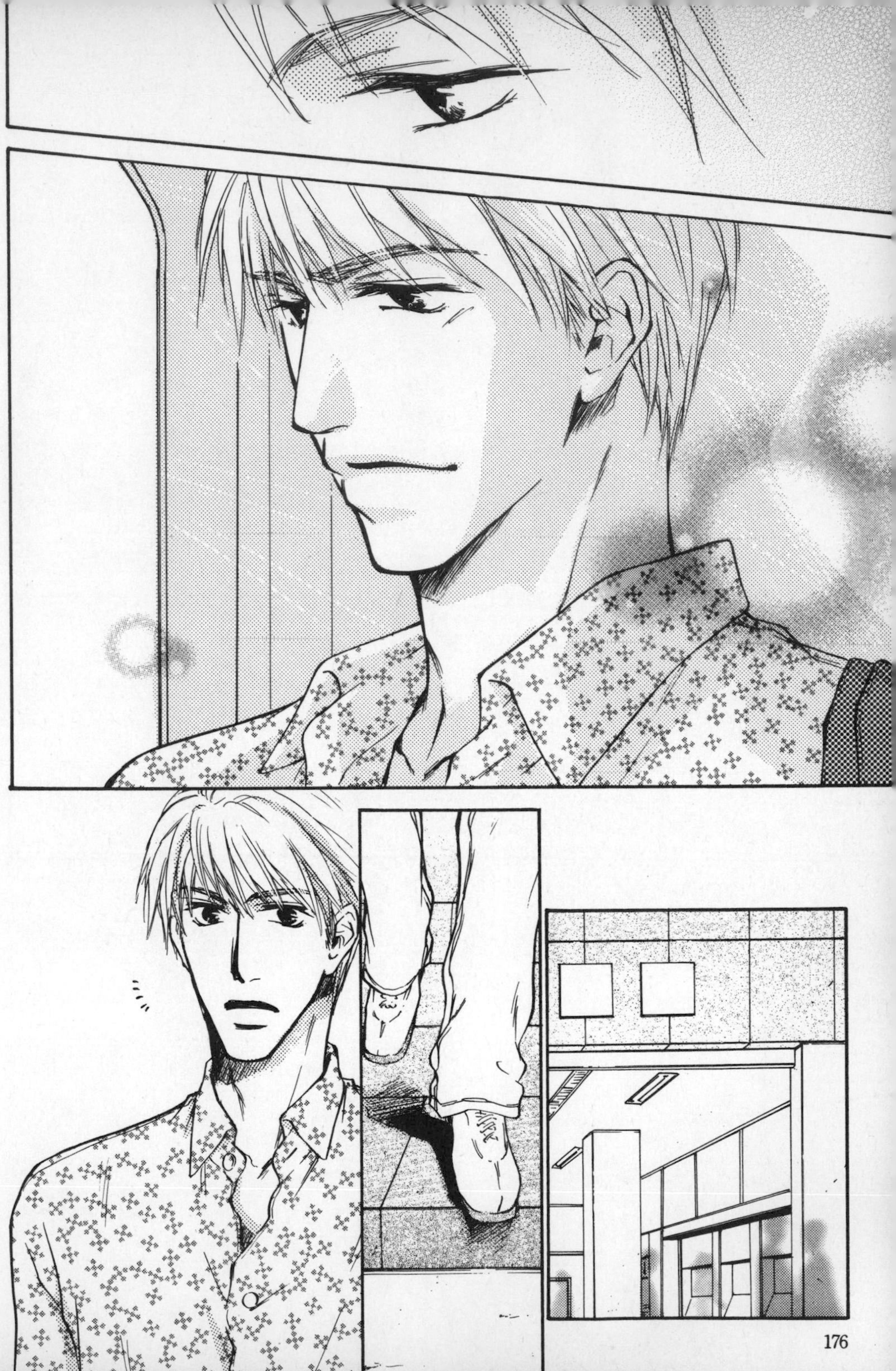

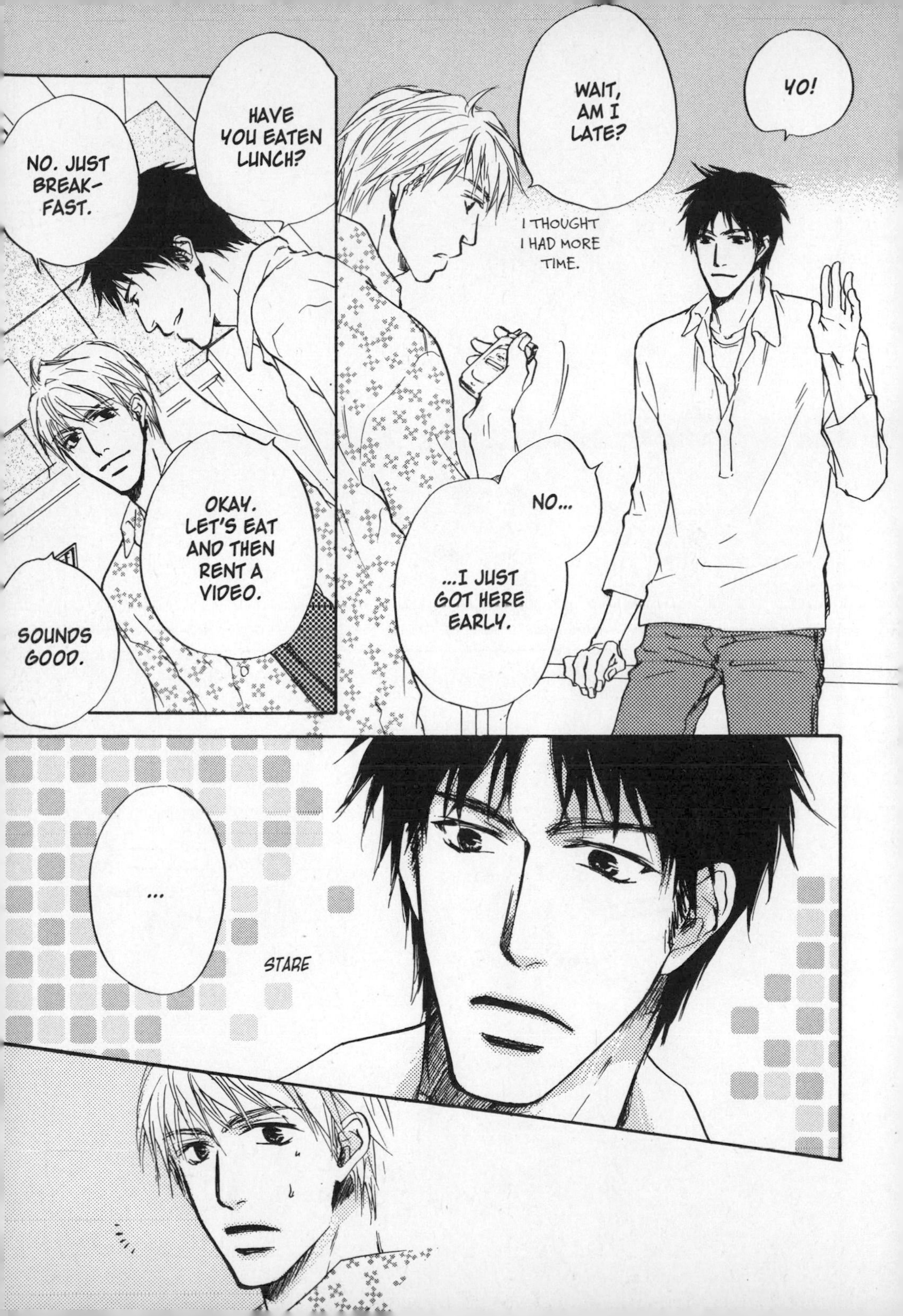
YO!
WAIT, AM I LATE?
I THOUGHT I HAD MORE TIME.
NO...
...I JUST GOT HERE EARLY.
HAVE YOU EATEN LUNCH?
NO. JUST BREAK-FAST.
OKAY. LET'S EAT AND THEN RENT A VIDEO.
SOUNDS GOOD.
...
STARE

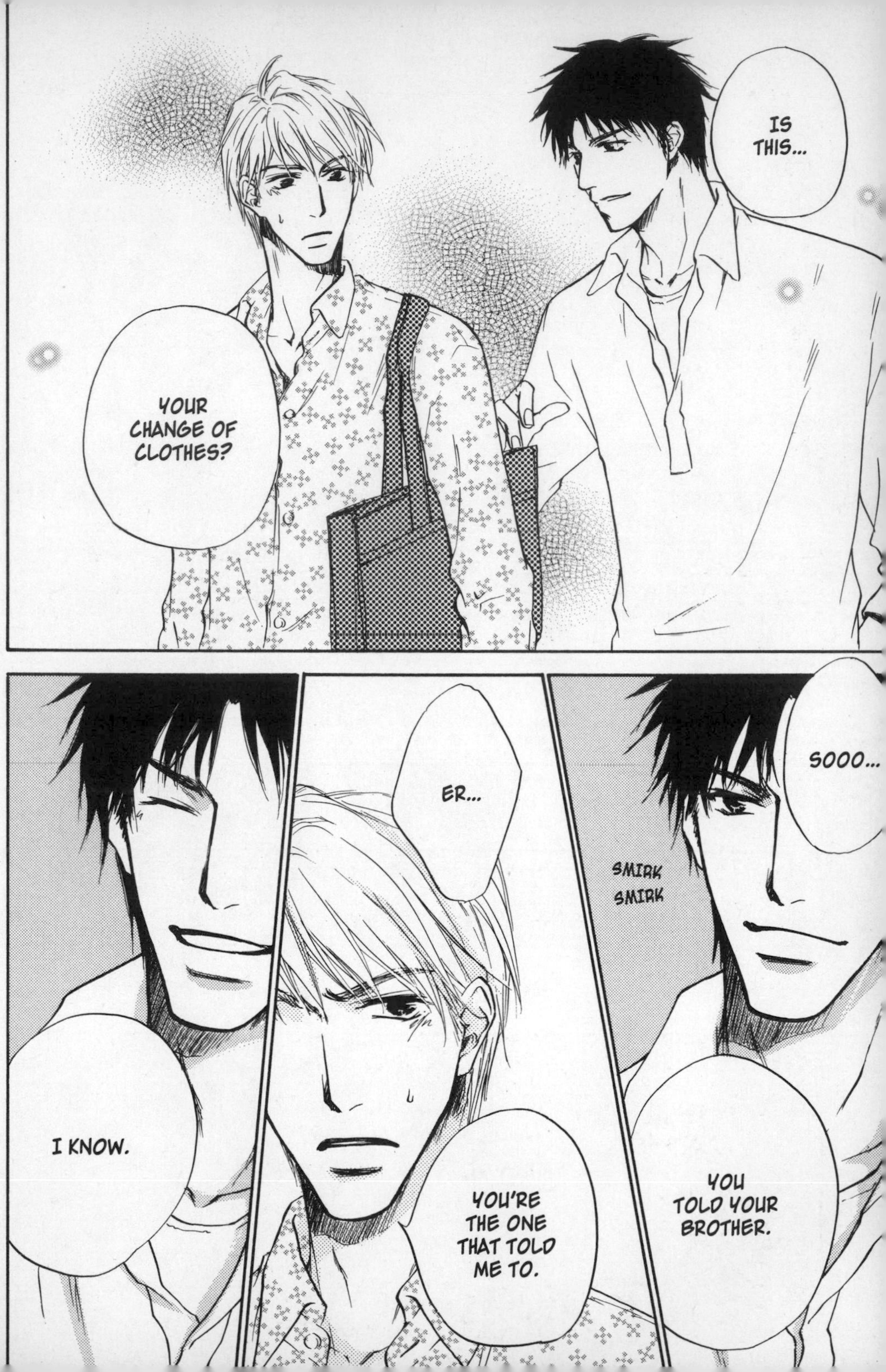
IS THIS...
YOUR CHANGE OF CLOTHES?
SOOO...
SMIRK SMIRK
YOU TOLD YOUR BROTHER.
ER...
YOU'RE THE ONE THAT TOLD ME TO.
I KNOW.

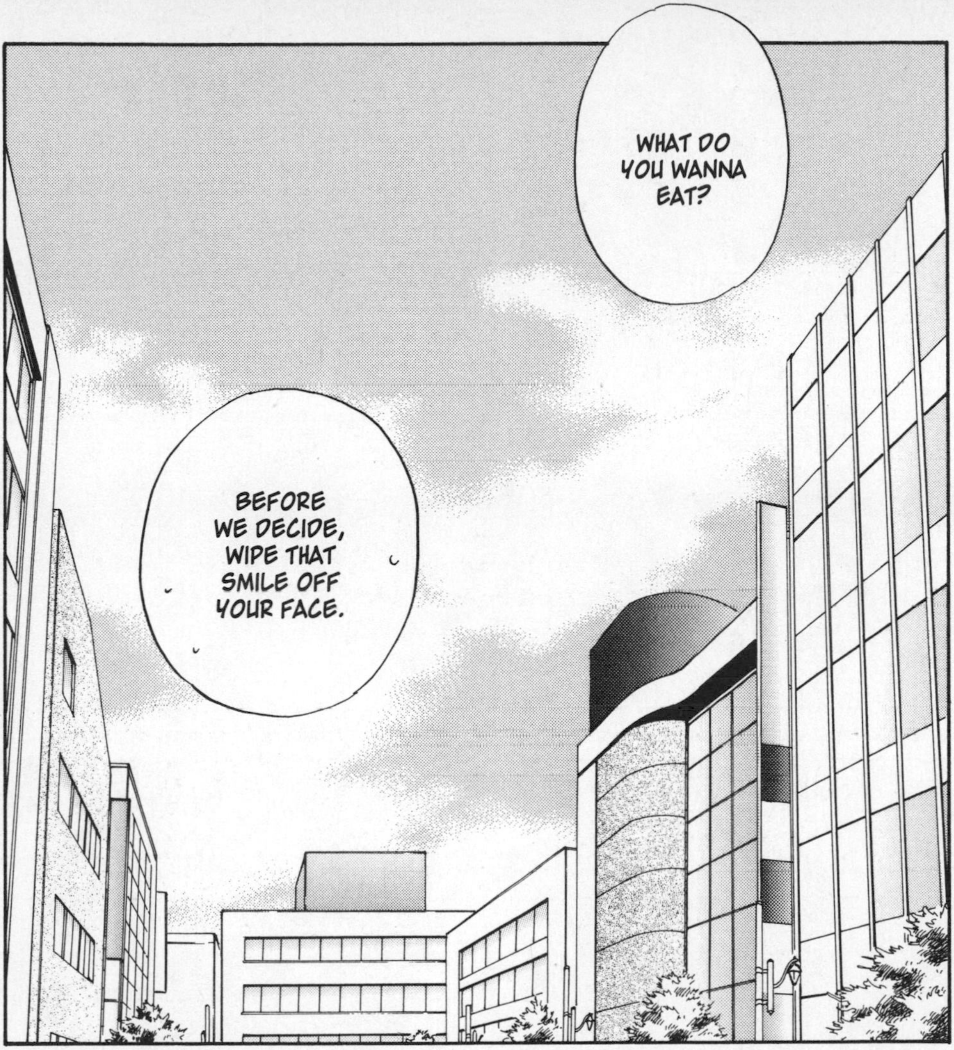
WHAT DO YOU WANNA EAT?
BEFORE WE DECIDE, WIPE THAT SMILE OFF YOUR FACE.

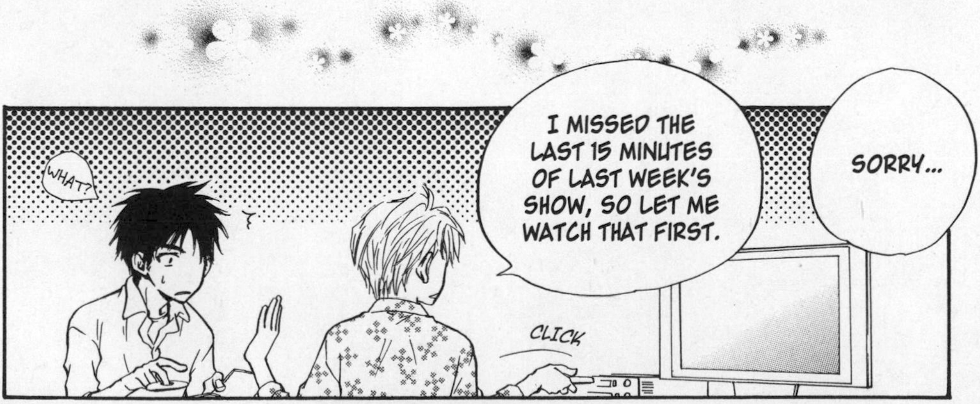
SORRY...
I MISSED THE LAST 15 MINUTES OF LAST WEEK'S SHOW, SO LET ME WATCH THAT FIRST.
WHAT?
CLICK

Freefall Romance
落下速度 fall5.5＊END

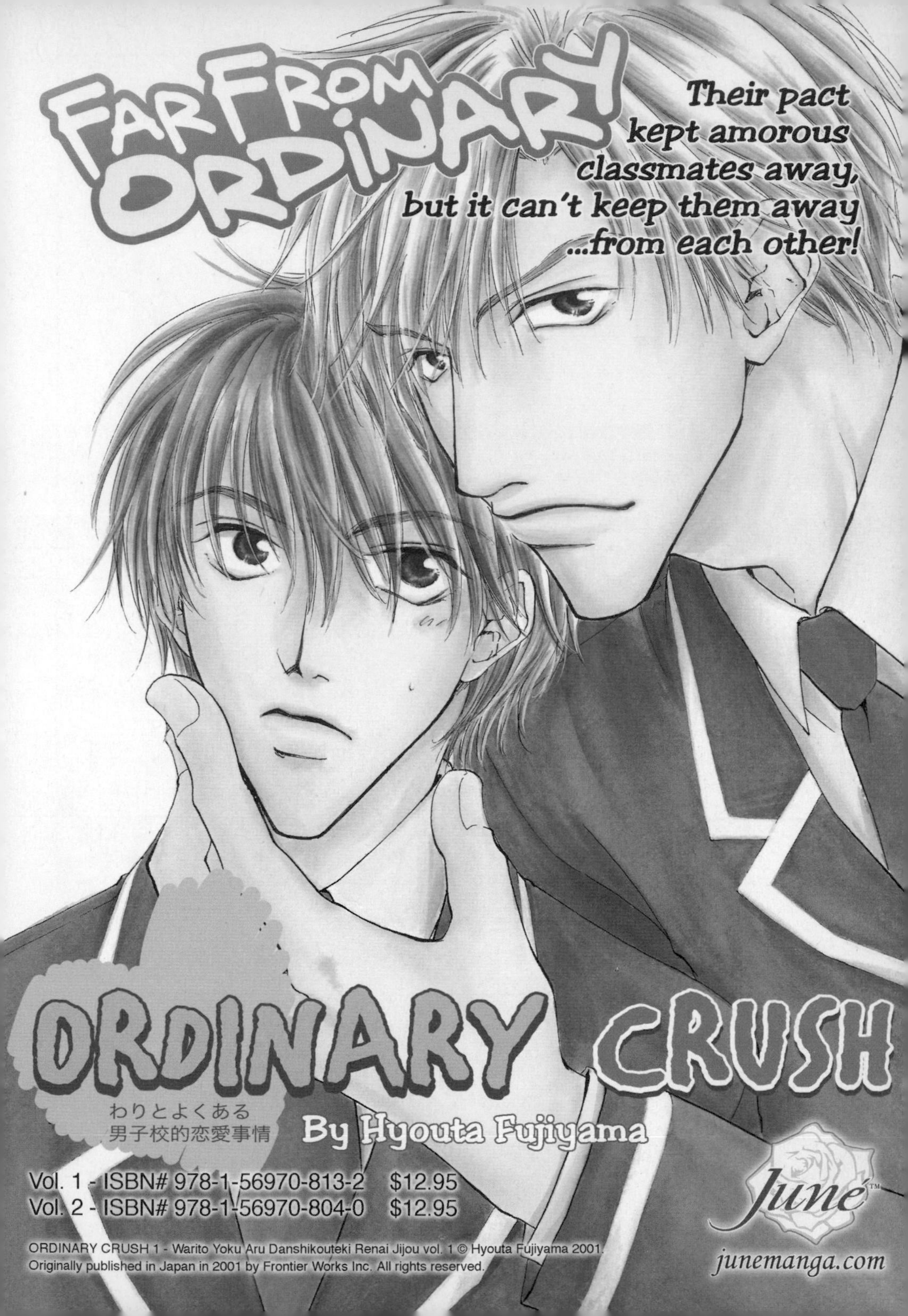

FAR FROM ORDINARY

Their pact kept amorous classmates away, but it can't keep them away ...from each other!

ORDINARY CRUSH

わりとよくある
男子校的恋愛事情

By Hyouta Fujiyama

Vol. 1 - ISBN# 978-1-56970-813-2 $12.95
Vol. 2 - ISBN# 978-1-56970-804-0 $12.95

June™

junemanga.com

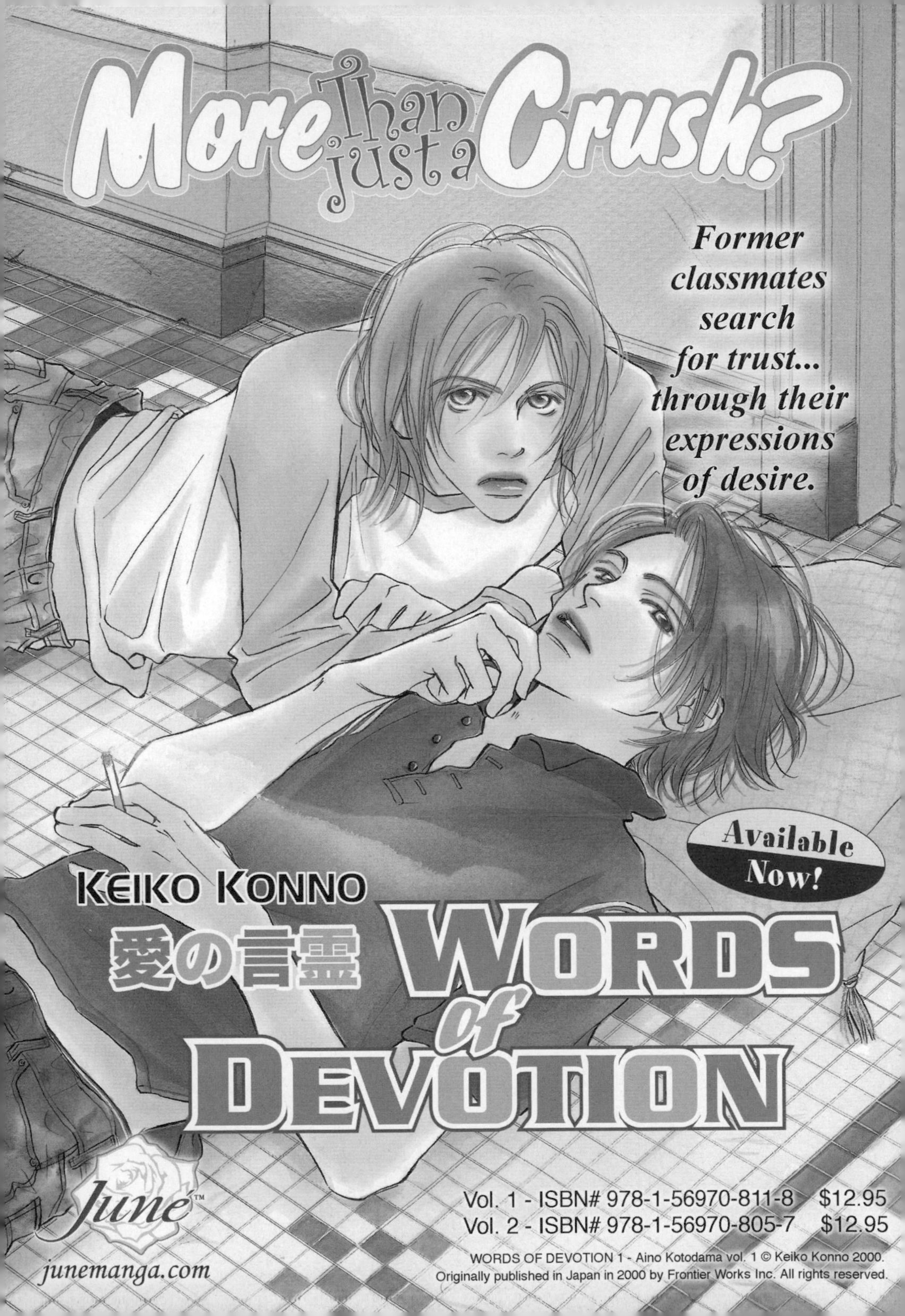

More Than just a Crush?
Former classmates search for trust... through their expressions of desire.
Available Now!
KEIKO KONNO
愛の言霊
WORDS of DEVOTION
June™
Vol. 1 - ISBN# 978-1-56970-811-8 $12.95
Vol. 2 - ISBN# 978-1-56970-805-7 $12.95
WORDS OF DEVOTION 1 - Aino Kotodama vol. 1 © Keiko Konno 2000.
Originally published in Japan in 2000 by Frontier Works Inc. All rights reserved.
junemanga.com

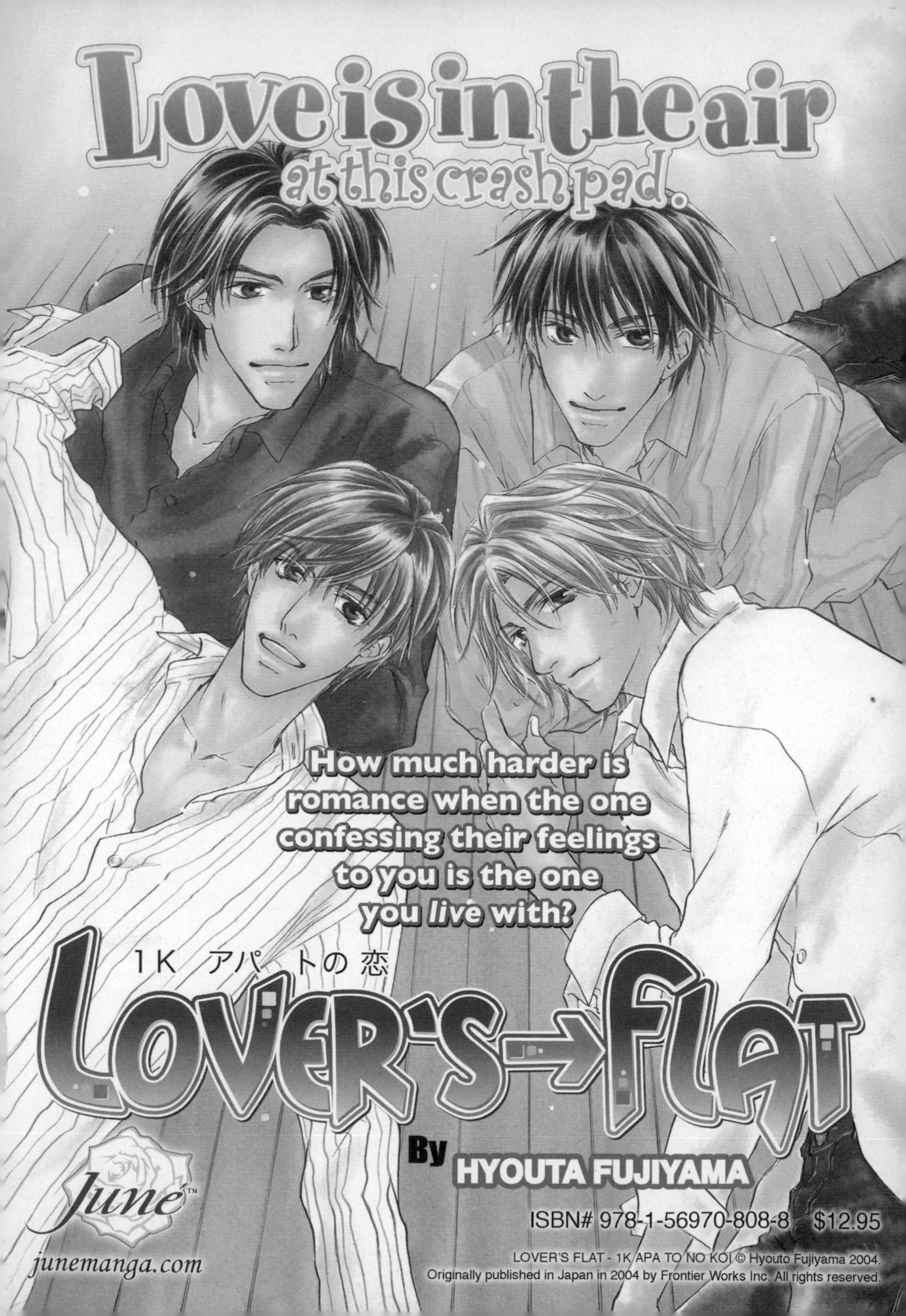

Love is in the air
at this crash pad.
How much harder is romance when the one confessing their feelings to you is the one you *live* with?
1K アパ トの 恋
LOVER'S→flat
By HYOUTA FUJIYAMA
June™
ISBN# 978-1-56970-808-8 $12.95
junemanga.com
LOVER'S FLAT - 1K APA TO NO KOI © Hyouto Fujiyama 2004.
Originally published in Japan in 2004 by Frontier Works Inc. All rights reserved.

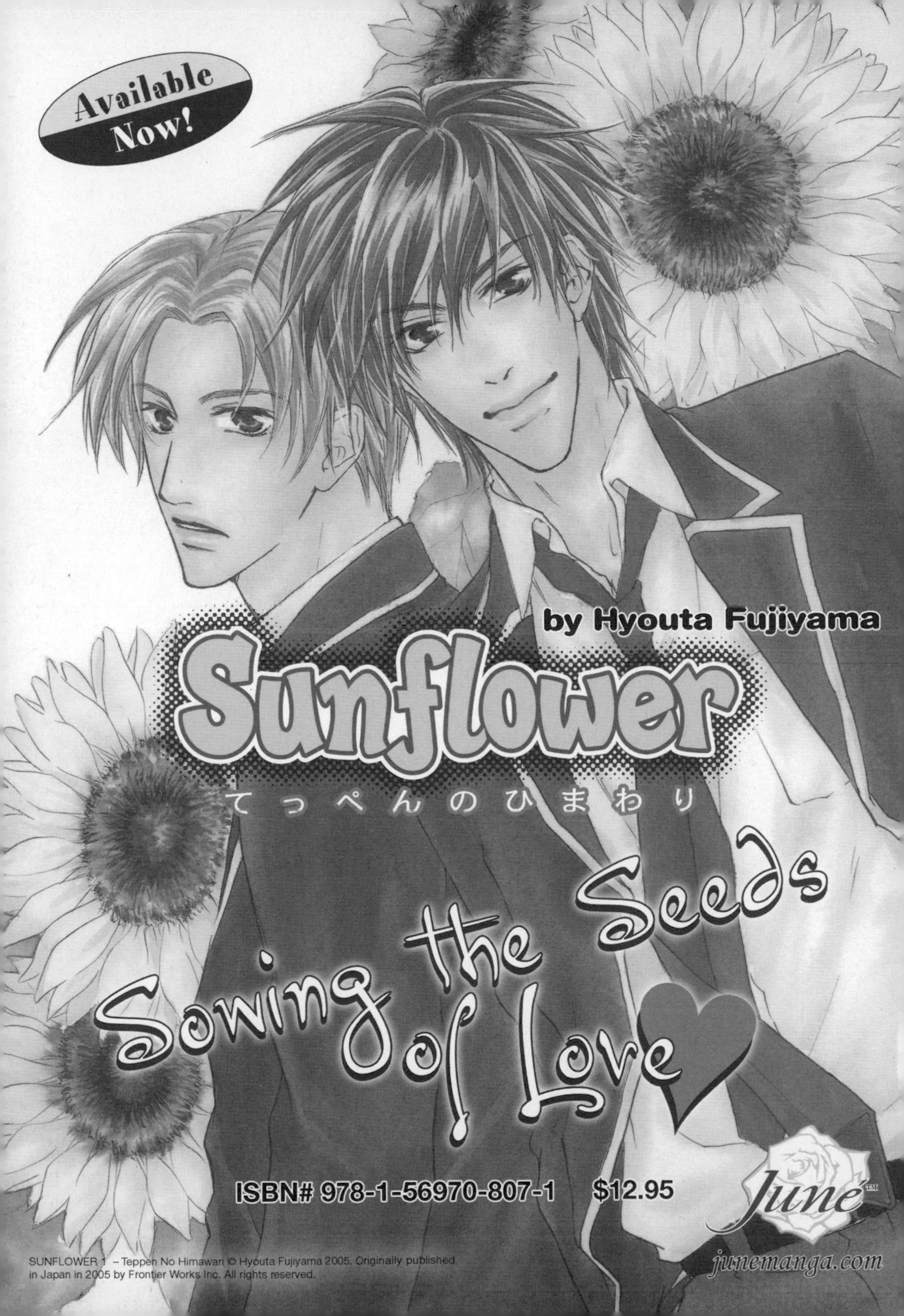
Available Now!
by Hyouta Fujiyama
Sunflower
てっぺんのひまわり
Sowing the Seeds of Love
ISBN# 978-1-56970-807-1
$12.95
June
junemanga.com
SUNFLOWER 1 – Teppen No Himawari © Hyouta Fujiyama 2005. Originally published in Japan in 2005 by Frontier Works Inc. All rights reserved.

kirico higashizato

LOVE RECIPE

2 pinches of PASSION and a cup of DESIRE...

Volume 1: ISBN# 978-1-56970-825-5 $12.95

june™

junemanga.com

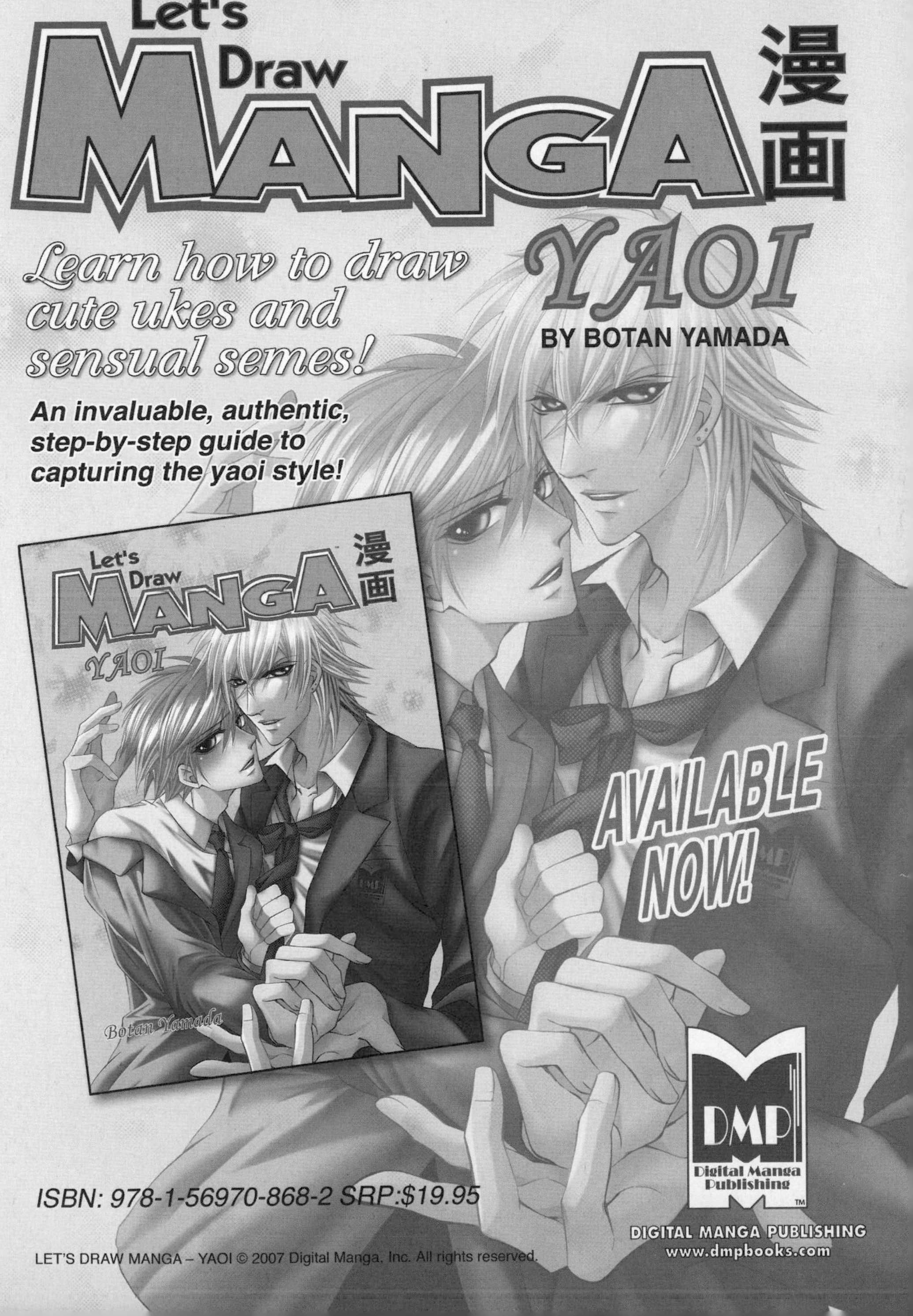
Let's Draw MANGA 漫画
YAOI
BY BOTAN YAMADA
Learn how to draw cute ukes and sensual semes!
An invaluable, authentic, step-by-step guide to capturing the yaoi style!
Let's Draw MANGA 漫画
YAOI
Botan Yamada
AVAILABLE NOW!
ISBN: 978-1-56970-868-2 SRP:$19.95
DMP
Digital Manga Publishing
DIGITAL MANGA PUBLISHING
www.dmpbooks.com
LET'S DRAW MANGA – YAOI © 2007 Digital Manga, Inc. All rights reserved.

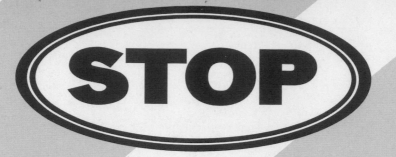

STOP

This is the back of the book! Start from the other side.

NATIVE MANGA readers read manga from *right to left*.

1
2
1
3
2
3
5
4
4
6
5
8
7
6

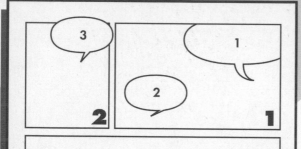

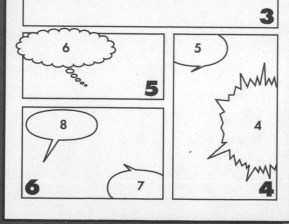

If you run into our ***Native Manga*** *logo on any of our books... you'll know that this manga is published in it's true original native Japanese right to left reading format, as it was intended. Turn to the other side of the book and start reading from right to left, top to bottom.*

Follow the diagram to see how its done.
Surf's Up!

NATIVE MANGA
READ RIGHT TO LEFT

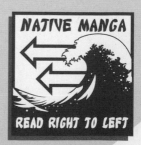